THE COMPARATIVE ARCHAEOLOGY
OF COMPLEX SOCIETIES

Part of a resurgence in the comparative study of ancient societies, this book presents a variety of methods and approaches to comparative analysis through the examination of wide-ranging case studies. Each chapter is a comparative study, and the diverse topics and regions covered in the book contribute to the growing understanding of variation and change in ancient complex societies. The authors explore themes ranging from urbanization and settlement patterns, to the political strategies of kings and chiefs, to the economic choices of individuals and households. The case studies cover an array of geographical settings, from the Andes to Southeast Asia. The authors are leading archaeologists whose research on early empires, states, and chiefdoms is at the cutting edge of scientific archaeology.

Michael E. Smith is Professor of Anthropology in the School of Human Evolution and Social Change at Arizona State University. He has published widely in scholarly journals on Aztec society, Mesoamerican archaeology, ancient urbanism, and the comparative analysis of early state societies. He is the author and editor of eight books, including *Aztec City-State Capitals*, *The Aztecs*, and *The Postclassic Mesoamerican World* (coedited with Frances F. Berdan).

THE COMPARATIVE ARCHAEOLOGY OF COMPLEX SOCIETIES

Edited by

Michael E. Smith

Arizona State University

CAMBRIDGE UNIVERSITY PRESS

CAMBRIDGE UNIVERSITY PRESS
Cambridge, New York, Melbourne, Madrid, Cape Town,
Singapore, São Paulo, Delhi, Tokyo, Mexico City

Cambridge University Press
32 Avenue of the Americas, New York, NY 10013-2473, USA

www.cambridge.org
Information on this title: www.cambridge.org/9780521142120

First published 2012

Printed in the United States of America

A catalog record for this publication is available from the British Library.

Library of Congress Cataloging in Publication data

The comparative archaeology of complex societies / [edited by] Michael E. Smith.
   p.   cm.
Includes bibliographical references and index.
ISBN 978-0-521-19791-5 (hardback) – ISBN 978-0-521-14212-0 (paperback)
1. Social archaeology.   2. Social groups.   3. Complex organizations.   I. Smith, Michael
Ernest, 1953–
cc72.4.c69   2011
930.1 – dc22   2011012709

ISBN 978-0-521-19791-5 Hardback
ISBN 978-0-521-14212-0 Paperback

CONTENTS

List of Tables   *page* ix

List of Figures   xi

Contributors   xiii

Foreword by Jeremy A. Sabloff   xvii

Preface   xxi

CHAPTER 1
COMPARATIVE ARCHAEOLOGY: A COMMITMENT TO
UNDERSTANDING VARIATION   I
Robert D. Drennan, Timothy Earle, Gary M. Feinman, Roland
Fletcher, Michael J. Kolb, Peter Peregrine, Christian E. Peterson,
Carla Sinopoli, Michael E. Smith, Monica L. Smith, Barbara L. Stark,
and Miriam T. Stark

CHAPTER 2
APPROACHES TO COMPARATIVE ANALYSIS IN
ARCHAEOLOGY   4
Michael E. Smith and Peter Peregrine

CHAPTER 3
COMPARATIVE FRAMES FOR THE DIACHRONIC ANALYSIS
OF COMPLEX SOCIETIES: NEXT STEPS   2 I
Gary M. Feinman

CHAPTER 4
WHAT IT TAKES TO GET COMPLEX: FOOD, GOODS, AND
WORK AS SHARED CULTURAL IDEALS FROM THE
BEGINNING OF SEDENTISM   44
Monica L. Smith

CHAPTER 5
CHALLENGES FOR COMPARATIVE STUDY OF EARLY
COMPLEX SOCIETIES   62
Robert D. Drennan and Christian E. Peterson

CHAPTER 6
PATTERNED VARIATION IN REGIONAL TRAJECTORIES
OF COMMUNITY GROWTH   88
Christian E. Peterson and Robert D. Drennan

CHAPTER 7
THE GENESIS OF MONUMENTS IN ISLAND SOCIETIES   138
Michael J. Kolb

CHAPTER 8
POWER AND LEGITIMATION: POLITICAL STRATEGIES,
TYPOLOGY, AND CULTURAL EVOLUTION   165
Peter Peregrine

CHAPTER 9
THE STRATEGIES OF PROVINCIALS IN EMPIRES   192
Barbara L. Stark and John K. Chance

CHAPTER 10
HOUSEHOLD ECONOMIES UNDER THE AZTEC AND INKA
EMPIRES: A COMPARISON   238
Timothy Earle and Michael E. Smith

CHAPTER 11
LOW-DENSITY, AGRARIAN-BASED URBANISM: SCALE,
POWER, AND ECOLOGY   285
Roland Fletcher

CHAPTER 12
ARCHAEOLOGY, EARLY COMPLEX SOCIETIES, AND
COMPARATIVE SOCIAL SCIENCE HISTORY   321
Michael E. Smith

Index   331

.

TABLES

2.1. Dimensions of comparison   *page* 10

7.1. Islands and their monuments: descriptive data   153

8.1. Kendall's Tau-b correlations between three dimensions of political strategy   171

8.2. Kendall's Tau-b correlations between dimensions of political strategy and classic neoevolutionary typologies   172

8.3. Correlations between dimensions of political strategy and other social variables. The top number for each variable is a Kendall's Tau-b correlation, while the bottom number is a partial correlation controlling for Service's (1962) classic neoevolutionary typology   175

8.4. Cross-tabulation of recoded sacred-profane and descent group membership variables   176

8.5. Kendall's Tau-b correlations between political strategies and selected cost and stability variables   179

8.6. States categorized by their relative stability as defined by their coding on three dimensions of political strategy   181

8.7. Codebook and data   184

8.8. Coding criteria for the dimensions of political strategy variables   187

8.9. Outline of coding criteria for Band, Tribe, Chiefdom, State variable   189

9.1. List of strategies of provincials in empires   193

10.1. Excavated contexts discussed in this chapter   249

10.2. Lithic tools at Inka sites   252

10.3. Ceramic forms at Inka sites   253

10.4. Ceramic wares at Inka sites   254

10.5. Metal objects at Inka sites   255

10.6.	Lithic tools at Aztec sites	258
10.7.	Ceramic forms at Aztec sites	259
10.8.	Ceramic wares at Aztec sites	260
10.9.	Craft production artifacts at Aztec sites	268
10.10.	Households engaged in obsidian tool production at Aztec sites	269
10.11.	Import distances at Inka sites	272
10.12.	Import distances at Aztec sites	275

FIGURES

0.1. Participants in the Amerind conference.   *page* xxii
2.1. Intensive and systematic comparative strategies.   7
6.1. Locations of regional trajectories.   91
6.2. Histograms and boxplots of initial neolithic community
     populations for seven regions.   95
6.3. Communities in the Marana regional trajectory.   98
6.4. Communities in the Pueblo Grande regional trajectory.   99
6.5. Communities in the Santa Valley regional trajectory.   101
6.6. Communities in the Basin of Mexico regional trajectory.   103
6.7. Communities in the Western Liao Valley regional
     trajectory (Chifeng survey area).   105
6.8. Communities in the Shandong Peninsula regional
     trajectory (Rizhao survey area).   107
6.9. Communities in the Valley of Oaxaca regional trajectory.   109
6.10. Communities in the Middle Niger Delta regional
      trajectory.   111
6.11. Communities in the Alto Magdalena regional trajectory
      (Western Valle de la Plata survey area).   112
6.12. Communities in the Tehuacán Valley regional trajectory
      (Quachilco survey area).   113
6.13. Communities in the Tehuacán Valley regional trajectory
      (Cuayucatepec survey area).   115
6.14. Summary of regional trajectories.   117
7.1. Locations of the islands mentioned in the text.   140
7.2. Schematic views of typical Oceanic monuments.   141
7.3. Schematic view of Pi'ilanihale temple on Maui.   145
7.4. Schematic views of typical Mediterranean monuments.   147
7.5. Schematic view of the palace at Knossos.   151

8.1. Three dimensions of strategy.   167
8.2. Scattergram of twenty-six ethnographic cases.   170
8.3. Scattergrams for each dimension of political strategy.   171
8.4. Three dimensions of political strategy grouped by
     neoevolutionary types of Service.   172
8.5. Three dimensions of political strategy grouped by
     neoevolutionary types of Fried.   173
8.6. Habermas's conception of Capitalist sociopolitical
     organization.   177
10.1. Map of the Mantaro region of the Inka Empire.   243
10.2. Elite and commoner residential compounds at
      Tunanmarca.   245
10.3. Map of the Morelos region of the Aztec Empire.   246
10.4. Elite and commoner residential compounds at Cuexcomate.   247
11.1. The east coast Megalopolis, USA, in 1963.   286
11.2. Tikal, Guatemala, ninth century A.D.   287
11.3. Angkor, Cambodia, thirteenth century.   289
11.4. Low-density agrarian cities today: Tikal, Anuradhapura,
      and Angkor.   291
11.5. Copan, Honduras, core zone, ninth century A.D.   293
11.6. Anuradhapura, Sri Lanka, twelfth century A.D.   294
11.7. Anuradhapura, twelfth century A.D.   295
11.8. Bagan, Myanmar, thirteenth century.   297
11.9. Greater Angkor, twelfth–thirteenth century A.D.   299
11.10. Greater Angkor, dispersed occupation and field systems.   301
11.11. Angkor Wat compared to central Tikal.   303
11.12. Caracol, Belize, ninth century A.D.   304
11.13. Anuradhapura, tank cascade.   305
11.14. Bagan region, rice production areas.   309

CONTRIBUTORS

John K. Chance is Professor of Anthropology at Arizona State University. His research interests include issues of class, identity, and political economy in colonial Mexico. He is the author of two books on the colonial ethnohistory of Oaxaca, Mexico, and coauthor of a volume on Mesoamerican ethnic identity. *Email:* john.chance@asu.edu.

Robert D. Drennan is Distinguished Professor of Anthropology and Director of the Center for Comparative Archaeology at the University of Pittsburgh. His current research focuses on the worldwide comparative study of patterns of organization in early complex societies. He has carried out field research on the archaeological remains of early chiefly communities in Mexico, Colombia, and China. *Email:* drennan@pitt.edu.

Timothy Earle is Professor of Anthropology, Northwestern University, where he served as Chair from 1995–2000 and 2009–2010. His archaeological research focuses on the political organization and economy of complex societies. He has conducted major excavations in Hawaii, the Andes (Peru and Argentina), and Europe (Denmark, Iceland, and Hungary). He has written ten books, including *How Chiefs Come to Power* (1997). *Email:* tke299@northwestern.edu.

Gary M. Feinman is the Curator of Mesoamerican Anthropology at the Field Museum. He has led systematic regional surveys, site surveys, and a series of household excavation projects to investigate long-term societal change in the Central Valleys of Oaxaca, Mexico. He also has co-directed a systematic archaeological settlement pattern study in eastern Shandong, China. Feinman has published on preindustrial economies, demographic and settlement pattern transitions, and variation and diachronic changes in political organizations. *Email:* gfeinman@fieldmuseum.org.

Roland Fletcher is Professor of Theoretical and World Archaeology at the University of Sydney. His research interests are the logic and philosophy of archaeological inquiry, global cross-comparison of settlement patterns, and the specific study of low-density urbanism. He has directed the Greater Angkor Project for the past decade. His major publication is *The Limits of Settlement Growth* (1995, Cambridge University Press). *Email:* roland.fletcher@sydney.usyd.edu.au.

Michael J. Kolb is Professor of Anthropology at Northern Illinois University, having received his Ph.D. from the University of California at Los Angeles in 1991. His specialty is examining the role monumental architectural construction plays in the rise of complex societies, with special attention to the Hawaiian islands in comparative perspective. Other interests include the link between ritual and warfare in the archaeological record, and how the creation of community is manifested through the creation of settlement. *Email:* aloha@niu.edu.

Peter Peregrine is Professor of Anthropology at Lawrence University in Appleton, Wisconsin. His research focuses on the evolution of complex societies and on developing cross-cultural data and methods to answer questions about large-scale cultural evolutionary processes. *E-mail:* peter.n.peregrine@lawrence.edu.

Christian E. Peterson is Assistant Professor of Anthropology in East Asian Archaeology at the University of Hawai'i at Mānoa. His research interests include Chinese archaeology, the comparative study of early complex societies ("chiefdoms"), regional settlement patterns, household archaeology, and quantitative methods. *Email:* cepeter@hawaii.edu.

Michael E. Smith is Professor of Anthropology in the School of Human Evolution and Social Change at Arizona State University. He has directed excavations at Aztec provincial sites in Mexico and publishes on the comparative analysis of preindustrial states, economies, cities, and households. *Email:* mesmith9@asu.edu.

Monica L. Smith is Professor of Anthropology at UCLA. Her research examines the origins and development of humans' interactions with objects, as well as the growth of urbanism as a social phenomenon. She is co-director of the Sisupalgarh archaeological research project in eastern India. *Email:* smith@anthro.ucla.edu.

Barbara L. Stark is Professor of Anthropology at Arizona State University. Her research interests include archaeological settlement patterns, long-term social and economic change in ancient complex societies, and the archaeology of the Gulf lowlands of Mexico. She has published articles and books about crafts, exchange, urbanism, and political changes in south-central Veracruz, Mexico. *Email:* blstark@asu.edu.

FOREWORD

The Comparative Archaeology of Complex Societies is a terrific book that should be read by every advanced undergraduate and graduate student with interests in the rise of preindustrial cultural complexity. Why am I so enthusiastic about the volume? My enthusiasm rests on both the high quality of its chapters and the signal importance of the subject matter and general approach in the book. This volume is a clarion call for archaeologists to take advantage of the rich database now available to them to significantly advance archaeological elucidation of the development of complex societies through time and space.

But such a goal seems so obvious. Why is a forceful argument for its importance necessary, especially because understanding the reasons for the rise of complex social, political, and economic organization has been of great interest to anthropological archaeologists for a long time?

In recent years, empirical data about this key emergent process, generated by a host of archaeological research projects, have grown quite strongly, and new insights into some of the principal elements involved in complex development have emerged. However, despite such attention and interest, strong theoretical explanations for the development of cultural complexity, in general, and the rise of the urban state, in particular, have not been in abundance.

The building of new theory on early state emergence has been hampered by a number of factors. One of the most important has been the relative lack of good comparative studies. The dearth of such studies is due in part to what can best be called pernicious postmodern influence, which at its most extreme does not see the utility or legitimacy of large-scale comparison (each case is seen as unique), and in part on a widespread concentration on site-specific empirical research. In addition, the relative lack of detailed regional settlement data until recently (not just single-site data) from around the world has impeded further theoretical thinking.

But now we have a sufficiently rich database from around the world that should allow theoretical advances that will provide clearer understandings of the reasons for this key evolutionary transition that provided the cultural foundation for the modern world, and this volume clearly illustrates a host of comparative approaches that promise to shed new light on and insights into the processes of complex cultural developments, and that make this volume's arguments even more promising.

My own interests in comparative archaeology are long standing, but so is my appreciation of the difficulties of this approach and the resistance of many archaeologists, albeit often passive, to such endeavors, particularly large-scale ones. Partly, my interest derived from the teaching of Gordon R. Willey, who championed the comparative approach in archaeology in his teaching and writing. For example, Willey's 1962 article "The Early Great Styles and the Rise of the Pre-Columbian Civilizations" remains a masterpiece in this regard. It also derives in part from my own teaching. Forty years ago, when C. C. Lamberg-Karlovsky and I began preparing an introductory general education course at Harvard University, modestly titled "The Rise and Fall of Civilizations," we quickly realized that there were no comparative ancient civilizations texts that would fit the goals of our course. Robert McC. Adams' superb 1966 volume *The Evolution of Urban Society* was available, but it was not really suitable as a freshman-level introduction to the subject. So, we ended up writing our own 1979 textbook, *Ancient Civilizations: The Near East and Mesoamerica*. We also edited a 1974 reader on the topic: *The Rise and Fall of Civilizations: Modern Archaeological Approaches to Ancient Cultures*, as well as a 1975 comparative volume, *Ancient Civilization and Trade*, that emanated from an earlier School of American Research advanced seminar.

However, in the 1970s, although we had strong interests in comparative archaeology of complex societies, we did not have the kinds of data available today that allow much more productive comparisons. Ironically, in the decades that followed, as the databases grew richer, the interests in comparison appeared to wane. Now with the combination of better information and a resurgence of attention to both small- and large-scale comparisons (see Gary Feinman and Joyce Marcus' 1998 edited volume *Archaic States*, Bruce Trigger's monumental 2003 book *Understanding Early Civilizations*, and Joyce Marcus and my 2008 edited volume *The Ancient City*, among many recent examples), the highly promising approaches discussed in

The Comparative Archaeology of Complex Societies should have great appeal and strong effects on scholarly understandings of this key subject.

Jeremy A. Sabloff
President, Santa Fe Institute
Santa Fe, New Mexico
December 2010

PREFACE

This volume presents the results of an advanced seminar dedicated to exploring new approaches in comparative archaeology. The seminar grew out of a planning meeting held at the School of Human Evolution and Social Change at Arizona State University in October 2007. Robert D. Drennan, Timothy Earle, Gary M. Feinman, Michael E. Smith, and Barbara L. Stark discussed current directions in research on early complex societies and agreed on the value of an invited advanced seminar focused on the diversity of rigorous comparative methods being used today.

The advanced seminar was held at the Amerind Foundation in Dragoon, Arizona, March 3–7, 2008. The session was organized by Michael E. Smith and sponsored by the Amerind Foundation and Arizona State University. The participants were: Robert D. Drennan (University of Pittsburgh), Timothy Earle (Northwestern University), Gary M. Feinman (Field Museum of Natural History), Roland Fletcher (University of Sydney), Michael J. Kolb (Northern Illinois University), Peter Peregrine (Lawrence University), Christian E. Peterson (University of Hawai'i at Mānoa), Carla Sinopoli (University of Michigan), Michael E. Smith (Arizona State University), Monica L. Smith (UCLA), Barbara L. Stark (Arizona State University), and Miriam T. Stark (University of Hawai'i). ASU graduate student Juliana Novic participated as an assistant and notetaker. Figure 0.1 shows the participants at the Amerind Foundation.

A strong consensus was reached about the importance of comparative analysis in archaeology and about the need for new approaches that encompass the vast variation within and among societies of different kinds. The participants wrote a joint programmatic statement on comparative analysis; that statement appears as Chapter 1 of this book. After the seminar, summaries of the main points were presented at a public forum at Arizona

Figure 0.1. Participants in the Amerind conference. Front row: Barbara L. Stark, Miriam T. Stark, Juliana Novic. Back row: Monica L. Smith, Gary M. Feinman, Robert D. Drennan, Timothy Earle, Michael J. Kolb, Roland Fletcher, Peter Peregrine, Carla Sinopoli, Christian E. Peterson, Michael E. Smith.

State University. Peter Wells (University of Minnesota) served as a respon-dent and provided insightful and helpful commentary on the presentations. Carla Sinopoli and Miriam T. Stark were unable to contribute a chapter to this volume, but their participation in the seminar was dynamic, interesting, and valuable.

I would like to thank the School of Human Evolution and Social Change, Arizona State University, for funding the initial planning meeting and the participant costs for the advanced seminar. The Amerind Foundation kindly hosted the seminar in a setting that was highly conducive to intellectual ex-change and advance. I thank John Ware and the entire staff of the Amerind Foundation for their help in making the seminar a success. ASU student Sara Robertson provided help with editorial and manuscript preparation tasks.

CHAPTER 1

COMPARATIVE ARCHAEOLOGY

A COMMITMENT TO UNDERSTANDING VARIATION

Robert D. Drennan, Timothy Earle, Gary M. Feinman, Roland
Fletcher, Michael J. Kolb, Peter Peregrine, Christian E. Peterson,
Carla Sinopoli, Michael E. Smith, Monica L. Smith, Barbara L.
Stark, and Miriam T. Stark

As archaeologists, we seek to understand variation and change in past human societies. This goal necessitates a comparative approach, and comparisons justify the broad cross-cultural and diachronic scope of our work. Without comparisons we sink into the culture-bound theorizing against which anthropology and archaeology have long sought to broaden social science research. By undertaking comparisons that incorporate long-term social variability, archaeologists not only improve our understanding of the past, but also open the door to meaningful transdisciplinary research. Archaeologists have unique and comprehensive data sets whose analysis can contribute to dialogues surrounding contemporary issues and the myriad challenges of our era.

In the past two decades, the pendulum seems to have swung away from comparative research in archaeology. Many archaeologists focus on detailed contextual descriptions of individual cases, and only a few have dedicated themselves to explicit comparative work. Yet in that same time span, fieldwork has expanded tremendously throughout the world, leading to an explosion of well-documented diachronic data on sites and regions. We now have substantial detail on the variation inherent in phenomena such as cultural assemblages, settlement patterns, and economic activity. New methods, from dating techniques to digital data processing, promote comparative analysis and greatly advance our understanding of human societies and change. The time is ripe for a renewed commitment to comparative research in archaeology.

Rigorous new methods are needed to achieve an explicit comparative understanding of the past. Particularly fruitful domains for comparative research in archaeology include households, settlement patterns, and the built landscape. These are categories of data that are both widely available in the archaeological literature and important for understanding the dynamics of past societies. It is a healthy sign that a variety of approaches to comparative research are now being pursued, including the documentation and exploration of the range of variation over time, the evaluation of potential causes for variation and change, and the exploration of the impact of particular variations on long-term patterns of stability and change. Productive comparative research ranges from statistical analysis of large samples to rich contextual comparisons of a few cases; there is no single best method. A holistic perspective for studying the past requires a range of comparative approaches in concert.

Work presented at the seminar focused on explicit comparative analyses of archaeological (and other) data and the participants plan to continue an approach that encompasses multiple regions or contexts in a single study rather than merely juxtaposing case studies in an edited volume. Seminar papers compared, for example, the process of Spanish colonization in different continents, the development of chiefdom-level settlement patterns and monuments in multiple world regions, the artifact inventories of households in diverse settings, tropical low-density urban centers across the globe, and the variation in political dynamics across and within polities. Such comparative research not only illuminates the past, but also produces surprising findings and identifies commonly held notions that may be incorrect or misleading.

Some archaeologists may associate the comparative method with the neoevolutionism of Steward, Service, and Fried. In fact, the comparative method and neoevolutionism are separate arenas of thought and activity; one does not imply the other. A central problem with neoevolutionism was its focus on normative societal types such as bands and tribes that tended to compress or ignore variation and concentrated on generalized similarities. As archaeological data have expanded at the end of the twentieth century, the utility of such societal types has declined because they mask the variation that is one of the most obvious aspects of human societies, past and present. The most productive comparative approaches do not focus on general societal types; instead they involve the analysis of archaeological data at multiple spatial and social scales and they emphasize societal variability and change.

Comparative archaeology can lead to the reevaluation of conventional categories such as community, polity, or urbanism. Its varied approaches have the potential to provide powerful syntheses that focus on and analyze the true complexity of past human life and society. Comparative methods are essential if archaeologists are to contribute to transdisciplinary research in the historical and social sciences and thereby broaden the scientific understanding of the past, the present, and the future of human society.

CHAPTER 2

APPROACHES TO COMPARATIVE ANALYSIS IN ARCHAEOLOGY

Michael E. Smith and Peter Peregrine

Archaeology is inherently comparative. Comparison is necessary to understand the material record, for one cannot identify or understand an object never before seen without comparing it to a known object. Comparison is also necessary to understand variation over time and space, for one cannot identify or investigate variation unless one has examples spanning a range of variation, nor can one examine change without examples spanning a range of time. Comparative analysis is the only way to identify regularities in human behavior, and it is also the only way to identify unique features of human societies. Indeed, to Bruce G. Trigger the comparative nature of archaeological data and analysis places archaeology at the heart of the most important issues in the social sciences:

> The most important issue confronting the social sciences is the extent to which human behavior is shaped by factors that operate cross-culturally as opposed to factors that are unique to particular cultures. (Trigger 2003:3)

In this chapter we outline the ways archaeologists have used comparison to understand the material record and to explore variation over time and space. After a brief history of comparative research on ancient societies, we review the variety of approaches used by the authors of this volume using seven dimensions of the comparative method in archaeology.

History of Comparative Research

The comparison of material traits to explore variation over space and time has a long history in archaeology. Indeed, one could argue that such comparisons were one of the major contributions made by nineteenth-century antiquarians in shaping what would become the discipline of archaeology (Trigger 2006). In one of the earliest examples of scientific archaeology in the New World, Cyrus Thomas (1898) compared ancient earthen mounds in the eastern United States to one another and to historic accounts of mound building and mound use. Through this comparison, Thomas established that there were several distinct mound building traditions, and all appear to have been built by the ancestors of contemporary Native Americans. In Europe, Gustav Oscar Montelius (1888) traveled extensively to museums and archaeological sites comparing the artifacts found in sealed deposits such as burials and hoards. Montelius used the information about objects that were never found in association to define six major periods within the Bronze Age, each of which, he posited, represented a different cultural tradition that spread across all of Europe.

In contemporary archaeology, the comparison of material traits for culture-historical purposes has been largely supplanted by chronometric dating techniques, although comparison as a means to perform seriation and stratigraphy still has a place (O'Brien and Lyman 1999). More commonly, comparisons are performed to aid in the interpretation of the archaeological record or to better understand variation. One major form of this has been the comparison of societal types (e.g., bands, tribes, chiefdoms, and states).

Comparative studies of societal "types" that allegedly encompass a core package of nonmaterial traits became increasingly common in archaeology with the rebirth of evolutionism in the 1960s, and particularly following the publication of Elman Service's *Primitive Social Organization* (1966). However, the comparison of societal types was also fostered by research on the origins of states and the recognition that early states appeared to share numerous features, despite being located in different parts of the world and evolving over varying spans of time. Few works focused on the comparison of societal types can easily be divorced from questions of process and origin; indeed, it was the origin of these societal types that underlay most comparative efforts (e.g., Adams 1966; Childe 1950; Sanders and Price 1968). However, a better way to examine evolutionary processes, such as the origins of urban societies or states, is to examine them over time, that is, diachronically.

Diachronic comparison was a staple method among the founders of the discipline of anthropology. In *Principles of Sociology*, for example, Herbert Spencer (1898–99) attempted to construct a general law of cultural evolution in part by providing examples of various stages of cultural evolution that included pre-Columbian Mexico, Pharonic Egypt, and the Roman Empire, among others. Similarly, Edward Tylor in *Primitive Culture* (1871) used a crude form of diachronic comparison to trace cultural "survivals" and build evolutionary sequences. Lewis Henry Morgan used diachronic comparison in *Ancient Society* (1878) to establish a universal sequence of cultural evolution. Unfortunately, these early attempts at diachronic comparison were doomed to fail because the available archaeological data were crude and lacked absolute dates, preventing the establishment of an empirical sequence of change. The lack of true diachronic data was a significant flaw in the work of the early evolutionists, a flaw that was rightly seized upon by Boas and his students, who launched a damning criticism of both comparative analyses and evolutionary theory (a critical perspective that continues to this day – see, e.g., Giddens 1984; Hodder 1986; Nisbet 1969; and Pauketat 2001).

Although the paucity of data and the Boasian reaction against these early evolutionists halted comparative research for a time, a second generation of evolutionists followed with comparisons based on better data and more rigorous theory (Hallpike 1986; Harris 1968; Sanderson 1999; Trigger 2006). Foremost among these scholars was Vere Gordon Childe, whose *Social Evolution* (1951) provided something of a blueprint for diachronic cross-cultural comparisons using archaeological data. His basic position was that "archaeology can establish sequences of cultures in various natural regions. And these cultures represent societies or phases in the development of societies. Potentially, therefore, archaeological sequences reveal the chronological order in which kinds of society did historically emerge" (Childe 1951:17). To unleash this potential, Childe (pp. 22–29) suggested that archaeologists needed to focus their efforts on clarifying archaeological sequences based on what can be most clearly observed in the archaeological record: technology and economy. Such changes in technology and economy, Childe argued, led to changes in other aspects of culture and, in turn, to cultural evolution.

What Childe and others (e.g., Fried 1967; Parsons 1966; White 1959) demonstrated is that diachronic comparison is an excellent way to study cultural evolution (for a recent discussion, see Yoffee 1993). Through diachronic comparison, presumed causes can be demonstrated to precede presumed effects, and evolutionary patterns and processes can be identified and studied over time. These conclusions are in no way groundbreaking – historians and evolutionary biologists had been working in a comparative framework for generations – but, as a consequence of the Boasian reaction against comparative research, it took anthropology much longer to realize the value of comparative methodology (for further discussion, see Harris 1968; Sanderson 1990; Yengoyan 2006). Recent books by Bruce Trigger (1998, 2003) explore the conceptual and empirical record of comparative research in anthropology and archaeology.

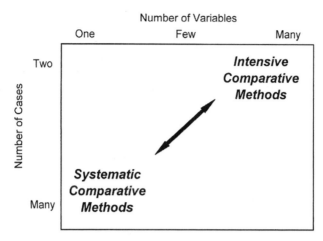

Figure 2.1. Intensive and systematic comparative strategies. After Caramani (2009:15); drawing by Miriam Cox.

Approaches to Comparison

There are many different approaches to comparative analysis in the social and historical sciences (e.g., C. R. Ember and Ember 2001; Gingrich and Fox 2002; Grew 1980; Hunt 2007; Mace and Pagel 1994; Mahoney 2004; Ragin 1987; Smelser 1976; Tilly 1984; Ward 2009; Westcoat 1994). Divergent approaches to comparison are sometimes discussed in terms of a contrast or continuum between what can be called systematic and intensive comparative methods (e.g., M. E. Smith 2006). Systematic studies, exemplified in anthropology by the cross-cultural research associated with the Human Relations Area Files, employ large sample sizes and typically use formal statistical methods of inference. In the social science literature on comparative analysis, systematic studies are often called "large-scale" or "variable-oriented" studies (Caramani 2009). Intensive comparative research, on the other hand, focuses on a small number of cases, each analyzed in more depth and with greater contextualization (i.e., consideration of many variables). This approach is often called "small-scale" or "case-oriented" (Caramani 2009). Figure 2.1 illustrates the relationship between the systematic and intensive approaches in terms of the numbers of cases and variables typically employed. Although each approach has its value and usefulness (as do studies intermediate between the polar extremes), most researchers tend to be comfortable working with a particular kind of comparative analysis, and statements of the advantages of one or the other approach are common in the literature.

Comparative historians tend to be much more comfortable using intensive comparisons. Within the discipline of history, comparative studies occupy only a small number of scholars. As noted by Jürgen Kocka, "Many cherished principles of the historical discipline – proximity to the sources, context, and continuity – are sometimes in tension with the comparative approach" (2003:39). Those historians who do pursue comparative research argue forcefully in favor of context-heavy comparisons of only a few cases (Grew 1980; Haupt 2001; Kocka 2003; Tilly 1984). Charles Tilly, for example, concludes his book on comparative historical research with this statement:

> It is tempting to look for finer and finer comparisons, with larger numbers of cases and more variables controlled. In the present state of our knowledge of big structures and large processes, that would be a serious error. It would be an error because with the multiplications of cases and the standardization of categories for comparison the theoretical return declines more rapidly than the empirical return rises. (Tilly 1984:144)

Some archaeologists agree with Tilly and other comparative historians and argue for the superiority of intensive comparisons over systematic approaches. Adam T. Smith, for example, explicitly positions his book toward the intensive end of the continuum:

> The book is intended to help resuscitate a genre of anthropological writing that explores material in a comparative spirit without yielding to the reductionist tendencies that tend to cripple many such works. Thus, it was critical that each case be allowed to develop in its own right without the compression that results from traditional comparison. (A. T. Smith 2003:28)

The intensive approach to comparison has long been popular among anthropologists (Eggan 1954; Gingrich and Fox 2002; Yengoyan 2006) and archaeologists (Adams 1966; Earle 1997; Trigger 2003). Recently, comparative analysis has become an important approach among some Classicists, whose research clearly lies at the intensive end of the continuum (e.g., Dal Lago and Katsari 2008; Morris and Scheidel 2009; Scheidel 2009; Webster 2008). Within archaeology and anthropology, however, intensive comparative analysis has received little explicit methodological attention. Systematic comparative research, on the other hand, is the target of a significant body of methodological work. It seems logical that systematic comparison would be of great interest to archaeologists, because this approach is particularly well suited to the study of cultural evolution. As discussed earlier, the founders of the discipline (Spencer, Tylor, and Morgan) employed systematic comparison, but their work was flawed by poor data and rudimentary statistical methods. The stigma of those flaws still haunts systematic comparison (e.g., autocorrelation bias is often called "Galton's problem," a reference to a question Francis Galton raised during one of Tylor's presentations to the Royal Anthropological Institute in 1889!), but well-designed samples like the Standard Cross-Cultural Sample (Murdock and White 1969), access to good ethnographic data through archives such as the Human Relations Area Files, and the development of statistical methods that can identify and correct flawed samples and data have led to greater confidence in systematic comparison (Peregrine 2001, 2004).

During the 1970s, archaeologists began to use comparative ethnology to interpret the archaeological record. Comparative ethnology refers to the statistical evaluation of theories or hypotheses using data from large (often worldwide) and clearly defined samples of cultures (C. R. Ember and Ember 2001). The importance of this approach is that if one can find a strong association in a worldwide sample of cultures, then one can assume that the association fits human behavior in general, and not just the customs of a particular culture or historically related group of cultures (Sanderson 1990:211–32). And, particularly important for the archaeologist, there is no a priori reason for this generalization not to hold for prehistoric cultures as well (M. Ember and Ember 1995:95–96). Although a large number of material indicators of human behavior have been identified (Blanton and Fargher 2008; C. R. Ember 2003; M. Ember and Ember 1995; McNett 1979; Peregrine 2004), comparative ethnology has yet to develop into an important archaeological tool. As McNett (1979:40) succinctly puts it, "One is rather at a loss to explain why this method has not been used more for archaeological purposes."

Dimensions of Comparison

Although contrasting the systematic and intensive approaches to comparison highlights some of the important issues of comparative research, most comparative work in archaeology today transcends this dichotomy or continuum. As exemplified by later chapters, contemporary comparative research by archaeologists covers a wide range of approaches, methods, and styles. To describe this variety adequately, we break the intensive–systematic continuum into nine separate dimensions of comparison (see Table 2.1): sample size (how many cases are compared?); sample selection (how are the cases selected?); contextualization (how thoroughly are the

Table 2.1. Dimensions of
comparison

Sample size
Sample selection
Contextualization
Scale
Primary vs. secondary data
Archaeological vs. historical data
Synchronic vs. diachronic
Stage in the research trajectory
Spatial and temporal domain

cases contextualized?); scale (do the comparisons focus on whole societies or a limited domain?); primary versus secondary data; archaeological versus historical data; synchronic versus diachronic comparisons; stage in the research trajectory at which comparison is invoked; and spatial and temporal domain.

1. Sample Size. The sizes of samples that archaeologists use in their comparative research vary widely. As a study in the holocultural tradition, Peregrine (Chapter 8) employs a larger sample than most of the case studies in this volume; at the other extreme is the chapter by Earle and Smith (Chapter 10), who compare just two examples: Aztec and Inka provincial societies. Their study shows that "sample size," however, is not always a simple construct. Although they are comparing two societies, each of those societies is represented by several archaeological sites, each of which contributes several individual excavated domestic contexts. Although quantitative measures are calculated for each of these domestic contexts, they are arrayed and combined in a form that illustrates the fundamental social comparison of interest (Aztec and Inka provincial societies). Most of the other studies in this volume employ sample sizes somewhere between two and ten cases. Stark and Chance (Chapter 9) draw on many more empirical cases than the other chapters, but their use of these examples differs from most of the others. As discussed later under "Stage in the Research Trajectory," their analysis is directed at documenting and understanding the range of variation in their topic (provincial imperial strategies) rather than at controlled comparisons of individual societies or empires.

2. Sample Selection. The ability of holocultural research to employ random sampling, coupled with the extensive discussions of methodological issues of sampling in this literature (C. R. Ember and Ember 2001;

Peregrine 2003), give this approach a significant advantage over other comparative approaches in sample selection. On the other hand, research projects positioned at the more intensive end of the continuum typically *cannot* employ random sampling because there are simply too few cases with the requisite richness of data and contextual control. For many archaeological studies, the sample consists of all of the cases that the author(s) can assemble with sufficient data that the authors feel they can comprehend and analyze. For example, Stark and Chance (Chapter 9) have assembled cases from nearly all of the known empires in the ancient and historical New World. At the extreme of small sample size, Earle and Smith (Chapter 10) limit their sample to cases in which they have personally conducted fieldwork. The reasons for this limitation have to do with the difficulties of generating extensive comparable primary data from published accounts for rich, artifact-based analyses like this, coupled with the paucity of projects that have gathered extensive relevant household-level data.

Unique in this collection, Peterson and Drennan (Chapter 6) employ a dynamic approach to sample size and sample selection. They began their comparative research on the historical trajectories of early complex societies with a comparison of three cases (Drennan and Peterson 2006). They subsequently identified an additional eight cases and added them to the original three for their discussion. These authors are actively seeking out additional cases that meet their data requirements (see Chapters 5 and 6), and thus their sample size will continue to grow.

One interesting approach to sample selection is to choose cases that are rich and diverse to explore new conceptual terrain. The goal of such comparisons is to build theory that will permit more rigorous and systematic comparisons at a later stage. Urban scholar Xavier de Souza Briggs (2004), for example, compares three "revelatory cases" (classical Rome, medieval Córdoba, and contemporary Los Angeles) to develop models of how large urban polities manage ethnic and cultural diversity. This was the context of one of the most influential comparative studies of early complex societies, Robert McC. Adams's (1966) *The Evolution of Urban Society*. Although Teotihuacan might have been a more appropriate choice of an early Mesoamerican urban society than much later Aztec Tenochtitlan, the richness of the historical data available for the latter case allowed Adams to develop a more sophisticated theoretical model for the rise of states, cities, and empires.

3. Contextualization. Contextualization in comparative research refers to the extent to which social, cultural, and historical details are provided to support and illuminate specific comparisons. As noted in the previous discussion of systematic and intensive approaches, the nature and level of contextualization in comparative studies tend to vary inversely with the sample size. For example, the chapters with the largest sample sizes for formal comparisons – Peterson and Drennan (Chapter 6) and Peregrine (Chapter 8) – employ lower levels of contextualization than do chapters with smaller sample sizes such as Fletcher (Chapter 11). But the level of contextualization also depends heavily on the scale of the comparisons (see next section). Earle and Smith (Chapter 10) have the smallest sample size (two cases), but because their comparison occurs on a narrow scale (households within economies), their level of contextualization is relatively low.

4. Scale. Productive archaeological comparisons can cover a wide range of analytical scales, from treatments of a single phenomena – such as the shapes of houses (Whiting and Ayres 1968) or sedentism (Odell 1998) – to comparisons of whole societies (Adams 1966; Trigger 2003). Most of the studies in this volume occupy a middle range, combining comparisons of specific features or institutions with broader contextual comparisons of societies as well. A common approach is to use one or more comparisons of specific traits in different cases to make inferences about the wider societies in question, with some discussion of how the societies compare on the broader scale. Whole-society comparisons can be interesting and illuminating, but at this stage of our understanding of ancient complex societies, comparisons at a more restricted scale may be more productive.

5. Primary Data, Secondary Data, and Interpretations. One of the important precepts of this book is that one should compare archaeological data rather than comparing interpretations of those data as made by diverse scholars (see discussion by Drennan and Peterson, Chapter 5). But the concept of data (defined as observations and measurements of empirical phenomena) is complex and multifaceted. Do we need to go back to original counts and descriptions of artifacts, or can we rely on published tabular data? What if not all analyzed contexts are included in the published reports? What if the contexts being compared have differing data-standardization procedures (e.g., percent vs. density, or percent of rim sherds vs. percent of all sherds)? These seemingly mundane issues present some of the biggest obstacles to formal comparative research using archaeological data. Earle and Smith (Chapter 10) discuss some of the problems of this sort that arose in their comparative study.

Most of the authors in this volume make an effort to base their analyses on primary archaeological data (and, in some cases, historical data). Stark and Chance (Chapter 9) and Monica L. Smith (Chapter 4) differ somewhat from the other chapters in that their early-stage research relies, by necessity, on interpretations rather than primary data to a greater extent than the other chapters. One of the promising aspects of Drennan and Peterson's approach (Chapters 5 and 6) is their attempt to devise analytical approaches that are sufficiently robust to be applied to data sets that were not all collected or published in the same manner.

6. Archaeological and Historical Data. The interrelationships among archaeological and historical data are much-discussed topics among archaeologists working on complex societies (e.g., Moreland 2006; M. E. Smith 1992b; Storey 1999). Several of the following case studies employ both types of data, using the insights of each as necessary for the problem at hand (e.g., Fletcher, Chapter 11; Stark and Chance, Chapter 9). Earle and Smith use historical data to establish the general parameters of the societies being compared, but then focus their analysis on archaeological data. Finally, a number of chapters deal entirely with archaeological data; these are Smith (Chapter 4), Peterson and Drennan (Chapter 6), and Kolb (Chapter 7).

7. Synchronic versus Diachronic. Although the most fundamental strength of archaeological data is their chronological context – their record of change over long periods of time – the most common approach to comparative analysis in archaeology focuses on synchronic comparisons. The reasons for this are complex and involve the nature of time, social change, archaeological chronology, and the relationships among these domains (Bailey 2007; Dunnell 1982; Holdaway and Wandsnider 2008; M. E. Smith 1992a). There is a large body of literature on methods for synchronic anthropological (and archaeological) comparisons (e.g., C. R. Ember and Ember 2001) and numerous published case studies. In contrast, the topic of diachronic comparisons – in archaeology and other disciplines – is less well developed (see earlier discussion). One of the few methodological treatments of diachronic comparisons is that of Bartolini (1993). In this volume Monica Smith (Chapter 4) and Peterson and Drennan (Chapter 6) contribute important new perspectives on diachronic archaeological comparisons. The remaining case studies all treat time and change in some manner, but they are fundamentally synchronic comparisons.

8. Stage in the Research Trajectory. Historian Raymond Grew (1980: 769) states that "comparison can aid historians at four stages of their work: (1) in asking questions, (2) in identifying historical problems, (3) in designing the appropriate research, and (4) in reaching and testing significant conclusions." Although this four-part classification seems too schematic to apply directly to archaeological research, the notion that comparisons can be useful at a number of points along the trajectory of research on a particular problem is important. Many of the chapters in this book employ comparisons relatively late in the research sequence, drawing conclusions based on carefully selected samples (e.g., Chapters 7 and 10). Others, however, employ comparisons much earlier in the research process (e.g., Chapters 4 and 9).

Stark and Chance (Chapter 9), for example, explore the concept of provincial strategies. Because this topic had not previously been synthesized or subject to comparative or theoretical analysis, their study is positioned relatively early in the trajectory of comparative research on provincial strategies. Now that they have identified a number of such strategies and their implications, the next step would be a more formal comparison of the provincial strategies employed in a sample of empires. Such early-stage comparisons differ from late-stage comparisons, such as Earle and Smith's study. In contrast to provincial strategies, there are large bodies of research on households in agrarian states (e.g., Allison 1999; Netting et al. 1984) and on ancient economies (Earle 2002; Feinman and Nicholas 2004; M. E. Smith 2004). This material permits Earle and Smith to ask rather detailed questions about the differences between provincial household economics in the Inka and Aztec empires.

The issue of stage in the research trajectory can be complex. For example, Smith's initial view was that the research by Peterson and Drennan (Chapter 6) falls at the later end of this scale (i.e., later in the research process), because they have relatively well-developed concepts and measures. Peterson and Drennan, on the other hand, would place their research earlier in the research trajectory, in at least some ways. They see their work as exploratory in the sense that it will lead to the generation of new questions about the dynamics that produce this variability. Drennan stated in an email to Smith (November 5, 2008), "The actual work that we've done, especially in the Peterson and Drennan chapter [Chapter 6] though, is at a much, much earlier stage. In our view, we've only just scratched the surface of characterizing the variation that we seek ultimately to understand better. So, we see the empirical comparisons here as at a very initial exploratory stage in research." Perhaps these views can be reconciled by suggesting that their research fits within Grew's stage 4, but at a very early position within that stage.

9. Spatial and Temporal Domain. Most recent comparative research by archaeologists fits within two broad domains: regional comparisons and global comparisons. Regional comparisons consider the archaeological cultures within a specific region and compare them over time to understand similarities and differences in cultural evolutionary processes (e.g., Blanton et al., 1993; Cutright et al. 2010; Marcus and Flannery 1996). Often the attempt is focused on understanding variation in how cultures have adapted to a particular area. Global comparisons consider archaeological cultures from diverse parts of the world (e.g., Earle 1997; Maisels 1999). These types of comparison have typically focused on major questions in cultural evolution such as the origins of agriculture and states. Although variation is of interest in global comparative studies, the main focus is often on identifying a single or group of similar processes that led to the same result in many areas of the world.

The chapters in this book are situated in between the categories of regional and global comparisons. None limit their domain to a single geographical region, yet none are truly global in striving to compare *all* known examples of a particular phenomenon. Peterson and Drennan's analysis (Chapter 6) is the most "global" study in the volume in terms of inclusion of many world regions.

A third domain, discussed by Feinman (Chapter 3) but not represented here by an empirical study, is the comparison of ancient cases with contexts in the modern world. Drennan and Peterson's (Chapter 5) point that only recently have we generated sufficient high-quality archaeological data to make robust comparative claims applies to ancient–modern comparisons as well, but work in this area is even more poorly developed. Although early papers on this topic may now appear simplistic and naïve (e.g., Martin and Gregory 1973), archaeologists have yet to progress very far with rigorous and relevant comparisons of ancient and modern social phenomena. Elsewhere I focus on several urban issues to argue that the reasons for this lack of progress lie less in the lack of archaeological data than in the realms of concepts and methods. Archaeologists need to engage conceptually with work in other disciplines to make effective ancient–modern comparisons, and we need to analyze (or reanalyze) our data so that we can address the topics and concepts of interest (M. E. Smith 2010).

The delay of archaeologists in seriously engaging ancient–modern comparisons (see Feinman, Chapter 3) has not stopped nonarchaeologists from doing this, however, and they frequently use outdated information or misuse archaeological data (Childs 2007; Pugh 2000). We agree with Feinman (Chapter 3) that it is up to archaeologists to engage the present as well as the past in our comparative endeavors.

The Chapters that Follow

The chapters in this book encompass a great diversity of approaches to comparison along the nine comparative dimensions discussed earlier. They are arranged in a rough progression from more general accounts to more specific accounts, and from relatively simpler to more complex societies. Gary Feinman (Chapter 3) makes an eloquent plea for expanding the conceptual and empirical domains of comparison within archaeology. Monica Smith (Chapter 4) compares three regional Neolithic trajectories toward greater complexity (the Levant, the Indus Valley, and the U.S. Southwest), focusing on the actions and decisions of individuals as key elements of change and stability.

Robert Drennan and Christian Peterson (Chapter 5) present a sophisticated conceptual and methodological discussion of issues in the comparison of archaeological trajectories. Then in Chapter 6, Peterson and Drennan apply their insights through an innovative and productive method for the rigorous comparison of settlement data from around the world. In Chapter 7, Michael Kolb shows some of the benefits of using a carefully delimited domain for comparison in a study of monuments in island societies. Peter Peregrine (Chapter 8) follows with the most systematic comparison represented in the book, a statistical study of the political strategies of leaders. Chapters 9 and 10 address New World empires, but using very different approaches and data. Barbara Stark and John Chance (Chapter 9) assemble an impressive range of archaeological and historical data on both pre-Hispanic and Spanish Colonial empires to identify a series of strategies that provincial peoples (rulers, elites, commoners) employed when confronted by expanding empires. In Chapter 10, Timothy Earle and Michael Smith compare provincial household economies before and after conquest by the Inka and Aztec empires.

Roland Fletcher, in Chapter 11, discusses a type of urban settlement – the low-density agrarian city – that is documented archaeologically in a number of regions. Chapter 12 by Smith draws together some of the insights and implications of the other chapters for the continuing development of comparative analysis as a productive approach in archaeology.

References Cited

Adams, Robert McC. 1966 *The Evolution of Urban Society: Early Mesopotamia and Prehispanic Mexico.* Aldine, Chicago.
Allison, Penelope M. (editor) 1999 *The Archaeology of Household Activities.* Routledge, New York.

Bailey, Geoff N. 2007 Time Perspectives, Palimpsests, and the Archaeology of Time. *Journal of Anthropological Archaeology* 26:198–223.

Bartolini, Stefano 1993 On Time and Comparative Research. *Journal of Theoretical Politics* 5:131–67.

Blanton, Richard E. and Lane F. Fargher 2008 *Collective Action in the Formation of Pre-Modern States*. Springer, New York.

Blanton, Richard E., Stephen A. Kowalewski, Gary M. Feinman, and Laura Finsten 1993 *Ancient Mesoamerica: A Comparison of Change in Three Regions*. 2nd ed. Cambridge University Press, New York.

Briggs, Xavier de Souza 2004 Civilization in Color: The Multicultural City in Three Millennia. *City and Community* 3:311–42.

Caramani, Daniele 2009 *Introduction to the Comparative Method with Boolean Algebra*. Quantitative Applications in the Social Sciences, vol. 158. Sage, Los Angeles.

Childe, V. Gordon 1950 The Urban Revolution. *Town Planning Review* 21:3–17.

———. 1951 *Social Evolution*. Meridian Books, New York.

Childs, Craig 2007 Phoenix Falling? Will Phoenix Continue to Boom . . . or Bust Entirely? The Answer May Lie in the Ancient Hohokam City Buried Beneath. *High Country News* 37(April 16):10–16.

Cutright, Robyn E., Enrique López-Hurtado, and Alexander J. Martin (editors) 2010 Comparative Perspectives on the Archaeology of Coastal South America/Perspectivas comparativas sobre la arqueología de la costa Sudamericana. Center for Comparative Archaeology, Pontificia Universidad Católica del Perú, and Ministerio de Cultura del Ecuador, Pittsburgh, Lima and Quito.

Dal Lago, Enrico and Constantina Katsari (editors) 2008 *Slave Systems, Ancient and Modern*. Cambridge University Press, New York.

Drennan, Robert D. and Christian E. Peterson 2006 Patterned Variation in Prehistoric Chiefdoms. *Proceedings of the National Academy of Sciences* 103:3960–67.

Dunnell, Robert C. 1982 Science, Social Science, and Common Sense: The Agonizing Dilemma of Modern Archaeology. *Journal of Anthropological Research* 38:1–25.

Earle, Timothy 1997 *How Chiefs Come to Power: The Political Economy in Prehistory*. Stanford University Press, Stanford.

———. 2002 *Bronze Age Economics: The Beginnings of Political Economies*. Westview Press, Boulder, CO.

Eggan, Fred 1954 Social Anthropology and the Method of Controlled Comparison. *American Anthropologist* 56:743–63.

Ember, Carol R. 2003 *Cross-Cultural Research and its Relevance for Archaeological Inference*. Paper presented at the Santa Fe Institute, Working Group on Language and Prehistory, Santa Fe, NM.

Ember, Carol R. and Melvin Ember 2001 *Cross-Cultural Research Methods*. Alta Mira, Walnut Creek, CA.

Ember, Melvin and Carol R. Ember 1995 Worldwide Cross-Cultural Studies and Their Relevance for Archaeology. *Journal of Archaeological Research* 3:87–111.

Feinman, Gary M. and Linda M. Nicholas (editors) 2004 *Archaeological Perspectives on Political Economies*. University of Utah Press, Salt Lake City.

Fried, Morton H. 1967 *The Evolution of Political Society: An Essay in Political Anthropology*. Random House, New York.

Giddens, Anthony 1984 *The Constitution of Society: Outline of the Theory of Structuration*. University of California Press, Berkeley.

Gingrich, Andre and Richard G. Fox (editors) 2002 *Anthropology, By Comparison*. Routledge, New York.

Grew, Raymond 1980 The Case for Comparing Histories. *American Historical Review* 85:763–78.

Hallpike, Christopher R. 1986 *The Principles of Social Evolution*. Clarendon Press, Oxford.

Harris, Marvin 1968 *The Rise of Anthropological Theory: A History of Theories of Culture*. Thomas Y. Crowell, New York.

Haupt, Heinz-Gerhard 2001 Comparative History. In *International Encyclopedia of the Social and Behavioral Sciences*, edited by Neil J. Smelser and Paul B. Baltes, pp. 2397–403. Pergamon, Oxford.

Hodder, Ian 1986 *Reading the Past: Current Approaches to Interpretation in Archaeology*. Cambridge University Press, New York.

Holdaway, Simon and LuAnn Wandsnider (editors) 2008 *Time in Archaeology: Time Perspectivism Revisited*. University of Utah Press, Salt Lake City.

Hunt, Robert C. 2007 *Beyond Relativism: Comparability in Cultural Anthropology*. Altamira Press, Lanham.

Kocka, Jürgen 2003 Comparison and Beyond. *History and Theory* 42:39–44.

Mace, Ruth and Mark Pagel 1994 The Comparative Method in Anthropology. *Current Anthropology* 35:549–64.

Mahoney, James 2004 Comparative-Historical Methodology. *Annual Review of Sociology* 30:81–101.

Maisels, Charles Keith 1999 *Early Civilizations of the Old World: The Formative Histories of Egypt, the Levant, Mesopotamia, India, and China*. Routledge, New York.

Marcus, Joyce and Kent V. Flannery 1996 *Zapotec Civilization: How Urban Society Evolved in Mexico's Oaxaca Valley*. Thames and Hudson, New York.

Martin, Paul S. and David A. Gregory 1973 Prehistoric and Contemporary Problems. In *The Archaeology of Arizona: A Study of the Southwest Region*, edited by Paul S. Martin and Fred Plog, pp. 361–68. Doubleday, Garden City.

McNett, Charles W. 1979 The Cross-Cultural Method in Archaeology. *Advances in Archaeological Method and Theory* 2:39–76.

Montelius, Oscar 1888 *The Civilisation of Sweden in Heathen Times*. Macmillan, New York.

Moreland, John 2006 Archaeology and Texts: Subservience or Enlightenment. *Annual Review of Anthropology* 35:135–51.

Morgan, Lewis Henry 1878 *Ancient Society*. H. Holt, New York.

Morris, Ian and Walter Scheidel (editors) 2009 *The Dynamics of Ancient Empires: State Power from Assyria to Byzantium*. Oxford University Press, Oxford.

Murdock, George P. and Douglas R. White 1969 Standard Cross-Cultural Sample. *Ethnology* 9:329–69.

Netting, Robert McC., Richard R. Wilk, and R. J. Arnould (editors) 1984 *Households: Comparative and Historical Studies of the Domestic Group*. University of California Press, Berkeley.

Nisbet, Robert A. 1969 *Social Change and History*. Oxford University Press, New York.

O'Brien, Michael J. and R. Lee Lyman 1999 *Seriation, Stratigraphy, and Index Fossils: The Backbone of Archaeological Dating*. Kluwer, Norwell, MA.

Odell, George H. 1998 Investigating Correlates of Sedentism and Domestication in Prehistoric North America. *American Anthropologist* 90:335–56.

Parsons, Talcott 1966 *Societies: Evolutionary and Comparative Perspectives*. Prentice Hall, Englewood Cliffs.

Pauketat, Timothy R. 2001 Practice and History in Archaeology: An Emerging Paradigm. *Anthropological Theory* 1:73–98.

Peregrine, Peter N. 2001 *Outline of Cultural Materials*. Human Relations Area Files, New Haven.

———. 2003 Atlas of Cultural Evolution. *World Cultures* 14:2–88.

———. 2004 Cross-Cultural Approaches in Archaeology: Comparative Ethnology, Comparative Archaeology, and Archaeoethnology. *Journal of Archaeological Research* 12:281–309.

Pugh, Cedric 2000 Squatter Settlements: Their Sustainability, Architectural Contributions, and Socioeconomic Roles. *Cities* 17:325–37.

Ragin, Charles C. 1987 *The Comparative Method: Moving Beyond Qualitative and Quantitative Strategies*. University of California Press, Berkeley.

Sanders, William T. and Barbara J. Price 1968 *Mesoamerica: The Evolution of a Civilization*. Random House, New York.

Sanderson, Stephen K. 1990 *Social Evolutionism*. Blackwell, Oxford.

———. 1999 *Social Transformations: A General Theory of Historical Development*. Rev. ed. Rowman and Littlefield, Lanham, MD.

Scheidel, Walter (editor) 2009 *Rome and China: Comparative Perspectives on Ancient World Empires*. Oxford University Press, New York.

Service, Elman R. 1966 *Primitive Social Organization*. Random House, New York.

Smelser, Neil J. 1976 *Comparative Methods in the Social Sciences*. Prentice Hall Methods of Social Science Series. Prentice Hall, Englewood Cliffs, NJ.

Smith, Adam T. 2003 *The Political Landscape: Constellations of Authority in Early Complex Polities*. University of California Press, Berkeley.

Smith, Michael E. 1992a Braudel's Temporal Rhythms and Chronology Theory in Archaeology. In *Annales, Archaeology, and Ethnohistory*, edited by A. Bernard Knapp, pp. 23–34. Cambridge University Press, New York.

———. 1992b Rhythms of Change in Postclassic Central Mexico: Archaeology, Ethnohistory, and the Braudellian Model. In *Annales, Archaeology, and Ethnohistory*, edited by A. Bernard Knapp, pp. 51–74. Cambridge University Press, New York.

———. 2004 The Archaeology of Ancient State Economies. *Annual Review of Anthropology* 33:73–102.

———. 2006 How Do Archaeologists Compare Early States? Book Review Essay on Bruce Trigger and Adam T. Smith. *Reviews in Anthropology* 35:5–35.

———. 2010 Sprawl, Squatters, and Sustainable Cities: Can Archaeological Data Shed Light on Modern Urban Issues? *Cambridge Archaeological Journal* 20:229–53.

Spencer, Herbert 1898–99 *Principles of Sociology*. 3 vols. Appleton, New York.

Storey, Glenn R. 1999 Archaeology and Roman Society: Integrating Textual and Archaeological Data. *Journal of Archaeological Research* 7:203–48.

Thomas, Cyrus 1898 Report on Mound Explorations of the Bureau of American Ethnology. *Annual Report of the Bureau of American Ethnology* 12:3–742.

Tilly, Charles 1984 *Big Structures, Large Processes, and Huge Comparisons*. Russell Sage Foundation, New York.

Trigger, Bruce G. 1998 *Sociocultural Evolution: Calculation and Contingency*. Blackwell, Oxford.

_____. 2003 *Understanding Early Civilizations: A Comparative Study*. Cambridge University Press, New York.

_____. 2006 *A History of Archaeological Thought*. 2nd ed. Cambridge University Press, New York.

Tylor, Edward B. 1871 *Primitive Culture*. 2 vols. J. Murray, London.

Ward, Kevin 2009 Towards a Relational Comparative Approach to the Study of Cities. *Progress in Human Geography* 33:1–17.

Webster, Jane 2008 Less Beloved: Roman Archaeology, Slavery, and the Failure to Compare. *Archaeological Dialogues* 15(2):103–23.

Westcoat, James L., Jr. 1994 Varieties of Geographic Comparison in the Earth Transformed. *Annals of the Association of American Geographers* 84:721–25.

White, Leslie A. 1959 *The Evolution of Culture: The Development of Civilization to the Fall of Rome*. McGraw-Hill, New York.

Whiting, John W. and B. Ayres 1968 Inferences from the Shape of Dwellings. In *Settlement Archaeology*, edited by Kwang Chih Chang, pp. 117–33. Yale University Press, New Haven.

Yengoyan, Aram A. (editor) 2006 *Modes of Comparison: Theory and Practice*. University of Michigan Press, Ann Arbor.

Yoffee, Norman 1993 Too Many Chiefs? (or, Safe Texts for the '90s). In *Archaeological Theory: Who Sets the Agenda?* edited by Norman Yoffee and Andrew Sherratt, pp. 60–78. Cambridge University Press, New York.

CHAPTER 3

COMPARATIVE FRAMES FOR THE DIACHRONIC ANALYSIS OF COMPLEX SOCIETIES

NEXT STEPS

Gary M. Feinman

The top scientific discovery according to the journal *Science* in 2007 (Kennedy 2007) was the finding that the DNA of all humans is not alike. More specifically, the extent of person-to-person genomic diversity is much greater than was expected (Pennisi 2007). To place this breakthrough in context, it was less than ten years ago that the same publication proudly announced the unraveling of "*The* Human Genome" (Jasny and Kennedy 2001), although in fairness the future comparison of different human genomic sequences was anticipated. What geneticists initially conceived to be a species-wide genomic pattern encompassing relatively minimal elements of individual variation has even at this early date been shown to be more diverse than most scientists imagined.

Although these research findings in evolutionary biology have been played out at warp speed, perhaps this path of discovery and interpretation has a degree of analogical utility for those of us who study human societies over long temporal scales or deep history. More than a century ago, early social scientists recognized broad patterns of human societal diversity (e.g., Morgan 1877). Yet the first recognitions of such diversity were often mistakenly commingled with elements of human biology. More than a half century later, similar overarching schemes of human organization were resurrected and reframed as Marxist and neoevolutionary theoretical perspectives. But by this time (e.g., White 1959), these ideas were appropriately estranged from the simple biological explanations of prior eras. Nevertheless, the latter conceptual approaches, like those of an earlier era, stressed broad modes of societal diversity (such as Service's [1971] categories of bands, tribes, chiefdoms, states) that were organized and differentiated by distinct degrees of politico-economic complexity. As with the 2001 early genomic work, the emphasis in these studies was understandably on the broad-brush modal patterns. Thus key works of this era featured titles such as *The Evolution of Culture* (White 1959), *Primitive Social Organization* (Service 1971), *The Evolution of Political Society* (Fried 1967), and *The Evolution of the Prehistoric State* (Haas 1982). The focus of this comparative work was on similarity, and much discussion centered on evaluating the relative merits of different prime movers that might uniformly account for the transition to more hierarchical modes of organization (such as *the* state) in different regions of the globe.

Since the mid-twentieth century, a great deal has been learned about societal change and diversity by both anthropological archaeologists and scholars in adjacent disciplines. As with the investigation of the human genome, much of this new knowledge highlights significant aspects of patterned variation within the broad tiers of organizational complexity that were outlined decades ago. In fact, it seems evident that recent comparative efforts have recognized this greater diversity, adopting titles with plural nouns such as *Archaic States* (Feinman and Marcus 1998), *Empires* (Alcock et al. 2001), *Chiefdoms: Power, Economy, and Ideology* (Earle 1991), *Understanding Early Civilizations* (Trigger 2003), and *Collective Action in the Formation of Pre-Modern States* (Blanton and Fargher 2008). Nevertheless, it is a central tenet of this chapter that key frames that were part of that mid–twentieth-century framework remain in place and require judicious reevaluation and modification. Specifically, I argue for more systematic and cross-disciplinary approaches to examine the recognized variation within broad organizational modes (such as "states"). In other words, comparative approaches now focus on societal variation as well as similarities, and modified theoretical frames are necessary to accommodate and explain the variation in societies that could be lumped under the rubric "states" (or "chiefdoms," for that matter).

Furthermore, archaeological dialogues and frameworks for the consideration of hierarchically organized societies should be open to theoretical constructs and conceptual frames that are currently being employed in cognate disciplines where the study of societal change and variation is also a serious and ongoing focus. Our comparative archaeological perspectives on human groups and groupings should not necessarily be restricted to the past, but should ideally contribute to and profit from comparative studies of societal organization in the more recent past and even the present.

The Challenge: Understanding Societal Change and Diversity

Following decades of sustained fieldwork, in conjunction with innovative laboratory analyses, amplified computer technologies, and new archival investigations, diachronic studies of complex/hierarchical societies in anthropological archaeology are on a far firmer and geographically broader empirical footing today than ever before. In most global areas, the depth and quality of published/readily available information on past socioeconomic organizations have increased by several orders of magnitude over the state of knowledge fifty years ago. And, in certain key places, we now possess significantly amplified, even entirely novel, perspectives at the regional and domestic/house scales. These vantages provide empirical bases to assess settlement, economy, and power relations in ways that were not possible before.

In addition to anthropological archaeology, scholars situated in a large number of cognate disciplines (or sectors thereof), including history, classics, area studies, political science, economic history, and sociology, are also studying shifts (and theorizing about variation and change) in human socioeconomic arrangements over long time horizons. Ironically, there is precious little dialogue and almost no consensus across these disciplines regarding how to conceptualize complex sociopolitical formations, or even a broadly accepted metalanguage to facilitate the exchange of information and comparison. Within anthropological archaeology, where the investigation of these issues has long been recognized as a focal topic for research, a sizeable faction of practitioners seems to eschew systematic comparison, and relatively little effort is devoted to engaging those researchers with related interests outside of anthropology. In fact, while archaeologists have been effective in conveying to the press and the public their claims for the oldest or the richest, they have been less successful at disseminating the field's long-standing interests in and contributions to the rise of (and variation in) hierarchical political organizations.

The lack of effective bridges and communication to other disciplines has its costs. For example, recently *Science* (Kennedy and Norman 2005) outlined 125 big/important questions that were driving contemporary scientific research. These included "how can a skin cell become a nerve cell," "can the laws of physics be unified," and "are we alone in the universe." Regrettably, relatively few questions from the social sciences were even placed on the list, and a much smaller subset of them concerned the dynamics of human social formations. Nowhere to be found were issues such as (or related to) "how does inequality become institutionalized in human societies," and "what factors and conditions historically have engendered human societies to rise, fall, and reorganize." Such research issues are not only critical for understanding our history as a species, but they are relevant to evaluating shifting politico-economic dynamics today.

On *Science*'s list, the only question that was close in content to aforementioned focal questions about societal organization was "how does cooperative behavior evolve" (Pennisi 2005). Certainly this is a pertinent issue, relevant to our broad understanding of human societal change. Yet the path to future breakthroughs was framed almost exclusively within the domains of evolutionary biology and game theory. Absent was any mention of archaeological/empirical findings regarding how human social groupings and the equations of cooperative behavior have changed over time and varied over space (Pennisi 2005). By raising the issue of broad scientific agendas, I do not intend to critique the selections of *Science* so much as to express a concern regarding the ways that anthropological archaeology as a discipline communicates and bridges (or not) to other fields and the larger educated public. In this regard, it is curious, if not unsettling, that the most broadly read serious treatises on the rises and collapses of complex societies (Diamond 1999, 2005) were written by a nonarchaeologist.

The construction of theory and the comparative study of settlement, economy, and power over deep history is in many senses a version of a synthetic investigation of "world history" (Yoffee 2005:195; see also Northrup 2005; Sanderson 1990:223) that certainly reflects a focal concern on how human societies rise, expand, reconfigure, and vary over time. The pursuit of these aims falls within the broad mandate that Boas (1932:606) expressed for anthropology more than eighty years ago, when he stated that "we may . . . best define our objective as the attempt to understand the steps by which man has come to be what he is, biologically, psychologically, and culturally." What is critical about the scholarly enterprise that Boas envisioned is that it is globally inclusive, explicitly historical in character, and necessarily comparative.

As Smith (2006:6) has emphasized, in the face of several decades of relative theoretical stasis in archaeology, a reenergized and more explicit comparative approach to complex societies is in order. For in accord with Hunt (2007:ix), "there is no inquiry, and no knowledge, without comparison." It is also important to stress that comparisons ought not to be restricted to one dimension. In analogical parallel with the current paradigmatic approach to the history of life, the contemporary biological evolutionary synthesis, comparative analyses of social evolution should be considered and enacted along various dimensions and scales as they inform (and are appropriately framed by) overarching theoretical questions. Although this may seem obvious, I stress this point in contrast to a recent approach (Yoffee 2005) that argues that specific sequences of societal change (looked at in their entirety) are the principal grist for comparative study. The outcome of this approach is to find and emphasize the "uniqueness" of many particular diachronic series. Yet sequences of change tell us little of broader relevance about the past without filtering in some understanding of the dynamics of the social and economic formations and other broader principles that help us interpret and understand these sequences.

Here again, an analogy with the theoretical frame for the history of life is informative, as the overarching conceptual frame for the investigation of human social evolution will have to be just as complex and multifaceted, if not more so (Shermer 2007; Watts 2007). Specific branching sequences of biological evolutionary change are important for the synthetic theory of life's history (as they are for social evolution). Yet it is not those historical sequences (e.g., the evolution of horses or beetles) when examined on their own that have advanced biological knowledge. Rather, the application of more general, overarching principles – concerning reproductive strategies, predator and prey relations, sociality, population/resource dynamics (and certainly genetics) as well as many other broadly comparative relations to the study of those sequences – serves to explain the history of life, both in the general and specific sense.

The remainder of this discussion advances major initiatives to expand and enhance the comparative frame that archaeologists employ to examine complex societies. This broadening agenda ought to include both intensified efforts to dialogue and communicate with other disciplines, and explorations toward a metalanguage or theoretical frames that are less parochial in structure (see Pearson and Sherman 2005) and promote more systematic analyses of the variation in complex societies (particularly societies with comparable degrees of hierarchical complexity). If there are intellectual reasons to segregate the study of non-Western cases/histories, archaeologically known complex societies, or the subset of early (formerly considered "pristine") states, then these reasons should be demonstrated or oriented to specific problem foci. They should not reflect arbitrary or antiquated disciplinary barriers or residues that largely reflect scholarly practices or priorities set decades, if not centuries, ago and maintained for the most part by inertia/practice (Wallerstein 2003).

More specifically, I propose that an expansion of the basic two-dimensional frame (that emphasizes hierarchical complexity and idiosyncratic/cultural variation), employed for more than fifty years by anthropological archaeologists, is necessary to accommodate variation more systematically. Several theoretical propositions, drawn from different scholarly traditions, are introduced that are intended to define and account for important axes of variation noted in societies with similar degrees of hierarchical complexity. These independent, yet parallel, perspectives offer direction for theoretical expansion, while illustrating the potential gains from enhanced cross-disciplinary communication. At the same time, they challenge traditional ideas regarding restrictions or limitations in which historical cases may fittingly be compared.

Expanding the Comparative Frame

As outlined earlier, the examination of societal sequences (or more to the point, shifts in the artifactual record) of a given region over time are just as inadequate for understanding societal evolution as narrow treatments of the fossil record alone would be to explain the history of life. Nevertheless, when placed in a broader comparative theoretical context, the analytical advantages of diachronic perspectives over strictly synchronic analyses are evident (Adams 2004:349). For that reason, it is unfortunate that frameworks and findings derived from the comparative examination of archaic complex societies are so rarely engaged by scholarly considerations of later generations of states (e.g., Smith 2006) and vice versa. Clearly, a wide-ranging dialogue, if not even an overarching set of ideas comparing states and statecraft and the cycling (rises, falls, and shifts in implementation) of political power, would be highly informative and could enhance the kinds of patterned variation recognizable in the corpus of complex societies past and present (see Jones and Phillips 2005 for a parallel argument).

As Trigger (2003:3) stated succinctly: "The most important issue confronting the social sciences is the extent to which human behaviour is shaped by factors that operate cross-culturally as opposed to factors that are unique to particular cultures." Yet, given this call and the related argument to expand the scope of such comparisons, it is necessary to assess and reconsider how anthropological archaeologists generally have framed the issue of similarities and differences in archaic states/complex societies. Although focused attention has on occasion been given productively to subsets of complex societies, such as small (city-) states (e.g., Hansen 2000; Nichols and Charlton 1997) and empires (Alcock et al. 2001), less theory building and systematic comparison has been devoted to the construction of more general frames that integrate distinct organizational properties into cross-cultural theories (comparisons and contrasts) of dynamics and change (however, see Trigger 1993). I propose that a repositioning or expansion of the predominant neoevolutionary theoretical perspective would bring archaeological approaches more in line with comparative efforts in cognate disciplines while opening up the potential for more overarching frameworks for the study of past and present complex societies.

As implied earlier, the following discussion of variation in complex societies decouples that consideration from any necessary or uniform pathway of change (see Drennan 1991:114). In other words, in examining any specific regional or even global sequence, neither progress nor any broad-brush directional shift over time is assumed (e.g., Blanton et al. 1993:13–23; Claessen 2000:45–69). Empirically, there seems little support either for the notion that small city-states always precede larger polities (cf. Yoffee 2005), or the converse that territorial states generally always arise first only to collapse into smaller political units (cf. Marcus 1992, 1998). In fact, collapse and reconfiguration are consistent features of the historical record, and the histories of different regions indicate alternative paths. Where there are convergent patterns of change or even cross-cultural trends that seem directional in nature, such historical patterns require explanation and ought not be considered preordained or "natural." Nevertheless, to describe and understand societal diversity and change, comparative frameworks are necessary, and this is the central focus here.

In Anglophone anthropological archaeology, most comparative and neoevolutionary approaches have been grounded for the better part of five decades (if not longer) in the reconciliation crafted by Sahlins and Service (1960) of the seemingly contradictory evolutionary approaches advanced previously by their mentors White (1949, 1959) and Steward (1949). This mediation (see particularly Sahlins 1960) previously has been discussed, dissected, and amended by many theorists (Claessen 2000:191–95; Flannery 1983; Sanderson 1990:131–38; Segraves 1974; Trigger 1989:292). The reconciliation outlined two core aspects of the neoevolutionary research agenda, general and specific societal evolution. Basically, general evolution was envisioned as a focus on the broad, shared societal patterns directly associated with increasing organizational complexity (such as the core features of Service's [1971] model of band, tribe, chiefdom, state), whereas specific evolution was defined as the focus on the remnant and presumably rather unique aspects of societal variation linked to particular regional traditions and case-specific adaptations to varying socioenvironmental conditions.

The focus of specific evolution is the individual pathway followed by each sociocultural grouping, society, or regional population; in contrast, the main concern of general evolution is the definition/identification of the patterned variation (*sensu* Drennan and Peterson 2006) associated explicitly with stepped increases in organizational complexity. From this theoretical frame, which has been at least implicitly employed in many archaeological analyses, cross-cultural similarities are generally searched for and recognized as indicators or properties of distinct levels of hierarchical complexity, whereas variation within these modes is presumed to have a basis in more case-specific or idiosyncratic factors.

The proposed framework suggested here builds on these prior studies that have recognized broad cross-cultural patterns of variation associated with increasing hierarchical complexity. At the same time, my point is not to take issue with the obvious and important influences of local histories or environs on societal diversity or change in order to account for certain specific features (*sensu* Harris 1968:645). Clearly, local, cultural, seemingly idiosyncratic factors are one dimension of societal variation. Factors associated with different degrees of hierarchical complexity are a second, although this is not an effort to reify societal types (such as "chiefdoms" and "states"). My strong reservations regarding the rigid adherence to (or reification of) such societal taxonomies have been expressed elsewhere (Blanton et al. 1993:13–23; Feinman and Neitzel 1984). Nevertheless, if one unpacks such organizational types or modes, it is reasonably clear that cross-culturally there is a strong correlation across societies between hierarchical complexity and elements of organizational scale, namely polity size and the size of a society's largest community (e.g., Feinman 1995:259–61; Kosse 1990; also Drennan and Peterson, this volume). As has been long documented in many prior studies, other societal variables broadly correlate with these two factors as well (e.g., Fried 1967; Johnson and Earle 2000; Service 1971).

Yet the aim here is to expand the extant interpretive frame to include a new comparative dimension, in order to recognize and systematically explore the patterned variation associated with different cross-cultural practices of socioeconomic integration. Diverse yet patterned modes of socioeconomic integration may be found across societies with relatively comparable degrees of hierarchical complexity.

The basic premises of the Sahlins and Service (1960) theoretical reconciliation have been widely influential for the interpretation of similarities and differences by anthropological archaeologists over the last decades. The influence of this two-dimensional approach to understanding societal diversity may partly stem from its parallels to earlier approaches including neo-Marxian analyses (e.g., Armillas 1957) and Coon's (1962) terminology of "grade" and "line" (see Sanders and Price 1968:217–18). Nevertheless, this basic framework has had much less impact in other disciplines that study states. To begin a dialogue regarding the structural parallels and transformational histories of states, early and more modern, certain basic theoretical principles or elemental axioms ideally should be broadly shared and not left unexplored by one discipline or subset of scholars. More importantly, and in accord with the wide body of knowledge on states from across the academy, it is becoming clear that key structural similarities or cross-cultural patterns of variation cannot be tied exclusively to stepped tiers of hierarchical complexity (or so-called general evolutionary "Bauplan" [*sensu* Spencer 1997:234]). Additional axes of patterned variation are explored in the next section.

Organizing Diversity within Hierarchical Modes

Although the broad axes of cross-cultural variation have rarely been drawn explicitly (see Trigger 1993 for a notable exception), patterned variability in the large corpus of ancient states has been recognized, particularly in regard to the properties associated with polity scale and/or major technological/communication breakthroughs. A number of studies have found that small states, part of regional networks (and often sharing a cultural tradition), tend to share features (such as high degrees of connectivity with neighboring states, smaller bureaucratic infrastructure, and a reliance on inter-polity exchange) that differ from common properties of larger states (e.g., Feinman 1998; Friedman 1977; Trigger 1993). In the same vein, there are properties of empires (size, ethnic/cultural heterogeneity, emergence through conquest/coercion) that distinguish them from smaller polities (Alcock et al. 2001; Doyle 1986; Sinopoli 2001:444–47). Likewise, legal/formal sovereignty and more finite borders (defined territories) are two of a number of features that tend to differentiate many modern states from those of the deeper past regardless of their relative size (Claessen 1985; Spruyt 2002). Industrial-era states generally claim effective legal sovereignty over a territorial domain and its population in the name of the nation in a manner less common deeper in the past (Hansen and Stepputat 2006). Nevertheless, other distinctive properties hypothesized to be associated with Western political "modernity" (Rokkan 1969; Tilly 1975) may also be present in the deeper past (Blanton and Fargher 2008:290–99). Finally, as Marcus (2008:259–61) has argued, it is conceivable that the processes associated with the rise of pristine states (the first to be established in a region) were distinct from the processes that led to the formation of secondary/later states, but that does not imply that the organizational properties of these pristine states were more similar as a group as compared to later states.

If scale and certain communication/transport technologies can be linked to (or pattern with) other characteristics of states, then other cross-cultural axes of variation in complex societies are also worth investigating. Here, I focus on different modes of politico-economic integration in complex societies.

Through an array of different approaches, some more theoretically driven (whereas others work more empirically from a more targeted contrast of specific cases), a range of scholars, working independently in different disciplines and different global regions, have noted that states with highly centralized, individualized power also tend to be characterized by high degrees of inequality and a dependence on externally derived resources. Alternatively, political formations with more diffuse access to power or power-sharing arrangements frequently co-occur with lesser degrees of inequality and greater reliance on basic economic production. In the remainder of this discussion, I principally review the broadly parallel patterns of variation that have been noted by researchers in different fields with an eye toward the definition of another axis or dimension of cross-cultural societal variation that requires examination in comparative analyses of long-term societal change and diversity. However, before discussing these specific studies, I first briefly review what I mean by societal integration and why cross-cultural variation in integrative modes is deeply rooted in the human career.

Means of Integration

Along with scale, complexity, and boundary conditions, integration has been proposed as a core feature or characteristic that is basic to all societies and comparable over time and space (Blanton et al. 1993:14–19). Specifically, integration refers to the interdependence between societal units and the means or mechanisms used to achieve the degree of connectivity. The integration of societal segments, such as households or larger units, can be achieved or implemented through various means – the most prominent include economic and political modes of integration. In complex, hierarchical societies, political integration is related to the sources or funds of power (e.g., Brumfiel 1992:554–55; Wolf 1982:97) that can be mobilized by political actors to accrue followers and pursue their political agendas.

Lehman (1969) contrasts power wielded systemically, largely through institutions or groups, with inter-member power, which is found in individual-centered social networks developed through personal social ties. As Blanton (1998:141–49) has argued, both of these means of wielding power encompass material resources as well as cognitive-symbolic bases of power – albeit in different ways that have distinct ramifications on other aspects of society. Of course, none of these strategies or bases of power are mutually exclusive, and they often are employed jointly, but in different ways and to varying degrees.

Because a degree of inequality (at least by gender, age, ability, and temperament) exists in just about every human social system (e.g., Cashdan 1980; Flanagan 1989), hierarchical or uneven relations of some sort are a key aspect to human social integration. Such hierarchical relations have their roots in many parts of the animal kingdom, including primates (Chase et al. 2002). Yet, in addition to these deeply rooted practices, cooperation and the social learning skills necessary to form and thrive in groups also have been argued (Herrmann et al. 2007; Tomasello 1999) to be a defining feature that distinguishes humans from other animals. These social practices helped keep overtly hierarchical behaviors largely in check for a long era in human history and in many smaller scale societies (e.g., Boehm 1993). Therefore, it is not surprising that very different mixes of these seemingly contradictory practices, hierarchy and cooperation, might characterize how human groupings interrelate (Stone 2008:77–80), and that given the deep roots of these characteristics in what it means to be human, the consequent integrative strategies might pattern in a suite of different but repetitive ways.

Analytical Parallels in the Societal Modes of Integration

More than a decade ago, my colleagues and I (Blanton 1998; Blanton et al. 1996; Feinman 1995; Feinman et al. 2000) juxtaposed corporate and exclusionary (network) modes of politico-economic organization in the corpus of complex societies. Our original comparative frame built on established cross-cultural contrasts between individualizing and group-oriented chiefdoms (Renfrew 1974; see also Renfrew 2001), and staple and wealth finance (D'Altroy and Earle 1985). Although our original formulation had a longer list of contrastive characteristics associated with each of these ends of a comparative continuum (e.g., Feinman et al. 2000:453), here I emphasize those key characteristics at the core of these alternative organizational patterns. In this section I unpack or trim down those features associated with the corporate or exclusionary strategies of integration. Corporate organization is broadly associated with shared power, less ostentatious manifestations of stratification, and an economy focused on basic/local production, whereas more exclusionary power arrangements are keyed to highly centralized/individualized rule, networks of personal power, more expressed degrees of inequality, and an economy heavily unpinned by long-distance networks and flows.

The corporate-exclusionary axis has proven conceptually useful to understand seemingly "enigmatic" archaeological cases (Feinman 2000, 2001; Feinman et al. 2000) in which scale, centralization, hierarchy, and inequality do not co-vary in strict (stepped) conformance with each other. In other words, these cases tended to lie outside the predictive parameters of the aforementioned two-dimensional frame in which variation is a consequence either of general evolutionary "Bauplans" or specific, idiosyncratic factors. From this vantage, with the consideration of an additional axis of variation, the notion of corporate yet hierarchically organized polities helps conceptualize historical instances where political power was unequally distributed but, perhaps, not concentrated in the hands of a single ruler or family and/or where the expression of stratification was muted or (inequality relatively unpronounced) despite the presence of supra-household, hierarchical, decision-making institutions.

It is important to note that corporate-exclusionary strategies are not meant to be culture-bound. That is, one would expect to see shifts along this continuum in a given region or for a specific society over time. Integrative strategies may change as opportunities arise and conditions warrant. For example, such transitions already have been illustrated for both the pre-Hispanic Maya (Blanton et al. 1996) and the Ancestral Pueblos (Feinman et al. 2000). Contrary to Yoffee's (2006:400) assertion, these alternative forms of integration were never intended to be used as a reformulation or resurrection of societal types; rather, the intent is to recognize repetitive patterns of societal variation that can help us understand human organizational diversity and patterns of societal change.

As I have examined different integration modes across diverse geographic regions, eras, and disciplines, it has become evident that scholars in an array of academic fields have noted rather similar patterned axes of variation or contrast in the global corpus of complex societies. This includes a number of empirically based studies (e.g., Lehman 1969; Renfrew 1974) that helped inspire the original contrast of corporate and exclusionary strategies (Blanton et al. 1996). Nevertheless, the prime focus of this remaining discussion is on more recently published parallel/independent conceptual perspectives. At the same time, it is also worth noting that a number of archaeologists have independently and constructively employed the corporate-exclusionary axis to discuss and explicate diversity and change in complex societies (e.g., Earle 1997; King 2006; Mills 2000; Trubitt 2000; Willey 1999).

An important corresponding perspective, advanced by Grinin (2004), draws a contrast between "monarchic" and "democratic" states. He argues that the latter, typified by ancient Athens and the Roman Republic, have most of the basic properties of early states elsewhere, but that political power was not monopolized by a single ruler (rather it was more shared, delegated, and checked). Grinin's argument is significant in that it recognizes that the Athenian state and the Roman Republic were hierarchically organized like other early states, but that the modes of political integration were less centralized, not focused on a single all-powerful ruler.

Similar to many corporately organized states, for the "democratic" states (as analyzed by Grinin) agrarian production was critically important for the economy, and its taxation largely financed the government. Socioeconomic stratification, although certainly present, was less ostentatiously expressed than in other archaic states (Grinin 2004:110–11). As with corporate polities, broad social mechanisms and pressures such as ostracism were voted on by the Athenian Assembly (see Ober 2008:75–76). Such sanctions were employed to encourage conformance to cultural codes in the absence of royal fiat or coercion. Grinin tends to associate his "democratic" states principally with the West, but some of the basic integrative properties are shared with non-Western cases described as "corporate," so less hegemonic practices of rule and government should not be considered unique to Europe or Western societies.

Independently, and shifting to a consideration of more recent times, the positive association between high degrees of (broad) political participation and relative economic equality has also been described in a cross-national study of contemporary polities (Russett 1964) and a large cross-cultural ethnographic sample (Ember et al. 1997). That these patterns were found in such synchronic samples is significant because factors such as relative income inequality reflect long intergenerational histories of wealth creation and transfer in specific historical contexts.

Conversely, the recurrent properties of exclusionary power arrangements are not unique to ancient kingdoms, medieval monarchies, or non-Western contexts. For example, the increasing concentration of executive power and a growing disparity of wealth, both of which have occurred over the last decades in the contemporary United States, are unlikely to be serendipitous, unrelated trends (American Political Science Association Task Force Report 2004; Domhoff 2006; Feinman 2010). Correspondingly, mathematical modeling directed at contemporary societies has illustrated in general how strong unitary executives reliant on personal networks to enhance their own power (through economic transactions) are advantaged in contexts already characterized by marked income inequities (Acemoglu 2005; Acemoglu et al. 2004). In other words, when marked disparities of wealth exist, leaders may find it easier to act unilaterally. Such relationships provide one potential mechanism through which shifts in power and wealth disparities can move in parallel ways in different specific historical contexts over time.

These perspectives from studies of contemporary states illustrate that the variation in states may have patterned structural characteristics with broad time–space applicability. For example, the co-occurrence of concentrated political power (and associated individualizing behavior), marked socio-economic stratification, and an emphasis on exchange-based (as opposed to basic productive) economic activity may have broader applicability than was envisioned originally (Blanton et al. 1996). At the same time, if these studies in concert serve to outline repetitive patterns of variation in states that explicitly do not correspond to broad stepped tiers of organizational complexity, then a new, more comprehensive frame for analyzing and explaining the variability in states is needed. Conceptually, we could profitably implement a research program to define and account for patterned and modal variation in the corpus of states (over time and space), recognizing that the variation in states is not strictly due to either unique historic pathways or culture-specific, idiosyncratic factors.

A Path toward Broader Understandings

Critiques of the corporate-exclusionary dimension have questioned why these societal properties tend to co-occur, while also wondering why integrative strategies might shift in a given societal context along this continuum. One productive avenue of research on these specific patterns of societal variation may extend to a consideration of the collective action problem (Olson 1965) and related works that have built upon this approach (in particular, Blanton and Fargher 2008; Levi 1988; Lichbach 1996). These ideas endeavor to bridge the micro–macro problem (e.g., Collins 1988) by exploring the extent to which individuals who share common aims may find it in their personal interest to carry the costs of organizational effort (Levi 1988:8). As Lichbach (1996:32) states, a collective action problem or the cooperator's dilemma "arises whenever mutually beneficial cooperation is threatened by individual strategic behavior." Although this line of discussion may seem abstract, the fundamental issue is really the key dilemma posed by Hobbs (2003). "What holds society together given the tendency of individuals to pursue their self-interest?" (Blanton and Fargher 2008:6; also Lichbach 1995). In other words, what kinds of integrative strategies and practices keep social systems intact and why might different societal compacts seem to be favored in certain contexts as opposed to others? To assess these questions, the interests of rulers and the ruled must be considered.

To explain variability in governing regimes, Levi's (1988) research in particular examined the link between the ways governments are financed and the relative dispersal of political power/voice. Levi's (1988:2) focus is on ruling strategies, political integration, revenue, and resources with an emphasis on the ways in which the latter two finance power. These factors largely encompass those unpacked characteristics of the corporate-exclusionary axis that are our central concern as well as the parallel contrasts/comparison drawn by other scholars (e.g., Ember et al. 1997; Grinin 2004; Russett 1964). Basically, Levi's thesis is that the more rulers depend on the extraction of localized resources, the more checks and voice the ruled will have. Alternatively, the more external and monopolized a ruler's financial base (e.g., patron–client relations), the more concentrated power is apt to be (Fargher and Blanton 2007). This perspective offers a testable alternative to traditional models that often associate heavily agrarian states with the manifestation of absolute power (Bates and Lien 1985:53–54).

In a large global sample of historical cases, Blanton and Fargher (2008) provide strong support for these expectations, while also illustrating that the basic model is supported across the world and in the analysis of cases from the deeper past as well as more recent history. The latter study provides a theoretical underpinning for the patterned variability noted in the suite of core features that marks the poles of the corporate-exclusionary axis. Significantly, parallel politico-economic arrangements can emerge through distinct historical pathways (likely under certain pre-conditions) just as we know that chiefdoms and/or states with similar hierarchical formations/properties can develop in diverse geographic/cultural settings when a set of necessary/sufficient conditions are met (Tilly [2000] makes a similar point for democracies). When examining long-term sequences of societal change, a framework that enables us to document and explicate both shifts in organizational complexity as well as changes in the modes of political and economic integration will yield a more holistic and explanatory perspective on "world history" and the diverse pathways that it encompasses.

Concluding Thoughts and Future Directions

As outlined earlier, anthropological archaeology can potentially learn a great deal from (and also contribute to) an expansive cross-disciplinary dialogue that explores the diversity of complex societies, ancient and modern; Fletcher (Chapter 11) and Smith (Chapter 12) also explore this theme. In our field, we might better come to understand the patterns of variation, particularly in regard to the means and modes of societal (economic and political) integration, which have been too little explored in a systematic, cross-cultural fashion. Specifically, we also might begin to more explicitly probe and define the differences that exist between preindustrial and industrial polities. Too often that gulf has been assumed rather than documented. Modern states clearly have key differences from those in the past, but not all of the claimed differences necessarily bear up to empirical scrutiny. Such dialogues would likely promote careful examinations of the theoretical and interpretive divides that artificially ghettoize the "Rest" from the West (see Blanton and Fargher 2008; Fargher and Blanton 2007). At a time when our models call for greater consideration of agency and voice, it is important to realize that such a focus naturally leads to an analysis of the different integrative modes and mechanisms that interconnect societies. However, efforts to study and model agency in deep history should not only empower those few voices that had power in the past (cf. Baines and Yoffee 1998).

As Claessen and Skalník (1978) illustrated decades ago, broad cross-disciplinary comparisons require the unbundling or unpacking of the features and properties of states and the societies in which they are part. Such a theoretical approach would need to explore (as one example) how degrees of stratification patterned with the relative concentration of political power as discussed earlier. Such a perspective not only would help define axes of variability, but it would enable the recognition of causal connections and dynamics that might account for that patterned variation. This is a critical point; it implies that to understand variation in states it is essential to go beyond the largely synchronic comparisons that composed *The Early State* and other subsequent comparative works (e.g., Feinman and Neitzel 1984; Hansen ed. 2000).

Recently and along these lines, Drennan and Peterson (2006:3960; see also Tilly 1984:14) have made a forceful case that patterned variation in human social formations can only be understood if various cases or examples are examined and compared over long sequences. Although I applaud the kinds of multi-case diachronic comparisons being carried out (Drennan and Peterson 2006; Peterson and Drennan, Chapter 6), there is no reason that such analyses need be undertaken in a purely bottom-up, inductive fashion. There is a danger that ad-hoc interpretations may betray the unexpressed biases of the investigators at the expense of more theoretical framing. If this happens, it can lead to mischaracterizations of specific empirical cases and the false disconfirmation of extant models (see Kiser and Hechter 1991).

As previously noted, it is important to analyze how different attributes of states change in correspondence with co-occurring changes in other features. When such patterns are explored over a wide range of sequences, then we will gain a better perspective not just on the generalized properties of states and the idiosyncratic features unique to specific histories, but we should be able to find the patterned and structured variation between different states (e.g., corporate vs. exclusionary or democratic vs. ruler-centric). I suspect patterned variation that has little connection to the dimension of hierarchical complexity will often be defined, and that such structured diversity will help identify key axes of differentiation between states. At the same time, no model or framework, no matter how robust, can ever singly or fully account for a significant aspect of societal diversity, and so a consideration of historical, cultural, and local factors remains important in a comparative context.

Although I see diachronic comparisons as a primary theoretical component in an overarching framework to study states and their diversity and their cycles of decline and regeneration, such an ambitious multidisciplinary framework focused on states across space and time clearly would necessitate the bootstrapping (*sensu* Blanton 1990) of an array of different, mutually reinforcing theoretical exercises, approaches, and frames, some of which are synchronic. As Fracchia and Lewontin (1999:78) state: "Transformational theories of cultural evolution have the virtue that they at least provide a framework of generality with which to give human long-term history the semblance of intelligibility. But the search for intelligibility should not be confused with the search for actual process." There are many ways to try to make sense of global history, and we may ultimately need a number of these approaches in concert to understand settlement, economy, and politics in deep history.

This kind of broad encompassing theoretical infrastructure or frame (incorporating more than the two standard dimensions of variation stressed in much archaeological interpretation) may seem ambitious to some or cumbersome to others (see Smith and Peregrine, Chapter 2). Yet a theoretical frame designed for understanding and explaining the differences and similarities in states is in reality a frame for exploring the global history of human societies, certainly a highly complex set of interrelated questions. So it is not surprising that ultimately we in the social and behavioral sciences will require a theoretical frame analogous in form to the bootstrapped theories, some diachronic and others synchronic, that together aim to explain a comparable grand topic or set of questions: the history of life through biological evolution (see Mayr 1982). Although the theory designed to explain that historical phenomenon (biological evolution) is not appropriately designed or structured to address and account for the suite of research questions of concern to us (e.g., Bryant 2004; Fracchia and Lewontin 1999; Gould 1987), I do suspect that a comparable or analogical multifaceted structure that encompasses phenomena at multiple scales ultimately will be required to explain human societies, their histories, rich diversity, and how and why they change through time (Goldstone 1998). To move toward this broader theory, a concerted initiative toward wider communications and more systematic comparative investigations must be undertaken.

References Cited

Acemoglu, Daron 2005 Constitutions, Politics, and Economics: A Review Essay on Persson and Tabellini's The Economic Effects of Constitutions. *Journal of Economic Literature* 18:1025–48.

Acemoglu, Daron, James A. Robinson, and Thierry Verdier 2004 Kleptocracy and Divide-and-Rule: A Model of Personal Rule. *Journal of the European Economic Association* 2:162–92.

Adams, Robert McC. 2004 Review of Understanding Early Civilizations: A Comparative Study. *The International History Review* 26:349–51.

Alcock, Susan E., Terrence N. D'Altroy, Kathleen D. Morrison, and Carla M. Sinopoli (editors) 2001 *Empires: Perspectives from Archaeology and History.* Cambridge University Press, Cambridge.

American Political Science Association Task Force Report 2004 American Democracy in an Age of Rising Inequality. *ASPA Task Force Report* 2:651–66.

Armillas, Pedro 1957 *Cronología y Periodificación de la Historia de América Precolumbina.* Escuela Nacional de Antropología e Historia, Mexico.

Baines, John, and Norman Yoffee 1998 Order, Legitimacy, and Wealth in Ancient Egypt and Mesopotamia. In *Archaic States*, edited by Gary M. Feinman and Joyce Marcus, pp. 199–260. School of American Research Press, Santa Fe.

Bates, Robert H., and Da-Hsiang Donald Lien 1985 A Note on Taxation, Development, and Representative Government. *Politics and Society* 14:53–70.

Blanton, Richard 1990 Theory and Practice in Mesoamerican Archaeology: A Comparison of Two Modes of Scientific Inquiry. In *Debating Oaxaca Archaeology*, edited by Joyce Marcus, pp. 1–16. Anthropological Papers of the Museum of Anthropology 84. University of Michigan, Ann Arbor.

———. 1998 Beyond Centralization: Steps toward a Theory of Egalitarian Behavior. In *Archaic States*, edited by Gary M. Feinman and Joyce Marcus, pp. 135–72. School of American Research Press, Santa Fe.

Blanton, Richard, and Lane Fargher 2008 *Collective Action in the Formation of Pre-Modern States.* Springer, New York.

Blanton, Richard E., Gary M. Feinman, Stephen A. Kowalewski, and Peter N. Peregrine 1996 A Dual-Processual Theory for the Evolution of Mesoamerican Civilization. *Current Anthropology* 37:1–86.

Blanton, Richard E., Stephen A. Kowalewski, Gary M. Feinman, and Laura M. Finsten 1993 *Ancient Mesoamerica: A Comparison of Change in Three Regions*. Second Edition. Cambridge University Press, Cambridge.

Boas, Franz 1932 The Aims of Anthropological Research. *Science* 76:605–13.

Boehm, Christopher 1993 Egalitarian Society and Reverse Dominance Hierarchy. *Current Anthropology* 34:227–54.

Brumfiel, Elizabeth M. 1992 Distinguished Lecture in Archeology: Breaking and Entering the Ecosystem – Gender, Class, and Faction Steal the Show. *American Anthropologist* 94:551–67.

Bryant, Joseph M. 2004 An Evolutionary Social Science? A Skeptic's Brief, Theoretical and Substantive. *Philosophy of the Social Sciences* 34:451–92.

Cashdan, Elizabeth A. 1980 Egalitarianism among Hunters and Gatherers. *American Anthropologist* 82:116–20.

Chase, Ivan D., Craig Tovey, Debra Spangler-Martin, and Michael Manfredonia 2002 Individual Differences versus Social Dynamics in the Formation of Animal Dominance Hierarchies. *Proceedings of the National Academy of Sciences* 99:5744–49.

Claessen, Henri J. M. 1985 From the Franks to France: The Evolution of Political Organization. In *Development and Decline: The Evolution of Sociopolitical Organization*, edited by Henri J. M. Claessen, Pieter van de Velde, and M. Estellie Smith, pp. 196–218. Bergin and Garvey, South Hadley, MA.

———. 2000 *Structural Change: Evolution and Evolutionism in Cultural Anthropology*. Research School CNWS, Leiden University, Leiden, The Netherlands.

Claessen, Henri J. M., and Peter Skalník (editors) 1978 *The Early State*. Mouton Publishers, The Hague.

Collins, Randall 1988 The Micro Contribution to Macro Sociology. *Sociological Theory* 6:242–53.

Coon, Carleton S. 1962 *The Origin of Races*. Alfred A. Knopf, New York.

D'Altroy, Terence N., and Timothy K. Earle 1985 Staple Finance, Wealth Finance, and the Inka Political Economy. *Current Anthropology* 26:187–206.

Diamond, Jared 1999 *Guns, Germs, and Steel: The Fates of Human Societies*. W.W. Norton, New York.

———. 2005 *Collapse: How Societies Choose to Fail or Succeed*. Viking, New York.

Domhoff, William G. 2006 C. Wright Mills 50 Years Later. *Contemporary Sociology* 35:547–50.

Doyle, Michael W. 1986 *Empires*. Cornell University Press, Ithaca.

Drennan, Robert D. 1991 Cultural Evolution, Human Ecology, and Empirical Research. In *Profiles in Cultural Evolution*, edited by A. Terry Rambo and Kathleen Gillogly, pp. 113–35. Anthropological Papers of the Museum of Anthropology 85. University of Michigan, Ann Arbor.

Drennan, Robert D., and Christian E. Peterson 2006 Patterned Variation in Prehistoric Chiefdoms. *Proceedings of the National Academy of Sciences* 103:3960–67.

Earle, Timothy 1997 *How Chiefs Came to Power: The Political Economy in Prehistory*. Stanford University Press, Stanford.

Earle, Timothy (editor) 1991 *Chiefdoms: Power, Economy, and Ideology*. Cambridge University Press, Cambridge.

Ember, Melvin, Carol R. Ember, and Bruce Russett 1997 Inequality and Democracy in the Anthropological Record. In *Inequality, Democracy, and Economic*

Development, edited by Manus I. Midlarsky, pp. 110–30. Cambridge University Press, Cambridge.

Fargher, Lane F., and Richard E. Blanton 2007 Revenue, Voice, and Public Goods in Three Pre-Modern States. *Comparative Studies in Society and History* 49:848–82.

Feinman, Gary M. 1995 The Emergence of Inequality: A Focus on Strategies and Processes. In *Foundations of Social Inequality*, edited by T. Douglas Price and Gary M. Feinman, pp. 255–79. Plenum Press, New York.

———. 1998 Scale and Social Organization: Perspectives on the Archaic State. In *Archaic States*, edited by Gary M. Feinman and Joyce Marcus, pp. 95–134. School of American Research Press, Santa Fe.

———. 2000 Dual-Processual Theory and Social Formations in the Southwest. In *Alternative Leadership Strategies in the Prehispanic Southwest*, edited by Barbara J. Mills, pp. 207–24. The University of Arizona Press, Tucson.

———. 2001 Mesoamerican Political Complexity: The Corporate-Network Dimension. In *From Leaders to Rulers*, edited by Jonathan Haas, pp. 151–75. Kluwer Academic/Plenum Publishers, New York.

———. 2010 Dual-Processual Perspective on the Power and Inequality in the Contemporary United States: Framing Political Economy for the Present and the Past. In *Pathways to Power*, edited by T. Douglas Price and Gary M. Feinman, pp. 255-88. Springer, New York.

Feinman, Gary M., Kent G. Lightfoot, and Steadman Upham 2000 Political Hierarchies and Organizational Strategies in the Puebloan Southwest. *American Antiquity* 65:449–70.

Feinman, Gary M., and Joyce Marcus (editors) 1998 *Archaic States*. School of American Research Press, Santa Fe.

Feinman, Gary M., and Jill Neitzel 1984 Too Many Types: An Overview of Sedentary Prestate Societies in the Americas. *Advances in Archaeological Method and Theory* 7:39–102.

Flanagan, James G. 1989 Hierarchy in Simple "Egalitarian" Societies. *Annual Review of Anthropology* 18:245–66.

Flannery, Kent V. 1983 Divergent Evolution. In *The Cloud People: Divergent Evolution of the Zapotec and Mixtec Civilizations*, edited by Kent V. Flannery and Joyce Marcus, pp. 1–4. Academic Press, New York.

Fracchia, Joseph, and Richard C. Lewontin 1999 Does Culture Evolve? *History and Theory* 38:52–78.

Fried, Morton H. 1967 *The Evolution of Political Society: An Essay in Political Anthropology*. Random House, New York.

Friedman, David 1977 A Theory of the Size and Shape of Nations. *Journal of Political Economy* 85:59–77.

Goldstone, Jack A. 1998 Initial Conditions, General Laws, Path Dependence, and Explanation in Historical Sociology. *American Journal of Sociology* 104:829–45.

Gould, Stephen J. 1987 The Ghost of Protagoras. In *An Urchin in the Storm: Essays about Books and Ideas*, edited by Stephen J. Gould, pp. 62–72. W.W. Norton, New York.

Grinin, Leonid E. 2004 Democracy and Early State. *Social Evolution and History* 3:93–149.

Haas, Jonathan 1982 *The Evolution of the Prehistoric State*. Columbia University Press, New York.

Hansen, Mogens Herman (editor) 2000 *Comparative Study of Thirty City-State Cultures*. The Royal Danish Academy of Sciences and Letters, Copenhagen.

Hansen, Thomas B., and Finn Stepputat 2006 Sovereignty Revisited. *Annual Review of Anthropology* 35:295–315.

Harris, Marvin 1968 *The Rise of Anthropological Theory: A History of Theories of Culture*. Thomas Y. Crowell Company, New York.

Herrmann, Esther, Joseph Call, María Victoria-Lloreda, Brian Hare, and Michael Tomasello 2007 Humans Have Evolved Specialized Skills of Social Cognition: The Cultural Intelligence Hypothesis. *Science* 317:1360–66.

Hobbes, Thomas 2003 *Leviathan*, edited by G. A. J. Rogers and Karl Schuhmann. Thoemmes Continuum, Bristol.

Hunt, Robert C. 2007 *Beyond Relativism: Comparability in Cultural Anthropology*. Altamira, Lanham, MD.

Jasny, Barbara R., and Donald Kennedy 2001 Human Genome. *Science* 291:1153.

Johnson, Allen W., and Timothy Earle 2000 *The Evolution of Human Societies*. Second Edition. Stanford University Press, Stanford.

Jones, Rhys, and Richard Phillips 2005 Unsettling Geographical Horizons: Exploring Premodern and Non-European Imperialism. *Annals of the American Association of Geographers* 95:141–61.

Kennedy, Donald 2007 Breakthrough of the Year. *Science* 318:1833.

Kennedy, Donald, and Colin Norman 2005 What Don't We Know? *Science* 309:75.

King, Adam 2006 Leadership Strategies and the Nature of Mississippian Chiefdoms in North Georgia, edited by Brian M. Butler and Paul D. Welch, pp. 73–90. *Center for Archaeological Investigations, Occasional Paper*, 33. Southern Illinois University, Carbondale.

Kiser, Edgar, and Michael Hechter 1991 The Role of General Theory in Comparative Historical Sociology. *American Journal of Sociology* 97:1–30.

Kosse, Krisztina 1990 Group Size and Societal Complexity: Thresholds in the Long-Term Memory. *Journal of Anthropological Archaeology* 9:275–303.

Lehman, Edward W. 1969 Toward a Macrosociology of Power. *American Sociological Review* 34:453–65.

Levi, Margaret 1988 *Of Rule and Revenue*. University of California Press, Berkeley.

Lichbach, Mark Irving 1995 *The Rebel's Dilemma*. University of Michigan Press, Ann Arbor.

————. 1996 *The Cooperator's Dilemma*. University of Michigan Press, Ann Arbor.

Marcus, Joyce 1992 Dynamic Cycles of Mesoamerican States: Political Fluctuations in Mesoamerica. *National Geographic Research and Exploration* 8:393–411.

————. 1998 The Peaks and Valleys of Ancient States: An Extension of the Dynamic Model. In *Archaic States*, edited by Gary M. Feinman and Joyce Marcus, pp. 59–94. School of American Research Press, Santa Fe.

————. 2008 The Archaeological Evidence for Social Evolution. *Annual Review of Anthropology* 37:251–266.

Mayr, Ernst 1982 *The Growth of Biological Thought*. Belknap Harvard, Cambridge.

Mills, Barbara J. (editor) 2000 *Alternative Leadership Strategies in the Prehispanic Southwest*. The University of Arizona Press, Tucson.

Morgan, Lewis H. 1877 *Ancient Society*. World Publishing, New York.

Nichols, Deborah L., and Thomas H. Charlton (editors) 1997 *The Archaeology of City-States: Cross-Cultural Approaches*. Smithsonian Institution Press, Washington, DC.

Northrup, David 2005 Globalization and the Great Convergence: Rethinking World History in the Long Term. *Journal of World History* 16(3). Located at www.historycooperative.org.

Ober, Josiah 2008 What the Ancient Greeks Can Tell Us about Democracy. *Annual Review of Political Science* 11:67–91.

Olson, Mancur 1965 *The Logic of Collective Action: Public Goods and the Theory of Groups*. Harvard University Press, Cambridge.

Pearson, Robert W., and Lawrence W. Sherman 2005 The Achievements, Frustrations, and Promise of the Social Sciences. *Annals, American Academy of Political and Social Science* 600:6–13.

Pennisi, Elizabeth 2005 How Did Cooperative Behavior Evolve? *Science* 309:93.

_____. 2007 Breakthrough of the Year: Human Genetic Variation. *Science* 318:1842–43.

Renfrew, Colin 1974 Beyond Subsistence Economy: The Evolution of Social Organization in Prehistoric Europe. In *Reconstructing Complex Societies: An Archaeological Colloquium*, edited by Charlotte B. Moore, pp. 69–95. Supplement to the Bulletin of the American Schools of Oriental Research, No. 20. Massachusetts Institute of Technology, Cambridge.

_____. 2001 Commodification and Institution in Group-Oriented and Individualizing Societies. In *The Origin of Human Social Institutions*, edited by W. G. Runciman, pp. 93–117. Oxford University Press, Oxford.

Rokkan, Stein 1969 Models and Methods in the Comparative Study of Nation-Building. *Acta Sociologica* 12:53–73.

Russett, Bruce M. 1964 Inequality and Instability: The Relation of Land Tenure to Politics. *World Politics* 16:442–54.

Sahlins, Marshall D. 1960 Evolution: Specific and General. In *Evolution and Culture*, edited by Marshall D. Sahlins and Elman R. Service, pp. 12–44. University of Michigan Press, Ann Arbor.

Sahlins, Marshall D., and Elman R. Service (editors) 1960 *Evolution and Culture*. University of Michigan Press, Ann Arbor.

Sanders, William T., and Barbara J. Price 1968 *Mesoamerica: The Evolution of a Civilization*. Random House, New York.

Sanderson, Stephen K. 1990 *Social Evolutionism: A Critical History*. Blackwell Publishers, Cambridge, MA.

Segraves, Barbara A. 1974 Ecological Generalism and Structural Transformation of Sociocultural Systems. *American Anthropologist* 76:530–52.

Service, Elman R. 1971 *Primitive Social Organization: An Evolutionary Perspective*. Second Edition. Random House, New York.

Shermer, Michael 2007 The Really Hard Science. *Scientific American* 297 (4):44–46.

Sinopoli, Carla M. 2001 Empires. In *Archaeology at the Millennium: A Sourcebook*, edited by Gary M. Feinman and T. Douglas Price, pp. 439–71. Kluwer Academic/Plenum Publishers, New York.

Smith, Michael E. 2006 How Do Archaeologists Compare Early States? *Reviews in Anthropology* 35:5–35.

Spencer, Charles S. 1997 Evolutionary Approaches in Archaeology. *Journal of Archaeological Research* 5:209–64.

Spruyt, Hendrick 2002 The Origins, Development, and Possible Decline of the Modern State. *Annual Review of Political Science* 5:127–49.

Steward, Julian H. 1949 Cultural Causality and Law: A Trial Formulation of the Development of Early Civilizations. *American Anthropologist* 51:1–27.

Stone, Brad Lowell 2008 The Evolution of Culture and Sociology. *The American Sociologist* 39:68–85.

Tilly, Charles 1975 Western State-Making and Theories of Political Transformation. In *The Formation of States in Western Europe*, edited by Charles Tilly, pp. 601–38. Princeton University Press, Princeton.

———. 1984 *Big Structures, Large Processes, and Huge Comparisons*. Russell Sage Foundation, New York.

———. 2000 Processes and Mechanisms of Democratization. *Sociological Theory* 18:1–16.

Tomasello, Michael 1999 Human Adaptation for Culture. *Annual Review of Anthropology* 28:509–29.

Trigger, Bruce G. 1989 *A History of Archaeological Thought*. Cambridge University Press, Cambridge.

———. 1993 *Early Civilizations: Ancient Egypt in Context*. American University in Cairo Press, Cairo.

———. 2003 *Understanding Early Civilizations*. Cambridge University Press, Cambridge.

Trubitt, Mary Beth D. 2000 Mound Building and Prestige Goods Exchange: Changing Strategies in the Cahokia Chiefdom. *American Antiquity* 65:669–90.

Wallerstein, Immanuel 2003 Anthropology, Sociology, and Other Dubious Disciplines. *Current Anthropology* 44:453–65.

Watts, Duncan J. 2007 A Twenty-First Century Science. *Nature* 445:489.

White, Leslie A. 1949 *The Science of Culture: A Study of Man and Civilization*. Grove, New York.

———. 1959 *The Evolution of Culture: The Development of Civilization to the Fall of Rome*. McGraw-Hill, New York.

Willey, Gordon R. 1999 Styles and State Formations. *Latin American Antiquity* 10:86–90.

Wolf, Eric R. 1982 *Europe and the People without History*. University of California Press, Berkeley.

Yoffee, Norman 2005 *Myths of the Archaic State: Evolution of the Earliest Cities, States, and Civilizations*. Cambridge University Press, Cambridge.

———. 2006 Afterword: Lenses on Mississippian Leadership. In *Leadership and Polity in Mississippian Society*, edited by Brian M. Butler and Paul D. Welch, pp. 398–401. Center for Archaeological Investigations, Occasional Paper, 33. Southern Illinois University, Carbondale.

CHAPTER 4

WHAT IT TAKES TO GET COMPLEX

FOOD, GOODS, AND WORK AS SHARED CULTURAL IDEALS FROM THE BEGINNING OF SEDENTISM

Monica L. Smith

The majority of chapters in this volume consider ancient and modern societies at their most developed stages, with a particular focus on chiefdoms and states. In this chapter, I look back into prehistory to examine the individual cognitive and social capacities manifested in human societies before the development of institutionalized political hierarchies. As Kyle Summers (2005:108) has observed, the last ten thousand years of human evolution has not changed gene frequencies sufficiently to account for new behavioral patterns; instead, preexisting propensities have led to the capacity of individuals to develop and adjust to new technological and social environments. Prior to ten to twelve thousand years ago, human group size was relatively small and organized along lines of kinship and affinity in which the majority of interactions were undertaken with already-known persons. In this chapter, I argue that those characteristics provided the necessary social foundation for the subsequent development of chiefdoms, states, and empires (see also Peterson and Drennan, Chapter 6).

Our species' ability to deliberately alter the environment, create complex tools, and make choices about food consumption and goods acquisition is evident by the Upper Paleolithic period starting fifty thousand years ago. Sophisticated investments in cognition and communication were exhibited in the creation of non-utilitarian "art" such as paintings and carvings, the development of portable symbol systems in the form of durable ornamentation, and the elaboration of burial customs. These actions, undertaken by individuals in a shared rubric of cultural understanding about intent and meaning, were elaborated through continued investments in objects and fixed-place settlements. After the adoption of sedentism, the transition to social complexity was manifested in the elaboration of ritual, the emergence of permanent leadership, and the specialization of economic inputs. Decisions exercised by individuals about actions at the household level continued even after the development of institutionalized political hier-archies, a factor that underwrote the capacity of elites to achieve large-scale outcomes through the appropriation of *some* food, the control of *some* goods, and the cooption of *some* labor.

Food, Goods, and Work: The Material Signatures of Individual Decision Making

The materialization of human cognitive capacities is carried out daily in three basic realms: food, objects, and work. Each of these activities leaves archaeological traces that can be utilized to evaluate both change over time and the stasis of systems (or "traditions") that remain unchanging. Both stasis and change are the result of conscious acts by individuals who expend energy; while much human action is habituated, the parameters of that habituation can be challenged when natural or social inputs change, result-ing in a stable-yet-fluid dynamic of production and consumption that is consciously maintained and furthered by each individual action.

Food is a basic human need that must be addressed by every living person, but food is utilized by people in many and diverse ways. Not everything that is edible is eaten, and not everyone is sanctioned to eat from the same menu. Within socially acceptable parameters, it is the individual who chooses to eat or not eat from the array of available foods. Through the expression of both food preferences and food taboos, people affirm their individual and group identity on a daily basis. Preference can be seen as a very deeply held component of the human food quest, evident as early as the begin-ning of the Upper Paleolithic when humans became the only predators to consistently target prime animals (Stiner 1994:chapter 11). In a study of the subsequent Mesolithic, Preston Miracle (2002) urges that we consider the development of food preferences and "cuisine" for hunter-gatherers as an important component of the social development of eating. Factors such as food availability, preference, and choice appear to have affected domestication as well (Fuller 2002), and it is clear that even after the advent of agriculture people continued to utilize a variety of "wild" resources as integral components of the diet (Mabry 2005; Smith 2006). Agriculture and sedentism encompassed many more types of decisions about food, including calculations of energy investment in intensification and food processing as well as the use of memory and social planning to create and manage storage systems for seasonally harvested foods.

Objects are another essential component of daily life, through which humans modify their environment and communicate with others. The use of objects as a human trait began as early as two and a half million years ago with the Oldowan chopper complex, and became increasingly diverse and sophisticated by about forty thousand years ago when ornaments as a symbolic manifestation supplemented the diversity of objects that could be used for practical tasks (Bar–Yosef 2002; Kuhn et al. 2001). People afterwards used objects to project social roles as well as to affirm both private and public identity (Smith 2007, 2010). The ubiquity of objects in the archaeological record enables us to discuss modes of acquisition (gift, exchange, theft), as well as the use of objects for practical purposes and for their display value. Even discard is important: humans cease their interactions with objects in a variety of ways, ranging from ostentatious removal through burial with the dead, to daily removal of trash in middens that are often located in front of houses in a way that signals social status and prosperity.

Work is a process through which individuals modify their social and physical environments. Although the anthropological evaluation of work tends to focus on "labor" and its attendant exploitative connotations, a broader definition of work as energy expenditure enables us to see how individuals direct themselves physically to address short-term, medium-term, and long-term outcomes. Even the simplest decisions about work involve the individual capacity to engage in calculations about time, space, and value: for example, grain can be prepared through labor-intensive grinding and baking, fuel-intensive boiling, or time-intensive fermentation. "Work" occurs not only in the form of physical energy expenditure, but also includes intangible activities such as storytelling, memory-work, adjudication, and other forms of communication. Given the need to respond to dynamic natural and social surroundings, individuals engage in selective energy expenditure in which each decision has an impact on subsequent activities. The outcomes of work are conditioned by factors of skill, for example when individuals apprentice themselves in specialized occupations such as ritual and medicine. Outcomes also are conditioned by factors of temporality as individuals age and either acquire virtuosity in quotidian tasks through practice or lose physical strength and reduce their task set.

In their decisions about food, goods, and work, individuals thoughtfully consider the results of their actions and purposefully engage with the material world. Individual decision-making as an active component of quotidian practices was the social basis upon which increasingly sophisticated social and economic systems were crafted at least fifty thousand years ago. The increasingly intensive manipulation of the environment in many parts of the world ten to twelve thousand years ago, often resulting in the adoption of domesticated plants and animals, further required the elaboration of individual decision-making capacities and "multi-tasking" to address new obligation and opportunities. Domesticated plants, for example, require a significant recalibration in expectations about the relationship of energy expenditure to results. The incremental efforts of tending plants until the moment of harvest represent a daily increment of "sunk costs" in planting, weeding, watering, and pest control. Energy that is expended in plant management cannot simultaneously be devoted to gathering wild foods, and the payoff of domesticates for the farmer is a long-term one that requires future planning from the moment of planting through the harvest and beyond. The harvest itself engenders further decision-making and energy inputs: storage facilities must be designed and built to keep out rodents, damp, and unauthorized human access. Each time a storage facility is opened, the user must calculate how much to remove and how much to keep behind for future use, and how far in the future that use will be.

All of these decisions about food, goods, and work are exercised at the quotidian level and through individual thought processes. Evident in sophisticated form as early as ten to twelve thousand years ago, they continued to increase as populations grew and as social complexity became materially defined through new demands placed on households by leaders who collected resources and pooled them for political, ritual, and communal activities. From the individual perspective, the emergence of hierarchical leadership meant that decisions about daily and annual energy expenditure were interwoven with new requirements such as taxation and corvée labor requirements. To examine the way in which quotidian decisions were exercised at the individual level as a integral component of increased social complexity, we can examine three areas of the world in which there are robust data sets covering long time spans: the Indus Valley, with a particular emphasis on the example of the Neolithic community at Mehrgarh (Pakistan); the Levant from the beginnings of the Natufian culture; and the American Southwest starting with the Archaic and ending with the Pueblo period.

Trajectories in the Levant

The hinterlands of the Eastern Mediterranean have been described as one of the "cradles of civilization" and one of the first places in the world where people experimented with the domestication of plants and animals (Kuijt and Goring-Morris 2002; Richerson et al. 2001; Salamini et al. 2002; Watkins 2005). In this region, shared cultural beliefs were developed at the same time as a shared basis of foodways and other daily domestic components of life, resulting in a highly ritualized set of beliefs about food, goods, and energy expenditure.

The social context of food preference is seen first in the Upper Paleolithic by a diversification of hunted food sources to include more small game (the "broad spectrum revolution"; Flannery 1969; Stiner 2001). By the Epipaleolithic (starting around twenty thousand years ago), environmental and archaeological studies show that humans utilized a wide range of plant and animal resources, including seasonal high-calorie, storable resources such as nuts, fruits, and seeds (Watkins 2005). A long history of research in the Levant enables us to examine the subsequent, intertwined ecological and social changes that afterwards developed in the Natufian (14,000–11,600 B.C.), Pre-Pottery Neolithic A (11,700–10,500 B.C.) and Pre-Pottery Neolithic B (10,500–8400 B.C.; see Kuijt and Goring-Morris 2002, Watkins 2005 for dates).

The development of the early Levantine agricultural economy is encapsulated by Randi Haaland (2007), who examines the development of Near Eastern foodways based on starchy staples such as wheat and barley. Noting that the earliest use of wild grasses dates to as early as 19,000 B.C. at Ohalo II, Haaland discusses the long trajectory of a pre-pottery period of grass seed use in the form of grinding tools. In her view, a focus on human decision making as an incremental, quotidian process shifts the understanding of early agriculture to emphasize the methods, rather than merely the product, of this transition. She notes that the "first important step in the emergence of agriculture was thus cultivation, not domestication. Cultivation is a socioeconomic process that constitutes the selection pressures affecting the biological process leading to the evolution from wild to domesticated . . . " (2007:172).

Although much of the adjustment in behavior tends to be interpreted by archaeologists from the perspective of the *longue durée*, Haaland's work reminds us that each of the actions undertaken to manage the environment and mitigate environmental fluctuation was undertaken by individuals engaged in daily activities of resource procurement and food preparation. Adaptations varied considerably from place to place within the Levant, meaning that individuals could watch the result of decisions made by others and elect to repeat or ignore the innovations of their neighbors. Pioneering settlements such as Ohalo II were inhabited in full view of other communities who did not immediately take up this mode of life; as Watkins (2005:207) summarizes, "Ohalo II is not typical of its period, for other Kebaran sites show evidence of repeated, short occupations by mobile hunter-gatherer bands. But Ohalo II does demonstrate that some groups were already tending toward sedentism and the year-round exploitation of an ecologically diverse home territory."

Environmental variability in both spatial and temporal terms provided the parameters for individual decision making on a daily, seasonal, annual, and lifetime basis. As Kuijt and Goring-Morris (2002:365) note, "Gradual changes in the environment could sometimes be accommodated whereas abrupt changes would have necessitated radical readjustments." Climate fluctuated considerably in the Levant throughout the past twenty thousand years, resulting in a variety of adjustments ranging from migration into better-favored areas during dry periods (e.g., at the end of the Natufian; see Kuijt and Goring-Morris 2002:371) to changes in household-level risk management that included communal storage and food sharing (see Flannery 2002).

The incremental development of sedentism, agriculture, and herding in the Levant can be discerned in the archaeological record through artifacts and features including hearths, storage facilities, grinding tools, and farming equipment. People altered many aspects of the built environment to accommodate new ways of procuring food, new types of foods, new ways of seeing the landscape, and even the growth of population that accompanied the advent of foods such as porridge that could be used to sustain both the very young and the very old (e.g., Molleson 1995). Even basic configurations of houses changed, with the transition from round houses to square ones observed by Flannery (1972) as a means of creating architecture that could be more easily added onto as households grew in size. Although leadership was probably evident in some elements of communal activity such as large-scale ritual events, the household's many daily decisions about cooking, eating, building, storage, resource allocation, domestic ritual, cleaning, and clothing were still undertaken one person at a time.

In an expansion of his 1972 article, Flannery (2002) provides an example of how small-scale changes within sites were generated at the household level and manifested in material remains. Using the example of Tell Hasuna in Iraq, he observes how changes in domestic architectural styles to accommodate larger-than-nuclear families were first made through the haphazard adjoining of rooms. In later phases, houses were purposefully laid out as larger, compartmentalized spaces that indicate their builders' intent to house a larger number of people as an acknowledgment of shifts in family size ideals. Although the site of Hasuna is relatively late (sixth millennium B.C.), the careful elucidation of phase-by-phase changes in the excavations cited by Flannery provides a model for looking at changes elsewhere that were undertaken one building and one generation at a time, in which decisions were materialized based on individual memory, planning, and predictive capacity. Flannery's more recent perspective on the variable adaptations seen in the early agricultural period leads him to conclude that the relatively rigid equivalencies of subsistence modes, storage and risk acceptance, and architectural configurations that he proposed in his 1972 paper were overdrawn. Instead, he concludes, "It appears that, far back in time, human agents made strategic decisions among alternatives for reasons which are not always apparent archaeologically" (2002:422).

Near Eastern burial treatments also show incremental decision making in the development and sustaining of ritual traditions. Increasingly elaborate, purposeful burials of individuals are seen at Epipaleolithic sites such as Neve David, where a young male was buried in a slab-lined grave pit accompanied by a grinding slab and a stone bowl (Kaufman 1989:277), indicative of the increasing symbolic importance of new subsistence practices. In the following Natufian period, "Most burials are primary and of a single individual, although secondary and multiple burials are also observed. Burial offerings are sometimes found on or around the interred" (Eshed et al. 2004:316). By the subsequent Neolithic period, burials became much more elaborate, including secondary mortuary treatments and ritual behaviors that combined architectural and burial activities in highly symbolic terms. The diversity of burial treatments in the Neolithic period, which included secondary burial, the re-use of skulls, the creation of figurines and half-size human effigies, painted heads on animal bones, and the occasional presence of stone masks, is evidence of "a remarkable regional similarity in mortuary practices and, at the same time, a high degree of variation in those practices between settlements" (Kuijt 2008:172). Decisions to participate in the regional tradition, as well as the forms of practice within a site or at a given time, were undertaken by individuals who assessed expectations and capacities at the moment of the specific ritual act.

Even ancillary behavioral patterns, such as trash disposal, were subject to modifications. In the Neolithic, changes in trash deposition indicate individuals' creation and acceptance of changing social parameters of behavior: "In contrast to the preceding Natufian, a major innovation begun during the PPNA and becoming widespread during the PPNB in the Mediterranean zone was systematic house cleaning and the dumping of refuse in clearly defined adjacent refuse areas" (Kuijt and Goring-Morris 2002:373). Along with the elaboration of ritual practices, routine activities ranging from house-building to foodways show that for Neolithic people, there was more work, and more types of work, in which individuals and households could be engaged.

In the ancient Near East, decisions related to food, objects, and energy expenditure undertaken at the village level continued to be made by individuals who became incorporated into successively larger physical entities such as the city and progressively larger social institutions such as the state starting in the Uruk period (4200–3000 B.C.). Sustained regional interactions throughout periods of dramatic episodes of state formation, including those identified through the study of trade connections, indicate the extent to which ordinary domestic activities resulted in the cultural cohesion that underwrote and sustained several subsequent millennia of complex political hierarchies.

Trajectories in the Indus Valley

The Indus Valley region is located in the alluvial plains of present-day Pakistan and western India. Best known archaeologically for the Bronze-Age Harappan culture (2500–1800 B.C.), the Indus region also has significant remains relating to earlier periods. With a long trajectory of human population development, the Indus region is an excellent place to look at the processes of initial agriculture and sedentism. The relatively close geographic proximity between the alluvial plains of the Indus and the "fertile crescent" of the Near East has prompted attempts to link technologies and social groupings from one area to the other. Examined from the South Asian perspective, however, there were many opportunities for the independent domestication of some plants and animals (MacHugh et al. 1997; Morrell and Clegg 2007; Possehl 2002).

One limitation to the comparative study of this region is that few sites of the earliest phases have been investigated; however, extensive investigations at the site of Mehrgarh (Jarrige 2004, Jarrige et al. 1995) serve as a proxy for regional patterns of cultural development. Mehrgarh, occupied from 7000–1600 B.C., is located in the western part of Pakistan at an ecotone where alluvial plains and upland meet. In this environment, people could readily exploit multiple natural resources in a manner that would reduce risk as well as provide opportunities for diversified production intensification in both plants and animals. Extensive excavations at the site show the development of agricultural strategies, architectural investments, and ritual activities in long-term patterns of stasis and change indicative of individual and household-level decision making.

From the beginning of the occupation, Mehrgarh's architecture consisted of structures described as freestanding, multiroomed, rectangular houses (Jarrige 2004:27). However, it was not until the sixth millennium that clay containers are recovered in association with this architecture, indicating that Mehrgarh (like the Levant) sustained a pre-pottery Neolithic tradition. By the fifth millennium, people were simultaneously investing more labor in storage, food processing, and architecture. Jean-François Jarrige (2004:29) notes that structures were more elaborate, and that "a more careful threshing of the cereals ... is clearly indicated by an almost complete disappearance of the impressions of seeds or whole ears that are so frequent in the Neolithic walls." Another change in foodways is seen at the midpoint of the occupational sequence when pig bones increased in frequency and then decreased again, leading the project's faunal analyst Richard Meadow to propose that there might have been an attempt at pig domestication in the fourth millennium that was later abandoned (reported in Jarrige 1995:77).

Figurines are another way in which social and ritual traditions can be examined. Figurines appear throughout the Indus Valley starting in the seventh millennium B.C.; at Mehrgarh, they are found in a wide variety of contexts and show an evolution from a generalized anthropomorph through a stage of bovine forms to a corpus of predominantly female figures, often with elaborate coiffures (Jarrige 1991). The hairstyles, along with the rolled clay layers that appear to represent jewelry, change from one era to the next and include various types of ringlets, coils, and even wigs. In nearly all cultures, hairstyles are one of the most basic ways in which people project their identity in the public sphere, along with clothing, headgear, and ornaments. The Mehrgarh figurines constitute one of the ancient world's few archaeologically documented examples of the dynamic ephemera of hair.

Figurines – and the living sartorial traditions they mirrored – were part of a regional culture in which there was a fluid distribution of styles across space and over time providing evidence for the often archaeologically invisible quotidian decisions made on an individual basis long before the advent of the state. Frequent changes in the shape, style, and decoration of the Mehrgarh figurines show a dynamic engagement with the production and consumption process by people who would have been experiencing many other cultural and environmental shifts including increased dependence on agricultural products and the engagement with highland peoples in cycles of transhumance that eventually linked the Indus region to the Iranian plateau and to Central Asia. Not all practices involved innovation, however, indicating that choices also included the deliberate selection of traditions and stasis. At Mehrgarh, burial practices are represented by what the excavator characterizes as "great homogeneity of grave goods, which are limited to necklaces and bracelets of baked white steatite micro-beads and a few pendants of lapis lazuli and other semiprecious stones" (Jarrige 1995:73).

Throughout the millennia of Mehrgarh's development, individuals and households were expending more energy in a variety of ways simultaneously, resulting in pressure for time management and planning throughout the economic spectrum. By about 3500 B.C., there is evidence of supra-household labor investment in the form of a ditch discovered at the edge of the settlement that the investigators interpreted as an irrigation canal (Jarrige et al. 1995:451). Energy expenditures for these supra-household allocations would have been added to the activities that people already scheduled for themselves. As in the case of the Levant, elaborate social, economic, and ritual traditions were sustained at the individual level and became the basis upon which increasingly complex sociopolitical configurations were established.

Although Mehrgarh itself did not become a city, by the middle of the third millennium B.C. the Indus region featured genuine urban configurations at sites such as Dholavira, Harappa, and Mohenjo-daro. People living in those urban centers continued to use the same agricultural base as the preceding Neolithic, as well as the same techniques of craft production and the types and styles of ornaments, architecture, and culinary practices seen at Mehrgarh and other nearby sites where the latest Neolithic figurines "already incorporate in embryonic form all the elements of the Indus civilization figurines with their elaborate hairstyles, loin-cloths and applied ornaments" (Jarrige 1991:92). These long-standing traditions, deliberately maintained, were augmented by new expressions of social hierarchy: walls around urban subdivisions, an elaborate script system, and the development of standardized ornaments made from a variety of raw materials. Writing about the Indus patterns of accommodating new hierarchies upon sustained cultural patterns, Mark Kenoyer notes that the "reproduction of identical shapes and styles using different raw materials helps to unify people within a single culture and belief system, even though not everyone enjoys the same wealth or status" (Kenoyer 1998:143).

Trajectories in the American Southwest

The American Southwest provides an extensive data set for assessing the development of social complexity, principally focused on the Four Corners area of Colorado, Arizona, Utah, and New Mexico. As in the Levant and the Indus, the time frame for the transition from foraging to farming is a long one, with about two millennia of experimentation with local plants before the adoption of fully-domesticated maize from Mexico circa 2100 B.C. (Mabry 2005:63). The culmination of the developmental trajectory from initial plant experimentation to sedentary farming to chiefdom (or chiefdom-like) levels of complexity are easily readable in the form of massive pueblo architecture concentrated in sequentially occupied locations (e.g., Chaco Canyon, 900–1150 A.D.; Mesa Verde, 1150–1300 A.D., and the northern Rio Grande region of New Mexico 1300–1450 A.D.).

Yet each act of foraging, farming, and construction was carried out one person at a time, building on centuries-old patterns of adaptation to the landscape through a process of cognitive assessment of each day, each season, and each lifetime. As in the case of the Indus and the Levant, *longue-durée* perceptions of agricultural increase are a scholarly abstraction of a process that resulted from many thousands of households' decisions about the parameters of successful resource extraction. Jonathan Mabry (2005:47) notes that during the period 4500–2500 B.C. when climate studies show a late-Holocene moist interval, "agriculture was introduced to the region and became the focus of subsistence, runoff farming and flood farming were possible on regularly flooding alluvial fans and floodplains, dry farming was possible on active sand dunes that dammed springs and conserved soil moisture, and irrigated farming was possible near permanent springs and along perennial reaches of rivers." The creative use of microclimate zones by early farmers was an extension of foragers' knowledge about resource variation in the landscape. This perspective brings to fruition Winterhalder and Goland's (1997:123–24) exhortation that we should look at localized decision making that made use of topographic variations and "field dispersion . . . to reduce risk in the same manner as does sharing among hunter-gatherers."

The landscapes of the American Southwest, with their distinctive topography and limited pockets of fertile ground, are likely to have instilled in each person not only the knowledge of resource availability but also a sense of memory as well as social and emotional ties encapsulated in landscape terms (for much later periods, see Basso 1996). People added stylistic markers to these natural demarcations of the landscape, producing ceramic vessels with regionally specific designs that were widely traded throughout the Southwest and that probably served as the vehicles for language-based communication about social ties and communal memory over large landscapes. By the late first millennium A.D., even utilitarian pottery appears to have moved over considerable distances, prompting Toll (2001:60) to note that these transfers were probably "based on more than pure need" (see also Abbott 2010).

Ritual expansion also occurred as a component of social networks. The most spectacular manifestation of a shared ideology can be seen at Chaco Canyon, a collection of large masonry pueblos in northwestern New Mexico. At Chaco, we can trace "ritualized" (cf. Bradley 2005:33) aspects found in basic activities such as food procurement. Extensive catchment systems were constructed that channeled water running off of canyon rims into local field systems (Cordell 1984). Although labor-intensive, these efforts were insufficient to feed the large numbers of people who lived and visited, so residents and visitors developed supplemental systems of resource provisioning. Analysis of maize found at Chaco Canyon indicates that it was grown in a variety of regions and thereafter transported 80–90 kilometers (Benson et al. 2003). Research on other domestic needs indicates that timber for construction and pottery for cooking were also brought from similar distances (e.g., Toll 2001; Windes and McKenna 2001). Although most researchers would agree that Chaco was "a highly organized, centralized, hierarchical, regional sociopolitical system" (Cordell 1984:273), evidence for coercion is slight (Windes and McKenna 2001:135). Instead, Chaco appears to have been sustained by many thousands of acts of individual decision making to allocate time and energy for the production of food and transportation of resources to a place of symbolic importance.

The simple fact of food production, distribution, and consumption provides a fine-scaled window of insight that humanizes the discussion of the American Southwest beyond the climate-driven, often mechanistic models of complexity offered for the region (e.g., Kohler et al. 2000; Reynolds et al. 2005). The adoption of cultigens seems to be part of a long trajectory of plant husbandry; although older explanations of maize adoption in the Southwest proposed that it was the result of a dramatic introduction from Mesoamerica, the accumulation of data on different rates and places of adoption show a multifaceted, lengthy, and idiosyncratic process of adoption. Moreover, this adoption appears to have enhanced a preexisting process of tending indigenous plants such as chenopodium and amaranth, such that the introduction of maize was a modification and extension of practices already in place (Mabry 2005).

The use of many different types of plants suggests that for the Southwest, the development of agriculture, irrigation, and sedentism was the result of a suite of knowledge held by individuals and incrementally implemented and modified to fit prevailing conditions. The adoption of cultigens was just one of many steps in the development of foodways, as there were subsequent decisions made about the storage, preparation, cooking, and serving of the domesticated product. Acknowledging the variation in the adoption of new ways of preparing food, including pottery and metates, Patricia Crown (2001:245–46) has noted that "data from smaller areas of the Southwest reveals considerable variation in the timing of changes in ground-stone tool morphology and size (Hard, Mauldin, and Raymond 1996), indicating the importance of individual decisions and strategies in adopting new technology."

Discussion

As archaeologists, we investigate the material remains that represent the actions of individual people engaged in daily activities involving food, goods, and energy expenditure. Long before the development of social complexity, individuals were intimately familiar with the concepts of multitasking, time management, spatial and temporal allocations of energy, future planning, and memory-enhanced quotidian decision making. These individual perceptions are evident in deep prehistory and were acted on in a constant series of trade-offs to address short-term, medium-term, and long-term outcomes. Even prior to the emergence of fully modern *Homo sapiens*, our ancestors individually capitalized on a number of cognitive skills: the collection and carrying of stone suitable for working by 1.6 million years ago, the control of fire by about 400,000 years ago, and the use of composite tools by 250,000 years ago. The cognitive skills exhibited in these individually-managed activities in turn provided the foundations for the increasingly sophisticated management of both natural landscapes and cultural interactions by the Upper Paleolithic era fifty thousand years ago.

The engagement with increasingly complex foodways starting as early as twenty thousand years ago, including the eventual domestication of plants and animals, provided an increasingly diverse arena for our species' cognitive skills. Memory and planning were necessary components of new subsistence patterns; not only were they needed for the allocation of land and the production of food, but they were critical in the allocation of stored resources. Farmers and their households watched their stockpiles of comestibles inflate seasonally but dwindle daily, requiring a long-term investment in allocation against which there was always a pressure to trade off future needs with present wants. The archaeological record indicates that at the same time that agricultural investments were increasing, people also increased the time and attention devoted to ritual, such that the transformation to agriculture and sedentism increased workloads at the household level in a number of ways simultaneously.

Even in the most advanced states and empires that developed after the transition to settled agricultural lifeways, most decisions about quotidian events continued to be made at the individual and household level, away from the control – or even perception – of elites. Individuals interwove the demands of political and social hierarchies into their already-existing commitments to short-term, medium-term, and long-term processes. The evidence of leadership starting in the Neolithic includes many artifactual and architectural components with high archaeological visibility: large-scale construction projects indicative of sustained management, widespread destruction at a scale beyond household violence and disruption, and/or the appearance of distinctive styles in portable objects. However, each of these materializations was added onto the diverse economic and social repertoire already sustained by individuals and households.

Leaders were likely to be most successful when they exhorted participants to undertake activities with which ordinary people were already familiar, such as ritual and agriculture. Leaders added the novel component of scale, providing a certain psychological "safety in numbers" as increasing numbers of individuals participated in community projects. Richard Sosis (2003) has explored the way in which ritual behavior is both externally projected and internally realized through acts of costly signaling that demonstrate their participants' commitment, a factor that may help to describe individuals' willingness to participate in ritualized behavior of all kinds including that which produces architecture, irrigation works, and other secular monuments.

Conclusion

Archaeological investigation works at a larger time frame than the individual life span, meaning that the understanding of ancient activities is often subsumed into interpretative frameworks that emphasize the *longue durée*. However, we do not excavate "cultural systems"; instead, what we recover from the archaeological record are the remains of individuals' actions in the form of houses, hearths, middens, workshops, storage pits, and burials. In antiquity, most goods and features were designed to be used by one person at a time. Most objects also were made by one person from start to finish, with manufacture dependent on the ability of an individual to envision the entire process of transforming raw materials into a finished product.

Even the largest archaeological monuments, directed by political or religious leaders, were the result of individual hands under conditions in which each working person undertook many other forms of energy expenditure when not working on a leader-directed task.

A prehistory of ordinary people illustrates the dynamic way in which each individual engaged an autonomous cognitive capacity to address both the natural and the social landscape. Much human activity was routinized and habituated, but people also possessed the ability to cognize those routine actions and creatively modify them. Daily activities are precisely the place in which we can investigate the decision-making processes that are materialized in loci of production, distribution, and consumption. For ordinary people as well as elites, the relationship among food, objects, and work is one that involves constant fine-tuning, thinking, planning, and energy expenditure on the part of individuals. The cognitive elements used in daily activities were active in deepest prehistory and were the component, sustaining parts of social complexity.

Acknowledgments

I would like to thank Michael E. Smith for inviting me to participate in the conference "Settlement, Economy, and Power in Deep History" held at the Amerind Foundation, and John Ware for the warm hospitality during our stay. Many thanks go to the other conference participants for the stimulating discussion generated in the course of the meeting and sustained afterward through the publication process.

References Cited

Abbott, David R. 2010 The Rise and Demise of Marketplace Exchange among the Prehistoric Hohokam of Arizona. In *Archaeological Approaches to Market Exchange in Ancient Societies*, edited by Christopher P. Garraty and Barbara L. Stark, pp. 61–83. University Press of Colorado, Boulder.

Bar-Yosef, Ofer 2002 The Upper Paleolithic Revolution. *Annual Review of Anthropology* 31:363–93.

Basso, Keith H. 1996 *Wisdom Sits in Places: Landscape and Language Among the Western Apache*. University of New Mexico, Albuquerque.

Benson, Larry, Linda Cordell, Kirk Vincet, Howard Taylor, John Stein, G. Lang, Farmer, and Kiyoto Futa 2003 Ancient Maize from Chacoan Great Houses: Where Was It Grown? *Proceedings of the National Academy of Sciences* 100(22):13111–115.

Bradley, Richard 2005 *Ritual and Domestic Life in Prehistoric Europe*. Routledge, London.

Cordell, Linda S. 1984 *Prehistory of the Southwest*. Academic Press, New York.

Crown, Patricia L. 2001 Women's Role in Changing Cuisine. In *Women and Men in the Prehispanic Southwest: Labor, Power, and Prestige*, edited by Patricia L. Crown, pp. 221–66. School of American Research Press, Santa Fe.

Eshed, Vered, Avi Gopher, Timothy B. Gage, and Israel Hershkovitz 2004 Has the Transition to Agriculture Reshaped the Demographic Structure of Prehistoric Populations? New Evidence from the Levant. *American Journal of Physical Anthropology* 124:315–29.

Flannery, K. V. 1969 Origins and Ecological Effects of Early Domesticates in Iran and the Near East. In *The Domestication and Exploitation of Plants and Animals*, edited by P. J. Ucko and G. W. Dimbleby, pp. 73–100. Duckworth, London.

————. 1972 The Origins of the Village as a Settlement Type in Mesoamerica and the Near East: A Comparative Study. In *Man, Settlement, and Urbanism*, edited by P. J. Ucko, R. Tringham, and G. W. Dimbleby, pp. 23–53. Duckworth, London.

————. 2002 The Origins of the Village Revisited: From Nuclear to Extended Households. *American Antiquity* 67(3):417–33.

Fuller, D. Q. 2002 Fifty Years of Archaeobotanical Studies in India: Laying a Solid Foundation. In *Indian Archaeology in Retrospect, Vol. 3: Archaeology and Interactive Disciplines*, edited by S. Settar and R. Korisettar, pp. 247–364. Manohar, New Delhi.

Haaland, Randi 2007 Porridge and Pot, Bread and Oven: Food Ways and Symbolism in Africa and the Near East from the Neolithic to the Present. *Cambridge Archaeological Journal* 17(2):165–82.

Hard, Robert J., Raymond P. Mauldin, and Gerry R. Raymond 1996 Mano Size, Stable Carbon Isotope Ratios, and Macrobotanical Remains as Multiple Lines of Evidence of Maize Dependence in the American Southwest. *Journal of Archaeological Method and Theory* 3(4):253–318.

Jarrige, Catherine 1991 The Terracotta Figures from Mehrgarh. In *Forgotten Cities on the Indus: Early Civilization in Pakistan from the 8th to the 2nd Millennium B.C.*, edited by Michael Jansen, Máire Mulloy, and Günter Urban, pp. 87–93. Verlag Philipp von Zabern, Mainz.

Jarrige, Catherine, Jean-François, Richard H. Meadow, and Gonzague Quivron (editors) 1995 *Mehrgarh Field Reports 1974–1985 From Neolithic Times to the Indus Civilization*. Department of Culture and Tourism, Government of Sindh, Karachi.

Jarrige, Jean-François 1995 Introduction. In *Mehrgarh Field Reports 1974–1985 – From Neolithic Times to the Indus Civilization*, edited by Catherine Jarrige, Jean-François Jarrige, Richard H. Meadow, and Gonzague Quivron, pp. 51–103. Department of Culture and Tourism, Government of Sindh, Pakistan.

————. 2004 Le néolithique des frontières Indo-Iraniennes: Mehrgarh. In *Aux marges des grand foyers du néolithique: Périphéries débitrices ou créatrices?* edited by Jean Guilaine, pp. 31–60. Editions Errance, Paris.

Kaufman, Daniel 1989 Observations on the Geometric Kebaran: A View from Neve David. In *Investigations in South Levantine Prehistory*, edited by O. Bar Yosef and B. Vandermeersch, pp. 275–85. BAR International Series 497, Oxford.

Kenoyer, Jonathan Mark 1998 *Ancient Cities of the Indus Valley Civilization*. Oxford University Press, Karachi.

Kohler, Timothy A., James Kresl, Carla Van West, Eric Carr, and Richard H. Wilshusen 2000 Be There Then: A Modeling Approach to Settlement Determinants and Spatial Efficiency among Late Ancestral Pueblo Populations of the Mesa Verde Region, U.S. Southwest. In *Dynamics in Human and Primate Societies*, edited by T. Kohler and G. Gumerman, pp. 145–78. Oxford University Press, New York.

Kuhn, Steven L., Mary C. Stiner, David S. Reese, and Erksin Güleç 2001 Ornaments of the Earliest Upper Paleolithic: New Insights from the Levant. *Proceedings of the National Academy of Sciences* 98(13):7641–46.

Kuijt, Ian 2008 The Regeneration of Life: Neolithic Structures of Symbolic Remembering and Forgetting. *Current Anthropology* 49(2):171–97.

Kuijt, Ian and Nigel Goring-Morris 2002 Foraging, Farming, and Social Complexity in the Pre-Pottery Neolithic of the Southern Levant: A Review and Synthesis. *Journal of World Prehistory* 16(4):361–440.

Mabry, Jonathan B. 2005 Changing Knowledge and Ideas about the First Farmers in Southeastern Arizona. In *The Late Archaic across the Borderlands*, edited by Bradley J. Vierra, pp. 41–83. University of Texas, Austin.

MacHugh, David E., Mark D. Shriver, Ronan T. Loftus, Patrick Cunningham, and Daniel G. Bradley 1997 Microsatellite DNA variation and the Evolution, Domestication, and Phylogeography of Taurine and Zebu Cattle (Bos taurus and Bos indicus). *Genetics* 146:1071–86.

Miracle, Preston 2002 Mesolithic Meals from Mesolithic Middens. In *Consuming Passions and Patterns of Consumption*, edited by Preston Miracle and Nicky Milner, pp. 65–88. McDonald Institute Monographs, Cambridge.

Molleson, Theya 1995 The Importance of Porridge. In *Nature et Culture*, edited by M. Otte, pp. 479–86. Université de Liège, Brussels.

Morrell, Peter L. and Michael T. Clegg 2007 Genetic Evidence for a Second Domestication of Barley (Hordeum vulgare) East of the Fertile Crescent. *Proceedings of the National Academy of Sciences* 104(9):3289–94.

Possehl, Gregory L. 2002 The Indus Civilization: A Contemporary Perspective. Altamira, Walnut Creek, CA.

Reynolds, Robert G., Ziad Kobti, Timothy A. Kohler, and Lorene Y. L. Yap 2005 Unraveling Ancient Mysteries: Reimagining the Past Using Evolutionary Computation in a Complex Gaming Environment. *IEEE Transactions on Evolutionary Computation* 9(6):707–20.

Richerson, Peter J., Robert Boyd, and Robert L. Bettinger 2001 Was Agriculture Impossible During the Pleistocene but Mandatory During the Holocene? A Climate Change Hypothesis. *American Antiquity* 66(3):387–411.

Salamini, Francesco, Hakan Özkan, Andrea Brandolini, Ralf Schäfer-Pregl, and William Martin 2002 Genetics and Geography of Wild Cereal Domestication in the Near East. *Nature Reviews Genetics* 3:429–41.

Smith, Monica L. 2006 How Ancient Agriculturalists Managed Yield Fluctuations Through Crop Selection and Reliance on Wild Plants: An Example from Central India. *Economic Botany* 60(1):39–48.

_____. 2007 Inconspicuous Consumption: Non-Display Goods and Identity Formation. *Journal of Archaeological Method and Theory* 14:412–38.

_____. 2010 *A Prehistory of Ordinary People*. University of Arizona, Tucson.

Sosis, Richard 2003 Why Aren't We All Hutterites? Costly Signaling Theory and Religious Behavior. *Human Nature* 14(2):91–127.

Stiner, Mary C. 1994 *Honor among Thieves: A Zooarchaeological Study of Neandertal Ecology*. Princeton University Press, Princeton.

———. 2001 Thirty Years on the "Broad Spectrum Revolution" and Paleolithic Demography. *Proceedings of the National Academy of Sciences* 98(13):6993–96.

Summers, Kyle 2005 The Evolutionary Ecology of Despotism. *Evolution and Human Behavior* 26:106–35.

Toll, H. Wolcott 2001 Making and Breaking Pots in the Chaco World. *American Antiquity* 66(1):56–78.

Watkins, Trevor 2005 From Foragers to Complex Societies in Southwest Asia. In *The Human Past*, edited by Chris Scarre, pp. 200–33. Thames and Hudson, New York.

Windes, Thomas C., and Peter J. McKenna 2001 Going Against the Grain: Wood Production in Chacoan Society. *American Antiquity* 66(1):119–40.

Winterhalder, Bruce, and Carol Goland 1997 An Evolutionary Ecology Perspective on Diet Choice, Risk, and Plant Domestication. In *People, Plants, and Landscape: Studies in Paleoethnobotany*, edited by Kristen J. Gremillion, pp. 123–60. The University of Alabama Press, Tuscaloosa.

CHAPTER 5

CHALLENGES FOR COMPARATIVE STUDY OF EARLY COMPLEX SOCIETIES

Robert D. Drennan and Christian E. Peterson

Early complex society studies, like anthropology in general, are strongly rooted in comparative analysis. Cultural evolutionists of the mid-nineteenth century (Tylor 1865; Morgan 1877; Spencer 1880–97) relied entirely on comparative ethnography to create speculative accounts of the antecedents of contemporary societies. A century later, Sahlins (Sahlins and Service 1960), Service (1962), Fried (1967), and other scholars did the same without assuming that "savages" would naturally aspire to better things, and slowly work their way through "barbarism" toward the "civilized" condition of Victorian Britain. Value-neutral vocabulary was sought and forces driving social change were considered, but the entire comparative enterprise still depended on imagining that some contemporary societies were like the unknown ancestors of other more complex contemporary societies. There was virtually no direct information about human societies before those that could be observed in the ethnographic present or through historical sources.

By the beginning of the twenty-first century, that situation has changed dramatically. It is no longer necessary to speculate about diachronic processes from synchronic snapshots of societies not historically related to each other, because of a flood of direct archaeological evidence about long-term trajectories of social change. We still do not know as much about the past of any region as we would like to, but we do now know more about many regions than we are fully able to make sense of. Comparative study is important to this task of, quite literally, making sense of abundant detailed information. It was exactly this that the early cultural evolutionists were doing with their comparative ethnography: making sense of a welter of ethnographic detail. Scholars from Morgan to Service and Fried offered understanding by placing ethnographically known contemporary societies in an imaginary developmental sequence. Since the sequence was based on nothing more than ethnographic information about contemporary unrelated societies, it is remarkable how much the cultural evolutionists got right about the past ten thousand years of human history.

We can now confirm archaeologically that these millennia did, indeed, see the development of larger and larger social formations, usually becoming sedentary and agricultural, and organized in increasingly complex ways, usually according to hierarchical principles. This was not a ubiquitous, steady, or uninterrupted process, but on a global scale, there was hardly a moment during the past ten thousand years when it would not have been accurate to say, "Somewhere on earth today there are larger populations integrated into a single society than ever before." This general notion has become so much a part of archaeology's conventional wisdom that it is easy to forget that it was not even much suspected before the formulation of cultural evolutionary schemes, and that it was not actually archaeologically documented until quite recently.

Consistent with nineteenth-century values, mid-twentieth-century archaeological attention to long sequences of change focused especially on the spectacular human "success stories" of the handful of pristine civilization regions that shone in the archaeological firmament for their conspicuous monumental remains and their unusually "advanced" social development. That their patterns of social organization were similar in a number of respects, despite their wide geographic separation, seemed the most interesting observation, and the similarities archaeologists began to observe took center stage in comparative studies of early civilizations. These similarities were customarily regarded as the interesting and enlightening findings, while differences were dismissed as idiosyncratic detail (cf. Trigger 2003:12). As more archaeological attention turned to earlier stages of development ("barbarism" for Morgan or "chiefdoms" for Service), it was recognized that societies of quite substantial scale had developed not only in the pristine civilization regions, but in many other places as well.

The impulse toward increasing demographic scale, for example, manifested itself repeatedly. Growth was neither steady nor uninterrupted, but region after region experienced episodes of often dramatic increase. This is not surprising for a biologically successful species that, as of ten thousand years ago, had just spread itself through all the world's major land masses. Higher regional population densities brought larger numbers of people into closer patterns of interaction than ever before, and new social relationships were organized in increasingly complex ways, very frequently in hierarchical forms of organization. Hierarchy is, after all, a highly effective principle of organization, and it is clear that the biological basis for hierarchical organization of small social groups was present in early humans, as in many other species (cf. Mazur 2005). Cultural variability in the expression of such tendencies may exist in nonhuman species as well (cf. Rendell and Whitehead 2001; Lycett, Collard, and McGrew 2007). These broadly similar trends toward demographic growth and more complex and varied, often hierarchical, organization are thus not difficult to understand.

Richer Archaeological Information and Societal Variation

New archaeological information has documented not only just how widespread some general tendencies recognized by cultural evolutionists really are but also how widely varied are their manifestations in different regional trajectories. This realization has, however, come slowly because it has been difficult to escape the straightjacket of unilineal cultural evolutionary thinking. Some have responded to the recognition of variability by jettisoning cultural evolutionary types such as the chiefdom. Others have instead broadened the definitions of such categories to encompass a wider array of organizational forms, including some only known archaeologically because ethnographic examples have never been seen. This is often taken to be a fundamental divergence of opinion, but in reality it is only a difference in ways of talking about a shared observation.

To say that there is a great deal of variability among chiefdoms is only to say that as various human societies grew toward thousands of inhabitants or more, they developed varied ways of organizing social relationships. Surely by now we can all agree that societies in this size range with more or less hierarchical social organization are not all just like Hawai'i at the time of European contact. We know this because we have much more archaeological information relevant to the issue than we had fifty (or even twenty or ten) years ago. We have that information largely because so many archaeologists in so many parts of the world were inspired by work such as that of Service (1962, 1975) to see if the Hawai'i suit fit the societies of their respective regions. Some such efforts have been rightly criticized for persistent inability to recognize a bad fit with the archaeological data when they saw it, but others have clearly shown that, while the suit might fit across the shoulders, the sleeves were too short.

All this variability among the earliest complex societies (now that we have recognized it) represents an unprecedented opportunity to advance our understandings of the forces of social change. The sample of chiefdoms is large enough, not only to force us to notice how varied these societies are, but to give us a chance to find patterns in this variability. If such patterns can be discovered, it suggests that the variability is not just idiosyncratic and random, but rather that the forces of social change tend generally to operate in a limited number of consistent ways that we can potentially specify. The available archaeological information about trajectories of chiefdom development in many regions is now becoming adequate to sustain such research. It can proceed from abstract models toward empirical data or in the reverse direction: models that make sense can be evaluated by seeking the patterns they lead us to expect in chiefdom variability, or chiefdom variability can be explored for patterns that can be the basis for formulating new models. Productive research is likely to work back and forth between models and empirical patterns.

A number of attempts have been made to characterize the meaningful aspects of chiefdom variability. The observation that some chiefdoms were much more highly developed than others led to splitting the chiefdom class into simple and complex chiefdoms (Wright 1984; Johnson and Earle 1987), creating a five-part evolutionary sequence of band, tribe, simple chiefdom, complex chiefdom, and state out of Service's four-part scheme. More common are concepts that crosscut the evolutionary trajectory. Renfrew (1974) distinguished individualizing from group-oriented chiefdoms, and D'Altroy and Earle (1985) distinguished between wealth and staple finance in the development of the Inka Empire. These distinctions have subsequently both been applied all along the evolutionary scale of complex societies from simple chiefdoms to very large states. They are principal elements in the composite notion of corporate versus network modes of organization (Blanton et al. 1996), posed originally as contrasting paths that complex society development followed in different regions (see Feinman, Chapter 3). Although the intensity of one mode or the other varied somewhat through time, the central Mexican pathway was seen to emphasize corporate organization all along, while the persistent tendency on the Maya pathway was network.

Other authors have given stronger developmental implications to the staple-financed corporate and wealth-financed network modes. A shift from one mode of organization to the other seems a sort of evolutionary advance, although for some corporate organization is an advance over network and for others it is the other way around (Earle 1991; King 2003; see also Earle and Smith, Chapter 10). The notion of varied sources of social power (Mann 1986; Earle 1997) has been put to similar use. Trajectories of societal development differ in character according to the relative importance of the military, religious, political, or economic roles played by leaders, but economic power is seen to have particularly strong developmental potential. The enthusiastic adoption of such concepts in archaeology shows the vigor of efforts to make sense of the variability we have recently begun to see in early complex societies.

All the concepts just mentioned revolve around notions of leaders, power, inequality, and hierarchy, but it has been argued that some societies grow to quite large scale and are integrated by complex forms of organization, but seem far less hierarchical in nature (Ehrenreich, Crumley, and Levy, eds., 1995; McIntosh 1999). The very existence of such societies is practically ruled out by definition in approaches such as that of Mann (1986:1), in which "societies are constituted of multiple overlapping and intersecting sociospatial networks of power," a concept that, for Mann, "gives us the best available entry into the issue of what is ultimately 'primary' or 'determining' in societies." A society entirely lacking in power relationships of any kind is indeed hard to imagine. It is increasingly evident that this is true, not only for human societies, but for those of macaques, baboons, dolphins, whales, elephants, wolves, and other species as well (cf. Connor, Smolker, and Richards 1992; Harcourt and de Waal, eds., 1992; Maestripieri 2007). How variable the centrality of unequal power relationships is, though, should be an empirical question rather than an article of faith. This is facilitated by an approach that takes the emergence of larger and larger scale social formations through recent millennia as the center of gravity of research rather than hierarchy, inequality, or power itself. Instead of labeling some larger-scale but not so hierarchical societies "heterarchical" and setting them apart from comparative study of "chiefdoms," an approach focused on growing social scale includes both and makes it easier to investigate the sources of variation in how central power relationships are to human social organization.

Archaeologists, then, have responded to the challenge of making sense of a flood of new information about ancient societies by recognizing more variability than these societies were once thought to have and by developing new concepts to characterize it. It would be easy to simply take these concepts and run with them, finding more and more examples of staple finance, wealth finance, corporate organization, network organization, heterarchy, and so on, as if fitting ever-larger numbers of societies into these categories were itself a conceptual advance. Still more conceptual development is needed, however, to do justice to the richness of the new information; existing concepts have only scratched the surface of the meaningful variability we can now observe. If we allow the concepts we now work with to become reified by simply using them as typological constructs for labeling different societies (as there are already signs of in the literature), we would be doing no better than those who have been rightly criticized for using cultural evolutionary concepts like chiefdom in this way.

Although it is challenging to find ways of working with the quantity of archaeological information we now have for so many regions, careful culti-vation of empirical approaches is needed to complement abstract modeling and help us to avoid reifying a set of concepts that is not yet subtle and sophisticated enough to help us learn as much as we can about processes of social change. This chapter (and its companion, Chapter 6) takes an essen-tially empirical approach that begins with archaeological observations and works toward more abstract generalizations, not to contradict or displace work that takes abstract models as its starting point, but to complement such work.

Archaeological Reconstruction and the Secondary Literature

In comparing social organization in different regions, archaeologists are, of course, relying on reconstructions of what that social organization was. These reconstructions are based on interpretation of the archaeological data that can actually be observed, and are thus already at some remove from it. It seems inevitable, though, that reconstruction of what happened in each region in prehistory must precede the act of comparing societies. Trigger (2003:30–31) has taken this even one step further by seeking "to understand each of the seven early civilizations as a functioning system before I compared them." Trigger relied, for the most part, on the social reconstructions and understandings offered by the secondary literature for this handful of regions. This has seemed the only way to encompass multiple regions in comparative studies, since the primary sources seem too extensive for any one scholar to master for very many regions. Trigger (2003:53) found that he had to limit his reading of even the secondary sources, opting to stop reading on a civilization when he was no longer learning much new about it.

Dealing with the much more numerous complex societies that never reached such a large scale is an even more prodigious task. Comparisons of larger samples have been attempted in archaeology (Peregrine and Ember, eds., 2001–2002; Peregrine 2003) by following the lead of cross-cultural research in ethnography (Murdock and White 1969; Murdock 1981). The codings of standard variables for large numbers of archaeological cases in such approaches have relied heavily, not just on the secondary literature, but even on tertiary summaries like encyclopedia entries.

Comparison of large samples of archaeological cases has come only at the cost of an ever-widening gap between the comparisons and the archaeological evidence upon which our knowledge of ancient societies is based (see Smith and Peregrine, Chapter 2). This gap has been crossed in a series of steps, starting with the actual archaeological observations ("Stratum 3 in Test F yielded 19 sherds of Atoyac Yellow-White ceramics . . ."). A primary source, like a site report, would customarily incorporate enough analysis and interpretation to arrive at a social reconstruction ("House 14 was the residence of a higher status family . . ."). The secondary literature would synthesize the conclusions of a number of primary reports ("Ascribed social status appeared in the Valley of Oaxaca at 1000 B.C. . . . "). Discussion and debate focuses at this level as regional specialists argue over ways of synthesizing, and dispute the conclusions primary reports draw from the observations. Sometimes regional specialists reach consensus and produce conventional wisdom; sometimes contested views persist. The summaries that appear in tertiary sources like encyclopedias and textbooks present conventional wisdom compactly, and resolve controversy in favor of the writer's views.

When regional specialists disagree in the secondary literature, the aspiring comparative analyst is faced with choosing one version or another – a decision he or she is probably ill-equipped to make for lack of region-specific expertise. Even when regional specialists agree, it is not clear that the consensus is truly comparable to that of specialists in a different region. Regional specialists can become very accustomed to particular ways of interpreting archaeological evidence and to particular reconstructions of past societies – reconstructions that become so rigidly codified into conventional wisdom that regional specialists no longer think critically about them. They can take on an existence altogether apart from the evidence that originally gave rise to them and lead comparisons badly astray.

For example, the secondary archaeological literature for North and Central America gives the clear impression that the societies represented by Moundville (Alabama) and Sitio Conte (Panama) were both led by spectacularly and similarly rich and powerful chiefs. In contrast, Pueblo Bonito (Colorado) is controversial, but the vision of it as an egalitarian society is strong. Even those who see social hierarchy at Pueblo Bonito often take pains to explain why this is not more conspicuous in the archaeological record, for instance by identifying it as a corporate complex society with anonymous or faceless leaders (Earle 2001; Peregrine 2001; Renfrew 2001).

While several kinds of archaeological evidence can relate to social hierarchy, it is burials (related to specific ethnohistory) that underpin the conventional wisdom for Moundville and Sitio Conte. In fact, virtually nothing is known of Sitio Conte except its burials, which are conventionally taken as classic instances of chiefly excess. The most elaborate contained a principal individual, surrounded by 22 others, possibly sacrificed to accompany the principal's interment. Included as offerings were 278 large gold ornamental items; 57 gold bells; 3,089 gold beads; 65 figures inlaid with gold; 2 copper ornaments; 143 ceramic vessels; 1,767 flaked and ground stone tools; and numerous teeth and claws of whales, sharks, felines, rabbits, dogs, and stingrays (Hearne and Sharer, eds., 1992; University of Pennsylvania Museum Archives 1999). At Moundville the most elaborate known burial, described as the "great chief of Mound C" in an early twentieth-century magazine article, contained one individual with a copper axe, 61 copper-covered beads, 3 sheet copper gorgets, a sheet copper hair ornament with a bison-horn pin, an amethyst human-head pendant, and a pearl necklace (Peebles 1974; Knight and Steponaitis 1998:18). The two burials may well indicate rich and powerful chiefs at Sitio Conte and Moundville, respectively, but if investment in burial treatment is the primary marker of wealth and power (and what else do we have in these cases?), then similarly rich and powerful chiefs are not indicated. The notion of chiefs who are, by definition, rich and powerful is a concept derived primarily from ethnography, a concept that we tend to use as a dichotomy – societies either have chiefs or they do not. Having said (for nearly a century) that both Moundville and Sitio Conte had rich and powerful chiefs makes them sound more similar than is really indicated by the evidence used to identify chiefs in the first place. The deeply entrenched acceptance of the conventional wisdom in the secondary literature for both sites has helped us to lose sight of that evidence.

Turning to Pueblo Bonito, the clear impression given by the secondary literature is that Pueblo Bonito lacks burials that could be taken as those of rich and powerful chiefs and is thus arguably a nonhierarchical society. Again, the entrenched conventional wisdom has obscured the archaeological evidence, which includes a burial in Room 33 of the great house with the central skeletons of two adult males (one of whom died violently); the disarticulated remains of 14 or 15 other men, women, and children; 2,032 pendants and other ornaments of turquoise, shell, jet, and other stone; 48,552 beads of turquoise, shell, and stone; 1,052 turquoise mosaic pieces; 2 mosaic-covered baskets; 43 pieces of malachite; 16 ceramic vessels; 1 shell trumpet; and 3 reed arrows (Pepper 1920; Akins 2001). If this burial had occurred at either Sitio Conte or Moundville, it would have been taken as evidence of strongly hierarchical social organization (and individualizing or network organization at that). That it is not interpreted in this way for Pueblo Bonito is attributable primarily to the dead hand of ethnography in the form of abundant descriptions of egalitarian Puebloan societies across the U.S. Southwest in the ethnographic present. Taken at face value, the presence of such an elaborate burial at Pueblo Bonito makes a substantially stronger case for rich and powerful chiefs than the Moundville burials do – chiefs more in the range of those inferred from the Sitio Conte burials. The sixteenth-century historical sources for both Panama and the U.S. Southeast give considerable encouragement to visions of rich and powerful indigenous chiefs, and the burial evidence for both regions was quickly interpreted in these terms, even though the support it actually provides for very powerful chiefs is much more emphatic in the Sitio Conte case. If we compare Moundville, Pueblo Bonito, and Sitio Conte societies on the basis of the conventional wisdom embodied in the secondary literature, Pueblo Bonito stands apart from the other two cases as substantially less hierarchical (or at least less clearly hierarchical). If, on the other hand, we compare the investment in mortuary ritual for most exalted individuals in each society using the primary evidence, it is Moundville that stands apart from the other two cases as lavishing less investment on important individuals. Irrespective of whether we conclude that the Moundville burial evidence indicates ascribed or achieved status, wealthy chiefs, paramount chiefs, or some other kind of leader, it is clear that far less was invested in the preservable elements of mortuary ritual for the most special individuals than at Sitio Conte or Pueblo Bonito.

We do not suggest that prevailing interpretations of social hierarchy in these three societies be overturned solely on the basis of these three burials, but the comparison of the most elaborate burials in the three regions comes as a considerable surprise in the context of what we are all accustomed to read in the secondary literature. Relying on the secondary literature makes us think that the most impressive burials at Moundville and Sitio Conte must be similarly elaborate, when in fact they differ quite substantially in this regard. And it makes us think that the most impressive burials at Pueblo Bonito and Sitio Conte must differ much more strongly than they really do. For a variety of reasons, the conventional wisdom about these three societies may actually be quite accurate, despite the comparison of investment in their most elaborate burials. Our point here is only that the detailed evidence of just what an elaborate burial was like must also be conspicuously present in any convincing social comparison so that the comparability of the synthetic accounts from the secondary literature can be adequately assessed. The details presented above on three burials are regularly blurred in synthetic accounts by normative descriptions of what burials, generically, were like in these societies; the full detail is only found by persistent searching into some deep dark recesses of the primary literature.

The intensity of regional specialization in archaeology means that specialists in one region typically know little about other regions or about how archaeology may be approached differently there. It is thus extremely easy to be entirely unaware of incompatibilities in archaeological interpretation. Carrying out field research in multiple regions can help develop greater awareness, and set comparative study on a sounder footing (Earle 1997; Drennan and Peterson 2006), but no one person or reasonably sized collaborative group can possibly carry out field research in very many regions. It is possible, however, to complement the reconstructions made by regional specialists by carrying out consistent analyses of primary archaeological data sets from many places so as to avoid the impact of incompatible ways of interpreting the evidence that are embedded in the conventional wisdom for different regions. Our aim here is not to supersede the work of regional specialists but to complement it by offering an approach to comparative study that takes direct hold of primary archaeological data sets (at the how-many-sherds-of-what-kind-were-recovered-where level). It delineates patterns in the data that derive their comparability from the consistency of an analytical approach that puts the same kinds of data from different regions through the same wringers. Comparison is then carried forward at much less remove from the data. It is fully integrated into the process of interpreting the patterns delineated in such a way that the social reconstructions for each region are hammered out on the forge of comparison.

Archaeological Data Threads

Concepts such as simple/complex chiefdoms, corporate/network organization, staple/wealth finance, and hierarchy/heterarchy have forced open the door to consideration of the variation in patterns of organization in early complex societies. Each of these dimensions amounts to a reconstruction of past organization that (ideally at least) relies on a number of lines of evidence interpreted in combination. Bringing comparative analyses more fully into the process of reconstruction or interpretation requires disentangling these lines of evidence for individual comparison between different regions. It is useful to think of a skein of data threads, each one comprising a particular kind of pattern that can be found by an appropriate analytical strategy applied to the same sort of data collected in compatible ways in various regions.

The previous example, comparing the most elaborate burials from Pueblo Bonito, Sitio Conte, and Moundville, represents such a data thread. The data themselves are direct observations of the skeletal remains and associated artifacts with minimal interpretation. Analysis, in this instance, is almost nonexistent, consisting simply of laying the quantitative and qualitative information for each case alongside the others. A more complicated analysis might assess the amount of energy invested to produce the nonperishable evidence recovered in each instance (see, for example, Tainter 1977, 1978; Brown 1981). We list below some data threads that can be dealt with separately and directly; most are important underpinnings of the concepts already proposed to characterize variability in early complex social organization. The analyses that tease out these data threads return repeatedly to a few very familiar domains of information in archaeological analysis, such as mortuary remains, household artifact assemblages, residential architecture, regional settlement, and monumental-scale construction.

Local Community Structure. The appearance in different regions of larger social formations must have quite small local communities as a starting point. These are generally envisioned in normative descriptions of "the Neolithic village." Even when sedentary agricultural subsistence is not taken as a necessary precondition of expanding social scale, the small communities that grow are often thought of in these same unitary terms – terms drawn strongly from ethnographic descriptions of village life. The daily face-to-face interaction of the inhabitants of the small communities is the matrix in which the growth of larger social formations takes place. We now have archaeological evidence, however, to show that ancient small communities did not all conform to a single Neolithic village blueprint, but were actually highly varied. The "small" local communities from which larger social formations grew vary substantially in size. They also show considerable variation in degree of nucleation, sometimes consisting of very compact groupings of residences clearly separated from other groupings by uninhabited space, sometimes comprising looser clusters of more widely spaced residences, and sometimes even disappearing entirely in a near-continuous dispersal of farmsteads across large areas. Elsewhere we have argued (Peterson and Drennan 2005) that tightly nucleated local communities reflect especially intense interaction patterns (social, political, economic, ritual, and/or other) among their inhabitants. Since community nucleation is an issue of how people distribute their residences across the landscape, the principal domain of archaeological information in which to seek such structure is regional settlement data. An analytical strategy is required that will delineate and characterize clustering of occupation at the greatest level of detail attainable in regional-scale studies. It must be possible to assess, in at least relative terms, differences between regions in the clarity or intensity of clustering.

Supra-Local Community Scale. The prototypical pattern for the growth of a larger-scale social formation from small local community roots involves the emergence by some means of a level of organization that encompasses and integrates multiple local communities. These supra-local entities are communities too, in the social interaction sense, but on a considerably larger spatial and/or demographic scale. They may be referred to as "polities" or "districts"; the spatial scale at which they exist is often described as "regional," although their spatial extents (like their population numbers) are highly variable. There may be many, few, or only one such supra-local community in a culturally meaningful geographic area. The emergence of such communities, more than any other one thing, actually constitutes the growth of larger social formations. This emergence is the phenomenon under study when archaeologists focus on the beginnings of social complexity or on "chiefdoms"; supra-local communities are these initial complex societies or chiefdoms (Carneiro 1981; Johnson and Earle 1987). The distinction between simple and complex chiefdoms rests mainly on differences in the scale of these supra-local communities. The two distinct aspects of their scale, spatial and demographic, must both be measured (separately – they are not necessarily correlated). The only domain of archaeological information in which supra-local communities are directly observable is regional settlement. An analytical strategy is required that makes it possible to delineate their territories consistently in different regions and periods and to estimate, in at least relative terms, the differences between regions in the supra-local community populations.

Supra-Local Community Centralization. Just as the emergence of supra-local communities is the prototypical pattern of social growth in the archaeological imagination, the emergence of a central place is the prototypical means by which we envision the formation of a supra-local community. Special activities carried out at a central place focus interaction of one kind or another on it, and exert a centripetal pull on outlying populations that create higher occupation densities closer to it. The centrally focused interaction could involve economic, political, social, ritual, and/or other affairs. We usually think of the central place as the top tier in a settlement hierarchy, which may contain several lower tiers as well. Centralization can occur, however, within supra-local communities even if no local communities or central places can be detected. As with supra-local community scale, the regional settlement domain is where information on centralization must be sought, since it is in reality a property of the supra-local communities. An analytical strategy is required that can assess, in at least relative terms, the differences between regions and periods in the strength of the centripetal forces that produce centralization – whether or not central places or local communities are present.

Demographic Density. Controversy concerning population growth and pressure on resources forms a broad current in the archaeological discussion of complex society development. Of greater interest to us in this and the companion chapter (Chapter 6) are the implications of population density for human interaction. At higher regional-scale population densities, interaction becomes less costly because more people are available to interact with at shorter distances, and the costs of interaction of any kind increase sharply with distance, especially under premodern technological regimes. Higher population densities thus can encourage interaction, although such interaction can take the form of conflict, offering not so much an opportunity as a problem. For these and other reasons, variation in demographic density is vital to studying the development of larger social formations. Comparing population densities in different regions does not require "correct" and precise absolute population estimates, only truly comparable analytical approaches to all regions. The best and most directly relevant information about ancient population densities comes from the regional settlement domain by way of the distribution of the remains of human occupation across the landscape. An analytical strategy is required that can assess, in at least relative terms, the differences between regions and periods in the abundance of those remains.

Public Works Investment. The mobilization of resources that comprise a political economy has been a widely recognized feature of complex sociopolitical organization. Public works cover a broad range of ways in which these resources are spent. Construction projects of a scale beyond, and often far beyond, the capacities of a single household are a classic archaeological signature of chiefdoms and states, either because large labor forces are thought to require the organizational efforts of managerial hierarchies and/or because control of considerable quantities of resources is required for their execution. This notion has led to controversies about the social organization of societies represented by sites like Hopewell (Ohio), Poverty

Point (Louisiana), Snaketown (Arizona), and others where large-scale public works projects are not accompanied by other signs of hierarchical organization. These controversies seem overly focused on establishing a threshold scale of public works that must indicate some qualitative leap in sociopolitical organization. For something as clearly variable in quantitative terms as scale of public works, this has led to a strange emphasis on a presence/absence approach: either a society has large-scale public works and is a "chiefdom," or it does not and it is not. In the spirit of disentangling data threads that are not necessarily related so that their possible relationships can be investigated empirically, we approach this subject from a different angle. Our central interest here is simply to assess the amount of labor invested in public works as one way of approaching variability in the scale of political economies (or collective labor efforts of some kind). Public works would include such constructions as temples and other religious or symbolic spaces, palaces, fortifications, roads and causeways, other public places and monuments, and agricultural infrastructure such as terraces, canals, or raised fields. Political economies or other collectively mobilized resources can, of course, be dedicated to other (and archaeologically less conspicuous) ends, but this should not discourage us from comparing different regions in regard to the magnitude of investment in public works projects and the nature of those public works projects. An analytical strategy is required that makes it possible to assess, in at least relative terms, how large the labor invested in public works is in different regions and periods. The relevant domain of archaeological information here, of course, is monumental-scale construction (see Kolb, Chapter 7).

Tax Rate. Investment in public works (or other collective labor efforts) is a burden carried by a human population. The magnitude of that burden can be thought of in terms of labor, irrespective of whether the population contributes labor or goods (such as food that sustains laborers) and irrespective of what means of collection is practiced (taxation, tribute extraction, voluntary contribution, or other). The size of the population is, of course, the other principal factor in determining how heavy the burden is per capita. In a region where one or more supra-local communities are definable, these would be the relevant units within which public works were presumably organized and carried out, since populations of these supra-local communities would constitute the available labor pool for public works. The data threads discussed earlier include estimates of both labor investment in public works and supra-local community population; these are easily combined into an estimate of the effective "tax rate" per capita for carrying out public works. As with the two data threads from which such tax rates are derived, a "correct" and precise assessment in absolute terms is unimportant; if regions and periods are accurately positioned relative to each other on scales of labor investment and supra-local community population, then they will be accurately positioned relative to each other on scales of tax rates.

Conflict. Individuals, families, communities, or other kinds of groups can enter into conflict with each other, and conflict – whether internal to societies or with external enemies – has played an important role in theorizing about early complex societies. Conflict can grow from a number of roots and take many different forms, which have different implications for its role in societal dynamics. Conflict generally, as well as in its particular varied forms, is much more strongly reflected in the archaeological record of some regions than others. An analytical strategy is required that can assess, at least in relative terms, the differences between regions and periods with regard to how strongly the archaeological record speaks of conflict of various kinds. The relevant domains of information are regional settlement, household artifact assemblages, residential architecture, monumental-scale public works (in the form of fortifications), and mortuary remains. As in the case of ritual differentiation (see next section), iconographic study is likely to be particularly important in some of these domains.

Wealth Differentiation. The accumulation of wealth through control of physical, human, spiritual, or other resources is one of the fundamental manifestations of unequal social relationships, and thus one of the hierarchical principles around which increasingly complicated networks of interaction can be structured in growing social formations. It has been the *sine qua non* of complex society emergence for some (Earle 1977, 1997; Gilman 2001), although others (Service 1962; Fried 1967) have argued that it emerges only after the chiefdom or ranked society stage. Wealth differentiation (like the other sorts of differentiation discussed below) involves a fine-grained view of differences between individuals, families, or groups of families, often within not only supra-local communities but small local communities as well. Wealth differences, where they exist, are one of the characteristics of the social relationships and interactions that comprise communities. Curiously, for a property with such an obvious continuously variable character, wealth differentiation has mostly been treated in presence/absence terms in the archaeological literature on early complex societies. There have been, however, a few attempts to quantify it more rigorously (McGuire 1983; Smith 1987), and these attempts, like the present effort, have sprung from an explicitly comparative interest. The relevant domains of information here are more numerous than those connected to the previous data threads, so wealth accumulation is actually better thought of, not as a single data thread, but as a bundle of related data threads that can be analyzed and compared separately. An analytical strategy is required that makes it possible to assess, in at least relative terms, how big the difference in archaeological evidence is between the wealthiest members of society and the poorest for different regions and periods. The most relevant domains of archaeological information are mortuary remains, household artifact assemblages, and residential architecture.

Ritual Differentiation. Wealth differentiation is not the only principle according to which unequal social relationships can be organized. Unequal access to the supernatural has also long been recognized in human societies. Preferential access to spiritual mana and elaborate taboos surrounding behavior toward those who possessed it are conspicuous in ethnographic accounts of contact-period Hawai'i, and these ethnographic sources were central to the mid-twentieth-century definition of the chiefdom social type (Service 1962). "Theocratic" was the adjective that often accompanied "chiefdom" in work that saw ritual differentiation as the initial form of social hierarchy, with wealth accumulation occurring only later in cultural evolutionary sequences (Service 1962; Fried 1967). In the late twentieth century, this became a question for empirical archaeological investigation concerning real societies in actual trajectories of social change, requiring the maintenance of analytical separation between wealth and ritual as principles of differentiation. An analytical strategy is required that makes it possible to assess for different regions and periods, in at least relative terms, how big the difference in archaeological evidence is between those members of society most engaged in ritual and those least engaged. Archaeological evidence for ritual differentiation can be sought in several domains of information: mortuary remains, monumental-scale construction, and household artifact assemblages. Iconographic study is likely to be particularly important in all three domains.

Prestige Differentiation. As a third principle recognizable in unequal social relations, prestige is based on respect, which is a question of social values. The respect in which some people are held can derive from their own personal qualities, charisma, generosity, or special abilities; it can come from family connections; its origins can be in any highly valued realm. Wealth can, in some value systems, be a source of prestige, although this is not necessarily so; precisely the reverse can also occur. Ritual differentiation can also lead to prestige, although those with special access to the supernatural can be less respected than feared. Feasting has particularly captured the archaeological imagination as a purely social means of accumulating prestige – one that does not necessarily depend on wealth or ritual differentiation. Such feasting-based prestige is taken by some as an even more "primitive" form of social inequality than ritual or wealth differentiation, coming earlier in what is formulated as a unilineal evolutionary sequence (Hayden 1995). Like postulated developmental relationships between ritual and wealth differentiation, this idea is most productively taken as a question for empirical archaeological investigation, which, of course, requires the analytical separation of prestige differentiation from other kinds, as well as ways of recognizing this principle in the archaeological record. An analytical strategy is required that makes it possible to assess for different regions and periods, in at least relative terms, how big the difference in archaeological evidence is between the most prestigious members of society and the least. The domains where prestige can be recognized include mortuary remains, household artifact assemblages, and residential architecture.

Productive Differentiation. Like wealth, ritual, and prestige differentiation, productive differentiation occurs between individuals, families, or groups of families. Productive differentiation can appear within communities, although it is commonly recognized that such differences may occur between local communities that are themselves internally homogeneous. A more common label for productive differentiation in the early complex society literature is craft specialization, and specialization is exactly what we mean by productive differentiation, although such economic specialization might well involve products not usually referred to as "crafts." Unlike wealth, ritual, or prestige differentiation, productive differentiation does not have an inherently hierarchical character, in that producers of different products, while they may be ranked relative to each other, are not necessarily so. Craft production has received considerable archaeological attention as a potentially important element in growing social formations and emerging hierarchy. Its variability has been characterized in a number of ways – for example, as full-time versus part-time, attached versus independent, or varying in terms of concentration or scale (Costin 1991). An analytical strategy is required that makes it possible to assess for different regions and periods, in at least relative terms, how big the difference in archaeological evidence is between the most specialized activity locations and the least. One very simple analytical strategy that facilitates full integration of interpretation and comparison is to assess how much differentiation there is with regard to productive activities carried out at different locations within a supra-local community. Information for such analysis can come from the domain of household artifact assemblages (although at least in this context "household" should be taken very broadly to refer to a variety of productive locations including, for example, those more accurately labeled "workshops").

Other Threads. Many more data threads relevant to early complex societies and amenable to comparative archaeological analysis could be enumerated. The ones we have discussed are only a small subset of the possibilities, and, while they all seem important, no pretense is made that they are the most important. A number of others come very quickly to mind. Productive differentiation implies exchange of some sort at a local scale, but there is also exchange at larger scales including quite long distances. Exchange over long distances is especially easy to work with in the archaeological record. Even when exact sources cannot be pinpointed, exotic or imported items are often easy to identify, and differences between regions in the magnitude of such exchange can be seen in ratios of such goods to locally produced ones in household artifact assemblages. Other data threads could concern various aspects of subsistence and the organization of subsistence production; these include labor requirements, storability of staple foods, nutritional adequacy, land tenure, roles of households or corporate groups, and others. Reaching beyond the realm of strictly archaeological data threads, environmental parameters of potential interest, like resource abundance and distribution or subsistence risk, can be approached in the same comparative way.

Dynamics of Societal Growth

With the expansion of primary archaeological information in recent decades, we have arrived at the possibility of truly expanding the range of known human social formations beyond those directly observed ethnographically or known historically. We are now for the first time able to describe, in enough detail to be truly useful, ancient societies that may be different in important respects from any seen in history or in the ethnographic present. This is interesting in its own right because of its implications for knowledge of the full range of variation in the human experience. Of far greater potential to enlighten us, however, are the implications for understanding the dynamics of societal growth as much larger-scale social formations have emerged over the past ten thousand years or so. We no longer need to rely on imagining that contemporary smaller-scale societies are like the smaller-scale ancestors of the very large social formations most of us live in today because we are finally coming to know these ancestors themselves. This knowledge vastly broadens the horizons of studying early complex societies in such a way as to advance our understandings of the dynamics of their growth through the complicated fits and starts and discontinuities that all regional trajectories, taken individually, show. Taking advantage of this opportunity requires powerful ways to move comparison beyond the customary level of comparing synchronic snapshots of societies in different regions, typically at their "peaks" of development.

The restriction of comparative studies of early civilizations to synchronic snapshots has usually been regarded as a necessary liability, imposed by the limitations of archaeological data and the necessity of relying heavily on written sources, although Trigger (2003:13) has made a virtue of it. Trigger's argument that comparison of synchronic snapshots "is even more useful for understanding sociocultural evolution than the study of actual sequences of change," however, is unconvincing. It springs from an undue pessimism about the possibilities for reconstructing ancient social and political organization from archaeological evidence alone (Trigger 2003:33), combined with an "attempt to understand each early civilization on the same terms as it was understood by its own people" (Trigger 2003:62). Some things about change can undoubtedly be learned from comparing synchronic snapshots, but to decline to examine what we can find out about actual trajectories of social change imposes an entirely unwarranted limitation. It is nonetheless true that the understandings of the dynamics of change that can be gained from studying archaeologically reconstructed trajectories have little to do with the terms in which people understand their own cultures. This latter kind of understanding is not among our objectives here.

The classic archaeological approach to trajectories of change also deals in synchronic snapshots, but these snapshots, instead of depicting societies in different regions, depict societies at different points of time in the same region. These sequential snapshots can be compared in much the same way that snapshots of societies in different regions can be compared, but this does not automatically utilize the critical additional element embedded in a series of sequential snapshots – that the societies in these snapshots are "genetically" related: they actually descended, one from the other, right down through time. It is this connectedness that provides the essential information for approaching the dynamics of change – for not only reconstructing the pathway change took but also for beginning to answer questions like "How did that trajectory of change come to happen?"; "How did social organization come to take the series of forms that it did in that region?"; "How did the changes come to happen when they did?"

We have worked previously with the archaeological data threads enumerated above by applying the same analytical strategies to a few regions we know firsthand. Following these threads through time produces an account of at least some aspects of the trajectory of societal change in each region. It is, then, through comparing these regional trajectories that one hopes to get beyond merely describing what they were like and to approach more closely the dynamic relationships that produced them. From our previous comparisons, three contrasting modes of societal growth have emerged. These modes are by no means explanations of the differences between the regional trajectories, but clearer accounts of different ways in which societal growth took place. Considering different modes of growth helps us frame more pointed questions about how different regional trajectories got on different paths.

One region we have worked with is the Valley of Oaxaca in the southern highlands of Mexico. This sequence has already played such a large role in chiefdom studies that it hardly needs to be described any further (Blanton et al. 1982; Flannery and Marcus, eds., 1983; Kowalewski et al. 1989; Marcus and Flannery 1996). This makes it an excellent anchor for comparative studies. The San José Mogote chiefdom that emerged in the Valley of Oaxaca over a period of six or seven hundred years was, compared to other early complex societies, relatively small demographically but large territorially. The local subunits of this supra-local community were small compact villages easily recognized in the archaeological settlement data. Their inhabitants lived close together surrounded by large expanses of open, unoccupied land where they farmed. San José Mogote was the largest such village from the beginnings of sedentary life. It grew ever larger for several centuries, by the end of which the hierarchical character of social organization was clear in mortuary remains and household artifact assemblages, not only at San José Mogote but also at other local communities. The demographic expansion of the local community at San José Mogote itself was part of the societal growth, but a stronger component was territorial expansion via the forcible domination of outlying communities, as seen in regional settlement and in the iconography displayed in monumental-scale construction. The mode of growth of the early complex society in the Valley of Oaxaca consolidated a larger sociopolitical unit out of smaller building blocks consisting of local communities by tightening control over them through elite conflict and conquest.

A rather different mode of growth is suggested for the Alto Magdalena in the Andes of southern Colombia (Drennan 2000; Drennan, ed., 2006) and for the Western Liao Valley in northeastern China (Chifeng 2003; Linduff, Drennan, and Shelach 2004; Guo 2005). In the Alto Magdalena, residence patterns consist so persistently of dispersed farmsteads that local communities are never clearly identifiable. The emergence and growth of supra-local communities is, nonetheless, easy to see in regional settlement, and the indications of their presence go back to the first centuries of settled life. The pace of growth was somewhat slower than in Oaxaca, but after about a millennium, these supra-local communities, centered on the monumental burials of high-ranking people, had populations several times larger than the San José Mogote chiefdom, although they had not grown any larger spatially. Larger sociopolitical units were not built of smaller blocks; their boundaries shifted somewhat over time, but it was not a process in which some grew larger at the expense of others. Rather, the mode of growth was purely internal, consisting of an infilling of the landscape with a growing number of farmsteads but without indication of conflict with neighbors or territorial expansion, which, in any event, could not have taken the form it did in Oaxaca, because there simply was no clear structure of local communities to be forcibly dominated.

In the Western Liao Valley, it took nearly two millennia after the beginning of sedentary life for much growth of larger social formations to become apparent. A structure of local communities was present, and supra-local communities emerged through internal population growth and the budding off of small outlying villages. In this sense, then, territories expanded, although supra-local communities were both demographically and spatially much smaller than in either Oaxaca or the Alto Magdalena. The earliest supra-local communities were centered on monumental constructions including the tombs of elites, as in the Alto Magdalena. The mode of growth, while not identical to that of the Alto Magdalena, and much slower, was quite similar and did not involve the territorial expansiveness that was fundamental in Oaxaca.

More cursory comparison with the Basin of Mexico in Mexico's central highlands suggests yet a third mode of societal growth (Sanders, Parsons, and Santley 1979). The initial sedentary local communities rapidly grew much larger than those of either Oaxaca or the Western Liao but remained extremely compact. After a few centuries, elites become visible in the archaeological evidence from mortuary remains and, later, from monumental construction. All the while, the populations of local communities were growing rapidly. Some budding off of small villages occurred, but an extraordinarily large proportion of the population lived in very large local communities widely separated by open landscape. Two of these large local communities grew especially rapidly, both by internal population expansion and by drawing in the populations of other large local communities, whose locations were progressively abandoned. The mode of growth, then, was not essentially internal, as in the Alto Magdalena and the Western Liao, but neither did it involve territorial expansion by conquest as in Oaxaca. Societal growth in the Basin of Mexico makes one think of a vacuum cleaner, hoovering up other communities and drawing their populations together into extraordinarily large compact settlements. The well-known ultimate result of this mode of growth was the metropolis of Teotihuacan in a near-empty landscape.

In addition to pointing the way toward recognition of these varied modes of growth, comparison of the same data threads across a few regions has suggested some elements of the recipes that might produce them, as well as some of the consequences they might have for the larger social formations they produce (Drennan and Peterson 2005, 2006, 2008; Peterson and Drennan 2005; Drennan and Haller 2007; Drennan, Peterson, and Fox 2010). In the companion chapter (Chapter 6), we expand the scope of the comparison to a larger sample of regions so as to explore whether these notions might be nurtured into accounts of consistent patterning in early complex society development. Our focus there is on the first seven of the data threads discussed above, those that focus most strongly on the domain of regional settlement, since this is central to the recognition of the larger social formations whose emergence is our central subject.

References Cited

Akins, Nancy 2001 Chaco Canyon Mortuary Practices: Archaeological Correlates of Complexity. In *Ancient Burial Practices in the American Southwest: Archaeology, Physical Anthropology, and Native American Perspectives*, edited by Douglas R. Mitchell and Judy L. Brunson-Hadley, pp. 167–90. University of New Mexico Press, Albuquerque.

Blanton, Richard E., Gary M. Feinman, Stephen A. Kowalewski, and Peter N. Peregrine 1996 A Dual-Processual Theory for the Evolution of Mesoamerican Civilization. *Current Anthropology* 37:1–14.

Blanton, Richard E., Stephen Kowalewski, Gary Feinman, and Jill Appel 1982 *Monte Albán's Hinterland, Part I: The Prehispanic Settlement Patterns of the Central and Southern Parts of the Valley of Oaxaca, Mexico.* Memoirs of the Museum of Anthropology, University of Michigan, No. 15.

Brown, James A. 1981 The Search for Rank in Prehistoric Burials. In *The Archaeology of Death*, edited by Robert Chapman, Ian Kinnes, and Klavs Randsborg, pp. 25–37. Cambridge University Press, Cambridge.

Carneiro, Robert L. 1981 The Chiefdom: Precursor of the State. In *The Transition to Statehood in the New World*, edited by Grant D. Jones and Robert R. Kautz, pp. 37–79. Cambridge University Press, Cambridge.

Chifeng International Collaborative Archeological Research Project 2003 *Regional Archeology in Eastern Inner Mongolia: A Methodological Exploration*. Science Press, Beijing.

Connor, Richard C., Rachel A. Smolker, and Andrew F. Richards 1992 Two Levels of Alliance Formation among Male Bottlenosed Dolphins (Tursiops sp.). *Proceedings of the National Academy of Sciences* 89:987–90.

Costin, Cathy L. 1991 Craft Specialization: Issues in Defining, Documenting, and Explaining the Organization of Production. *Archaeological Method and Theory* 5:1–56.

D'Altroy, Terence N., and Timothy K. Earle 1985 Staple Finance, Wealth Finance, and Storage in the Inka Political Economy. *Current Anthropology* 26:187–206.

Drennan, Robert D. 2000 *Las sociedades prehispánicas del Alto Magdalena*. Instituto Colombiano de Antropología e Historia, Bogotá.

_____ 2006 *Prehispanic Chiefdoms in the Valle de la Plata, Volume 5: Regional Settlement Patterns*. University of Pittsburgh Memoirs in Latin American Archaeology No. 16.

Drennan, Robert D., and Mikael J. Haller 2007 The Local Village Community and the Larger Political Economy: Formative and Classic Interaction Patterns in the Tehuacán Valley Compared to the Valley of Oaxaca and the Basin of Mexico. In *The Political Economy of Ancient Mesoamerica: Transformations during the Formative and Classic Periods*, edited by Vernon L. Scarborough and John E. Clark, pp. 65–81. University of New Mexico Press, Albuquerque.

Drennan, Robert D., and Christian E. Peterson 2005 Early Chiefdom Communities Compared: The Settlement Pattern Record for Chifeng, the Alto Magdalena, and the Valley of Oaxaca. In *Settlement, Subsistence, and Social Complexity: Essays Honoring the Legacy of Jeffrey R. Parsons*, edited by Richard E. Blanton, pp. 119–54. Cotsen Institute of Archaeology, UCLA, Los Angeles.

_____ 2006 Patterned Variation in Prehistoric Chiefdoms. *Proceedings of the National Academy of Sciences* 103:3960–67.

_____ 2008 Centralized Communities, Population, and Social Complexity after Sedentarization. In *The Neolithic Demographic Transition and Its Consequences*, edited by Jean-Pierre Bouquet-Appel and Ofer Bar-Yosef, pp. 359–86. Springer, New York.

Drennan, Robert D., Christian E. Peterson, and Jake R. Fox 2010 Degrees and Kinds of Inequality. In *Pathways to Power*, edited by T. Douglas Price and Gary M. Feinman, pp. 45–76. Springer, New York.

Earle, Timothy K. 1977 A Reappraisal of Redistribution: Complex Hawaiian Chiefdoms. In *Exchange Systems in Prehistory*, edited by Timothy K. Earle and Jonathon E. Ericson, pp. 213–29. Academic Press, New York.

_____ 1991 Property Rights and the Evolution of Chiefdoms. In *Chiefdoms: Power, Economy, and Ideology*, edited by Timothy Earle, pp. 71–99. Cambridge University Press, Cambridge.

———— 1997 *How Chiefs Come to Power: The Political Economy in Prehistory.* Stanford University Press, Stanford, CA.

———— 2001 Economic Support of Chaco Canyon Society. *American Antiquity* 66:26–35.

Ehrenreich, Robert M., Carol L. Crumley, and Janet E. Levy (eds.) 1995 *Heterarchy and the Analysis of Complex Societies.* Archaeological Papers of the AAA 6. American Anthropological Association, Arlington.

Flannery, Kent V., and Joyce Marcus (eds.) 1983 *The Cloud People: Divergent Evolution of the Zapotec and Mixtec Civilizations.* Academic Press, New York.

Fried, Morton H. 1967 *The Evolution of Political Society: An Essay in Political Anthropology.* Random House, New York.

Gilman, Antonio 2001 Assessing Political Development in Copper and Bronze Age Southeast Spain. In *From Leaders to Rulers,* edited by Jonathan Haas, pp. 59–81. Kluwer Academic/Plenum, New York.

Guo Dashun 2005 *Hongshan Wenhua.* Wenwu Chubanshe, Beijing.

Harcourt, Alexander H., and Frans B. M. de Waal (eds.) 1992 *Coalitions and Alliances in Humans and Other Animals.* Oxford University Press, Oxford.

Hayden, Brian 1995 Pathways to Power: Principles for Creating Socioeconomic Inequalities. In *Foundations of Social Inequality,* edited by T. Douglas Price and Gary M. Feinman, pp. 15–86. Plenum Press, New York.

Hearne, Pamela, and Robert J. Sharer (eds.) 1992 *River of Gold: Precolumbian Treasures from Sitio Conte.* University Museum of Archaeology and Anthropology, University of Pennsylvania, Philadelphia.

Johnson, Allen W., and Timothy Earle 1987 *The Evolution of Human Societies: From Foraging Group to Agrarian State.* Stanford University Press, Stanford.

King, Adam 2003 Over a Century of Explorations at Etowah. *Journal of Archaeological Research* 11:279–306.

Knight, Vernon James, Jr., and Vincas P. Steponaitis 1998 A New History of Moundville. In *Archaeology of the Moundville Chiefdom,* edited by Vernon James Knight, Jr., and Vincas P. Steponaitis, pp. 1–25. Smithsonian Institution Press, Washington, DC.

Kowalewski, Stephen A., Gary M. Feinman, Laura Finsten, Richard E. Blanton, and Linda M. Nicholas 1989 *Monte Albán's Hinterland, Part II: Prehispanic Settlement Patterns in Tlacolula, Etla, and Ocotlán, the Valley of Oaxaca, Mexico.* Memoirs of the University of Michigan Museum of Anthropology, No. 23.

Linduff, Katheryn M., Robert D. Drennan, and Gideon Shelach 2004 Early Complex Societies in NE China: The Chifeng International Collaborative Archaeological Research Project. *Journal of Field Archaeology,* 29:45–73.

Lycett, Stephen J., Mark Collard, and William C. McGrew 2007 Phylogenetic Analyses of Behavior Support Existence of Culture among Wild Chimpanzees. *Proceedings of the National Academy of Sciences* 104:17588–592.

Maestripieri, Dario 2007 *Machiavellian Intelligence: How Rhesus Macaques and Humans Have Conquered the World.* University of Chicago Press, Chicago.

Mann, Michael 1986 *The Sources of Social Power, Vol. 1: A History of Power from the Beginning to A.D. 1760.* Cambridge University Press, Cambridge.

Marcus, Joyce, and Kent V. Flannery 1996 *Zapotec Civilization: How Urban Society Evolved in Mexico's Oaxaca Valley.* Thames and Hudson, London.

Mazur, Alan 2005 *Biosociology of Dominance and Deference*. Rowman and Littlefield, Lanham, Maryland.

McGuire, Randall H. 1983 Breaking Down Cultural Complexity: Inequality and Heterogeneity. *Advances in Archaeological Method and Theory* 6:91–142.

McIntosh, Susan Keech 1999 Pathways to Complexity: An African Perspective. In *Beyond Chiefdoms: Pathways to Complexity in Africa*, edited by Susan Keech Mcintosh, pp. 1–30. Cambridge University Press, Cambridge.

Morgan, Lewis H. 1877 *Ancient Society*. Charles Kerr, Chicago.

Murdock, George Peter 1981 *Atlas of World Cultures*. University of Pittsburgh Press, Pittsburgh.

Murdock, George Peter, and Douglas R. White 1969 The Standard Cross-Cultural Sample. *Ethnology* 8:329–69.

Peebles, Christopher S. 1974 *Moundville: The Organization of a Prehistoric Community and Culture*. Ph.D. Dissertation, University of California at Santa Barbara.

Pepper, George H. 1920 *Pueblo Bonito*. Anthropological Papers of the American Museum of Natural History, Vol. 27. (1996 reprint edition, University of New Mexico Press, Albuquerque).

Peregrine, Peter N. 2001 Matrilocality, Corporate Strategy, and the Organization of Production in the Chacoan World. *American Antiquity* 66:36–46.

———— 2003 Atlas of Cultural Evolution. *World Cultures* 14:1–89.

Peregrine, Peter N., and Melvin Ember (eds.) 2001–2002 *Encyclopedia of Prehistory*. 9 vols. Kluwer Academic /Plenum, New York.

Peterson, Christian E., and Robert D. Drennan 2005 Communities, Settlements, Sites, and Surveys: Regional-scale Analysis of Prehistoric Human Interaction. *American Antiquity* 70:5–30.

Rendell, Luke, and Hal Whitehead 2001 Culture in Whales and Dolphins. *Behavioral and Brain Sciences* 24:309–24.

Renfrew, Colin 1974 Beyond a Subsistence Economy: The Evolution of Social Organization in Prehistoric Europe. In *Reconstructing Complex Societies: An Archaeological Colloquium*, edited by Charlotte B. Moore, pp. 69–85, Supplement to the Bulletin of the American Schools of Oriental Research, No. 20.

———— 2001 Production and Consumption in a Sacred Economy: The Material Correlates of High Devotional Expression at Chaco Canyon. *American Antiquity* 66:14–25.

Sahlins, Marshall D., and Elman R. Service (eds.) 1960 *Evolution and Culture*. University of Michigan Press, Ann Arbor.

Sanders, William T., Jeffrey R. Parsons, and Robert S. Santley 1979 *The Basin of Mexico: Ecological Processes in the Evolution of a Civilization*. Academic Press, New York.

Service, E. R. 1962 *Primitive Social Organization: An Evolutionary Perspective*. Random House, New York.

Service, Elman R. 1975 *Origins of the State and Civilization: The Process of Cultural Evolution*. Norton, New York.

Smith, Michael E. 1987 Household Possessions and Wealth in Agrarian States: Implications for Archaeology. *Journal of Anthropological Archaeology* 6:297–335.

Spencer, Herbert 1880–1897 *The Principles of Sociology*. D. Appleton and Co, New York.

Tainter, Joseph A. 1977 Modeling Change in Prehistoric Social Systems. In *For Theory Building in Archaeology: Essays on Faunal Remains, Aquatic Resources, Spatial Analysis, and Systemic Modeling*, edited by Lewis R. Binford, pp. 327–51. Academic Press, New York.

—— 1978 Mortuary Practices and the Study of Prehistoric Social Systems. *Advances in Archaeological Method and Theory* 1:105–41.

Trigger, Bruce G. 2003 *Understanding Early Civilizations: A Comparative Study*. Cambridge University Press, Cambridge.

Tylor, Edward B. 1865 *Researches into the Early History of Mankind and the Development of Civilization*. J. Murray, London. University of Pennsylvania Museum Archives.

University of Pennsylvania Museum Archives 1999 Sitio Conte, Panama, 1940. www.museum.upenn.edu/SitioConte/index.html.

Wright, Henry T. 1984 Prestate Political Formations. In *On the Evolution of Complex Societies: Essays in Honor of Harry Hoijer 1982*, edited by Timothy K. Earle, pp. 41–77. Undena Press, Los Angeles.

CHAPTER 6

PATTERNED VARIATION IN REGIONAL TRAJECTORIES OF COMMUNITY GROWTH

Christian E. Peterson and Robert D. Drennan

Societies in many regions all over the world started down the path toward large-scale social formations, so the number of trajectories available for comparative study is large. Although most of these regional trajectories are not well known, the few that are well enough documented for comparative study are more than comparisons can easily handle. A focus on early civilizations leads to comparing large world areas (Mesopotamia, Nile Valley, North China, Mesoamerica, Central Andes, etc.) because early civilizations are very large-scale social formations – finally, each of these world areas contained only one civilization. The beginnings of large social formations, which is the subject of this chapter, however, can be found in multiple separate regions within any of these areas. It is the specific trajectories of societal change within these smaller regions that we seek to compare, not culture-historical constructs like archaeological cultures, horizons, or traditions. For comparing trajectories, attention must be focused on human activities and the organization of social relationships in a place, and culture history is not the most effective or direct approach to these subjects. We treat each regional trajectory as a separate instance to be compared with others.

This chapter lays aside the data threads spun around differentiation in Chapter 5 in order to focus on those most directly connected to the emergence and growth of supra-local communities: local community structure, supra-local community scale, supra-local community centralization, demographic density, public works investment, tax rate, and conflict. Estimation of ancient populations and labor investment in public works lies at the core of the comparisons presented here. At least some archaeologists have long been willing to make such estimates, but the task should only be attempted by archaeologists willing to "dare to be inaccurate" (cf. Martens 2008:1160). Although the empirical basis for archaeological population and labor investment estimates is far better than it was twenty years ago, both still come with very wide error ranges. They can be put to effective use, but only if we adopt the attitude required for solving what have come to be called Fermi problems in the natural sciences, where the vital role played by quick calculations on cocktail napkins is thoroughly appreciated (Morrison 1963; Weinstein and Adam 2008). The comparisons we offer here are based on more rigorous use of empirical data than the solutions to Fermi problems often are, but the reader is forewarned that we have not let the imprecision of archaeological population or labor investment estimates stop us. We have been willing to work with sometimes uncomfortably large error ranges in order to see what kind of conclusions the best information now available leads toward. We offer them as cocktail napkin calculations; readers more interested in data precision than in the heuristic value of seeing where even imprecise data might lead should probably stop here. Those willing to join us in being as careful as possible with the data but riding roughshod when necessary, should read on. The sources of the empirical information we have used and the nature of our analyses are discussed in the appendix.

The social changes of the dozen regional trajectories dealt with here occurred at very different dates. Thus, for most productive comparison, the trajectories need to be aligned according to some principle other than absolute date. Although it happened in varied ways in different regions, there is, in each of the trajectories dealt with here, a point at which the essential elements of "neolithic" life coalesced. The elements that come together include increased sedentism, food production, and the use of ceramics. Their co-occurrence marks an important transition in these trajectories, and provides a common starting point we have used to lay them alongside each other. Time is thus consistently dealt with in years elapsed since this "zero point."

Among the regions discussed here, the establishment of neolithic life occurred earliest in north and northeastern China, starting with the Houli period in Shandong and the Xinglongwa period in the Western Liao Valley (Figure 6.1), both of which began about 6500 B.C. In the central and southern highlands of Mexico, neolithic life began about 1500 B.C., with the Ajalpan phase in the Tehuacán Valley, the Tierras Largas phase in the Valley of Oaxaca, and the Early Formative or Early Horizon in the Basin of Mexico. We have set the zero point for the Santa Valley of coastal Peru at the start of the Cayhuamarca phase at around 1000 B.C. By contrast, the antecedents of neolithic life are very poorly known for the Alto Magdalena in the Andes of southern Colombia. The earliest permanent house structures and ceramics appeared in Formative 1 times beginning at 1000 B.C.

Maize cultivation was practiced, although wild food resources continued to have considerable importance. Neolithic life began in southern Arizona with the Hohokam Formative or Pioneer period at about 1000 B.C. The Hohokam are represented here by two sequences, Pueblo Grande in the Phoenix Basin and Marana (including the adjacent Los Robles community) in the Tucson Basin. The hallmarks of neolithic life in Alabama's Black Warrior Valley include regional population growth, the appearance of large compact villages, and intensified reliance on cultivation (especially of maize), which all co-occur at the beginning of the West Jefferson phase at 900 A.D. Of all the regional trajectories examined here, Mali's Middle Niger Delta is perhaps the least expected inclusion. By 400 B.C., in this part of West Africa, neolithic ways of living had already existed for nearly two millennia. For environmental reasons, however, the Middle Niger Delta itself only became habitable at about this time, so our zero point for this regional trajectory is the initial colonization of the delta by plant cultivators, who not only produced ceramics, but also possessed well-developed iron technology.

This set of regional trajectories includes some "success stories," like the Valley of Oaxaca and the Basin of Mexico, that continued beyond the initial stages that concern us here to see the development of complex states and even large territorial empires. In the later stages of their trajectories, others of these regions were subsumed by just such expansive political or economic systems centered elsewhere. This was the fate of the Tehuacán Valley, the Santa Valley, the Western Liao Valley, and Shandong. The Black Warrior Valley and the Alto Magdalena trajectories, which are commonly seen as chiefdom development, did not lead to any larger-scale social formations. Societies of modest scale persisted in the Alto Magdalena, but lacked longevity in the Black Warrior Valley. Like the Black Warrior Valley, Marana and Pueblo Grande represent a cycle of development that came to an end – in these Hohokam cases, though, without being so widely recognized as chiefly societies. The Middle Niger Delta also saw a cycle of development ending in progressive abandonment of the region; despite its demographic scale, the classic hallmarks of social hierarchy are even harder to identify in this trajectory.

Initial Neolithic Communities

Initial neolithic communities were the starting point in the emergence and development of large social formations in each of these regions. The matrix of interaction that constitutes such a local community is where the human

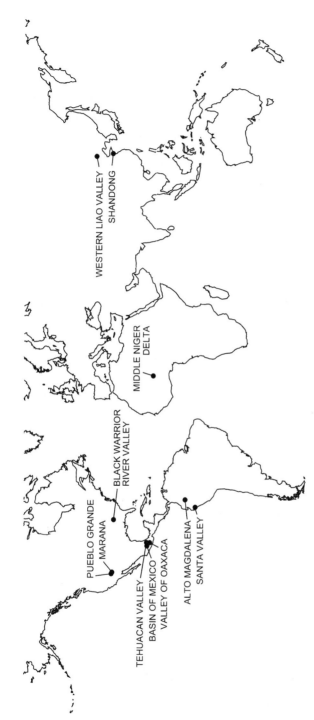

Figure 6.1. Locations of regional trajectories.

WESTERN LIAO VALLEY
SHANDONG

MIDDLE NIGER DELTA

BLACK WARRIOR RIVER VALLEY

PUEBLO GRANDE MARANA

TEHUACAN VALLEY
BASIN OF MEXICO
VALLEY OF OAXACA

ALTO MAGDALENA
SANTA VALLEY

activities and social relationships of an early neolithic society occur. It is logical to think that the nature of this interaction matrix has an impact on whether and how a small neolithic community grows toward a larger social formation. This impact is produced both through the opportunities for social action that particular community structures provide as well as through the constraints they impose. Local community structure comprises one of the data threads outlined in Chapter 5, approached via regional settlement data. With the lone exception of the Black Warrior Valley, all of the regional trajectories compared here are documented through systematic regional-scale settlement survey.

Population densities in all these regions were very low at the beginning of neolithic life. Actual estimates of population density cannot be made for the Black Warrior Valley because of the lack of systematic regional survey, or for the Middle Niger Delta because of a lack of clarity in the early part of the chronological sequence. For most of the other regions, estimated population density in the earliest neolithic period was less than 1 person/km², sometimes far less. The highest population density estimates at the beginning of the neolithic (for the Santa Valley and the Alto Magdalena) still do not place much more than a single nuclear family in each square kilometer on the landscape. Such population levels could not have created any pressure on subsistence resources. It would have been possible for families to live in widely dispersed fashion at considerable distances from their neighbors. In most regions, however, at least some families chose to live in closer proximity to others, forming clusters that we can identify in regional settlement data as small local communities.

Most of the regional settlement data sets examined here were collected with survey methodologies that would have recorded even the very small archaeological sites left by single-family farmsteads, making it possible to compare the roles of such tiny occupations in settlement systems across regions. The broad reliance in these surveys on the "site" as a unit of data collection, however, introduces a potential concern about comparability. It is easy to begin to think of each discovered early neolithic site in a region as a village, and to implicitly impute to it the characteristics of excavated village sites. Clearly, however, some such sites are very small compared to excavated villages – not surprising since the largest sites with the densest remains are likely to be selected for excavation. In other cases, small sites may cluster together to form a single larger community whose inhabitants must have been in face-to-face interaction on a daily basis. The discussion of local communities below is based on an examination of regional settlement data at its finest scale of resolution, forming clusters of "sites" where indicated according to the methodology outlined in Peterson and Drennan (2005). For the most part, the local communities identified correspond closely to the accounts of the investigators who carried out the surveys we rely upon. In some instances, however, this process has produced results that differ from previously published analyses.

Four regions stand out for the unusually large size of their initial neolithic communities. Some of the earliest settlements in the Basin of Mexico, the Santa Valley, Marana, and Pueblo Grande are villages numbering well up into the hundreds of inhabitants (Figure 6.2). In the Basin of Mexico and the Santa Valley there were also very small hamlets, but individual family farmsteads were virtually unknown at the beginning of neolithic life in any of these regions. In all four, early neolithic social interaction was strongly organized into large-village structures.

This does not appear to be the case for the other regions, although systematic surveys have covered only portions of some of these regions. For example, the frequency distribution of settlement sizes shown in Figure 6.2 for the Western Liao Valley comes from systematic settlement survey of 1,234 km² in the Chifeng region, although the entire Western Liao Valley is vastly larger. The most common kind of early neolithic local community in the Chifeng survey area was a one- or two-family farmstead (which is essentially what the leftmost bar in the histograms in Figure 6.2 represents), and no known community had much more than a dozen families. Excavated Xinglongwa sites in the Western Liao Valley outside the Chifeng survey area show that at least a handful of larger villages also existed. The prevalence of very small settlements in the Chifeng survey area, nonetheless, makes it clear that early neolithic life in the Western Liao Valley occurred in very small local social contexts compared to the four regions already discussed. Like the Western Liao Valley, only a very small part of Shandong has been systematically surveyed – the 1,120 km² of the Rizhao survey area. This time no early neolithic settlement at all occurred within the survey area, so Shandong cannot be represented in Figure 6.2. The few excavated Houli period sites elsewhere in Shandong, like Peiligang period sites farther west, seem generally to be even smaller than the Xinglongwa sites just discussed. Shandong thus seems to be another area where early neolithic life largely occurred in very small local communities. Likewise in the Valley of Oaxaca, where the entire region has been surveyed systematically, one initial village had 100 inhabitants or slightly more, but most people lived in much smaller groups, ranging from four or five families down to single-family farmsteads. In the Tehuacán Valley, systematic survey is limited to two small blocks: Cuayucatepec (59 km²) and Quachilco (56 km²). One very small Early Ajalpan phase site is known from excavation elsewhere in the valley, but neither survey area included any early neolithic settlement. Consequently, there are no data to represent Tehuacán in Figure 6.2, but initial settlements there were at least as small as in Oaxaca. Tehuacán, Oaxaca, Shandong, and the Western Liao form a second group of regions where early neolithic life took place in much smaller local communities, and many families even lived in individual farmsteads.

The Alto Magdalena is by itself in yet a third category, one in which no regular pattern of early neolithic local communities is discernible at all. Systematic settlement data does not cover the entire Alto Magdalena; here we rely on the western survey zone of the Valle de la Plata (totaling some 317 km²). Initial neolithic settlement consisted almost entirely of dispersed farmsteads. Occupation areas are usually quite small, although they sometimes merge into areas of several hectares. Artifact densities are so low, however, that even these larger areas seem more accurately described not as villages, but as scattered farmsteads. Interaction among initial neolithic families, then, would have been very diffuse – not focused into any recognizable local community structure at all. In order to include the Alto Magdalena in Figure 6.2, we have taken its settlement pattern to consist entirely of groupings of ten or fewer people, all of which, then, fall within the category represented by the leftmost bar in its histogram.

The Black Warrior Valley cannot be included in Figure 6.2 because no systematic regional-scale survey data exist. Abundant, less comprehensive information about settlement, however, documents the presence of compact villages, sometimes occurring in groups of two or three, spaced so closely that they should be taken as single local communities with populations numbering up into the hundreds. Individual farmsteads were also present; their abundance at the beginning of the neolithic is unclear, although they seem to have been more common than at the start of the Marana, Pueblo Grande, Basin of Mexico, or Santa Valley sequences. The Black Warrior Valley, then, falls into an intermediate position – similar to these four regions in terms of its large compact villages, but more like the other regions in regard to the importance of farmstead living. Little can be said about the earliest neolithic settlement in the Middle Niger Delta because its remains are particularly scarce. This fact in itself probably indicates that initial neolithic settlement did not take the form of large, compact villages, and that the Middle Niger Delta should be grouped with the Western Liao Valley and the Valley of Oaxaca.

The large earliest neolithic villages of the first four regions discussed would have generated particularly complex webs of interaction among their

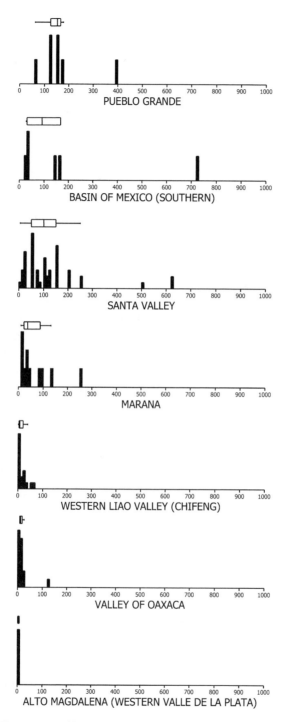

Figure 6.2. Histograms and boxplots of initial neolithic community populations for seven regions. The interval for histogram bars is an estimated ten inhabitants. Thus, the leftmost bar, for example, represents a farmstead of one or two families.

large numbers of inhabitants. Smaller villages would have had less potential of this kind, and dispersed farmstead occupations even less. This line of thinking, of course, is based on distance-interaction principles: the general notion that proximity facilitates interaction (and its converse, that interaction encourages proximity). This is the reason to suspect high levels of interaction in large villages. In addition to sheer numbers, the close proximity of neighbors in tightly packed villages would both produce and be the product of high levels of interaction. Direct information about the proximity of neighbors in earliest neolithic settlement is available for only a few of the regions. Of these, the Santa Valley and the Basin of Mexico had the most tightly packed settlements, with houses spaced an average of 30 to 40 m apart. Both are among the regions with the largest villages, reinforcing the impression of especially intense interaction there. In the Valley of Oaxaca and the Western Liao Valley, local communities were not only smaller, but also less tightly packed – with houses at 50 to 70 m spacing, consistent with less intense interaction patterns. The dispersed farmsteads of the Alto Magdalena were, of course, the most widely spaced, at not much less than 100 m, even in their greater concentrations. Isolated farmsteads hundreds of meters from their nearest neighbors were not at all uncommon. At such distances, daily interaction with neighbors was surely very much attenuated.

The regions with the largest villages among their earliest neolithic settlements, then, might have had a head start in building larger social formations. They already had larger, denser webs of social interaction than the other regions did, networks that would have provided rich opportunities for the kinds of social action that might have sparked change and growth. Superficially at least, it would seem that smaller villages would provide less room to maneuver for aspiring elites and/or other agents of change. The yet thinner tissue of interaction among dispersed farmsteads seems an even less likely foundation for social growth. Seeing whether these plausible expectations are met empirically requires going on to the regional trajectories that show how these initial neolithic communities grew.

Trajectories of Community Growth from Initial Large Villages

Community growth often takes the form of expansion to supra-local scale. Here we have delineated supra-local communities with a consistent approach to the analysis of regional settlement data, an approach based on mathematically smoothed surfaces representing the distribution of human occupation across the landscape (Peterson and Drennan 2005).

These surfaces make it easy to observe clusters of occupation taken (on the basis of distance–interaction principles, as above) to represent centrally focused interaction at the scale of the region. Figures 6.3 through 6.13 present the results of these analyses. The mathematically smoothed surfaces for each period in a regional trajectory appear at the right, organized chronologically from bottom to top. The limits of the territories covered by regional survey are indicated on the surfaces, and the boundaries of larger – and often supra-local – communities are represented as darker lines. On the left side of these figures, histograms and box plots show how the relative abundance of settlements in the smallest size categories changes as larger social formations develop. These depict only communities with fewer than 500 inhabitants, excluding the larger settlements. The time scale in the center is set with its zero point at the beginnings of neolithic life in each region, and the midpoints of each period discussed are indicated in years elapsed since this time.

It is not surprising that the two Hohokam trajectories follow broadly similar patterns. The first period in each sequence (Formative for Marana, and Pioneer for Pueblo Grande) already shows some clustering of local communities into supra-local units. Hohokam settlement units have customarily been defined based on watercourses or canal systems that sustained agricultural production in this arid region. Pueblo Grande is one such unit, and two others, the adjacent Marana and Los Robles communities, are both in the region we have labeled Marana. The same distance-interaction principles used to define communities in the surfaces in Figure 6.3 and 6.4 are the implicit basis for these traditional Hohokam settlement units, clearly set off from one another by sparsely occupied or even entirely unoccupied areas. Subdivisions can also be recognized within such settlement units, as indicated by dark lines in Figures 6.3 and 6.4, although the separation between them is not so dramatic. By Preclassic or Colonial times, these multiple supra-local communities that subdivided the Pueblo Grande, Marana, and Los Robles settlement units had populations estimated at up to about 2,500 although most were much smaller. The construction of ball courts and the activities that took place there seem to have played an important centralizing role. These supra-local communities became progressively less numerous and the separation between them less distinct, until by Classic times they entirely disappeared, leaving the three traditional Hohokam settlement units fully consolidated as the largest social formations to emerge in these trajectories, with 10,000 inhabitants or more. Ball courts gave way to platform mounds as the principal monumental manifestation of community centralization. Both trajectories came to an abrupt end after two and

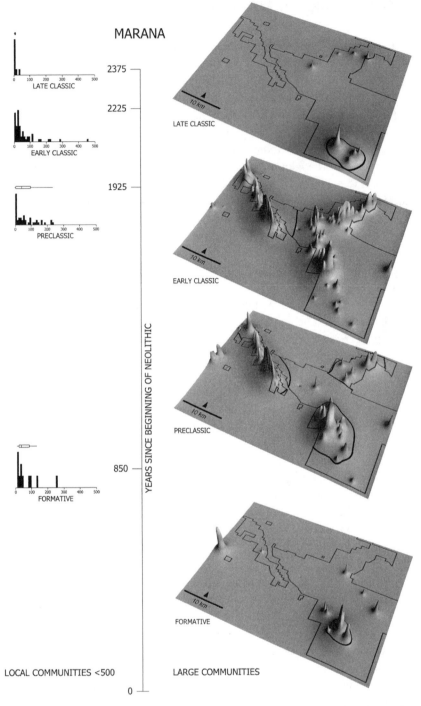

Figure 6.3. Communities in the Marana regional trajectory. The time scale indicates the midpoints of the four periods.

PUEBLO GRANDE

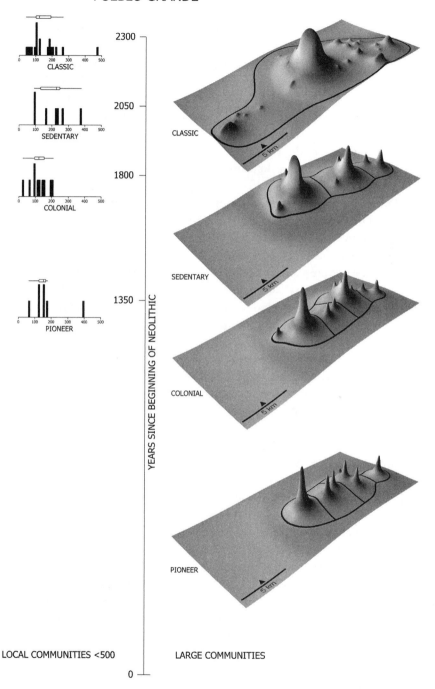

Figure 6.4. Communities in the Pueblo Grande regional trajectory. The time scale indicates the midpoints of the four periods.

a half millennia at about 1450 A.D., with the abandonment of the region. True to their neolithic beginnings, the settlement distributions of both regions focused very heavily on large-village living throughout their trajectories. Large initial villages were replaced by very large villages as the central places of supra-local communities. Over time in the Marana region, smaller villages, hamlets, and farmsteads did appear, but the portion of the population living in them was never large. Very small communities are even less evident in the Pueblo Grande region, although this impression may be due in part to the difficulty of documenting such small sites under the modern urban sprawl of Phoenix.

The large initial neolithic villages of the Santa Valley were already in the Cayhuamarca period the centers of five supra-local communities numbering 1,000 to 2,000 inhabitants (Figure 6.5). Numerous fortified hilltop "citadels" establish the importance defensive works had through the entire sequence. Multiple supra-local communities are a persistent feature of the Santa Valley trajectory, although their boundaries were in constant flux. It is easy to imagine competition and conflict between supra-local communities, although raiding from other coastal valleys is also a possibility. Substantial population shifts between the different parts of the valley also suggest changes in the organization of agricultural production. Some amalgamation occurred with the reduction to only two supra-local communities in the Early Suchimansillo period, along with the appearance of administrative centers with elite residences, storage facilities, and civic-ceremonial architecture. Platforms and plazas of civic or ceremonial function had been present from the beginning, but had not previously been incorporated into major population centers. Early Suchimansillo also represents a major surge in the size of the largest social formation, which now reached more than 15,000 inhabitants. This amalgamation did not, however, proceed to unification of the entire valley, since the largest Early Suchimansillo population center, which seemed poised to dominate the valley, instead shrank during Late Suchimansillo while a still larger center grew and fragmented the other earlier supra-local community into two. The waxing and waning of apparently competing centers and their supra-local communities ended only with the forcible conversion of the Santa Valley into a province of the Moche state. The smallest of local communities became slightly more numerous later on in the Santa Valley trajectory, but as in Pueblo Grande and Marana, the overall pattern of living remained persistently oriented around large villages and even larger centers.

The fourth of the trajectories characterized by large initial villages was the Basin of Mexico. In contrast to the other three regions, there is no sign

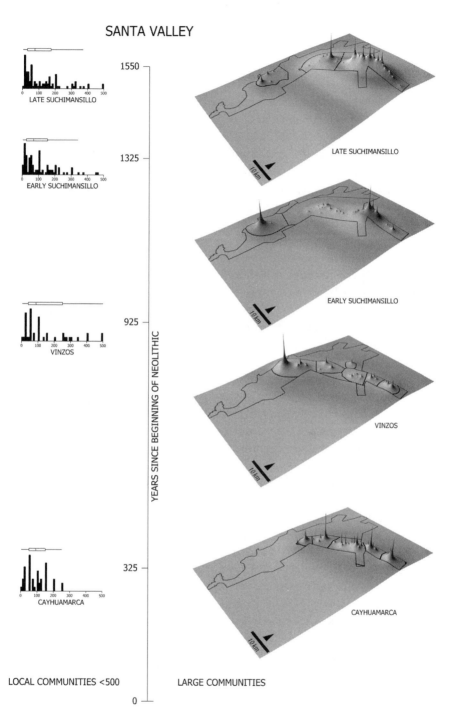

SANTA VALLEY

LATE SUCHIMANSILLO

EARLY SUCHIMANSILLO

VINZOS

CAYHUAMARCA

YEARS SINCE BEGINNING OF NEOLITHIC

1550

1325

925

325

0

LATE SUCHIMANSILLO

EARLY SUCHIMANSILLO

VINZOS

CAYHUAMARCA

LOCAL COMMUNITIES <500

LARGE COMMUNITIES

Figure 6.5. Communities in the Santa Valley regional trajectory. The time scale indicates the midpoints of the four periods.

that smaller settlements clustered around large villages to produce supra-local communities at the very beginning (Figure 6.6). Large villages grew for several centuries, with populations reaching toward 2,000, and they became considerably more numerous by First Intermediate One. They did not take on any supra-local character until First Intermediate Two, when at least a weak tendency for smaller villages to cluster around larger ones can be seen. By now, single large villages could approach 5,000 inhabitants, and featured platforms and plazas. Populations of the largest of perhaps a dozen supra-local communities exceeded 10,000 (including those outside the formally surveyed area, such as Cuicuilco in the southwest corner of the basin, which had grown to more than double the size of the next largest settlement). The number of supra-local communities remained roughly constant during First Intermediate Three, although some vanished only to be replaced by newly emerged ones where none had previously existed. One of these new central places was Teotihuacan, whose population grew rapidly to rival that of Cuicuilco at the opposite end of the basin. The large communities in the Basin of Mexico have usually been envisioned as competitors, much like those in the Santa Valley, although the Basin of Mexico lacks conspicuous fortifications. Perhaps conflict in the Basin of Mexico took other forms, or perhaps competition took forms other than conflict. In any event, as in the Santa Valley, competition between the largest communities appears to have reached a stalemate. Despite a considerable amount of flux, no one was initially able to grow much beyond the level of the others, or to forge a much larger or more inclusive interaction community. In the Santa Valley, the stalemate was broken by the intervention of an outside power; in the Basin of Mexico, it was broken internally by Teotihuacan, which then went on to dominate an area extending far beyond the Basin of Mexico.

As is well known, and can be clearly seen in the First Intermediate Four surface in Figure 6.6, Teotihuacan grew by drawing the populations of practically all the region's other communities into the city itself. What becomes clearer in comparative perspective is that precisely this had always been the dominant mode of community growth in the Basin of Mexico. Regional clustering is seen among the initial neolithic communities of the other three regions, but not in the Basin of Mexico. While supra-local communities can eventually be identified, their supra-local character is highly attenuated compared with the Santa Valley, for example. Their people and their activities were always heavily concentrated into their central local communities. Their waxing and waning was less a process of regional population movement than of shifts in location of central places, because there were only very few peripheral places to realign. Although the number of

BASIN OF MEXICO

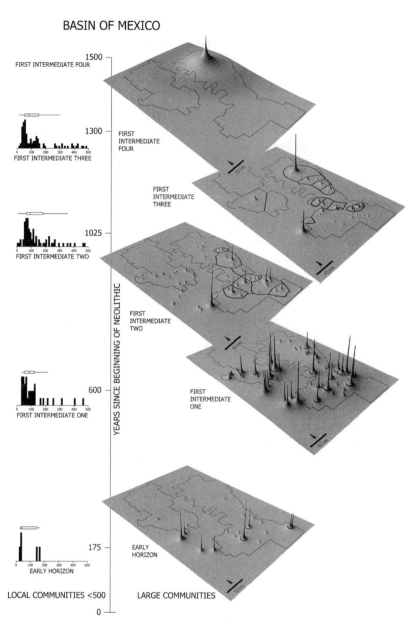

Figure 6.6. Communities in the Basin of Mexico regional trajectory. The time scale indicates the midpoints of the five periods.

smaller settlements increased through time in the Basin of Mexico (Figure 6.6), the proportion of the population that lived in them decreased. In First Intermediate Two and Three, only 20 percent of the regional population lived in communities of fewer than 500 inhabitants. Long before Teotihuacan, then, the growth of larger social formations had depended almost entirely on drawing people into larger and larger local communities, as opposed to expanding control over smaller ones. It is not surprising that this mode of growth is seen in a region whose initial neolithic communities were already very large, but as Pueblo Grande, Marana, and the Santa Valley make clear, it is not the inevitable outcome of such a starting place.

Trajectories of Community Growth from Initial Small Villages

Initial neolithic settlement in the Western Liao Valley contrasts sharply with the pattern of large village living in the Basin of Mexico, the Santa Valley, and the Hohokam sequences. The entire Chifeng survey area has not a single settlement accurately described as a village. Among the farmsteads and tiny hamlets were two local communities with populations larger than fifty, but the dozen or so households that each represents were spread across hundreds of meters. The few excavated village sites from elsewhere represent a way of life that was unusual for the Western Liao Valley's earliest neolithic residents. Although none of these excavated sites is in an area of systematic survey, they all appear to be isolated, without additional nearby settlement. Within the Chifeng survey area, this Xinglongwa occupation was widely scattered with no indication of regional scale clustering (Figure 6.7). Change came very slowly in the Western Liao Valley. By Zhaobaogou times, life in villages of 100 to 400 people had become the norm, with 80 percent of the regional population living in such communities. After two thousand years, the Western Liao Valley had arrived at a pattern of local communities similar in this regard to the neolithic starting points of the regions discussed above. In the Western Liao, though, small hamlets and farmsteads, like those of Xinglongwa times, remained a more prominent feature of the settlement pattern. These were widely scattered across the landscape with no tendency to cluster near large villages, indicating that the villages played little role in focusing regional scale patterns of interaction.

It was not until well into the third millennium of neolithic life, in Hongshan times, that villages became more numerous, slightly larger, and drew smaller settlements toward them in centrally focused patterns of

WESTERN LIAO VALLEY (CHIFENG SURVEY)

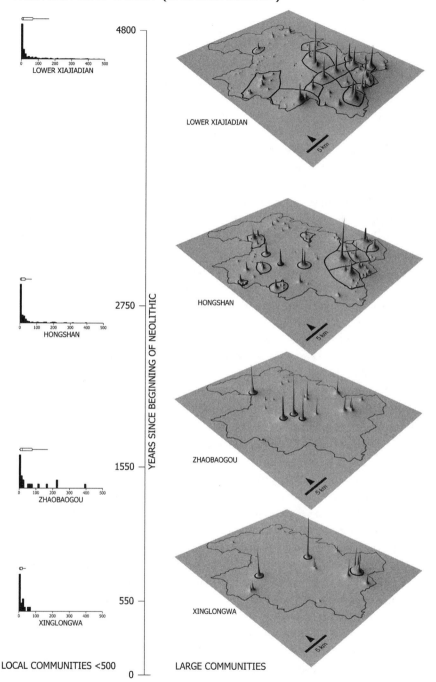

Figure 6.7. Communities in the Western Liao Valley regional trajectory (Chifeng survey area). The time scale indicates the midpoints of the four periods.

interaction. The central place activities of these large villages emphasized ceremonies carried out in complexes of plazas and platforms that incorporated the tombs of important people. With populations still less than 1,000, these supra-local communities were quite small and numerous compared to those of the regions already discussed. Hongshan supra-local communities were closely packed, but regional population levels were still much too low to have created conflict between them based on resource scarcity, and there is no defensive architecture or other evidence of conflict. Lower Xiajiadian period supra-local communities remained spatially small, but their populations had grown substantially, with some reaching more than 10,000. Many single villages had populations larger than 1,000. The Western Liao mode of growth, then, was dominated by demographic increase internal to supra-local communities, and by their proliferation, presumably through a process of budding off. The greater number of Lower Xiajiadian supra-local communities meant ever-tighter packing, and regional population had reached levels that make resource scarcity a possibility. Conflict put in a conspicuous appearance at this point, as fortifications became a feature of many sites. Some amalgamation of supra-local communities may have occurred subsequently, but unification of the Chifeng survey area did not occur until its conquest by outside powers nearly 6,000 years after the beginning of the neolithic.

In Shandong the development of full-scale village life was also very slow, and villages were, if anything, even scarcer. None at all appeared in the Rizhao survey area at the beginning of the neolithic, and by 2,000 years later there were only two tiny Beixin period settlements. In Dawenkou times, after another 1,000 years had passed, there were two villages with populations in the hundreds (Figure 6.8). One of these, Dantu, was surrounded by a rammed earth wall, although it is not clear that its function was defensive. Other smaller settlements were scattered through the survey area, but show only the slightest of tendencies to cluster near the large villages or each other. Dramatic change marks the Early Longshan period, whose midpoint falls fully 4,000 years after the beginning of neolithic life. Regional population surged, probably augmented by substantial immigration from farther inland; a half dozen local communities had populations of 10,000 or more (although only Dantu was walled); and multiple supra-local communities had emerged. The two largest supra-local communities continued to grow into Middle Longshan times by subsuming their neighbors, although a few smaller supra-local communities persisted. This trajectory is distinguished by the continuity in the locations of its two largest communities, Dantu-Liangchengzhen and Yaowangcheng, even after the incorporation

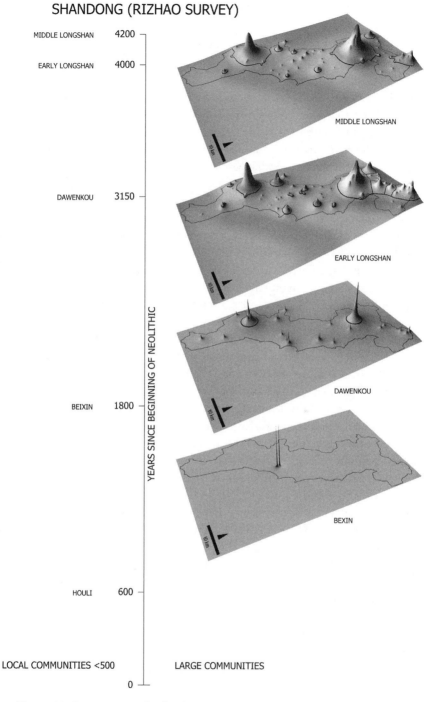

SHANDONG (RIZHAO SURVEY)

MIDDLE LONGSHAN   4200

EARLY LONGSHAN   4000

MIDDLE LONGSHAN

DAWENKOU   3150

EARLY LONGSHAN

YEARS SINCE BEGINNING OF NEOLITHIC

DAWENKOU

BEIXIN   1800

BEXIN

HOULI   600

LOCAL COMMUNITIES <500   LARGE COMMUNITIES

0

Figure 6.8. Communities in the Shandong Peninsula regional trajectory (Rizhao survey area). The time scale indicates the midpoints of the five periods.

of the Rizhao survey area by foreign polities some 5,000 years following the initial neolithic.

The population of the Valley of Oaxaca's only initial neolithic village, San José Mogote, was not much more than 100, but even so it was several times larger than the hamlets or farmsteads where the rest of the region's population lived. Fully half these hamlets and farmsteads were clearly drawn toward San José Mogote, forming a supra-local settlement cluster, which persisted and became somewhat larger as regional population grew through the next few centuries (Figure 6.9). Demographic scale remained modest, with only about 1,500 people in the supra-local community, but elite residences and civic-ceremonial architecture were concentrated in the central village from the San José phase onwards. In the Rosario phase, iconographic evidence suggests coercive domination of outlying communities by elites at San José Mogote. This did not correspond to an enlargement of the supra-local interaction community that had been present since the beginning, but probably represents its political consolidation. As this territorial control was established, population actually shifted from the center to peripheral settlements within the larger community. The dynamic of political consolidation by military force continued as the community's central place was relocated from San José Mogote to Monte Albán, from which control was then extended to the entire Valley of Oaxaca and its 15,000 inhabitants. Throughout this sequence Oaxaca's single supra-local community encompassed more than two-thirds of the regional population. San José Mogote was the center of this community for a full 1,000 years. Monte Albán was not a rival that won centrality away from San José Mogote; rather, it was founded as a new capital by elites from San José Mogote as a seamless continuation of their previous political strategy. Violent conflict clearly played an important role in the emergence of larger social formations in the Valley of Oaxaca, but it was not the same one played by conflict elsewhere.

The Middle Niger Delta provides an example of a large-scale social formation argued to differ strongly from the others included in this comparison. The regional settlement data available documents something of its character at the peak of its development, but gives little indication of its earlier trajectory. Regional population apparently grew and became more centralized at Jenné-jeno during about a millennium after the establishment of neolithic life (Figure 6.10). By this time, the supra-local community had more than 70,000 inhabitants – just how much more cannot be determined because it extended beyond the area surveyed. A few very small local communities did exist, although these were hamlets not farmsteads, but the vast

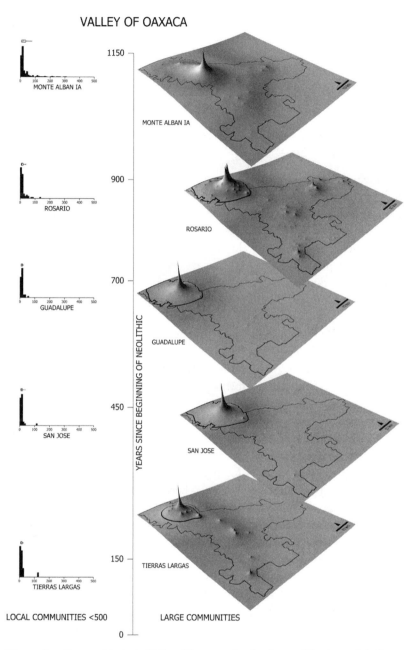

VALLEY OF OAXACA

MONTE ALBAN IA

ROSARIO

GUADALUPE

SAN JOSE

TIERRAS LARGAS

LOCAL COMMUNITIES <500

LARGE COMMUNITIES

YEARS SINCE BEGINNING OF NEOLITHIC

MONTE ALBAN IA

ROSARIO

GUADALUPE

SAN JOSE

TIERRAS LARGAS

Figure 6.9. Communities in the Valley of Oaxaca regional trajectory. The time scale indicates the midpoints of the five periods.

majority of the population lived in local communities numbering well up in the hundreds, or even into the thousands. Regional population then began to decline, especially at the periphery of the supra-local community, and this "urban" phenomenon withered away. After another thousand years, the region had been largely abandoned.

Trajectories of Community Growth and Dispersed Rural Occupation

Despite the absence of local communities in the Alto Magdalena to provide building blocks, supra-local communities are strongly in evidence from the earliest neolithic times (Figure 6.11). Although the farmsteads of Formative 1 times are widely scattered across the region with no sign of compact settlements, they did occur at closer spacing in some places. These form the nuclei of occupational concentrations, and the more sparsely occupied zones between them divide the entire territory into spatially extensive supra-local communities. For a millennium the landscape gradually filled with farmsteads, and supra-local community populations grew to approximately 2,000 each. In the Regional Classic, some swelled to more than 5,000. At their centers were complexes of ceremonial plazas and the monumental tombs of important people. While farmsteads were closer together near these complexes, they still did not form compact villages. Regional population continued to grow into the Recent period, and its tendency to concentrate in certain places strengthened somewhat, even though construction ceased at the ceremonial complexes. The territories of the supra-local communities shifted somewhat through time, but overall there is much continuity in their locations, more than for the multiple units of other trajectories. Whatever competition there may have been between them, it seems not to have resulted in conflict. The Alto Magdalena sequence came to an end after 2,500 years with abandonment of the region at the time of the Spanish Conquest, or possibly shortly before.

In the Tehuacán Valley, each of the two survey blocks documents the emergence of a central place and the core of its supra-local community. Less complete survey of the entire valley provides information about at least the larger sites. After about a millennium of neolithic life, a small village in the Quachilco survey area grew fairly quickly into a center of around 2,000 people (Figure 6.12). This first supra-local community in the Tehuacán Valley included 10,000 inhabitants within the survey area, and an undetermined number beyond. In the latter part of the Late Santa María phase, additional supra-local communities began to emerge in other

MIDDLE NIGER DELTA

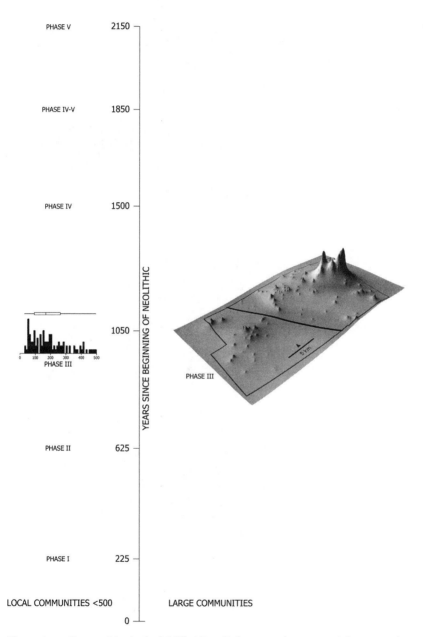

Figure 6.10. Communities in the Middle Niger Delta regional trajectory. The time scale indicates the midpoints of the six periods.

ALTO MAGDALENA (WESTERN VALLE DE LA PLATA SURVEY)

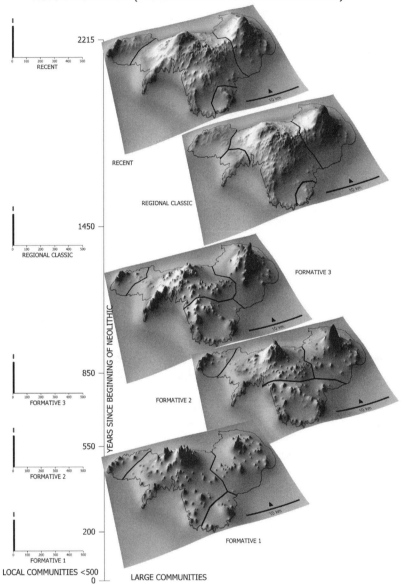

Figure 6.11. Communities in the Alto Magdalena regional trajectory (Western Valle de la Plata survey area). The time scale indicates the midpoints of the five periods.

TEHUACAN VALLEY (QUACHILCO SURVEY)

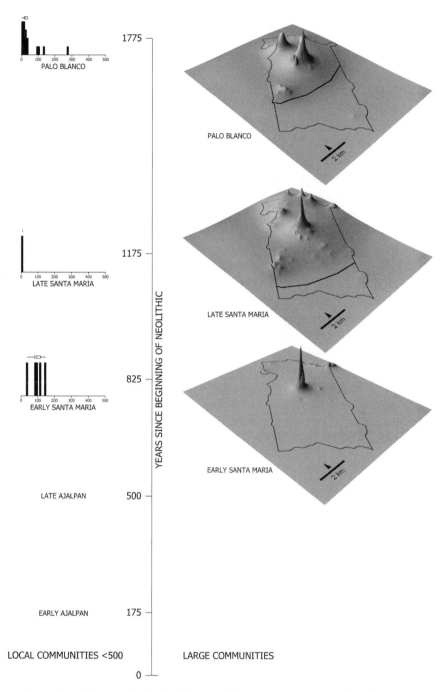

Figure 6.12. Communities in the Tehuacán Valley regional trajectory (Quachilco survey area). The time scale indicates the midpoints of the five periods.

parts of the valley. One of these is documented in the Cuayucatepec survey area (Figure 6.13). It reached its full development in the subsequent Palo Blanco phase with a population of 16,000, again plus an undetermined number beyond the boundaries of the survey area. At this point there were perhaps a dozen supra-local communities of similar size all along the valley. One of these was still centered in the Quachilco survey area, although its population had declined and a different local community had emerged as its center. By this time, the region was greatly overshadowed by its neighbor at Teotihuacan (some 200 km away in the Basin of Mexico), although it does not seem to have been consolidated into a Teotihuacan political entity.

The Tehuacán sequence shows particularly interesting changes in local community structure. In the Alto Magdalena, farmstead living dominated throughout the sequence; in other regions, either farmsteads were absent or they remained present throughout but represented a decreasing proportion of the population as larger local communities grew and supra-local communities developed. The Tehuacán Valley's population, on the other hand, lived initially in small villages and hamlets, but not farmsteads. As sizeable centers and supra-local communities emerged, substantial portions of their populations dispersed to live on individual farmsteads. In the Quachilco survey area this occurred principally toward the northeast along the Río Salado, where intensive cultivation of individual family plots would have been an effective strategy for feeding the supra-local community's growing population. Toward the southwest, agricultural intensification meant canal systems requiring high levels of cooperation and interaction, which would have encouraged the continuation of compact village living. The same phenomenon can be observed in the Cuayucatepec survey area with the growth of its supra-local community. Again, a substantial portion of the population dispersed into individual farmsteads, especially toward the northeast where agricultural intensification meant the development of very small-scale irrigation systems not requiring much cooperation or interaction. At their peaks, then, Tehuacán's supra-local communities combined compact village living for some with dispersed farmstead occupation for others. As the Quachilco supra-local community diminished in the Palo Blanco phase, the balance tipped back toward compact villages.

The Black Warrior Valley also shows shifts between compact villages and scattered farmstead living, although the lack of systematic survey leaves us unable to quantify these shifts or to produce a figure comparable to those for the other regions. The earliest villages, of the West Jefferson phase, have been attributed to both increased reliance on cultivated plants and to warfare. After only a century or two, population dispersed, shifting

TEHUACAN VALLEY (CUAYUCATEPEC SURVEY)

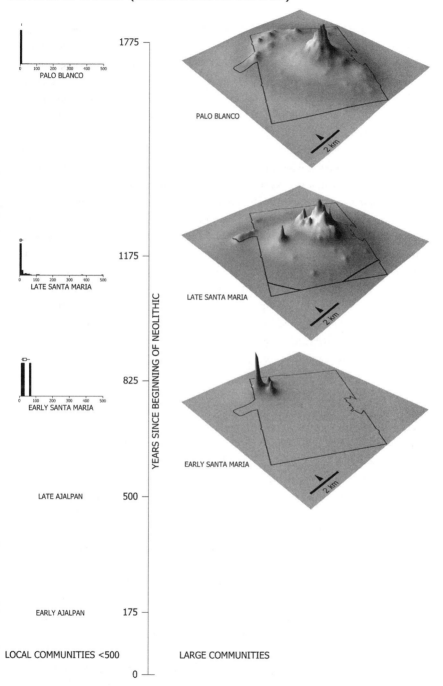

Figure 6.13. Communities in the Tehuacán Valley regional trajectory (Cuayucatepec survey area). The time scale indicates the midpoints of the five periods.

more toward farmstead living. Moundville began to emerge as a center and two truncated mounds were constructed there. It was not, however, a nucleated village; rather, farmsteads occurred at closer spacing, forming a concentration of population perhaps similar to those seen in the Alto Magdalena sequence. About 300 years after the beginning of the Black Warrior sequence, Moundville became a nucleated community of some 1,500 people surrounded by a massive palisade that also enclosed some 30 large mounds around an extensive plaza. The palisade certainly suggests that a renewed need for defense contributed to this dramatic nucleation, although most of the regional population continued to live in scattered farmsteads, and secondary mound centers had neither palisades nor large resident populations. In any event, the nucleated community lasted only a century or so, after which the palisade disappeared and most of its population dispersed to farmsteads. Moundville, nonetheless, continued for another century or two to be the center of the supra-local community of some 10,000 people that had emerged with the nucleated community inside the palisade. Eventually, the remaining elite occupation of Moundville disappeared as nucleated villages were reestablished in the region and the importance of maize cultivation declined. Regional population dwindled to almost nothing, bringing the sequence to an end some 750 years after it began.

Modes of Growth

Figure 6.14 sums up much of the previous discussion of the growth of large social formations. All eleven regional trajectories are represented with their initial neolithic zero points aligned. Regions with large initial neolithic villages appear toward the left; those with smaller initial villages are farther to the right; and the one without local community structure at all is the rightmost. Each period or phase in each trajectory is represented by a circle whose area is proportional to the estimated population of the largest social formation. Episodes of particularly strong regional population increase are marked by jagged lines.

The length of the Western Liao and Shandong sequences, so conspicuous in Figure 6.14, is attributable primarily to an initial two millennia or more during which very little happened in either region. Villages started small and slightly larger ones appeared only very slowly. After 2,000 or even 2,500 years, the social formations in these two regions had only just gotten to the scale of the earliest detectable villages in some other regions. Something similar could be said of the Marana and Pueblo Grande trajectories. Their zero points in Figure 6.14 correspond to the earliest dates for Hohokam

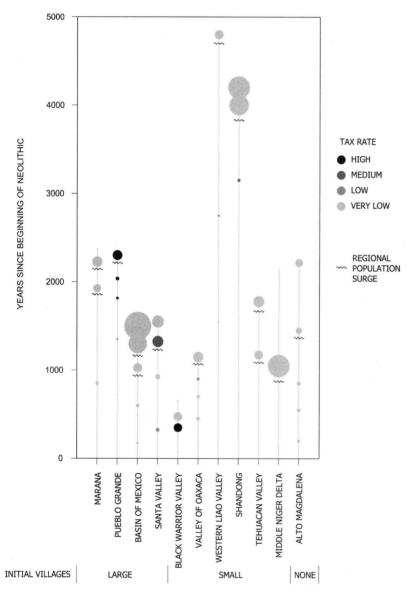

Figure 6.14. Summary of regional trajectories. Circle size represents the population of the largest social formation in each region and period.

villages, but village life began across the Hohokam region in a very scattered and spotty way. It was only after several centuries that neolithic life was as solidly established as at most other regions' zero points. After this very slow start in the Hohokam and Chinese sequences, the pacing of community growth was not so different from that seen in most of the other regions. Once this process was really underway, then, in 10 of the 11 regions, social formations of 10,000 people or more emerged within about 1,000 to 2,000 years. The Black Warrior Valley stands out as the real exception. The growth of a large social formation here was very rapid, requiring only about three centuries.

Community growth in all regions, except possibly the Alto Magdalena, was punctuated; periods of little change in scale were often followed by episodes of dramatic enlargement of social formations, regularly in a context of growing regional populations. Regional demographic processes, then, were the major source of the additional people required to create larger social formations; without them these larger social formations could not have existed. For the most part, regional population growth was of internal origin, presumably from a major increase in birthrates. In only a few regions (including Shandong and the Middle Niger) does immigration seem to have made a substantial contribution. Particular points of rapid demographic growth can be identified in all the trajectories except the Black Warrior Valley, where the lack of complete survey makes it impossible to monitor regional population change. These population surges are the context in which episodes of dramatic community enlargement occurred. Such episodes were not triggered when slow, steady population growth reached some threshold level. There is no reason, however, to treat these population surges as the causes of community enlargement episodes; they might be more result than cause. It is clear, though, that community enlargement tends to be episodic, and that these episodes include regional demographic surges as an important component. Understanding where these surges come from will be important to modeling the dynamics of the emergence of large social formations.

The Alto Magdalena stands apart as the only trajectory without an especially dramatic episode of community expansion associated with a demographic surge. The increase in the scale of supra-local communities that occurred about a thousand years after the beginning of neolithic life was slightly larger than those seen between other phases. The transitions identified in other regions, however, were much more dramatic. Much the same can be said about regional demography; there was a surge at this same point, but a very minor one compared with those of other regions.

In general, change in both regional population and social scale proceeded at a much more even pace than in other regions. This might be an effect of the more diffuse patterns of interaction suggested by dispersed farmstead living. The intense patterns of interaction in more compact and clearly defined local communities may have been essential for the critical mass necessary to produce the much more dramatic social transformations seen in other sequences.

The Alto Magdalena is the only trajectory where farmsteads persisted as the dominant mode of living throughout the sequence. They were never very numerous in other regions except in the Tehuacán Valley and the Black Warrior Valley. Farmsteads were not early in the Tehuacán sequence, but put in an appearance alongside compact villages later on as a result of agricultural intensification following the dramatic emergence of large social formations out of a compact village pattern. The Black Warrior Valley seems more of an exception to the rule that dispersed farmsteads do not produce major growth spurts. Here initial compact villages dispersed into a farmstead pattern out of which the Moundville polity sprang quite suddenly. The very beginnings of the Moundville center sound much like the Alto Magdalena – a concentration of more closely spaced farmsteads around the two earliest mounds. Unlike the Alto Magdalena, however, this community was very rapidly transformed into a compact, nucleated settlement surrounded by a palisade, even as the supra-local community it headed emerged. It apparently took an external threat from bellicose neighboring regions to effect this transformation, however; it seems not to have emerged *sui generis* from dispersed farmstead life. The Black Warrior trajectory thus does not really contradict the notion that forming a critical social mass for a major transformation is difficult in the absence of village living, and that social growth in a farmstead-based settlement system is accretional. The Alto Magdalena, however, is the only farmstead-based settlement system among these regions; studying additional such cases will be essential to pursuing these ideas empirically.

Among the regional trajectories where compact villages were the catalyst for dramatic social transformations, the presence of large villages at the very beginning of the sequence does not seem to constitute a head start. These sequences did not arrive at the dramatic emergence of large social formations any sooner than regions whose initial villages were smaller. Their larger social formations may, however, have been more strongly centralized, a subject we have dealt with in more detail elsewhere (Drennan and Peterson 2008). The four trajectories that began with large, compact villages and few if any farmsteads do, however, share one characteristic in the creation of large social formations. In all four regions the major episodes of community growth were produced not only by rapid regional population increase, but also by the amalgamation of smaller, previously distinct communities. Political fragmentation and conflict characterized the Santa Valley sequence from the beginning, and the major jump to larger social scale involved a reduction in the number of communities through amalgamation. Multiple units also characterized the Basin of Mexico; conflict is not as apparent, but proliferation of more units was followed by amalgamation, as in the Santa Valley, until only one vastly larger social formation was left. Amalgamation in the Basin of Mexico took the peculiar form referred to in the companion chapter as "hoovering." Rather than units combining to form more extensive territories, amalgamation occurred in the Basin of Mexico as some units disappeared from the landscape entirely, their populations having been completely siphoned off to fuel the growth of others. In the Marana and Pueblo Grande trajectories, the units that became the Classic Hohokam irrigation communities were visible from the beginning, but separate interaction foci create distinct subunits within them early in the sequence. The jump that created larger social formations came through the amalgamation of these units.

Amalgamation was not such an easy process in either the trajectories that began with small villages or the ones focused on farmsteads. As noted at the close of the companion chapter, the Alto Magdalena's extensive supra-local communities appeared very early, and grew internally as regional population increased. The same mode of growth is seen in the Tehuacán Valley and the Western Liao Valley, where supra-local communities stayed spatially small even as their populations grew. Amalgamation into larger units did not occur in any of these three regions; communities simply continued to proliferate. Proliferation of multiple units also characterized the Shandong sequence, although two stood out persistently as much larger than the others. These grew through a process more like the hoovering of the Basin of Mexico than the additive amalgamation of the Santa Valley – even after more than four millennia of neolithic life, though, not only these two large communities, but also several other smaller ones, remained. Although small by comparison with other regions, the largest village in Oaxaca far overshadowed the other tiny settlements in the valley. Its interaction cluster included most of the valley's population from the beginning, so there was little raw material for amalgamation. As political consolidation of this supra-local community proceeded, however, its population became increasingly decentralized, in a reversal of the hoovering process seen in the Basin of Mexico. This political consolidation involved the use of coercive force, which eventually turned outwards, producing territorial expansion, but not exactly the amalgamation of small units to form a large one.

The Roles of Conflict

Conflict is a popular theme in the literature on complex societies. It is no surprise, then, that its more violent forms are clear in over half the trajectories investigated here, and it may well have occurred in others without leaving such telltale signs. Conflict is often seen as the major mechanism of amalgamation in the creation of larger social formations. Something like this may have happened in the Santa Valley, where hilltop redoubts were present throughout the sequence, and larger social formations were built through amalgamation. This process eventually stalled, however. By the end of the period discussed here, no one unit had won out over the others in the valley. Armed conflict is unequivocal in the fortifications and hilltop redoubts of the Western Liao sequence, but only far too late to have contributed to the formation of the earliest supra-local communities. It does coincide with a late regional demographic surge and a sharp increase in social scale, though, and resource pressure cannot be ruled out as a source of conflict late in the Western Liao sequence. Population, however, had not just grown steadily to this point; it is equally plausible to posit conflict as the cause of a regional population surge, as contending factions found advantage in larger numbers. More likely both causal dynamics were at work at once, with competition over resources and population growth locked in an upward spiral. This spiral did not produce any larger social formation through conquest and domination, however, but rather balkanization and stalemate. The Tehuacán Valley sequence could be described in very similar terms. Conflict produced hilltop redoubts in the last period of the sequence considered here, coincident with a regional population surge, balkanization, and stalemate.

Conflict with neighbors in other valleys was sporadically important from early in the Black Warrior sequence. Nucleated villages early in the sequence were probably a response to it. Dispersal of these villages as farmsteads may have come from a reduction in this threat. Its return, testified to by massive palisade construction at Moundville, may have spurred development of the centralized supra-local community, and enabled its elites to expand their power. This scenario casts conflict in a vital role contributing to the emergence of a larger social formation, but it does not follow the familiar script in which forcible amalgamation creates larger units from smaller ones. Conflict's impact was felt in an entirely different way.

In the Valley of Oaxaca, conflict is indicated not by fortifications, but by carved stone reliefs depicting sacrificial victims thought to have been elites from peripheral communities. Although this conflict occurred around the time of a regional demographic surge, resource pressure cannot have been involved because population levels were far too low. A larger social formation did emerge, but not from the conquest and amalgamation of rivals that posed any serious military threat. Rather, the inhabitants of peripheral communities were forcibly reminded to obey the elites of the central community that had demographically dominated the valley from the beginning of the sequence. Some evidence from Shandong may suggest a similar dynamic involving conflict. The rammed earth wall at Dantu is part of a widespread late Dawenkou and Longshan phenomenon. Although no examples are known at Dantu, such walls, and the foundations of elaborate elite residences within them, are at other sites associated with the burials of individuals who had been beheaded, who had their arms tied behind their backs, or who were buried alive. As in Oaxaca, Dantu was a very large central community from early in the sequence, and the evidence of conflict suggests terrorizing an already dominated population into complete submission. Unlike Oaxaca, the Dantu supra-local community did not grow through territorial expansion, but rather through a process more like the Basin of Mexico's hoovering. A similarly large community, some 35 km away, persisted without either one dominating the other, although no rammed earth wall is known from it. Oaxaca, then, and possibly Shandong, sketch out yet a fourth role for conflict in the emergence of larger-scale social formations.

Public Works and Tax Rates

The emergence of large social formations in all the regions compared here involved monumental-scale construction in one way or another. Such public works are commonly taken as the materialization of social and political power. They often create spaces for ritual and public ceremony which can reinforce the power of elites. More purely "practical" public works, such as fortifications or agricultural infrastructure, also materialize power, at least if they are seen as a response to elite directives, but the contribution they make to a population's material well-being is usually seen as their principal value. Monuments perhaps make political economies most directly visible archaeologically (see Kolb, Chapter 7), and the labor investment in their construction opens an avenue for approaching resource mobilization in the political economies whose emergence is generally thought to be an essential component of large social formations. Estimates of the labor required to build large things are scattered through the archaeological literature for different parts of the world. By combining this familiar data thread with an assessment of supra-local community scale, the per capita burden of public works can be estimated as outlined in the companion chapter. This "tax rate" is, of course, not the only burden that living in a large social formation places on a population, but it is thought of as a heavy one, one that has occupied a prominent place in the archaeological imagination.

Surprisingly, for most periods in most trajectories, tax rates for public works were truly negligible (less than a quarter day's work per able-bodied worker per year – light gray circles in Figure 6.14). These include all of the largest social formations, ones where large amounts of labor were clearly committed to monumental construction. Four social formations with slightly higher tax rates (around one half day per worker per year – slightly darker gray circles) are all of quite modest size. Yet higher tax rates (around one day per worker per year – still darker gray) occur in one quite small and one fairly large social formation. The highest tax rates run to one week per worker per year (or a bit more), and often occur in relatively small social formations.

Talk of public works, tribute, and taxes springs readily from the emphasis in the archaeological literature on complex societies on elites pursuing their own selfish aims as the driving force behind the growth of large social formations. Even the notion of resistance, which reminds us that nonelite populations are not necessarily easy to push around, leaves the impetus for social change in elite hands. Public works have direct and obvious elite connections when they take the form of elaborate residences and burials. Such projects are an especially important element among the public works of the Black Warrior Valley (at Moundville's apogee), the Valley of Oaxaca (Rosario and Monte Albán Ia), the Western Liao Valley (Hongshan), Shandong (Dawenkou and Longshan), and the Alto Magdalena (Regional Classic). Creation of spaces for public ceremony and ritual is among the major objectives of monumental construction in all eleven regions except the Middle Niger Delta. This kind of public works project is conspicuously connected to elites as well when burial monuments or elaborate residences occupy prime positions, as they often do.

In some regions, the hand of elite activity is less directly evident in civic-ceremonial architecture, leading to talk of "faceless" elites. The notion that such projects materialize social relations and enhance social solidarity, though, goes unchallenged. Among these eleven regions, defensive constructions are the most common kind of public works whose practical benefits are seen to outweigh their purely social impact. They appeared throughout the Santa Valley sequence, and at particular points in the Black Warrior Valley and the Western Liao Valley. Massive walls at Dantu-Liangchengzhen (Shandong) and at Jenné-jeno (Middle Niger) might have been defensive but were more likely built for some other purpose. Public works in the realm of agricultural infrastructure are rare among these eleven regions. Canal irrigation was practiced in several, but only in the Hohokam sequences did canal systems attain the scale of public works. Large investments were made in agricultural infrastructure in other regions but only in periods later than those that concern us here.

The temple platforms, rammed earth walls, monumental sculpture, and other public works of some regions have regularly conjured visions of massive labor input. Some of these projects did indeed consume vast quantities of resources, but it comes as a surprise that this did not necessarily impose a heavy average burden per capita on the sustaining population. The estimated labor burden for public works in the various periods of the trajectories compared here does not exceed about one day per worker per year, except for a total of four periods in two regions. (The biggest surprise may be that the sequence with three periods exceeding this tax rate is the Hohokam Pueblo Grande trajectory.) Overall tax rates, of course, may include supporting a range of other activities in addition to major construction projects, so estimates of the labor required for large-scale construction may not represent the entire burden. We are nonetheless accustomed to thinking of major public works projects as an indicator of societies imposing a particularly heavy tax burden on their populations.

Dynamics of Political Economy

A more interesting factor in the relationship between construction scale and tax rate is population size. The scale of public works, the tax rate, and the size of the population are locked in a circular relationship. Elites might often wish to carry out larger-scale public works projects to reap greater benefits, whether symbolic, social, or purely practical in nature. The two fundamental options would be to raise tax rates or tax a larger population. The ability to raise tax rates, of course, depends on the amount of power already in elite hands for overcoming resistance. In a demographically large social formation, however, a construction burden can be spread across many people to accomplish substantial projects while keeping the tax rate modest. No one imagines that this escaped the attention of aspiring elites, who would naturally attempt to enlarge their communities, thus producing larger social formations.

This just-so story accounting for the social dynamics of emerging complex societies is plausible in the context of prevailing thinking at the close of the twentieth century and the beginning of the next. And much of what can be seen in Figure 6.14 about these eleven regional trajectories is empirically consistent with it. Public works were supported by tax rates that remained quite low throughout five trajectories, both because social formations grew in scale and because regional populations increased. These are Marana, the Basin of Mexico, the Tehuacán Valley, the Middle Niger Delta, and the Alto Magdalena. Three other regional trajectories (Oaxaca, Western Liao, and Shandong) are also consistent with this account. In these latter three sequences, a perceptible rise in tax rates is followed in the next period by both regional population growth and the emergence of substantially larger social formations. These new social formations carried out public works projects of unprecedented scale in their regions with tax rates that had fallen back into the lowest category. This combination of the motivations of self-aggrandizing elites, resistance, the social and practical functions of public works, and mobilization of labor makes sense of a pattern of growth that seems recurrent among this dozen trajectories at least.

It is worth noting in passing that both this empirical evidence and the logic of the just-so story may be at odds with our tendency to think that only the established elites of large social formations had developed and exercised the means to place very heavy tax and tribute burdens on their populations. Very high tax rates were achieved in some quite small social formations, but for larger societies, the tax burdens of expanded public works were kept low by increasing social scale even more rapidly. Tax rates may have increased less visibly if the resources mobilized were dedicated to purposes other than public works. Elites, for example, may simply have lived more lavishly; if so, the changes would be reflected in some of the other data threads enumerated in Chapter 5.

Three trajectories are not so easily squared with the idea of keeping tax rates low by increasing social scale. The Santa Valley shows noticeably high tax rates at the beginning of the neolithic, owing principally to the construction of a large number of fortified citadels. Conflict persisted throughout the part of the Santa Valley sequence examined here; tax rates dropped in the Vinzos phase only because existing fortifications continued to be used with little additional construction. In Early Suchimansillo times, a soaring regional population and the amalgamation of a half dozen supra-local communities into two produced much larger social formations. Nonetheless, the Santa Valley population did not enjoy any tax relief as a consequence, because the scale of both citadel and civic-ceremonial construction more than kept pace. Both kinds of construction leveled off somewhat in Late

Suchimansillo times, bringing tax rates down to a much more modest level. The more manageable political economy this might have created, however, was short-lived, as larger-scale political disruption across Peru's north coast took its toll.

Like the Santa Valley, the Pueblo Grande sequence had a noticeably higher tax rate for the initial neolithic than we usually associate with this period. Rather than defensive works, it was the construction of canal systems that produced this high rate for Pueblo Grande. Thus, in neither region was the high initial tax rate of purely internal social origin; it was a social response to an externally imposed condition, imposed in one case by the physical environment and in the other by the larger-scale political environment. Whether this is a consistent pattern or not can be investigated empirically by enlarging the sample of regional trajectories. Several other coastal Peruvian valleys would be especially interesting in this regard, because of their extremely early (late Preceramic) civic-ceremonial architecture. A larger sample of regions would also make it possible to explore whether substantial public works at a very early date have some consistent impact on the subsequent course of the trajectory. In the case of Pueblo Grande, tax rates for public works stayed high right through the sequence, even though both regional population and the scale of social formations increased. Over time, the balance shifted more toward civic-ceremonial construction, but the most expensive public works were always agricultural.

The Black Warrior Valley sequence is not the "classic" case of chiefdom development it is sometimes taken to be, but actually is very unusual in several respects. Not only is its tax rate the highest estimated for any period in any region, but this occurred in a period of growth in both regional population and scale of social formation. This growth and the construction that accounts for the high tax rate began suddenly and proceeded rapidly. After little more than two centuries, it was over. Populations dispersed and declined, and the scale of social formations diminished quickly. That the tax rate reached levels not seen in any other sequence makes it possible to suggest that elites placed heavier burdens on their population than they could continue to enforce over the long term. Like the high initial tax rates in the Santa Valley and Pueblo Grande sequences, those of the Black Warrior Valley may be attributable to external conditions. The rapid nucleation of 1,500 people living on farmsteads into a compact community surrounded by a massive palisade would have obvious practical benefits in defending against external threats. It was also a major social transformation that could have helped vault Moundville's nascent elites into a much more powerful position – one from which they could have imposed much higher tax rates, even though the lion's share of the public works was dedicated to civic-ceremonial construction. Even though these elites persisted into the next period, when the palisade was evidently no longer needed, tax rates plummeted as mound construction virtually ground to a halt. The downward slide of the political economy may have proved irreversible, and soon the entire supra-local community was gone, elites and all. This may be a case where external pressures encouraged and enabled an aspiring elite to rapidly overextend its political economy. This issue could be pursued empirically if there were complete settlement data for the Black Warrior Valley and adjacent regions.

Extending the Comparative Analysis

Having by now used up a good many more cocktail napkins than the editor of this volume intended to allow us, we will attempt briefly to take stock of where the exploration has led. There is clearly no one way in which large social formations begin to grow, but there are some modes of growth that recur in several regions. Some larger social formations are the product of amalgamation of smaller units through territorial expansion. In other trajectories, smaller units disappear as they are sucked into larger ones. Conflict often plays an important role in the process of amalgamation, although the nature of the role varies. In yet other trajectories, supra-local communities appear early and growth is largely internal to them. Aspects of some trajectories stand out as very unusual. The emergence and growth of supra-local communities, for example, is very rapid in the Black Warrior Valley and extremely slow in the Western Liao Valley and Shandong.

As the chiefdom literature has grown beyond its mid-twentieth-century roots, more attention has focused on human motivations, agency, and resistance. At center stage is the idea that larger social formations are the product of self-aggrandizing elites and the social resistance they spark in a process of faction-building and the creation of political economies. Such thinking about the central forces at work seems readily applicable to the patterns of demographic growth and changing tax rates seen in six of the trajectories: the Basin of Mexico, the Valley of Oaxaca, the Western Liao Valley, Shandong, the Tehuacán Valley, and the Alto Magdalena. The Black Warrior Valley can also be accommodated under this paradigm as a failed attempt; an excessively heavy tax burden, imposed on the strength of an external threat in the absence of sufficient regional demographic expansion to keep tax rates low, may simply have proved unsustainable. The Santa Valley trajectory, with its early high tax rates and low population growth, is also unusual. Unlike the Black Warrior Valley, though, this trajectory seems to have avoided complete collapse and finally underwent a major regional population surge, although with such an expansion of public works construction that tax rates also increased. We will never know whether this trajectory would have stabilized since it was cut off by the imperial expansion of neighbors. These issues can, nonetheless, be discussed sensibly under the prevailing paradigm of the chiefdom literature.

Three trajectories, however, are difficult to discuss in these terms. Hohokam archaeology does not speak strongly to us of the machinations of powerful elites, so thinking focused on hierarchical organization would have us imagine little development of political economy and relatively low tax rates. Nevertheless, the Marana trajectory looks very much like the previous group of six to which current chiefdom thinking applies easily – early low population levels and small social formations undergo a regional population surge that keeps tax rates low as large social formations emerge and consolidate. The Pueblo Grande trajectory is especially unusual in this group of eleven, but not for the low tax rates and modest public works that minimal elite development might suggest. To the contrary, Pueblo Grande tax rates are persistently very high, rivaled only by those in the last period of the "failed" Black Warrior trajectory. The Middle Niger trajectory has also been described as lacking in archaeologically conspicuous elites. It nonetheless sees a regional demographic surge that helps keep tax rates low even as one of the largest social formations in this comparison emerged. Accounts of how the Marana and Middle Niger trajectories came to look so "normal" for early complex societies and of how the Pueblo Grande trajectory sustained such heavy tax burdens that rely on self-aggrandizing elites, resistance, and faction-building are, then, suspect. The question of just how hierarchical these societies were, compared to others, becomes crucial. The four data threads concerning household-scale differentiation enumerated in the companion chapter are, of course, at the heart of this issue. It goes well beyond what can be accomplished in this chapter, but comparative analysis along these lines might sustain the view that these trajectories were persistently less hierarchical than the others, and thus not well accounted for by elite-anchored social dynamics. This point has been made by others, but simply labeling such trajectories "corporate," "heterarchical," or "self-organizing systems" does not really make their social dynamics any more comprehensible. The cocktail napkin calculations presented here, however, do show that these three trajectories share much in terms of community growth patterns and tax rates with those more conventionally described as chiefdoms. If trajectories of markedly hierarchical and nonhierarchical character are separated into two incomparable classes, it becomes impossible to make such observations. Whatever label(s) we apply to them, we can understand patterns of community growth better if we include them all within the same comparative frame.

The results of this heuristic empirical exploration make it seem worthwhile to enlarge the comparative sample considerably, so as to investigate whether patterns that look recurrent in this grab bag of a dozen trajectories really are, and whether additional examples can be found that are unusual in the same ways that some of these trajectories are. Trajectories where large social formations emerge with little evidence of hierarchy are needed in this enlarged sample, so we can model more successfully the forces behind community growth in such settings. A larger set of trajectories without nucleated local communities is needed to assess the impact dispersed settlement has on the pacing of community growth and other characteristics of the larger social formations that emerge. And weaving the data threads involving differentiation of various kinds into this fabric is essential to pursuing notions of hierarchy and political economy. Clearly a large supply of cocktail napkins will be required, along with considerable willingness to use them.

Appendix: Data Sources and Analysis

This chapter amounts to a trial run to see whether some modes of analysis we have suggested previously can be extended to a larger number of cases than we have worked with before. The selection of these eleven regions was largely a matter of convenience; they are cases that came readily to hand, with a modest effort to encompass some widely separated parts of the globe. Each is a region that encompasses one or a few of the larger social formations whose emergence is our subject. Most cover, at an order of magnitude, 1,000 km^2 (i.e., they are substantially larger than 100 km^2 and substantially smaller than 10,000 km^2). Generally they are substantially smaller than the archaeological culture areas they belong to (Pueblo Grande and Marana, not Hohokam; Black Warrior Valley, not Mississippian; etc.). The Western Liao Valley and Shandong are exceptions; these two regions are two orders of magnitude larger (upwards of 100,000 km^2) and are large homogeneous archaeological culture areas. It has been necessary to cast such a broad net for these two trajectories, however, in order to assemble the various kinds of information we have relied upon. In both the Western Liao and Shandong, there is settlement data for an area of more than 1,000 km^2, but much essential information comes from excavated sites far outside these survey areas. One can hope that future data collection will make it possible to focus in more tightly in both these culture areas on much smaller regions, ones more commensurate with the scales of the early sociopolitical entities this comparison concerns.

The very most central among the regional summaries we have relied on are the following: Basin of Mexico (Sanders, Parsons, and Santley 1979); Valley of Oaxaca (Flannery and Marcus, eds., 1983; Marcus and Flannery 1996); Tehuacán Valley (MacNeish, ed., 1967–72; Drennan and Haller 2007); Alto Magdalena (Drennan 2000); Santa Valley (Wilson 1988); Black Warrior Valley (Knight and Steponaitis, eds., 1998); Pueblo Grande and Marana (Gumerman, ed., 1991; Bayman 2001; Abbott 2003); Middle Niger (McIntosh and McIntosh 1993; McIntosh 2005); Western Liao Valley (Guo 1995, 2005; Shelach 1999; Linduff, Drennan, and Shelach 2004); Shandong (Liu 2004; Underhill et al. 2008).

The delineation of local and supra-local communities and the population estimates are our own analyses. The Black Warrior Valley, for which no systematic settlement data exists, is the exception; statements about communities and populations rely on Knight and Steponaitis, eds. (1998). Sanders, Parsons, and Santley (1979) present settlement data for the entire Basin of Mexico on maps indicating point locations for a series of settlement types; for the supra-local community analysis we have assigned each settlement the median population figure for its type. The local community analysis is based only on more detailed data available for the southern Basin of Mexico (Parsons 1971; Blanton 1972; Parsons et al. 1982; Parsons, Kintigh, and Gregg 1983). The total population estimates for each period made by Sanders, Parsons, and Santley for this part of the survey area have been divided across the sites in proportion to the site areas. Settlement locations and population estimates for the Valley of Oaxaca come from Blanton et al. (1982) and Kowalewski et al. (1989). Settlement data for the Tehuacán Valley are from the Palo Blanco Project (Drennan 1978; Drennan, ed., 1979; Drennan and Haller 2007); population estimates are based on an area-density index as for the Alto Magdalena and the Western Liao Valley (see below). Alto Magdalena settlement and population data are from Drennan, ed. (2006). Santa Valley settlement and population data are from Wilson (1988). Basic settlement data for Pueblo Grande are taken from Howard's (1993) maps of occupation in each period. Abbott (2003:41–46) has estimated the population of Pueblo Grande itself; his median Classic period estimate of 819 inhabitants works out to 14.4 persons/ha for the 56.9 ha Pueblo Grande covers on Howard's Classic period map. This density of 14.4 persons/ha was applied to all of the site areas on all of Howard's maps. Marana settlement data comes from Fish, Fish, and Madsen (1992) and Downum (1993). Fish, Fish, and Madsen (1992:26) provide a median Classic period population estimate of 1,000 for the Marana Mound site, and estimate that this is one-fourth of the total population for the Marana irrigation community. The corresponding total occupied area is just over 1,000 ha, meaning an average occupational density of 4 persons/ha. This figure has been applied to the occupied areas on all the Marana maps. Middle Niger settlement data are drawn from McIntosh and McIntosh (1980). McIntosh and McIntosh (1993:633) estimate 42,000 inhabitants for the Jenné-jeno "urban cluster," which contains 70 sites totaling 90 ha, for an average of 221 persons/ha. We have accepted the McIntoshes' argument that this high occupational density is warranted for Middle Niger settlements. Settlement data for the Chifeng region in the Western Liao Valley was produced by the Chifeng International Collaborative Archaeological Research Project (Chifeng 2003; Linduff, Drennan, and Shelach 2004); population estimates are based on an area-density index (Drennan et al. 2003). In Shandong, the settlement locations and areas for the Rizhao region come from the maps in Underhill et al. (2008). An occupational density of 93 persons/ha (the average for the roughly contemporaneous Lower Xiajiadian period in the Chifeng region) has been applied to these settlement areas. This yields population estimates quite similar to those of Fang et al. (2004), who use a density of 72 persons/ha derived from modern villages.

Like the demographic estimates, the estimates of monument construction labor are our own so as to make every effort to ensure consistency in the analyses. In all cases, one-third of the supra-local community's population was taken as the available work force for monument construction. Person-days of labor were based on an average work day of five hours. Usually it was not possible to determine the actual number of years during which construction took place, so the required construction effort was averaged out over the length of the period to which monuments were dated. In many cases monuments were surely constructed in shorter bursts, implying heavier burdens but only temporarily. In such cases, more intense periods of construction work were compensated for by periods of tax relief, and it is that longer-term, time-averaged tax burden that seems most relevant. In all regions, for earthen mound construction, we have used Erasmus' (1965) estimate of 5.25 person-days per m³ of fill; for excavation of ditches and subterranean features, Abrams' (1994) estimate of 2.6 days per m³; and for exterior masonry walls, facings, and platforms, Erasmus' (1965) estimate of 12.25 person-days per m³. The basis for estimates for other tasks is enumerated below.

In the Black Warrior Valley, almost all the monument construction was at Moundville. Mound volumes and information about the palisade come from Knight and Steponaitis, eds. (1998); 7.5 posts can be cut, transported, and placed per person-day (Blitz 1993), and filling between them with wattle and daub requires 1 person-day per m² (Carmean 1991). Very little comprehensive information is available for Formative period monuments in the Basin of Mexico. For the earliest ones, in First Intermediate Two, we used Sanders, Parsons, and Santley's (1979:97) descriptions of the magnitude of platform construction in "regional centers"; for First Intermediate Three, Cuicuilco's main pyramid was assumed to represent about half of its monument construction (Heizer and Bennyhoff 1958; Sanders, Parsons, and Santley 1979:76–77; Evans 2001); and for First Intermediate Four, Teotihuacan's monuments were taken to represent an order of magnitude more construction than Cuicuilco's. Descriptions of monuments in the Valley of Oaxaca are in Caso, Bernal, and Acosta (1967), Blanton (1978), Flannery and Marcus, eds. (1983:47–48, 60–62), and Flannery and Marcus (2005:409–43). The construction tasks included clay and rock fill (5.5 person-days per m³ [Erasmus 1965; Pozorski 1980]); stucco (43.9 person-days per m³ for preparation [Abrams 1994] and 0.2 person-days per m² for application [Smailes 2000]); wooden posts (7.5 per person-day [Blitz 1993]); wattle and daub (1 m² per person-day [Carmean 1991]); adobe (4.96 person-days per m³ of bricks and 0.17 person-days per m² of adobe plaster [Smailes 2000]; and stone facing (0.5 person-days per m² [Carmean 1991]). The Tehuacán Valley's monuments are earth and rubble platforms (Drennan 1978; Drennan, ed., 1979). The Alto Magdalena's monuments were earth mound tombs and statues (Drennan 1995; González Fernández 2008); carving a statue represents 25 person-days (Drennan 2000:19) and moving statues into place, 187.5 person-days per m³ (Abrams 1994). In the Santa Valley, the construction of defensive walls and ditches, plazas, and platforms (Wilson 1988) involved clay and rock fill (5.5 person-days per m³ [Erasmus 1965; Pozorski 1980]), adobes (4.96 days per m³ [Smailes 2000]), adobe plaster (0.17 person-days per m² [Smailes 2000]). Monumental construction for Pueblo Grande (Wilcox and Sternberg 1983; Howard 1993; Abbott 2003) and Marana (Wilcox and Sternberg 1983; Doelle and Wallace 1991; Fish et al. 1992; Bayman 1994:22) involved canal excavation (1.59 person-days per m³ [Billman 2002]), rock and adobe wall construction (5.2 person-days per m³ [Craig, Holmund, and Clark 1998]). For the Middle Niger, Jenné-jeno's wall (McIntosh, ed., 1995:118; McIntosh 2005:175) is adobe (4.9 person-days per m³ for bricks and 0.17 person-days per m² for plaster [Smailes 2000]). For the Western Liao Valley, the

Hongshan platforms and tombs (Guo 1995, 2005; Liaoning 1997; Li 2003; Chaoyang and Liaoning 2004) and the Lower Xiajiadian fortifications (Xu 1986; Wagner 2006:129–30) required setting wooden posts (7.5 per person-day [Blitz 1993]), wattle and daub (1 person-days per m² [Carmean 1991], wall plastering (80 m² per person-day [Abrams 1994]), tamped earthen floor (0.05 days per m² [Carmean 1991]), and rammed earth construction (1 person-day per m³ [Meng 1993]). The walls and moats of Shandong (Yang 2004:109–10) required transportation of excavated earth (3.17 m³ per person-day [Erasmus 1965]) for rammed earth construction (1 person-day per m³ [Meng 1993]).

Acknowledgments

Most of the data used here were compiled from published sources by members of the Chiefdom Datasets Project at the University of Pittsburgh: Robyn Cutright, Jake Fox, William Locascio, Enrique López-Hurtado, Adam Menzies, Scott Palumbo, and Sarah Taylor. We thank Stephen Kowalewski and David Wilson for providing additional digital data.

References Cited

Abbott, David R. 2003 *Centuries of Decline during the Classic Period at Pueblo Grande.* University of Arizona Press, Tucson.
Abrams, Elliott M. 1994 *How the Maya Built Their World: Energetics and Ancient Architecture.* University of Texas Press, Austin.
Bayman, James M. 1994 Craft Production and Political Economy at the Marana Platform Mound Community. Ph.D. Dissertation, Department of Anthropology, Arizona State University.
———. 2001 The Hohokam of Southwest North America. *Journal of World Prehistory* 15:257–311.
Billman, Brian R. 2002 Irrigation and the Origins of the Southern Moche State on the North Coast of Peru. *Latin American Antiquity* 13:371–400.
Blanton, Richard E. 1972 *Prehispanic Settlement Patterns of the Ixtapalapa Peninsula Region, Mexico.* Dept. of Anthropology, The Pennsylvania State University, Occasional Papers in Anthropology, No. 6.
———. 1978 *Monte Albán: Settlement Patterns at the Ancient Zapotec Capital.* Academic Press, New York.
Blanton, Richard E., Stephen Kowalewski, Gary Feinman, and Jill Appel 1982 *Monte Albán's Hinterland, Part I: The Prehispanic Settlement Patterns of the Central and Southern Parts of the Valley of Oaxaca, Mexico.* Memoirs of the Museum of Anthropology, University of Michigan, No. 15.
Blitz, John H. 1993 *Ancient Chiefdoms of the Tombigbee.* University of Alabama Press, Tuscaloosa.

Carmean, Kelli 1991 Architectural Labor Investment and Social Stratification at Sayil, Yucatan, Mexico. *Latin American Antiquity* 2:151–65.

Caso, Alfonso, Ignacio Bernal, and Jorge R. Acosta 1967 *La cerámica de Monte Albán*. Instituto Nacional de Antropología e Historia, Mexico City.

Chaoyang Shi Wenwubu, and Liaoning Sheng Wenwu Kaogu Yanjiusuo 2004 *Niuheliang Yizhi*. Xueyuan Chubanshe, Beijing.

Chifeng International Collaborative Archeological Research Project 2003 *Regional Archeology in Eastern Inner Mongolia: A Methodological Exploration/Neimenggu Dongbu (Chifeng) Quyu Kaogu Diaocha Jieduanxing Baogao*. Science Press, Beijing.

Craig, Douglas B., James P. Holmund, and Geoffrey J. Clark 1998 Labor Investment and Organization in Platform Mound Construction: A Case Study from the Tonto Basin of Central Arizona. *Journal of Field Archaeology* 25:245–59.

Doelle, William H., and Henry D. Wallace 1991 The Changing Role of the Tucson Basin in the Hohokam Regional System. In *Exploring the Hohokam*, edited by George J. Gumerman, pp. 279–346. Amerind Foundation, Inc., Dragoon, AZ.

Downum, Christian E. 1993 *Between Desert and River: Hohokam Settlement and Land Use in the Los Robles Community*. Anthropological Papers of the University of Arizona, No. 57. University of Arizona Press, Tucson.

Drennan, Robert D. 1978 *Excavations at Quachilco: A Report on the 1977 Season of the Palo Blanco Project in the Tehuacán Valley*. Technical Reports, No. 7. University of Michigan Museum of Anthropology.

———. 1979 *Prehistoric Social, Political, and Economic Development in the Area of the Tehuacán Valley: Some Results of the Palo Blanco Project*. Technical Reports, No. 11. University of Michigan Museum of Anthropology.

———. 1995 Mortuary Practices in the Alto Magdalena: The Social Context of the "San Agustín Culture." In *Tombs for the Living: Andean Mortuary Practices*, edited by Tom D. Dillehay, pp. 79–110. Dumbarton Oaks, Washington, DC.

———. 2000 *Las sociedades prehispánicas del Alto Magdalena*. Instituto Colombiano de Antropología e Historia, Bogotá.

———. 2006 *Prehispanic Chiefdoms in the Valle de la Plata, Vol. 5: Regional Settlement Patterns/Cacicazgos prehispánicos del Valle de la Plata, tomo 5: Patrones de asentamiento regionales*. University of Pittsburgh Memoirs in Latin American Archaeology, No. 16.

Drennan, Robert D., and Mikael J. Haller 2007 The Local Village Community and the Larger Political Economy: Formative and Classic Interaction Patterns in the Tehuacán Valley Compared to the Valley of Oaxaca and the Basin of Mexico. In *The Political Economy of Ancient Mesoamerica: Transformations during the Formative and Classic Periods*, edited by Vernon L. Scarborough and John E. Clark, pp. 65–82. University of New Mexico Press, Albuquerque.

Drennan, Robert D., and Christian E. Peterson 2008 Centralized Communities, Population, and Social Complexity after Sedentarization. In *The Neolithic Demographic Transition and Its Consequences*, edited by Jean-Pierre Bouquet-Appel and Ofer Bar-Yosef, pp. 359–86. Springer, New York.

Drennan, Robert D., Christian E. Peterson, Gregory G. Indrisano, Teng Mingyu, Gideon Shelach, Zhu Yanping, Katheryn M. Linduff, and Guo Zhizhong 2003 Approaches to Regional Demographic Reconstruction/Quyuxing Renkou

Guimo Chongjian Zhi Changshi. In *Regional Archeology in Eastern Inner Mongolia: A Methodological Exploration/Neimenggu Dongbu (Chifeng) Quyu Kaogu Diaocha Jieduanxing Baogao*, pp. 152–65. Science Press, Beijing.

Erasmus, Charles 1965 Monument Building: Some Field Experiments. *Southwestern Journal of Anthropology* 21:277–301.

Evans, Susan Toby 2001 Cuicuilco (D.F., Mexico). In *Archaeology of Ancient Mexico and Central America: An Encyclopedia*, edited by Susan Toby Evans and David L. Webster, pp. 198–99. Garland, New York.

Fang Hui, Gary M. Feinman, Anne P. Underhill, and Linda M. Nicholas 2004 Settlement Pattern Survey in the Rizhao Area: A Preliminary Effort to Consider Han and pre-Han Demography. *Bulletin of the Indo-Pacific Prehistory Association* 24:79–82.

Fish, Paul R., Suzanne K. Fish, and John H. Madsen (eds.) 1992 *The Marana Community in the Hohokam World*. University of Arizona, Anthropological Papers, No. 56.

Flannery, Kent V., and Joyce Marcus (eds.) 1983 *The Cloud People: Divergent Evolution of the Zapotec and Mixtec Civilizations*. Academic Press, New York.

————. 2005 *Excavations at San José Mogote 1: The Household Archaeology*. Memoirs of the Museum of Anthropology, University of Michigan, No. 40.

González Fernández, Víctor 2008 *Prehispanic Change in the Mesitas Community: Documenting the Development of a Chiefdom's Central Place in San Agustín, Huila, Colombia/Cambio prehispánico en la comunidad de Mesitas: Documentando el desarrollo de la comunidad central en un cacicazgo de San Agustín, Huila, Colombia*. University of Pittsburgh Memoirs in Latin American Archaeology, No. 18.

Gumerman, George J. (ed.) 1991 *Exploring the Hohokam*. Amerind Foundation, Inc., Dragoon, AZ.

Guo Dashun 1995 Hongshan and Related Cultures. In *The Archaeology of Northeast China: Beyond the Great Wall*, edited by Sarah M. Nelson, pp. 21–64. Routledge, London.

————. 2005 *Hongshan Wenhua*. Wenwu Chubanshe, Beijing.

Heizer, Robert F., and James A. Bennyhoff 1958 Archeological Investigation of Cuicuilco, Valley of Mexico, 1957. *Science* 127:232–33.

Howard, Jerry B. 1993 A Paleohydraulic Approach to Examining Agricultural Intensification in Hohokam Irrigation Systems. In *Research in Economic Anthropology, Supplement 7: Economic Aspects of Water Management in the Prehispanic New World*, edited by Vernon L. Scarborough and Barry L. Isaac, pp. 263–324. JAI Press, Greenwich, CN.

Knight, Vernon James, Jr., and Vincas P. Steponaitis (eds.) 1998 *Archaeology of the Moundville Chiefdom*. Smithsonian Institution Press, Washington, DC.

Kowalewski, Stephen A., Gary M. Feinman, Laura Finsten, Richard E. Blanton, and Linda M. Nicholas 1989 *Monte Albán's Hinterland, Part II: Prehispanic Settlement Patterns in Tlacolula, Etla, and Ocotlán, the Valley of Oaxaca, Mexico*. Memoirs of the University of Michigan Museum of Anthropology, No. 23.

Li Xinwei 2003 *Development of Social Complexity in the Liaoxi Area, Northeast China*. Ph.D. Dissertation, Archaeology Program, La Trobe University.

Liaoning Sheng Wenwu Kaogu Yanjiusuo 1997 *Niuheliang Hongshan Wenhua Yizhi yu Yuqi Jingcui*. Wenwu Chubanshe, Beijing.

Linduff, Katheryn M., Robert D. Drennan, and Gideon Shelach 2004 Early Complex Societies in NE China: The Chifeng International Collaborative Archaeological Research Project. *Journal of Field Archaeology*, 29:45–73.

Liu Li 2004 *The Chinese Neolithic: Trajectories to Early States*. Cambridge University Press, Cambridge.

MacNeish, Richard S. (ed.) 1967–72 *The Prehistory of the Tehuacán Valley*. 5 vols. University of Texas Press, Austin.

Marcus, Joyce, and Kent V. Flannery 1996 *Zapotec Civilization: How Urban Society Evolved in Mexico's Oaxaca Valley*. Thames and Hudson, London.

Martens, Stephan 2008 On the Back of an Envelope. *Science* 321:1160.

McIntosh, Roderick J. 2005 *Ancient Middle Niger: Urbanism and the Self-Organizing Landscape*. Cambridge University Press, Cambridge.

McIntosh, Susan K. (Editor) 1995 *Excavations at Jenné-Jeno, Hambarketolo, and Kaniana (Inland Niger Delta, Mali), the 1981 Season*. University of California Publications, Anthropology, Vol. 20. University of California Press, Berkeley.

McIntosh, Susan K., and Roderick J. McIntosh 1980 *Prehistoric Investigations in the Region of Jenne, Mali: A Study in the Development of Urbanism in the Sahel*. BAR International Series 89. B.A.R., Oxford.

———. 1993 Cities without Citadels: Understanding Urban Origins along the Middle Niger. In *The Archaeology of Africa: Food, Metals, and Towns*, edited by Thurston Shaw, Paul Sinclair, Bassey Andah, and Alex Okpoko, pp. 622–41. Routledge, London.

Meng Huaping 1993 Sanxia Diqu Xinshiqi Shidai Yicun de Puxi Yanjiu. *Huaxia Kaogu* 1993(3):35–51.

Morrison, Philip 1963 Fermi Questions. *American Journal of Physics* 31:626–27.

Parsons, Jeffrey R. 1971 *Prehistoric Settlement Patterns in the Texcoco Region, Mexico*. Memoirs of the University of Michigan Museum of Anthropology, No. 3.

Parsons, Jeffrey R., Elizabeth Brumfiel, Mary Parsons, and David Wilson 1982 *Prehispanic Settlement Patterns in the Southern Valley of Mexico: The Chalco–Xochimilco Region*. Memoirs of the University of Michigan Museum of Anthropology, No. 14.

Parsons, Jeffrey R., Keith Kintigh, and Susan A. Gregg 1983 *Archaeological Settlement Pattern Data from the Chalco, Xochimilco, Ixtapalapa, Texcoco, and Zumpango Regions*. Technical Reports, No. 14. University of Michigan Museum of Anthropology.

Peterson, Christian E., and Robert D. Drennan 2005 Communities, Settlements, Sites, and Surveys: Regional-scale Analysis of Prehistoric Human Interaction. *American Antiquity* 70:5–30.

Pozorski, Thomas 1980 The Early Horizon Site of Huaca de los Reyes: Societal Implications. *American Antiquity* 45:100–10.

Sanders, William T., Jeffrey R. Parsons, and Robert S. Santley 1979 *The Basin of Mexico: Ecological Processes in the Evolution of a Civilization*. Academic Press, New York.

Shelach, Gideon 1999 *Leadership Strategies, Economic Activity, and Interregional Interaction: Social Complexity in Northeast China*. Kluwer Academic/Plenum, New York.

Smailes, Richard 2000 *Building Chan Chan: The Application of Construction Project Management to the Analysis of Ancient Architecture*. Ph.D. Dissertation, Department of Anthropology, University of Florida.

Underhill, Anne P., Gary M. Feinman, Linda M. Nicholas, Fang Hui, Luan Fengshi, Yu Haiguang, and Cai Fengshu 2008 Changes in Regional Settlement Patterns and the Development of Complex Societies in Southeastern Shandong, China. *Journal of Anthropological Archaeology* 127:1–29.

Wagner, Mayke 2006 *Neolithikum und Fruhe Bronzezeit in Nordchina vor 8000 bis 3500 Jahren: Die Nordostliche Tiefebene (Studteil)*. Verlag Philipp von Zabern, Frankfurt.

Weinstein, Lawrence, and John A. Adam 2008 *Guesstimation: Solving the World's Problems on the Back of a Cocktail Napkin*. Princeton University Press, Princeton.

Wilcox, David R., and Charles Sternberg 1983 *Hohokam Ballcourts and Their Interpretation*. Arizona State Museum Archaeological Series, No. 160.

Wilson, David J. 1988 *Prehispanic Settlement Patterns in the Lower Santa Valley, Peru: A Regional Perspective on the Origins and Development of Complex North Coast Society*. Smithsonian Institution Press, Washington, DC.

Xu Guangji 1986 Chifeng Yingjinhe, Yinhe Liuyu de Shicheng Yizhi. In *Zhongguo Kaoguxue Yanjiu*, pp. 82–93. Wenwu Chubanshe, Beijing.

Yang Xiaoneng 2004 Urban Revolution in Late Prehistoric China. In *New Perspectives on China's Past: Chinese Archaeology in the Twentieth Century*, Vol. 1: *Cultures and Civilizations Reconsidered*, edited by Xiaoneng Yang, pp. 99–143. Yale University Press, New Haven.

CHAPTER 7

THE GENESIS OF MONUMENTS
IN ISLAND SOCIETIES

Michael J. Kolb

One important way archaeologists examine past social relationships is by studying durable monuments. Monuments, such as elaborate tombs, large temples, and elite palaces, are usually the products of complex societies, where they serve as testimonies of social authority and prestige. Unlike more private forms of architecture such as houses, monuments serve as public focal points and places of community interaction, built to communicate very specific meanings about how to become a member of a larger social whole, how to interact collectively. Their more complex architectural grammars (with plazas, expansive doorways, or passageways) create a spatial map that is acted on through movement, translated through spatial experience, and physically communicated by anchoring social meanings in space. And as individuals move around or through monumental spaces, they experience and translate these public meanings.

One of the most critical dynamics of large public monuments is the act of their physical construction. A motivated labor force orchestrating and executing a coordinated building plan represents no better example of how to generate collective thought. Up to thousands of laborers were utilized in constructing the most sophisticated and greatest of the world's monuments, demonstrating that as the size and complexity of a monument begins to exceed its practical function, so does its collective vision and symbolism expand. Monumental architecture directly communicates, in a public and enduring fashion, that the greater the monument the more orchestrated the collective effort involved. And as a form of collectiveness they create social messages that are fundamentally different than those conveyed by the domestic house. Monuments steer individuals away from any notions of privacy through discourses of the collective public.

In this chapter, I undertake a comparative analysis of island monuments to understand some of the variables associated with their construction and elaboration. Smith and Peregrine (Chapter 2) discuss the various approaches to comparative analysis in the archaeology of ancient complex societies. Islands represent excellent study areas because of the additional degree of geographic and social circumscription that is usually present, and because some of the most impressive examples of monumentality occur on islands. The test case studies include three islands from the Pacific and three islands from the Mediterranean. They are: (1) the *ahu* temples and mono-liths of Rapa Nui (Easter Island); (2) the *heiau* temples of Maui (Hawaiian Islands); (3) the *lulung* burial and habitation platforms of Pohnpei (Microne-sia); (4) the *talayot* towers of Menorca (Balearic Islands); (5) the temple and funerary complexes of Malta and Gozo; and (6) the palaces of Minoan Crete (Figure 7.1). The goal is to obtain a more precise understanding of how monuments are utilized. Three questions become predominant: (1) How and why do certain types of social and ritual elaboration assume monumen-tal proportions? (2) What are the functional and morphological similarities and differences of these monument types? and (3) What was the basis of power associated with the construction of these monuments? In this vol-ume, Peterson and Drennan (Chapter 6) and Fletcher (Chapter 11) also deal with related aspects of monument construction in ancient societies.

Pacific Islands

Rapa Nui. The first test case is the temples and stone statues of Rapa Nui (Easter Island) in eastern Polynesia. Rapa Nui is the smallest (164 km^2) and most geographically isolated of our island test cases and its colonizers migrated from central Polynesia no later than A.D. 600–700, beginning to construct a unique type of monument that included multi-ton stone torso statues for ancestor worship. Numerous syntheses exist for Rapa Nui and its monuments (e.g., Diamond 2005; Flenley and Bahn 2003; Kirch 2000; Martinsson-Wallin 1994; Pavel 1990; Van Tilburg 1994; Van Tilburg and Ralston 2005).

More than 300 *ahu* temples and 700 *moai* statues were rapidly constructed between A.D. 1100 and 1500. *Ahu* architecture evolved from the central Polynesian *marae* stone platform shrine with its altars, huts, and statues. *Ahu* are dispersed along the coastline at intervals of approximately 0.75 km (except for high cliff areas). The typical *ahu* measures 3 m in height and 720 m^2 in area (see Martinsson-Wallin 1994: Appendix A). A 1–m high retaining wall is found on the seaside edge, denoting the rear section of the *ahu*. The *ahu* platform was built using dry-laid rock fill, and then paved over with smooth stones. An entrance ramp was placed on the land-side

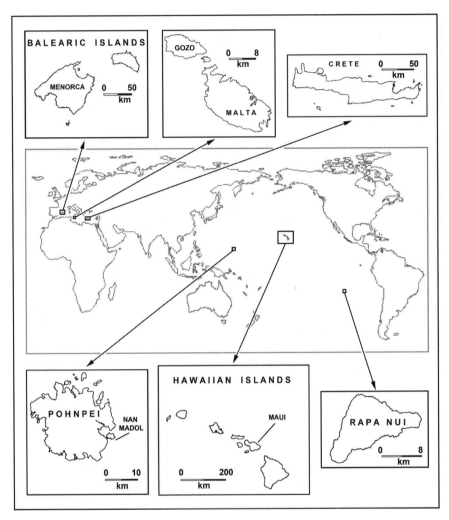

Figure 7.1. Locations of the islands mentioned in the text.

edge and was surrounded by more paving stones (Figure 7.2, A). Of the 313 remaining *ahu*, 125 contained *moai* statues that face land-side. The others may have had wooden statues.

The *moai* stone statues are truly unique. Archaeologists have documented 887 *moai*, the majority as carved human head and torso in minimalist style. Almost all come from the volcanic tuff of the Rano Raraku volcano; approximately 55 statues were carved from stone material from other parts of the island. The typical statue measures 4 m tall and 12 tons in weight. Because of

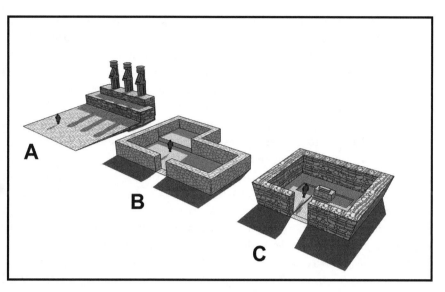

Figure 7.2. Schematic views of typical Oceanic monuments: A: Rapanuian *ahu* platform with *moai* statues; B: Mauian *heiau* temple; C: Pohnpeian *lulung* platform.

excessive transporting costs, only about 288 statues (25 percent) were successfully moved and installed on *ahu* platforms. Another 397 statues remain abandoned at the quarry of Raraku Rarku, including the largest statue (20 m tall and more than 200 tons). Another 92 were abandoned in transit along the prepared roads outside the main quarry. Statues were installed with their backs to the sea, facing the accompanying ceremonial area and nearby village. Many have bas-relief etchings on their backs (perhaps tattoos of rank) and carved loincloths. Most statues are sexually ambiguous, although some have traces of a beard or etched vulva. Most installed *moai* were given finishing touches, including carved eye sockets and headdress.

One of the earliest Rapa Nuian ritual structures is Ahu Tahai, located on the island's western shore. Ahu Tahai was originally a small platform dating to A.D. 690 and then rebuilt around A.D. 1200. It possessed an early-style red scoria statue that was tipped over into the fill of the later platform extension and then replaced with five Rao Raraku tuff statues. Other rebuilt platforms contain early statues as well, including Ahu Tongariki, Ahu Hekii, and the inland *ahu* of Ahu Akivi. The early-style red scoria statues found in the fill of these rebuilt platforms are less stylized that later statues and similar in design to the "tiki" images of central Polynesia, with naturalistic heads and ears. Many early single-statue open-air altars probably existed, some perhaps built with a courtyard in the typical central Polynesian fashion.

Monumental construction on Rapa Nui peaks by A.D. 1400. The most elaborate *ahu* is Ahu Tongariki, located on the south coast approximately 1 km from the quarry of Rano Raraku. Ahu Tongariki was constructed in multiple construction phases and has a length of 60 m and a volume of 23,000 m³. Given its proximity to the quarry, it houses fifteen *moai* statues including an 86-ton giant. Sometime after A.D. 1500 (and maybe as late as A.D. 1770), profound sociopolitical and religious changes in Rapa Nuian society resulted in the cessation of statue carving and the modification or destruction of most *ahu* platforms. *Moai* statues were intentionally toppled over, and many *ahu* became burial locations for human remains. The reasons behind such drastic change are debated (e.g., Diamond 2005); the most likely is the rise of internecine warfare tied to degradation of the environment, population pressure, and/or rising social stress.

The Rapanuian monuments document emerging elite religious power in a highly constrained environment. The *ahu* platforms with their *moai* statues were used as ceremonial "meeting places" for ancestor worship, similar to features in other Polynesian societies. Each statue immortalized a high-ranking ancestor of the local village (a deeply rooted Polynesian tradition), and the enhanced spiritual role given these statues was a trait shared with the Society Island upright stones and the Hawaiian carved wooden images. The Rapanuian statues stood protectively over a neighboring village, serving as a perpetual reminder of the villagers' link to both the spiritual world as well as a temporal link to the surrounding countryside.

It may appear that considerable effort was invested into *moai* statue carving and transportation from A.D. 1100 to 1500, especially given the small population size and extreme isolation of the Rapanuian inhabitants. However, twenty individuals could easily carve a statue in their spare time within one year (Pavel 1990), whereas fifty to seventy-five people could haul a statue 15 km in the course of a week (Van Tilburg and Ralston 2005). Transportation was clearly the greatest logistical effort; including the construction and maintenance of V-shaped roads, the manufacture of large qualities of rope, the growing of foodstuffs to be used as lubricants, and the culling of wood to serve as harnesses and leavers. The organic goods, particularly the rope and wood, were of limited quantity on such a small island. Total food requirements during the four hundred years of statue construction increased 25 percent (Van Tilburg and Ralston 2005), and may have contributed to overexploitation and eventually decline in availability of such materials, probably contributing to the end of statue carving.

At first glance, it may appear that the monuments of Rapa Nui were constructed by some sort of centralized hierarchy. The grandiosity of the statues, the detail of their stylistic design, and the laborious efforts of a small population to carve and construct all suggest some sort of controlled coercion. Nevertheless, ethnohistorical and archaeological evidence indicate that ritual power was in fact decentralized among a series of rival kin groups. The argument that intergroup social competition drove monumental elaboration is supported by the ease of *ahu* construction and *moai* statue carving, the fact that so many statues were carved but not moved, the lack of any clear central monumental place, and the equal distribution of monuments across the landscape.

Maui. The monumental structures of Maui in the Hawaiian archipelago of East Polynesia are called *heiau* temples. At the time of European contact in A.D. 1778, chiefs in the Hawaiian archipelago had implemented a temple network to provide the proper infrastructure for expressing the ideology of kingship, feudalizing land tenure practices, imposing ritual taboos on labor and production, and engaging in internecine warfare over territory (Cordy 2000; Earle 1997; Kirch 1985; Kolb and Dixon 2002). A number of ethnohistorical and archaeological syntheses have been published on the Maui *heiau* (Kolb 1992, 1994, 1997, 1999, 2006; Kolb and Dixon 2002; Valeri 1985).

Similar to the Rapanuian ahu platform, *heiau* architecture has its origins in the central Polynesian *marae* platform shrine. The typical *heiau* measures 2 m high and 424 m² in area. These features were dispersed along the coast or in the island interior. More than 250 *heiau* temples were present on Maui according to ethnohistoric data, although only 108 remain today. *Heiau* structures had dry-laid lava rock foundations with stone altars, offering pits, and the foundations of thatched houses and wooden images (Figure 7.2, B). Three general functional categories have been identified archaeologically with the excavation of eight Maui temples: (1) small open court ancestral shrines, (2) large platform temples used for major political rituals and feasts that helped glorify successful chiefly lines, and (3) smaller enclosed temples used for local rituals and feasts that promoted collective cosmological principles and encouraged consensus among political groups. Oral histories of the Hawaiian temple system indicate the presence of several functional types (Valeri 1985:172–83), and temples ranged in size from family structures (~200 m²) to medium-sized community shrines (~650 m²) and larger polity temples (upwards of ~2,000 m²).

The general trend of temple construction followed four phases between A.D. 1200 and 1800 (Kolb 2006), and those phases correlate with general sociopolitical trends distilled from ethnohistory. These include

(1) the formation of district-sized polities and the rise of chiefly prerogatives, (2) the expansion of the chiefly hierarchy and a bifurcation of the island into eastern and western kingdoms, (3) island unification and a shift in land tenure, and (4) inter-island competition and eventual absorption into a larger incipient state. An important shift in temple construction and use coincided with island unification and a shift in land-tenure and occurred by A.D. 1650.

The *heiau* temple of Pi'ilanihale in east Maui (Figure 7.3) represents the largest and most architecturally complex example in the Hawaiian archipelago (Kolb 1999). It was built in four building episodes with visible architectural seams that are indicative of the dynamic nature of the growth and function of the site. The first building episode (A.D. 1400) was the most impressive in terms of size and complexity (9,363 m²), rivaled only by the construction of the war temple of King Kamehameha in A.D. 1791 (Fornander 1969, 2:327). Adjacent terraces were added to the west and east by A.D. 1650, similar to the addition of wings on the Rapanuian *ahu* platform. Pi'ilanihale was originally used for some sort of public ritual or assembly function. The two winged additions served as affiliated residential areas for elites, and were closely associated with the ceremonial or public meeting area of the central terrace, which retained its function over time.

Overall, the Maui *heiau* temple system followed a cycle of construction and use characteristic of the incipient state development experienced by the Hawaiian archipelago. Temple construction phases coincided with distinct periods of political tension when it was important to encourage and control social allegiances.

Pohnpei. The monuments of Pohnpei in central Micronesia represent another example of architectural elaboration. Pohnpei is a high island (330 km²) that was initially inhabited before A.D. 1. Its population likely peaked at 20,000, organized into a series of nominally independent political units at the time of European contact. A number of syntheses discuss the Pohnpeian monuments and their chronology (e.g., Athens 1983; Ayres 1979, 1993; Ayres and Mauricio 1997; Bath and Athens 1990; Kirch 2000:194–201; Rainbird 2004, 2007).

The typical Pohnpeian monument was the *lulung* burial, a walled platform enclosure constructed of stacked basalt columnar prisms. The average basalt column was 8 m long and weighed several tons, placed in header-stretcher fashion similar to the knitting of logs when building a log cabin. The *lulung* functioned as a combined sleeping platform and walled tomb, its size reflecting the social status of both occupant and clan. The typical

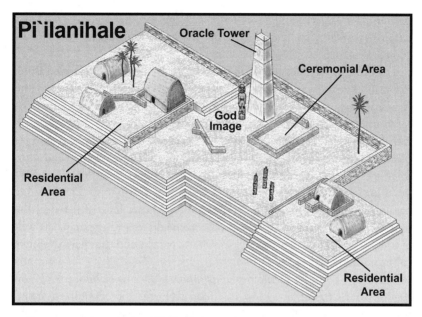

Figure 7.3. Schematic view of Piʿilanihale temple on Maui. Drawing by Niel Colwell.

lulung was 250 m² surrounded by a 3-m high circumference wall (Figure 7.2, C). It is unknown exactly how many *lulung* burials were constructed, but hundreds have been located. The tidal reef city of Nan Madol has the largest concentration of *lulung* burials; ninety-two *lulung* built as islets in the shallows of an 81-hectare lagoon. Islets were separated by narrow waterways that flood during high tide. Nan Madol had two separate wards: an inner cluster of thirty-four residential platforms and an outer seaward array of fifty-eight ritual and *lulung* islets. A massive sea wall (up to 10 m thick in places) protects the southeastern edge of Nan Madol, stretching at least 1,000 m along the border of the city (Morgan 1988). Nan Madol was constructed using more than 750,000 tons of columnar basalt, outcropped or quarried from various sources (Ayres, Goles, and Beardsley 1997).

The lagoon and sandy shoals of Nan Madol were first occupied by A.D. 900. Expansion continued until A.D. 1600, after which time residence was mostly abandoned. The earliest constructed islets were near shore, an area later comprised of large and small basalt and coral-filled platforms used as residences, meeting areas, and storage facilities. Four large islets (at least 8,000 m²) dominate this residential area, the largest (called Pahnkedira) being the reputed residence of island rulers. Pahnkedira is subdivided into five major courtyards by large basalt walls. These courtyards were used as residential areas, a sacred altar, and a meeting area for holding court and religious worship. The entire structure was built using 44,000 m³ of basalt and coral fill.

The outer array of fifty-eight *lulung* islets at Nan Madol that served as the ritual and mortuary sector was slowly expanded outwards from shore. The largest islet is called Nandauwas, a double-walled enclosure with an area of 3,100 m². Nandauwas was the sepulcher for a ruling line of Pohnpeian elites called the Saudeleur hegemony, a group who ruled all of Pohnpei. It consists of 18,000 m³ of fill and has a foundation that is 3 m above sea level and a 6 m thick and 5 m high enclosing wall. A second interior enclosure surrounds an inner burial chamber, which is a 7 × 6 × 1.5 m platform topped with twelve basalt columns 8 m in length. Additional burials are located between the outer and inner walls. Nandauwas is located adjacent to the main sea wall entrance, forcing all canoe-going visitors to pass by and thus pay reverence to the elites buried there.

Oral history and archaeological data indicate that the elaboration of Nan Madol from A.D. 1000 to 1500 was indicative of island centralization and formalization under the Saudeleurs, when the city served as a ritual and trade center (see Kirch 2000:200; Rainbird 2007). The city's restricted sea-side entrance, its array of *lulung* burials, and its elite residences formally organized and directed the activities associated with social exchange networking (e.g., collection, storage, and presentation of tribute, including canoes laden with basalt building materials). The eventual abandonment of Nan Madol likely coincided with the collapse of the Saudeleur hegemony, and it has been hypothesized that a possible expansion of other island political centers began at this time, including the fortified hilltops of Sapwtakai and Ohlapel (each approximately 2 hectares in size), as well the rise of a similarly designed city at Lelu on the island of Kosrae, some 600 km east of Pohnpei.

Mediterranean Islands

Menorca. The monumental phase of Menorca in the Balearic Islands of the Mediterranean is called the Talayotic Period and spans a broad period between about 1700 and 123 B.C. Less work has been done on these monuments than on those from other island groups, but a number of important syntheses do exist (Calvo Trias et al. 2001; Gómez Bellard 1995; Gasull et al. 1984; Patton 1996; Plantalamor and Rita 1984; Rita 1988; Waldren 1982, 1992). The *talayot*, a tower-like structure similar to the Sardinian nuraghic towers (Waldren 1982), is the predominant monument feature of

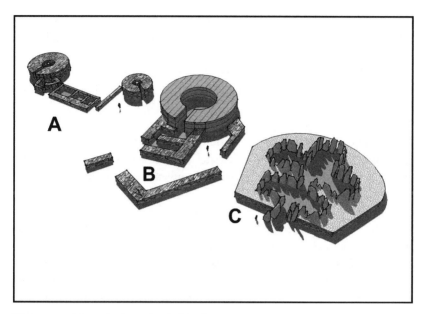

Figure 7.4. Schematic views of typical Mediterranean monuments: A: Menorcan *talayot*; B: Cretan *tholos* tomb (the site of Moni Odigitria after Meyers and Cadogan 1992); C: Maltese temple.

the island (although others exist such as the *naveta* burial tomb and *taula* sanctuary). A *talayot* may be square, round, oval, or stepped in form, averaging 12–20 m in diameter and containing a massive central roof pillar. The *talayot* tower is usually found at the center of a settlement, or built adjacent to defensive walls. Some settlements have more than one *talayot*. More than three hundred of the structures are still preserved on Menorca (Figure 7.4, A).

The *talayot* monuments were built during the Talayotic Period (1700–123 B.C.) but trace their origins to the megalithic chamber tombs, fortified enclosures, and standing menhir stones of the Pretalayotic Period (Gómez Bellard 1995; Rita 1988). Settlements from the Pretalayotic Period, such as Ferrandell-Oleza on Mallorca, often incorporate central tower-like structures (Waldren 1982). Material culture indicates a clear link with the Iberian mainland, and includes such things as metal and Bell-Beaker pottery (Chapman 1985:145). The circular *talayot* style was developed earliest and eventually evolved into the square and stepped forms (Waldren 1982). The functions of *Talayot* are unclear, but they may have served as defensive structures, community storage areas, or possibly as loci for ceremonial community feasting (see Gasull et al. 1984). The chronology of these monuments is still somewhat imprecise given the paucity of modern systematic excavations, but we do know all three monument types were built in the late Bronze Age, between 1400 and 800 B.C., and were used simultaneously. The *talayot* does bear a resemblance to the towers of Sardinia and Corsica even though the Balearic Islands are clearly linked to the Iberian mainland (Patton 1996:94).

Malta. The monuments of the Maltese islands are the oldest of the island test cases. They are located on two islands, Malta and Gozo (combined area of 383 km²). These temple and funerary complexes, built in the Copper Age (c. 3600–2500 B.C.), represent some of the earliest worldwide monuments ever built. Little is known about the builders of these structures. The original inhabitants of the Maltese Islands had clear affinities to the Neolithic Stentinello culture of Sicily (ca. 5000–4500 B.C.), and were farmers who grew cereal crops and raised domestic livestock. A number of syntheses exist regarding the Maltese temples and their chronology (Bonanno et al. 1990; Evans 1984; Lewis 1977; Patton 1996; Stoddart 1999; Stoddart et al. 1993; Trump 1972, 2002).

About forty temples are distributed on both Malta and Gozo, often in complexes. The seven largest complexes consist of a perimeter wall encircling two or more adjacent temples. Each temple is distinct in layout and size, but all have the apsidal chamber as a basic architectural element. The typical apse is a curved hemispheric room averaging 6 m in diameter, but tapered toward the top. It has a horizontal arch entryway consisting of a post-and-lintel trilithon. An apse had no stone roof, but was probably covered with suspended rafters covered in thatch, wattle and daub, or animal hides. Each temple was built with multiple apses, usually laid out in paired or trefoil (leaf-shape) groups. Styles ranged from three to six apses per temple (Figure 7.4, C).

Ggantija (or giantess' tower) on Gozo is the largest and best-preserved example, consisting of two temples built 6 m high. The southern temple was constructed about 3400 B.C. and is 27 m long with five chambers. The northern temple was constructed around 3000 B.C., and is 19.5 m long containing four chambers with a fifth central chamber the size of a small niche. A massive curvilinear wall surrounds both temples. The space between the temple walls and the perimeter wall is filled with earth and rubble. The most elaborate temple complex is at Tarxien (pronounced Tar-heen) on Malta, consisting of three temple structures built after 3100 B.C. A large central six-apse temple was built last. Doorjambs and holes were used to restrict access between apses. The remains of an older abandoned temple lie nearby. The Tarxien temples contained significant numbers of "cult" objects found in the innermost apses, including pottery, carved female figurines, animal bones, and spiral wall cravings. The earliest temple is located at Skorba on Malta, a small shrine dating to 4100 B.C. and the precursor to later monumental structures. This shrine was the largest building of a small village with a D-shaped room and paved courtyards. The shrine contained female figurines, polished cow bones, and mutilated goat skulls.

Two large funerary complexes are associated with the Maltese temples. Both are below ground but follow the same modular design as the temples, being composed of carved rock niches and cavities. The Hal Saflieni Hypogeum at Tarxien is an expansive subterranean structure with large uprights of coralline limestone. It remains the most extensively excavated funerary complex, and was built in three successive phases. The first was a simple tomb built around 3000 B.C., about 2 m in diameter and averaging 2 m below ground. This cemetery space was eventually extended both above and below ground over time. The Brochtorff Circle on Gozo is centered between the Ggantija group and another temple complex (see Bonanno et al. 1990). Artifacts include articulated and disarticulated human remains, small terracotta female figurines and statuettes, and imported goods.

The chronology of construction for the Maltese temple and funerary complexes is lengthy (see Stoddart et al. 1993). The antecedents of these monuments are the shrines and upright stones of the Skoba and Zebbug phases (ca. 4500–3800 B.C.). The temples and funerary complexes were first constructed during the Ggantija phase (ca. 3600–3000 B.C.), and expanded and elaborated during the Tarxien phase (ca. 3000–2500 B.C.). The temples were abandoned during the Tarxien Cemetery phase, at which time funerary rituals switched to the use of new cremation cemeteries (ca. 2500–1500 B.C.). The earliest temple style was the simple lobed design, with a central court and irregular-shaped apses. Then followed the trefoil style that had three apses opening symmetrically off the central court. Some five-apse temples were also built. By 3000 B.C., five-apse temples were converted to four-apse structures by walling off one apse to make a small niche. Many central apses of earlier trefoil temples were also walled off.

The Maltese monuments provide a glimpse into the nature of emerging elite religious power (e.g., Stoddart 1999; Stoddart et al. 1993). One important debate has focused on territorial control of rival and competing social groups (Stoddart et al. 1993:17). Renfrew and Level (1979) argue that these temples signal inter-group competition and political centralization. As temple centers and their population increased (perhaps as many as two thousand per group), competing groups built successively larger

monuments as emerging elites organized and directed temple construction and use (Renfrew 1974). Others have argued that ritual power was
instead decentralized with competing religious factions (Meillassoux 1964,
1967). The lack of any single central place, coupled with the recurrent pair-
ing of temples, supports the argument of decentralized intra-group social
rivalry and completion (Bonanno et al. 1990). In either case, it is clear that
emerging leaders increased control over ritual practice and the ceremonies
associated with the afterlife.

Another debate centers on the rise of the cremation cemeteries after
2500 B.C. (see Bonanno et al. 1990; Stoddart et al. 1993; Trump 1977). One
argument is that this shift represents the abandonment settlements on Malta
and Gozo, followed by eventual migration of new peoples to the islands
(Trump 1977). Stratigraphic evidence at Tarxien has revealed a long period
of abandonment before the conversion to a cemetery. Another argument
is that these cemeteries represent an internal shift in religious expression
(Bonanno et al. 1990). A third possibility is that this shift represents a new
way that elites are doing business, with religious control "giving way" to
a broader-based economic control of external trade (Stoddart et al. 1993).
With their ritual power slowly waning in the wake of increased external
trade contacts, the Maltese elite followed their peers on Crete by exerting
their control on trade goods.

Crete. The last example of Mediterranean monumental elaboration is the
labyrinthine structures of Middle to Late Bronze Age Crete (ca. 2200–
1200 B.C.), the largest of island test cases (8,336 km²). Much has been
written about the Minoan culture and its "palaces" of Homeric legend
(e.g., Driessen et al. 2002; Graham 1987; Hägg and Marinatos 1987;
Hamilakis 2002; Kolb 2004; MacGillivray 2000; Manning 1994; Patton
1996; Rehak and Younger 1998; Renfrew 1972; Watrous 1994), even
though their true function is debatable. The Minoans are regarded as the
Mediterranean's first large complex society, replete with political centralization, organized government, recordkeeping, specialization of labor, and
mass-produced trade goods.

Four labyrinthine palaces were constructed on Crete by 1900 B.C.:
Knossos (13,000 m²), Mallia (7,600 m²), Phaistos (6,500 m²), and Zakros
(2,800 m²). They were built using cut-stone masonry and recessed façades,
embellished with decorated engravings, painted stucco, veneering, and clay
ornamentation. Each palace was a multi-story building consisting of a series
of recessed and projecting rectilinear architectural units, giving the entire
structure an irregular shape and labyrinthine appearance. Vertical pillars

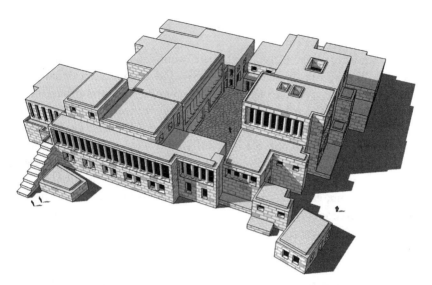

Figure 7.5. Schematic view of the palace at Knossos. Modified after Evans (1921).

included a startling variety of forms, often clustered in particular combinations. The palace at Knossos is shown in Figure 7.5. Palaces were located at places thought to have religious significance and/or provide easy access to the sea.

All palaces contain key architectural features that include: (1) public spaces; (2) clusters of similar room/hall units; and (3) storage magazines and grain silos affiliated with sunken cult rooms. The most prominent feature is a rectangular central court, oriented slightly east of a north–south axis with dimensions that are 2:1 in size proportion. This orientation dictated the general layout of the entire structure, important for optimal sunlight exposure, recognizing sacred mountains and caves, or exposing certain rooms to the rising sun (Shaw 1973). Minoan art and frescoes suggest a variety of court rituals such as bull leaping and group dancing (Davis 1987; Sipahi 2001; Younger 1995), but other possibilities include feasting, astronomical observation, and ceremonial displays. The central court at Knossos held as many as 5,435 people (Gesell 1987), the equivalent of one quarter of the estimated total population of Neopalatial Knossos (Whitelaw 2001:27). Additional public spaces include a plaza entryway at Knossos, Mallia, and Phaistos (see Davis 1987; Marinatos 1987; cf. Driessen et al. 2002), a second-story reception hall at all the palaces, and small auditoriums at Knossos and Phaistos. Possible activities for these secondary public spaces may have included political assemblies, religious gatherings, sporting events, or entertainment.

In contrast to public spaces, the private room/hall units give each palace its maze-like appearance (see Graham 1987). These units, dubbed "Minoan halls," consist of two unequally sized rectangular rooms separated by a row of pillars and piers where a retractable door was set for permitting or restricting the access of movement, air, or light. Some halls also include a third, more private room that contains a short flight of doglegged stairs leading to a toilet and a decorated "lustral basin." This third room may have been used for simple bathing or ritual initiation/purification/rite of passage. In sum, each unit probably served a multi-functional role as living/meeting/ceremonial spaces. A stairway fresco at Knossos and the presence of tablets or sealing archives suggest these rooms may have been used as a meeting place for bureaucratic recordkeepers.

A large amount of palatial space was devoted to storage magazines. These long and narrow rooms were located to the west and north, and commonly contained *pithoi*, large clay storage jars often several feet tall (see Christakis 1999). Storage items probably included grain, wine, olive oil, textiles, and smaller pottery vessels. Large cylindrical semi-subterranean grain silos are also present. At the three largest main palaces these silos were placed in prominent locations outside the west façade in or near the west plaza, suggesting they also served a ritual or symbolic function. Cult rooms known as "pillar crypts" with single or double pillars (see Graham 1987) are closely associated with the storage magazines. The pillars frequently bear carved mason insignias, particularly the prominent Minoan cult symbol of the double-axe. Some also contain pyramidal stone stands for mounting double-axes or other cult emblems.

The construction chronology of Minoan palaces is long and complex. The palaces were first constructed during the Protopalatial Period (ca. 1900–1720 B.C.) and were rebuilt or modified during the Neopalatial (ca. 1720–1470 B.C.), and declined and then abandoned after the violent eruption of Thera ca. 1470 B.C. (cf. Driessen and. Macdonald 1997). Discussions of palatial emergence have emphasized local social, economic, and political factors (e.g., Cherry 1983, 1986; Graham 1987; Hägg and Marinatos 1987; Hamilakis 1999; Hansen 1988; Knappett and Schoep 2000; Manning 1994; Renfrew 1972; Sherratt 1981). General consensus is that the palaces helped an emerging elite class to accumulate and redistribute vital resources such as food and specialized craft items, although specific economic and social motivations are debatable and may include forced specialization, environmental instability, economic control, or trade monopolization.

Table 7.1. Islands and their monuments: descriptive data

	Island		Monuments			
	Area (km²)	Isolation index[a]	Number	Density (/km)	Avg (m²)	Total area (ha)
Rapa Nui	164	149	313	1.9	341	10.7
Maui	1,903	118	250	0.1	924	23.1
Pohnpei	316	108	92 + (1 center)	0.3	1,708	15.7
Menorca	693	35	300	0.4	177	5.3
Malta/Gozo	383	35	40	0.1	324	1.3
Crete	8,336	28	5	0.0006	7,475	3.7

[a] The index of island isolation is calculated by totaling the square roots of the distances to the nearest equivalent or larger island, the nearest island group or archipelago, and the nearest continent. As presented by the United Nations Environmental Programme, located at http://islands.unep.ch.

More research is required to clarify the architectural origins of the Minoan palaces. One potential forerunner of the palaces is the rectangular-shaped "house tomb" and beehive-shaped "*tholos* tomb" of the Pre-Palatial Period (e.g., Branigan 1970, 1993; Goodison 2001; Watrous 1994:715). These slab-lined, collective-style tombs are built on a monumental scale, with house tombs averaging more than 1,000 m² and *tholos* tombs often built with adjacent enclosed courts and an annex of auxiliary rooms built against the circular wall near the entrance (Figure 7.4, B). Sacrificial and ritual activity in some of the adjacent room annexes suggests some sort of worship tied to the dead (Murphy 1998). Perhaps these tombs served as inspiration for a burgeoning Minoan elite class, who after being bolstered economically by trade contacts with Egypt and Mesopotamia, were roused to create a series of administrative and religious "palaces" that followed their own culturally distinctive design.

Comparisons

Quantitative Data. Table 7.1 presents some general descriptive data regarding the six test cases and their monumental sequences. The following variables are used for comparison:

1. Island area (km²).
2. Island isolation index. Based on the United Nations Environmental Programme (http://islands.unep.ch), this measure is calculated by totaling the square roots of the distances to the nearest equivalent or larger island, the nearest island group or archipelago, and the nearest continent.

3. Total number of monuments on an island.
4. Density of monuments (monuments per km²). Variables 3 and 4 measure the degree of dispersal of monumental space.
5. Average monumental size in m². This is a measure of relative labor investment.
6. Total monumental area. This is the sum of the areas of individual monuments; it represents an approximation of how overall space was utilized for collective social activities.

The earliest monuments are the Malta and Gozo temples. They flourished between 3600 and 2600 B.C. in a region that was somewhat isolated within the Mediterranean itself, but according to the Isolation Index (II = 35, 96 km to nearest isle, 96 km to nearest island group, and 240 km to the nearest continent) had easy to moderate access to neighboring landforms. The average monumental structure on Malta/Gozo was quite small, the total area of monumental construction was also small, and they were fairly evenly dispersed across the landscape. The Minoan palaces are next in age, rising into prominence in the eastern Mediterranean from 1900 to 1000 B.C., and functionally/stylistically different from the Maltese monuments. Crete was slightly less insular than Malta/Gozo, and had easy and ready access to neighboring landforms (II = 28, 70 km to nearest isle, 100 km to nearest island group, and 100 km to the nearest continent). At 7,475 m², the average monumental structure on Crete dwarfs those of other islands, although the total of monumental construction was small, and the monument density is 167 times lower than any other island test case (0.0006 monuments/km). The Talayotic period of Minorca stretched from 1700 to 123 B.C., and served as community houses for defense, storage, and sacrifice. Similar to the other Mediterranean isles, Minorca also had easy access to neighboring landforms (II = 35, 40 km to nearest isle, 200 km to nearest island group, and 200 km to the nearest continent). The average *talayot* tower on Minorca was relatively small. There was a moderately small total area of monumental construction, and monuments were relatively dispersed across the landscape.

In the Pacific, the Pohnepian *lulung* of Micronesia was the earliest monuments, utilized between A.D. 1000 and 1500. Most were conglomerated into the city of Nan Madol, but other smaller centers exist as well. Pohnpei was highly insular (II = 108, 20 km to nearest isle, 1,350 km to nearest island group, and 4,500 km to the nearest continent) compared to any of the Mediterranean examples. The average monumental structure on Pohnpei was moderate in size and had a large total area of monumental construction.

The *heiau* temples of Maui, utilized between A.D. 1200 and 1800, were dispersed fairly evenly across the island landscape, yet clusters of temples were located at political centers. Maui was extremely insular (II = 60 km to nearest isle, 2,000 km to nearest island group, and 4,018 km to the nearest continent). The average monumental structure on Maui was moderate in size, and the island had the largest area of monumental construction (n = 250; 23.1 ha). The *ahu* temples of Rapa Nui dominated the landscape of this remote Pacific island from A.D. 1100 to 1500, the most isolated island on earth (II = 149, 2,001 km to nearest isle, 2,001 km to nearest island group, and 3,568 km to the nearest continent). The average monumental structure on Rapa Nui was moderate in size, resulting in a large quantity of monumental construction. The *ahu* temples were highly dispersed across the island landscape, and had highest density among the test cases (1.9 monuments/ha), almost five times greater than any other island monument.

The data in Table 7.1 appear to be interconnected in two ways. First, island isolation positively correlates with monumental elaboration in the form of the total space available for monumental construction. Second, the density of monuments per km² is relatively constant except where island size is very small and very large. Although local processes of social and ritual elaboration for each of the four test cases were undoubtedly important, I argue that two interrelated variables – productive circumscription and social competition – influenced the rise and use of monumental trajectories on islands.

Productive Circumscription. Islands, more so than most other environments, are highly susceptible to geographic circumscription. Circumscription (Carneiro 1970) occurs when social distress peaks as increasing populations become stymied because no new suitable locations are available for economic expansion. This leads to either increased conflict or hierarchical formations that regulate existing resources. Productive circumscription is a product of how concentrated or controllable resources are in any given environment (Earle 1991:10–11), and thus predicts social complexity, especially for early agrarian societies that focus on staple production. Among the test cases, a correlation seems to exist between island isolation index and the total area of monumental construction (see Table 7.1). Rapa Nui, Maui, and Pohnpei have isolation indices that are at least three times greater than any of the Mediterranean islands. Moreover, the Pacific islands also possess a total monumental area that is at least double that of any Mediterranean islands, which measures available space utilized for collective social activities.

Isolation, of course, may represent a proxy measure of environmental circumscription and therefore agro-economic potential. Archaeological evidence indicates that farmers and foragers traveled back and forth from the Mediterranean islands for millennia (see Barker 2004), and therefore could have easily provided an economic and social buffer for those who resided on either island. Crete, given its size and carrying capacity, was self-sustainable throughout antiquity. Malta and Menorca, although perhaps less sustainable in the long term, were no more than 250 km from large landforms. The Pacific islands were probably just as self-sustainable as Malta, particularly Maui, but did not have comparably proximal productive buffers, and so would have more quickly reached maximum carrying capacity and sustainability. The archaeological record is quite clear that Pohnpei was involved in some long-distance trade (probably nonsubsistence goods); the Pacific trade networks were highly sophisticated and regularly spanned thousands of kilometers (see Irwin 1992; Kirch 2000). Rapa Nui, the most isolated place in the world, may have had at least some degree of intermittent contact and exchange with the outside world for a brief period, but not enough to provide an adequate productive buffer.

Social Competition. Social competition is also important to monumental elaboration. Certainly one of the most perplexing facets of island monumentality is the fact that the caloric and economic investments required for monumental construction seem counterproductive in such circumscribed environments. Rapa Nui and its 25 percent increase in food production/caloric intake for monumental construction is a case in point. Obviously, monuments become an important form of currency for social conflict or competition that results in channeling and controlling a set of limited productive resources.

One way to examine the relationship between monumental elaboration and conflict or competition is through the continuum of corporate and exclusionary strategies of social organization (see Feinman, Chapter 3). Corporate strategies are political relations that emphasize collective unity rather than personal aggrandizement, suppressing economic differentiation and deemphasizing personal wealth (Blanton 1998; Blanton et al. 1996; Feinman 1995; Feinman et al. 2000). Corporate organization is linked with local economic production, shared political power, and architecture emphasizing cooperative religious rituals, food production, and boundary maintenance (see Kolb 1997). Exclusionary or networked organization is linked with long-distance economic networks, more centralized/individualized rule, higher degrees of social inequity, and architecture expressing exclusionary elite aggrandizement (such as the palaces and tombs of ancient Egypt).

The dispersed nature, horizontal differentiation, and centrality of the monumental landscape are important measures for assessing the nature of social competition. Interestingly, monument density/dispersal (per km^2) is relatively constant except for the smallest (Rapa Nui) and largest (Crete) islands (see Table 7.1). Rapa Nui has a density at least five times greater than all other islands, and more than a thousand times more than Crete, yet the island is only 1/50th the size of Crete. But Crete has a monument density at least a hundred times less than other islands. This suggests that corporate competition, as measured by monumental dispersal, intensifies on islands that are more environmentally or social circumscribed. A dispersed monumental landscape suggests greater island-wide political participation (and therefore competition), as well as less-centralized control over productive resources. Viewing island monuments as territorial markers (Kolb 1994; Renfrew 1976), or as levers for negotiating religious or ideological activities in exchange for food or economic resources (Rainbird 2007; Stoddart et al. 1993), are two arguments that may explain this type of monumental functionality.

The Rapanuian, Menorcan, and Maltese monuments are good examples of the use of corporate social power. All have small monuments equally distributed across the landscape. They hosted important group-oriented rituals that allowed various social groups to exercise political, spiritual, and economic control. As these monuments became more architecturally complex over time, they served as markers for expressing territorial conflagrations and social dissent between social groups. It is unclear whether power became centralized under one or more elites/social groups over time, but it appears that social friction was on the rise. The eventual shift to cremation burials at both the Maltese temples and the Rapanuian *ahu* platforms indicate a subsequent breakdown of corporate power; on Malta, rule became more authoritative to access external metal exchange and maintain elite power (see Stoddart et al. 1993), and on Rapa Nui, social cohesion collapsed from environmental degradation and civil strife (see Diamond 2005:108).

The Mauian *heiau* temples reveal a mixed pattern of corporate and exclusionary social competition. Their initial use was associated with corporate group competition, coinciding with distinct periods of political tension when it was important to encourage and control social allegiances. It was at this time that some of the largest temples were built. After island unification, temple numbers increased and their size stabilized. Their function shifted to maintaining territorial control and social consensus within a broader exclusionary network of elite centralization.

The Minoan palaces represent the most drastic departure from the corporate strategy of social competition. On Crete, long-distance trade of prestige goods fostered more exclusionary social control, where palaces with their magnificent frescos served as centralizing nodes of organizational development, enhancing the social and ideological stature of local elites. Undoubtedly the rapid changes experienced in the east Mediterranean during the second millennium (e.g., increasing population, more intensive farming, Near Eastern contact, rise of metallurgy) stressed more exclusionary forms of ritual practice and leadership by enhancing social distinctions among individuals. On the other hand, a diverse set of palatial functions seem to indicate the expression of corporate relationships control, even if it were a vestige of the past. These include the public spaces and processional ways, the decentralized use of apartment spaces, and the lack of elite spaces.

The Pohnpeian *lulung* burials/platform structures represent the most fascinating test case, demonstrating an interesting amalgam of corporate and exclusionary monumental elaboration. In one sense, they represent clear indicators of corporate expression: single structures commissioned and built by individual families with the clan support. Their function as residential platforms and burial mounds also denote horizontal differentiation of social control and competition. However, placement of many large *lulung* platforms at the centralizing node of Nan Madol is indicative of exclusionary social competition with a centralized decision-making process. The lack of any larger defining monument at Nan Madol suggests the nature of social competition was still staple-based, not fully exclusionary, and may have been in social transition. The location as a coastal site may have been an attempt to generate long-distance trade networks. But given Nan Madol's isolation, minimal inter-island social network, and lack of any really unique trade goods that enhanced elite control, its centralized society based eventually collapsed.

Conclusions

The goal of this chapter has been to examine the genesis and elaboration of some of the world's most interesting and impressive island monuments through comparative analysis. Although substantial differences exist in the construction, chronology, and location of these monuments, two key similarities exist. First, the nature of monumental construction is intrinsically linked to island isolation and social circumscription. A certain threshold of isolation seems to stimulate a divergence in the way monuments are constructed and utilized. Second, those who built and used these monuments made logical choices for undertaking social competition and negotiating social consensus. As social inequality and economic intensification increased over time, island communities struggled with ways to maintain their collective unity in the face of emerging elites. These monuments represent a variety of expressions for economically and ideologically enhancing long-term authority. In those cases where political and territorial cohesion could be maintained (such as on Maui and Crete), very tangible economic benefits emerged for elites. The pattern of monumental use in island societies has significance for the development of complex societies throughout the world, where the processes of political formation and ritualized ideology can be interwoven with architectonic and economic questions in discussions of historical or archaeological change.

References Cited

Athens, J. Steven 1983 The Megalithic Ruins of Nan Madol. *Natural History* 92(12): 50–61.
Ayres, William S. 1979 Archaeological Survey in Micronesia. *Current Anthropology* 20:598–600.
————. 1993 *Nan Madol Archaeological Fieldwork: Final Report*. Historic Preservation Office, Pohnpei State, Federated Sates of Micronesia.
Ayres, William S., and Rufino Mauricio 1997 Pohnpei Archaeology Component. Salapwuk Archaeology: A Survey of Historic and Cultural Resources on Pohnpei, Federated States of Micronesia. Micronesian Endowment for Historic Preservation, Federated States of Micronesia, U.S. National Park Service, San Francisco.
Ayres, William S., Gordon G. Goles, and Felicia R. Beardsley 1997 Provenance Study of Lithic Material in Micronesia. In *Prehistoric Long-Distance Interaction in Oceania: An Interdisciplinary Study Approach*, edited by Marshal Weisler, pp. 21, 53–67. New Zealand Archaeological Association Monograph, Volume 21.
Barker, Graeme 2004 Agriculture, Pastoralism, and Mediterranean Landscapes in Prehistory. In *The Prehistoric Archaeology of the Mediterranean*, edited by Bernard A. Knapp and Emma Blake, pp. 46–76. Blackwell, London.
Bath, Joyce, and J. Stephen Athens 1990 Prehistoric Social Complexity on Pohnpei: The Saudeleur to Nahnmwarki Transition. In *Recent Advances in Micronesian Archaeology, Micronesia, Supplement 2*, edited by R. L. Hunter-Anderson, pp. 275–90. University of Guam Press, Mangilao.
Gómez Bellard, Carlos 1995 The First Colonization of Ibiza and Formentera (Balearic Islands, Spain): Some More Islands Out of the Stream? *World Archaeology* 26:442–45.

Blanton, Richard 1998 Beyond Centralization: Steps toward a Theory of Egalitarian Behavior. In *Archaic States*, edited by Gary M. Feinman and Joyce Marcus, pp. 135–72. School of American Research Press, Santa Fe.

Blanton, Richard E., Gary M. Feinman, Stephen A. Kowalewski, and Peter N. Peregrine 1996 A Dual-Processual Theory for the Evolution of Mesoamerican Civilization. *Current Anthropology* 37:1–86.

Bonanno, Anthony, Tancred Gouder, Caroline Malone, and Simon Stoddart 1990 Monuments in an Island Society: The Maltese Context. *World Archaeology* 22: 90–205.

Branigan, Keith 1970 *The Tombs of Mesara: A Study of Funerary Architecture and Ritual in Southern Crete, 2800–1700 B.C.* Duckworth, London.

———. 1993 *Dancing with Death: Life and Death in Southern Crete c. 3000–2000 B.C.* Adolf M. Hakkert, Amsterdam.

CalvoTrias, Victor Manuel, Victor M. Guerrero Ayuso, and Bartomeu Salvà Simonet 2001 Arquitectura Ciclópea del Bronce Balear. *El Tall del Temps* 37. El Tall, Mallorca.

Carneiro, Robert L. 1970 A Theory of the Origin of the State. *Science* 169:733–38.

Chapman, Robert W. 1985 The Later Prehistory of Western Mediterranean Europe: Recent Advances. In *Advances in World Archaeology* 4, edited by Fred Wendorf and Angela Close, pp. 115–87. Academic Press, New York.

Cherry, John F. 1983 Evolution, Revolution, and the Origins of Complex Society in Minoan Crete. In *Minoan Society*, edited by O. Krzyszkowska and L. Nixon, pp. 33–45. Bristol Classical Press, Bristol.

———. 1986 Polities and Palaces: Some Problems in Minoan State Formation. In *Peer Polity Interaction and Socio-Political Change*, edited by Colin Renfrew and John F. Cherry, pp. 19–45. Cambridge University Press, Cambridge.

Christakis, Kostas S. 1999 Pithoi and Food Storage in Neopalatial Crete: A Domestic Perspective. *World Archaeology* 31:1–20.

Cordy, Ross 2000 *Exalted Sits the Chief*. Mutual Publishing, Honolulu.

Davis, Ellen N. 1987 The Knossos Miniature Frescoes and the Function of the Central Courts. In *The Function of the Minoan Palaces*, edited by Robin Hägg and Nanno Marinatos, pp. 157–161. Svenska Institutet i Athen, Stockholm.

Diamond, Jared M. 2005 *Collapse: How Societies Choose to Fail or Succeed*. Viking, New York.

Driessen, Jan and Colin Macdonald 1997 *The Troubled Island. Minoan Crete Before and After the Santorini Eruption*. Aegaeum 17. Université de Liège, Liège.

Driessen, Jan, Ilse Schoep, and Robert Laffineur, eds. 2002 *Monuments of Minos: Rethinking the Minoan Palaces*. Aegaeum 23. Université de Liège, Liège.

Earle, Timothy 1991 The Evolution of Chiefdoms. In *Chiefdoms: Power, Economy, and Ideology*, edited by Timothy Earle, pp. 1–15. Cambridge University Press, Cambridge.

———. 1997 *How Chiefs Come to Power*. Stanford University Press, Stanford.

Evans, Arthur 1921 *The Palace of Minos*. Macmillan, London.

Evans, J. D. 1984 Maltese Prehistory: A Reappraisal. In *The Deyà Conference of Prehistory. Early Settlement in the West Mediterranean Islands and the Peripheral areas*, edited by William H. Waldren, Robert Chapman, James Lewthwaite, and

Rex-Clair Kennard, pp. 489–97. International Series, no. S229. British Archaeological Reports, Oxford.

Feinman, Gary M. 1995 The Emergence of Inequality: A Focus on Strategies and Processes. In *Foundations of Social Inequality*, edited by T. Douglas Price and Gary M. Feinman, pp. 255–80. Plenum Press, New York.

Feinman, Gary M., Kent G. Lightfoot, and Steadman Upham 2000 Political Hierarchies and Organizational Strategies in the Puebloan Southwest. *American Antiquity* 65:449–70.

Flenley, John and Paul G. Bahn 2003 *The Enigmas of Easter Island: Island on the Edge.* Oxford University Press, Oxford.

Fornander, Alexander 1969 [1878–80] *An Account of the Polynesian Race, Its Origins and Migration and the Ancient History of the Hawaiian People to the Times of Kamehameha I.* Tuttle, Rutland.

Gasull, Pepa, Vicente Lull, and Encarna Sanahuja 1984 *In Son Fornes I: La Fase Talayotica. Ensayo de reconstrucción socioeconómica de una comunidad prehistórica de la Isla de Mallorca.* International Series, vol. S209. British Archaeological Reports, Oxford.

Gesell, Geraldine C. 1987 The Minoan Place and Public Cult. In *The Function of the Minoan Palaces*, edited by Robin Hägg and Nanno Marinatos, pp. 123–28. Svenska Institutet i Athen, Stockholm.

Goodison, Lucy 2001 From Tholos Tomb to Throne Room: Perceptions of the Sun in Minoan Ritual. In *Potnia. Deities and Religion in the Aegean Bronze Age*, Aegaeum 22, edited by Robert Laffineur and Robin Hägg, pp. 77–88. Université de Liège, Liège.

Graham, J. Walter 1987 *The Palaces of Crete.* Princeton University Press, Princeton.

Hägg, Robin and Nanno Marinatos (editors) 1987 *The Function of Minoan Palaces. Proceedings of the Fourth International Symposium at the Swedish Institute at Athens.* Paul Åströms Förlag, Göteborg.

Hamilakis, Yannis. 1999 Food Technologies/Technologies of the Body: The Social Context of Wine and Oil Production and Consumption in Bronze Age Crete. *World Archaeology* 31:38–54.

Hamilakis, Yannis (editor) 2002 *Labyrinth Revisited: Rethinking Minoan Archaeology.* Oxbow Books, Oxford.

Hansen, Julie M. 1988 Agriculture in the Pre-Historic Aegean: Data versus Speculation. *American Journal of Archaeology* 92:39–52.

Irwin, Geoffrey 1992 *The Prehistoric Exploration and Colonisation of the Pacific.* Cambridge University Press, New York.

Kirch, Patrick V. 1985 *Feathered Gods and Fishhooks.* University of Hawai'i Press, Honolulu.

———. 2000 *On the Road of the Winds.* University of California Press, Berkeley.

Knappett, Carl and Ilse Schoep 2000 Continuity and Change in Minoan Palatial Power. *Antiquity* 74:365–71.

Kolb, Michael J. 1992 Diachronic Design Changes in Heiau Temple Architecture from the Island of Maui, Hawai'i. *Asian Perspectives* 31:9–37.

———. 1994 Monumentality and the Rise of Religious Authority in Pre-Contact Hawai'i. *Current Anthropology* 35:521–47.

———. 1997 Labor, Ethnohistory, and the Archaeology of Community in Hawai'i. *Journal of Archeological Method and Theory* 4:265–86.

———. 1999 Monumental Grandeur and Political Florescence in Pre-Contact Hawai'i: Excavations at Pi'ilanihale heiau, Maui. *Archaeology in Oceania* 34:71–82.

———. 2004 The Genesis of Monuments among the Mediterranean Islands. In *The Prehistoric Archaeology of the Mediterranean*, edited by Bernard A. Knapp and Emma Blake, pp. 156–79. Blackwell, London.

———. 2006 The Origins of Monumental Architecture in Ancient Hawai'i. *Current Anthropology* 46(4):657–64.

Kolb, Michael J. and Boyd Dixon 2002 Landscape of War: Rules and Conventions of Conflict in Ancient Hawai'i (and elsewhere). *American Antiquity* 67:514–34.

Lewis, H. 1977 *Ancient Malta: A Study of Its Antiquities*. Smythe, Gerrards Cross.

MacGillivray, J. A. 2000 *Minotaur. Sir Arthur Evans and the Archaeology of the Minoan Myth*. Hill and Wang, New York.

Manning, Sturt 1994 The Emergence of Divergence: Development and Decline on Bronze-Age Crete and the Cyclades. In *Development and Decline in the Mediterranean Bronze Age*, edited by Clay Mathers and Simon Stoddart, pp. 221–70. J. Collis, Sheffield.

Marinatos, Nanno 1987 Public Festivals in the West Courts of the Palaces. In *The Function of the Minoan Palaces*, edited by Robin Hägg and Nanno Marinatos, pp. 135–43. Svenska Institutet i Athen, Stockholm.

Martinsson-Wallin, Helene 1994 *Ahu, the Ceremonial Stone Structures of Easter Island: Analyses of Variation and Interpretation of Meanings*. Societas Archaeologica Upsaliensis, Uppsala University, Uppsala.

Meillassoux, Claude 1964 *Anthropologie économique des Gouro de Côte d'Ivoire: De l'économie de subsistance à l'agriculture commerciale*. Mouton, The Hague.

———. 1967 Récherche d'un niveau de détermination dans la société Cynégétrique. *L'Homme et la Société* 6:24–36.

Morgan, William N. 1988 *Prehistoric Architecture in Micronesia*. University of Texas Press, Austin.

Murphy, Joanne 1998 The Nearness of You: Proximity and Distance in Early Minoan Funerary Landscapes. In *Cemetery and Society in the Aegean Bronze Age*, edited by Keith Branigan, pp. 27–40. Sheffield Academic Press, Sheffield.

Myers, Eleanor E. and Gerald Cadogan, eds. 1992 *The Aerial Atlas of Ancient Crete*. University of California Press, Berkeley.

Patton, Mark 1996 *Islands in Time: Island Sociogeography and Mediterranean Prehistory*. Routledge, London.

Pavel, Pavel 1990 Reconstruction of the Transport of Moai. In *State and Perspectives of Scientific Research in Easter Island Culture*, edited by Heide-Margaret Esen-Bauer, pp. 141–44. Courier Forschungsinstitut Senckenburg, Frankfurt.

Plantalamor, L. and M. C. Rita 1984 Formas de población durante el segundo y primero milenio B.C. en Menorca: Son Merver de Baix, transición entre la cultura Pretalayotica y Talayotica. In *The Deyà Conference of Prehistory. Early Settlement in the West Mediterranean Islands and the Peripheral Areas*, edited by William

H. Waldren, Robert Chapman, James Lewthwaite, and Rex-Clair Kennard, pp. 797–826. International Series, vol. S229. British Archaeological Reports, Oxford.

Rainbird, Paul 2004 *The Archaeology of Micronesia.* Cambridge University Press, Cambridge.

———. 2007 *The Archaeology of Islands.* Cambridge University Press, Cambridge.

Rehak, Paul and John G. Younger 1998 Review of Aegean Prehistory VII: Neopalatial, Final Palatial, and Postpalatial Crete. *American Journal of Archaeology* 102: 91–173.

Renfrew, Colin 1972 *The Emergence of Civilization.* Methuen, London.

———. 1974 Beyond a Subsistence Economy. In *Reconstructing Complex Societies*, edited by Charlotte B. Moore, 20, pp. 69–96. Supplement to the Bulletin of American School of Prehistoric Research, Cambridge, MA.

———. 1976 Megaliths, Territories, and Populations. In *Acculturation and Continuity in Atlantic Europe*, edited by S. DeLaet, pp. 198–220. Dissertationes Archaeologicae Gandenses, Ghent.

Renfrew, Colin and Eric V. Level 1979 Exploring Dominance: Predicting Polities from Centers. In *Transformations: Mathematical Approaches to Culture Change*, edited by Colin Renfrew and Kenneth L. Cooke, pp. 145–67. Academic Press, New York.

Rita, C. 1988 The Evolution of the Minorcan Pretalayotic Culture as Evidenced by the Sites of Morellet and Son Mercer de Baix. *Proceedings of the Prehistoric Society* 54:241–47.

Shaw, J. W. 1973 The Orientation of the Minoan Palaces. *Antichità Cretesi Studi in onore di Doro Levi* 2:47–59.

Sherratt, Andrew 1981 Plough and Pastoralism: Aspects of the Secondary Products Revolution. In *Pattern of the Past: Studies in Honour of David Clark*, edited by Glynn Isaac, Ian Hodder, and Norman Hammond, pp. 261–305. Cambridge University Press, New York.

Sipahi, Tunc 2001 New Evidence from Anatolia Regarding Bull-Leaping Scenes in the Art of the Aegean and the Near East. *Anatolica* 27:107–25.

Stoddart, Simon 1999 Long-Term Dynamics of an Island Community; Malta 5500 B.C. – 2000 A.D. In *Social Dynamics of Prehistoric Central Mediterranean*, edited by Robert H. Tykot, Jonathan Morter and John E. Robb, pp. 137–47. Accordia Specialist Studies on the Mediterranean 3. Accordia Research Institute, University of London, London.

Stoddart, Simon, Anthony Bonanno, Tancred Gouder, Caroline Malone, and David Trump 1993 Cult in an Island Society: Prehistoric Malta in the Tarxien Period. *Cambridge Archaeological Journal* 3:3–19.

Trump, David H. 1972 *Malta: An Archaeological Guide.* Faber and Faber, London.

———. 1977 The Collapse of the Maltese Temples. In *Problems in Economic and Social Archaeology*, edited by Gale d. G. Sieveking, Ian H. Longworth, and K. E. Wilson, pp. 605–09. Westview, Boulder.

———. 2002 *Malta: Prehistory and Temples.* Midsea Books, Valetta, Malta.

Valeri, Valerio 1985 *Kingship and Sacrifice.* University of Chicago Press, Chicago.

Van Tilburg, Jo Anne 1994 *Easter Island: Archaeology, Ecology, and Culture.* Smithsonian Institution Press, Washington.

Van Tilburg, Jo Anne and Ted Ralston 2005 Megaliths and Mariners: Experimental Archaeology on Easter Island. In *Onward and Upward: Papers in Honor of Clement W. Meighan*, edited by Keith L. Johnson, pp. 279–306. Stansbury Publishing, Chico, CA.

Waldren, William H. 1982 *Balearic Prehistoric Ecology and Culture*. S149. British Archaeological Reports, Oxford.

———. 1992 *Radiocarbon and Other Isotopic Age Determinations from the Balearic Islands: A Comprehensive Inventory*. 26. Deyà Archaeological Museum and Research Centre, Mallorca.

Watrous, Livingston V. 1994 Review of Aegean Prehistory III: Crete from Earliest Prehistory through the Protopalatial Period. *American Journal of Archaeology* 98: 695–753.

Watrous, Livingston V., Despoina Chatzåe-Vallianou, Harriet Blitzer, and John Bennet 2004 *The Plain of Phaistos: Cycles of Social Complexity in the Mesara Region of Crete*. Cotsen Institute of Archaeology, Los Angeles.

Whitelaw, Todd 2001 From Sites to Communities: Defining the Human Dimensions of Minoan Urbanism. In *Urbanism in the Aegean Bronze Age*, edited by Kevin Branigan, pp. 15–37. Sheffield Studies in Aegean Archaeology. University of Sheffield, Sheffield.

Younger, John G. 1995 Bronze-Age Aegean Representations of Aegean Bull-Games, III. In *Politeia: Society and State in the Aegean Bronze Age. Aegaeum 12*, edited by Robert Laffineur and W. D. Niemeier, pp. 507–45. Université de Liège, Histoire de l'art et archéologie de la Grèce antique, Liège.

CHAPTER 8

POWER AND LEGITIMATION

POLITICAL STRATEGIES, TYPOLOGY, AND CULTURAL EVOLUTION

Peter Peregrine

Tell Mardikh lies on an arid plain to the east of Hamas, Syria. It is not an unlikely place for an ancient city, nor is it a particularly obvious one. It is surrounded by tillable land, and is adjacent to the Orontes River valley. It is not a particularly impressive site. It has massive walls, the ruins of which can be seen for several miles, but they are no larger than those surrounding many tell sites in northern Syria. What makes Tell Mardikh special are the more than 15,000 clay tablets discovered *in situ* in what appears to have been a royal archive, tablets that offer a remarkable portrait of an ancient empire (Matthiae 1981). Without the archive of tablets, Tell Mardikh is one among several Early Bronze Age city-states in northern Syria, each controlling a modest hinterland of agricultural fields and pasturage (e.g., Wilkinson 1994). With the archive, Tell Mardikh becomes the center of control for an empire that stretched across much of what is today northern Syria and Iraq and southeastern Turkey (Pettinato 1991).

Tell Mardikh illustrates an assumption that underlies the rest of this chapter: The past is more complex than the archaeological record makes it appear. This assumption is, in my opinion, a fairly uncontroversial one, and is a logical extension of what we know about the archaeological record. However, it also problematizes much of traditional thought in archaeology, for example, Yoffee's Rule, which asserts that "if you can argue whether a society is a state or isn't, then it isn't" (Yoffee 2005:41).

Yoffee's Rule (and, by extension, much of traditional thought in archaeology) represents an inherently conservative approach to prehistory. It suggests that political complexity (the state) does not arise easily or commonly, and if the presence of a state cannot be demonstrated beyond any doubt, an archaeologist is forced to withhold statehood from the political entity. It also suggests (despite arguments to the contrary, e.g., Yoffee 2005:31) regularity and stability in political formations, that once a state arises, its presence will be obvious to any knowledgeable observer. Finally, Yoffee's Rule suggests clarity in the archaeological record, that what is found is unambiguous to scholars, and accurately represents political formations as they existed in the past.

I have a far different approach to prehistory, an approach that I think is nicely illustrated by the example of Tell Mardikh. In my approach, political formations are best perceived as fluid and changing, representing the strategies of political leaders as they attempt to establish and maintain authority (Blanton et al. 1996; cf. Yoffee 2005:176–79). These strategies sometimes involve actively promoting the leader's authority; other times they involve masking it (Peregrine 1999). For this reason I do not assume that the archaeological record provides a stable or unambiguous record of political formations; rather, I believe the archaeological record requires careful examination and a coherent theory of political behavior in order to be understood (cf. Yoffee 2005:31–41). Scholars with different theories may come to different conclusions, and this is to be expected. The final judgment of which conclusion is correct must be based on explanatory power, not simply whether or not all parties agree.

More importantly, my approach assumes that conclusions about prehistory will change as more archaeological work is done (e.g., Bloch 1953:23, 58). Archaeologists by necessity work with nonrandom samples of the past. We have no idea what the population we study looks like, and therefore we have no way to generate a truly representative sample from it. What this means for us is that whatever we identify from the samples we obtain probably masks a great deal of diversity that we are not finding, because the probability of finding low-frequency items is very small. In other words, it is likely that we are missing a lot, and thus it is reasonable to assume that there is more diversity than what we appear to be finding.

Variation and Typology

The inherent complexity of the archaeological record forces us to categorize, if only to make sense of what we find. This categorization has often been done using descriptive criteria, that is, particular traits or constellations of traits regularly found in association. For example, a state is variously defined as a polity having three or more levels of settlement hierarchy (Wright and Johnson 1975), as a society having marked differences in access to resources (e.g., Flannery 1972), or one having monumental architecture (e.g., Flannery 1998), or a combination of such traits. Each of these is a plausible material indicator of the presence of a political state, yet each seems to avoid the reality that states are not monolithic and immutable

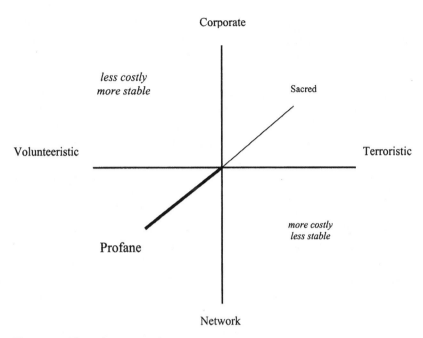

Figure 8.1. Three dimensions of strategy. The X dimension reflects strategies for implementation of power. The Y dimension reflects strategies for construction of power. The Z dimension reflects strategies for the source of power.

things, but rather vary and are subject to change over time. One problem with the typological approach is that it masks the variation known to be present within defined types.

A second problem with the typological approach is that, when considering change, typologies encourage us to think in terms of neoevolutionary "stages" (e.g., bands, tribes, chiefdoms, states). It is against this kind of simplistic neoevolutionary-stage thinking that Yoffee's Rule is really meant to stand. We should not envision a state just because we think it should be there, following a chiefdom; rather, Yoffee would argue, states are both unique and diverse political formations that no simple categorization accurately captures. I agree, but I also argue that a more nuanced approach to the neoevolutionary problem is needed. Because the past is always more complex than the archaeological record makes it appear, no typology can accurately reflect the past, as we cannot know what range of variation we have captured and what we have missed. What we should do, instead, is to consider social formations from a multidimensional perspective, focusing on variation and ranges of variation rather than on traits and their presence or absence.

Figure 8.1 displays my conception of a multidimensional approach to the typology of political formations. It presents three separate dimensions, each of which shows a range of possible strategies that political leaders employ in the exercise of power. The Y dimension has been discussed at length by Blanton et al. (1996) and has been employed by scholars working in the Southeast, the Southwest, and Mexico (e.g., Blanton 1998; King 2006; Peregrine 2001). On this dimension, which I call here the construction of political power, corporate strategies are those in which leaders attempt to build a power base by developing and promoting activities that reinforce the corporate bonds tying members of the polity together. A common corporate strategy is, for example, to mobilize goods from across a polity for large public rituals or construction projects that bring members of the polity together in corporate-affirming activities. On the opposite end of this dimension are network strategies. Leaders following a network strategy attempt to build a power base by controlling access to networks of exchange and alliance both within and outside the polity. Thus a network strategy is one in which leaders attempt to monopolize sources of power, whereas a corporate strategy is one in which leaders attempt to share power across different groups and sectors of a polity (see discussion by Feinman, Chapter 3).

The X dimension reflects what I call strategies for the implementation of political power. At one end is the implementation of power to terrorize individuals within the polity. In this strategy, political leaders essentially force individuals, through the threat of persecution and death, to follow them. It is a strategy that seems all too familiar today. On the other end of this dimension is the implementation of power to encourage individuals within the polity to volunteer their time, talents, and resources to support the polity. In one sense, this might be similar to the kind of selfless volunteerism that brings people together to build houses for the homeless or to enlist in the military when they see their society threatened. In another sense, volunteerism can be seen akin to the way Foucault (1977) envisions polities creating self-disciplined individuals by defining the conditions of a "natural" or "just" society, and creating mechanisms through which individuals feel compelled (internally, if possible) to seek to obtain those conditions. Utopian communes certainly fall on this end of the implementation of power continuum, but for Foucault (and others, e.g., Toulmin 1990) the entire Enlightenment "project" was one promoted by political elites to establish and maintain a new political system in the aftermath of the Thirty Years' War. For these scholars, Westfalian nation-states are rooted in what I am here calling a volunteeristic strategy for the implementation of political power.

The Z dimension in Figure 8.1 represents strategies for establishing the source of power. At one end of this dimension is a purely supernatural source, a strategy in which political leaders claim the source of their power comes directly from the supernatural, the gods, magical knowledge, ancestors. At the other end of this dimension is a purely profane, earthly, social source, in which power comes from the will of the people through, for example, direct election. Kin-based strategies lie somewhere in the middle. A political leader might claim the source of their power is rank within a clan (a more socially oriented strategy) and the clan's relationship to the original founder of the polity (a more supernaturally oriented strategy). Divine kingship and Western democracies perhaps define the ends of the spectrum of strategies for establishing the source of power.

To illustrate and explore this multidimensional approach, I employ a comparative method that is somewhat different from those employed by others in this volume (see discussion in Smith and Peregrine, Chapter 2). Termed holocultural, this method employs a random sample of cases, each a single community at a single point in time, drawn from a well-defined population of cases designed to reflect the range of variation in the cultures of the world (see Ember and Ember 2009). Variables of interest are coded from primary ethnographic documents, and then compared to identify patterns of variation and intervariable correlations that, because they are found in a random sample, can be (at least probabilistically) generalized to all the cultures of the earth. The Human Relations Area Files (HRAF) provides an online, digitized population of such cases, each with an extensive collection of indexed primary source material for coding variables. Numerous variables coded by other researchers are also available through the journals *Ethnology*, *Cross-Cultural Research*, and *World Cultures*.

For this analysis a random sample of twenty-six ethnographic cases from the HRAF probability sample were coded for each dimension of political strategy (Bramm 2001). Coding was conducted by a single coder, who recorded all the information pertinent to each of the dimensions, and then gave each case a rating on a five-point scale for each dimension (Bramm 2001:45–47). The coder also determined whether the case was a band, tribe, chiefdom, or a state according to criteria derived from Service (1962). Both the codebook and data are presented here as an appendix.

Figure 8.2 presents a scattergram of the ethnographic cases as coded on the three dimensions of political strategy. Clearly these dimensions provide an adequate way to separate the cases, and thus, seem an appropriate set of variables to discuss similarities and differences among the cases.

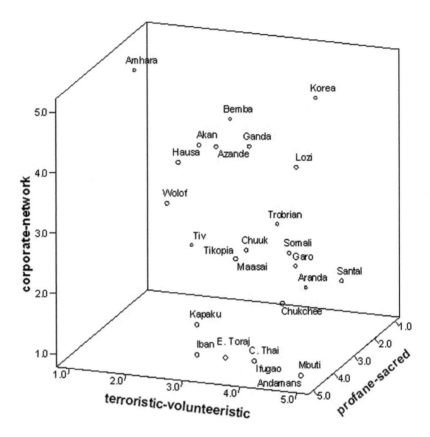

Figure 8.2. Scattergram of twenty-six ethnographic cases as coded on three dimensions of political strategy.

However, there does appear to be a trend among the variables such that more corporate-oriented strategies are also more profane and volunteeristic in their orientation (multiple regression R-squared of .497 with corporate-network as the dependent variable). Figure 8.3 shows separate scattergrams for each dimension, and also illustrates modest but statistically significant intercorrelations between the corporate-network variable and the two other dimensions of political strategy (also see Table 8.1). So, the three dimensions are not completely independent, but, because they separate the cases well, they do seem to be useful variables for exploring diversity in political formations.

How does this multidimensional approach relate to "classic" neoevolutionary typologies? Table 8.2 illustrates the relationship between the three

Table 8.1. Kendall's Tau-b correlations between three dimensions of political strategy

Political strategy	Corporate-Network	Terroristic-Volunteeristic	Sacred-Profane
Corporate-Network	1.000		
Terroristic-Volunteeristic	−.407(*)	1.000	
Sacred-Profane	−.507(*)	.251	1.000

* Correlation is significant at the 0.01 level (2-tailed).

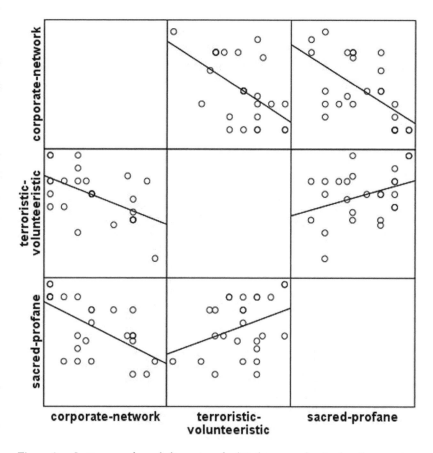

Figure 8.3. Scattergrams for each dimension of political strategy, showing best fit regression line.

Table 8.2. Kendall's Tau-b correlations between dimensions of political strategy
and classic neoevolutionary typologies

	Corporate-Network	Terroristic-Volunteeristic	Sacred-Profane
Service (1962)	.620(**)	−.381(*)	−.357(*)
Fried (1967)	.355(*)	−.418(*)	−.168

** Correlation is significant at the 0.01 level (2-tailed).
* Correlation is significant at the 0.05 level (2-tailed).

dimensions of political strategy and two classic neoevolutionary typologies, those of Service (1962) and Fried (1967). Interestingly, there are
a number of statistically significant correlations. Indeed, the correlation
between the corporate-network variable and Service's neoevolutionary
types is fairly strong, and both the other dimensions of political strategy
also show statistically significant correlations, although more modest. Does
this imply that the dimensions of political strategy are just another neoevolutionary scheme? No. What it shows is that these dimensions do reflect

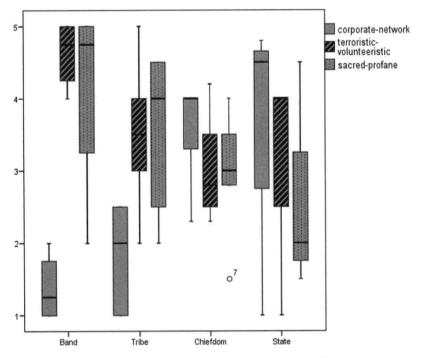

Figure 8.4. Boxplot of three dimensions of political strategy grouped by neoevolutionary
types as defined by Service (1962).

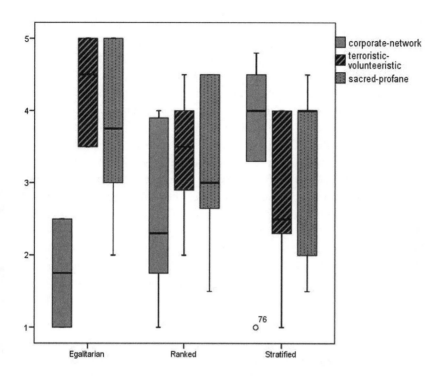

Figure 8.5. Boxplot of three dimensions of political strategy grouped by neoevolutionary types as defined by Fried (1967).

general trends in human societies, just as do neoevolutionary typologies. But because they are continuous dimensions, they do not limit our ability to see or explore variation in the way that neoevolutionary classifications do.

The relationship between the dimensions of political strategy and classic neoevolutionary typologies can be seen more clearly in Figures 8.4 and 8.5. Figure 8.4 is a boxplot of the three dimensions grouped by Service's band, tribe, chiefdom, and state types, whereas Figure 8.5 shows the dimensions grouped by Fried's egalitarian, ranked, and stratified types. In Figure 8.4, it is apparent that bands and tribes are strongly associated with corporate strategies, while chiefdoms and states have a tendency to be associated with more network-oriented strategies. This makes some sense if we think about the organization of bands and tribes (and, of course, recognizing that there is a range of variation within these types). They are rooted in kinship; in other words, in corporate groups. There are little possibilities for aggrandizement, and indeed there are often active social control mechanisms preventing it. Thus, purely network-oriented strategies are not practical in bands or tribes. The same argument could be made for egalitarian societies as shown in Figure 8.5. It is interesting that states demonstrate the full range of corporate-network strategies. This suggests a fuller range of political strategies may be available to leaders in states.

States demonstrate a range of strategies for the implementation and legitimation of power as well, whereas bands (and egalitarian societies as shown in Figure 8.5) tend to be strongly volunteeristic. Again, this may be because of the limited ability of emergent leaders in bands to use force – it simply is not an option. And the use of true, terroristic force and strongly sacred strategies seems limited to states – neither tribes nor chiefdoms employ them, nor do the ranked societies shown in Figure 8.5. This is likely because of limits on leaders' authority in these societies. Because, by definition, there are no formal social classes in either chiefdoms or ranked societies, it may be impossible for leaders to adopt a strategy that differentiates them as "divine" rulers or gives them absolute power to use force. Thus, once again, limitations inherent in the sociopolitical formations of these societies limit the range of strategies that leaders in these polities might employ.

Political Strategy and Typology

There are regular associations between the dimensions of political strategy I have defined here and classic neoevolutionary typologies. I hypothesize that these associations exist because the strategies used by leaders impact and can shape other aspects of culture; that is, the correlations between neoevolutionary types and political strategies exist because particular political strategies tend to create particular constellations of social forms. Thus political strategies, although not in themselves social or political "types," may function to create what might be seen as social or political "types." Table 8.3 presents the results of bivariate and partial correlations designed to illustrate this point.

Table 8.3 demonstrates that more corporate-oriented societies tend to have multifamily dwellings, while more network-oriented societies tend to have dwellings where single families or individuals reside alone. This trend is present even when controlling for classification into Service's band, tribe, chiefdom, and state typology. What this suggests is that people tend to live more communally in more corporately oriented societies, and to live in more isolation in more network-oriented societies. Although a causal relationship cannot be established by these correlations, it seems that political strategy and household form tend to co-vary in a way that suggests that

Table 8.3. Correlations between dimensions of political strategy and other social variables. The top number for each variable is a Kendall's Tau-b correlation, while the bottom number is a partial correlation controlling for Service's (1962) classic neoevolutionary typology

	Corporate-Network	Terroristic-Volunteeristic	Sacred-Profane
Household Form	.482(**)	−.298	−.242
	.490(*)	−.257	−.139
Family Size	.171	−.430(**)	−.140
	.088	−.519(**)	−.092
Descent-Membership in Corporate Kinship Groups	−.348(*)	.247	.525(**)
	−.378	.174	.599(**)

** Correlation is significant at the 0.01 level (2-tailed).
* Correlation is significant at the 0.05 level (2-tailed).

both reflect a basic ideology – one more group-oriented, the other more individualistic. I further suggest that this variation stems from the political leaders and the strategies they employ to construct power. Their strategies flow outward and permeate society, affecting many aspects of life, including household form.

The strategies leaders use to implement power, I suggest, also affect society, and evidence to support this suggestion is presented in Table 8.3. The second line of the table shows that more terroristic-oriented societies tend to have extended families, whereas more volunteeristic-oriented societies tend to have nuclear families. This may seem an odd relationship, but I suggest it makes sense if we think of a permeating ideology shaping family life. In more terroristic societies, leaders implement power through the threat of force. In this situation, families might consolidate – brothers joining one another, fathers and sons cooperating – as a form of resistance to power. No such resistance is necessary when volunteerism is the prevailing ideology. In such a society, a nuclear family can thrive even in times of difficulty because the family knows that others are available to help.

Finally, Table 8.3 suggests that societies in which leaders legitimate power through more sacred means tend to be more matrilineal in orientation, whereas those in which leaders use more profane means tend to be more bilateral in orientation. It is important to note that there is a statistically significant correlation between this variable and household form (matrilineal societies tend to have larger dwellings – see, e.g., Ember 1973), and thus also with strategies for the construction of power. The correlation, however, weakens when membership in Service's neoevolutionary

Table 8.4. Cross-tabulation of recoded sacred-profane
and descent group membership variables.

	More sacred	More profane	
Descent groups present	11 (8.5)	6 (8.5)	17
Descent groups absent	2 (4.5)	7 (4.5)	9
TOTAL	13	13	26

Chi-squared = 4.248; p =.039; Fisher's exact p = .048.
Kendall's Tau-b = .404; p =.024.
Expected values are shown in parentheses.

typology is controlled for, probably because both bands and states tend to have bilateral kinship. The correlation between sacred power strategies and matrilineality is a less obvious one than the others presented in the table. I believe it stems from the focus on ancestor veneration and the totems and taboos that are present in many societies with descent groups. In this way the correlation is more one between sacred strategies and the presence of descent groups versus profane strategies and the lack of them. This association is presented in Table 8.4, which shows that descent groups are more likely to be present in more sacred-oriented societies than expected, whereas they are more likely to be absent in more profane-oriented societies than expected.

Tables 8.3 and 8.4, then, demonstrate an association between sacred strategies for legitimating power and the presence of descent groups. Is it reasonable to suggest that political leaders actively create descent groups through implementing a sacred strategy? No. But it is reasonable to suggest that leaders implementing a sacred strategy might emphasize and utilize existing sacred beliefs in descent-based societies, and thus make a sacred strategy more practical, and more likely, in a society where descent groups are present. In this way political strategy and social organization respond one another dialectically, each changing to adapt as the other changes and adapts in response. It is this dynamic process of leaders implementing strategies in the face of existing social conditions, and by doing so, affecting the social conditions and perhaps the political strategy itself, which I suggest underlies political process in human societies.

Political Strategy and Cultural Evolution

When considering political strategy from the perspective of leaders, I assume that maintaining power is the basic, underlying goal of political

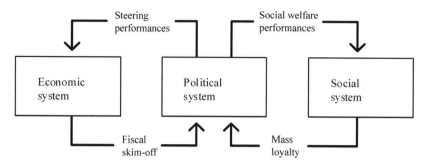

Figure 8.6. Habermas's conception of Capitalist sociopolitical organization.

actions (e.g., Machiavelli 1513). The most basic political activity from this perspective is one of legitimation (see Stark and Chance, Chapter 9), and the primary threat to legitimation is what has been called a "legitimation crisis" (Habermas 1973; Peregrine 1999).

Figure 8.6 is a diagram of Habermas's (1973) conception of the Capitalist system. On the far left is the economic system, the privately owned enterprises that produce goods and services for profit. The arrows going to and from it show how it is aided by the political system, which develops laws and policies beneficial to economic interests, and which works with other polities to maintain favorable conditions for growth. In this way, the political system helps to steer the economic system to maximum performance for private, profit-driven interests. In return, the economic system financially supports the political system, which cannot maintain itself otherwise because it produces nothing beyond steering the economic system and providing social welfare, which leads to the other side of the diagram.

The right side of Figure 8.6 shows the sociocultural system, basically the traditions, beliefs, norms, values, expectations, and the like that are shared by members of the polity. As the figure shows, these traditions are aided by the polity through social welfare programs that support them, leading, in turn, to mass popular support for the polity. The political system uses financial resources generated through the economic system to support the sociocultural system, which, in turn, legitimates the polity's existence and right to govern; that is, its right to create and implement laws and policies beneficial to the maximum operation of the economic system. This interdependency is the basis of Habermas's view of Capitalist societies and the basis of his conception of legitimation crises.

Because the three systems are tightly interdependent, a crisis in any one of them may lead to a systemic crisis of the whole. However, Habermas (1973) suggests that the weak point in the system is in the "mass loyalty" arrow leading from the sociocultural system to the political system. His reason for this is complicated, but is basically that the political system can control everything except people's "rational" minds, and crises in any part of the system are going to tend to produce crises in legitimation, precisely because it cannot be readily controlled. Habermas argues that an environmental calamity or crisis in the subsistence economy is not a necessary, or even common, precondition for collapse; rather, a crisis in the sociocultural system, a legitimation crisis, is a more likely source of political collapse.

As I have argued elsewhere (Peregrine 1999), legitimation crises are not confined to Capitalist economies alone, but can be seen in a wide range of economic systems, especially those in which economic stability is considered something a political leader can provide. Stability may come from active management of the economic system (as in the case of Capitalism), or from perceived manipulation of natural and supernatural forces. But in either case, where it is part of a political leader's job to ensure economic stability, to ensure, at minimum, that people have enough to survive, a legitimation crisis may ensue far sooner than an economic crisis if the people perceive an economic crisis is imminent, even possible. To stave off a legitimation crisis, a leader might turn to an alternate strategy of maintaining mass loyalty, a strategy to contain the emergent crisis – a "strategy of containment" (Jameson 1981).

The concept of political strategies of containment was, like that of legitimation crises, developed to understand the modern Capitalist system, but there is no inherent reason it cannot be usefully applied to non-Capitalist societies (Jameson 1981:9–10). A strategy of containment is intended "to 'manage' historical and social, deeply political impulses, that is to say, to defuse them, to prepare substitute gratifications for them, and the like" (Jameson 1981:266). Such strategies can take many forms, and are often developed in the face of specific political or economic challenges (Jameson 1981:267). These strategies are also not a pure creation of political leaders, but are produced in the context of resistance: "This process cannot be grasped as one of sheer violence . . . nor as one inscribing the appropriate attitudes on a blank slate, but must necessarily involve a complex strategy of rhetorical persuasion in which substantial incentives are offered for ideological adherence" (Jameson 1981:287).

I also assume that leaders facing a potential crisis will adopt strategies of containment that they can implement without much social endorsement; that is, ones they can implement largely by themselves. Looking at Figure 8.2, these strategies might include network means of constructing

Table 8.5. Kendall's Tau-b correlations between political strategies and selected cost and stability variables

		Corporate-Network	Terroristic-Volunteeristic	Sacred-Profane
Cost factors	Jurisdictional Hierarchy Beyond Local Community	.580**	−.326*	−.309*
	Political Role Differentiation: Full-Time Specialists	−.515**	.272	.366*
	Enforcement specialists (police, tax collectors)	−.577**	.272	.457*
	Taxation paid to community	−.632**	.109	.444*
Stability factors	Unstable Political Power Index	−.071	−.429*	−.138
	Food Stress or Hunger	.411**	−.164	−.317*
	Perceptions of Political Leaders' Benevolence	−.530*	.218	.681**
	Conflict (Social or Political) in the local community	−.091	.070	.404*

* Correlation is significant at the 0.05 level (1-tailed).
** Correlation is significant at the 0.01 level (1-tailed).

power, terroristic means of implementing power, and supernatural means of establishing the source of power.

I hypothesize that there are different "costs" associated with implementing different strategies and that some are more difficult to maintain. Table 8.5 presents evidence supporting these hypotheses. In Table 8.5, each strategy is correlated with a series of variables intended to measure the relative cost and stability of the strategy. The first four row variables in the table are cost factors. They are considered "costly" because they require more individuals to be supported by the polity or, in the case of taxation, are a direct measure of costs borne by the polity. The last four row variables are stability factors. They are intended to measure the relative degree of social stress or unrest in the polity. None of these variables is a direct measure of either cost or stability, but together they provide a general picture of the relative cost and stability of the various strategies.

The corporate-network strategy demonstrates the clearest pattern in terms of relative cost. More corporate-oriented polities tend to have fewer levels of hierarchy, less role differentiation, fewer specialists, and fewer taxes than more network-oriented polities. In terms of terroristic-volunteeristic strategies, the relative costs are not clear, although terroristic-oriented polities appear to require greater levels of jurisdictional hierarchy. Finally, sacred-oriented polities appear to require greater levels of jurisdictional hierarchy than more profane-oriented ones, as well as greater role differentiation, more specialists, and more taxes. It would appear from these variables that corporate and profane strategies are less costly than others, and that volunteeristic strategies may be less costly.

In terms of relative stability, both corporate-network and sacred-profane strategies again demonstrate a fairly clear pattern. Corporate-oriented polities tend to have less food stress than network-oriented ones, and leaders appear to be perceived as more benevolent. In sacred-oriented polities, the opposite appears to be true, and both conflict and food stresses are more pronounced than in more profane-oriented polities. There is not a clear trend for terroristic-volunteeristic strategies, but it appears that terroristic-oriented polities are more generally unstable than volunteeristic-oriented polities. From this it would appear that corporate and profane strategies are more stable than others, and volunteeristic strategies may be more stable.

I further hypothesize that less costly, more stable formations of these strategies will survive for longer time periods than more costly and less stable ones. However, in the face of crisis, leaders will implement more costly and unstable strategies to contain the crisis. The ensuing struggle is the process of history. But why would leaders choose more costly, less stable strategies? I propose that in a crisis a leader will choose a strategy over which they have relatively strong control (e.g., network, terroristic, sacred), and where only a handful of key supporters are needed to implement the strategy. Corporate, volunteeristic, and profane strategies require societal endorsement, a time-consuming and often difficult process, especially in the face of crisis. This means that leaders' choices are constrained. Although they may want to implement a more stable and less costly strategy, the opportunity may not be present.

Examples from the cases coded for this study nicely illustrate the relative stability of different strategies, and provide initial support for my hypothesis that more stable strategies persist longer than more unstable ones. Three modern states were coded for the study – Amhara (Ethiopia), Central Thai, and Korea. If we consider the time period one hundred years before the focal time for which the case was coded (which differs for each) to the present, and look at the relative stability of the polity over that time period, we would expect to see the pattern shown in Table 8.6, with the Central Thai being the most stable, the Koreans being intermediate, and the Amhara being

Table 8.6. States categorized by their relative stability as defined by their coding on three dimensions of political strategy

	Construction of power	Implementation of power	Legitimation of power	Predicted stability
Amhara	network	terroristic	sacred	unstable
Korea	network	volunteeristic	sacred	intermediate
Central Thai	corporate	volunteeristic	profane	stable

relatively unstable. Indeed, the history of these polities seems to match this pattern.

The focal time for Central Thai is 1955. If we go back one hundred years, we find the kingdom of Thailand settling into a new capital in Bangkok and beginning to feel pressure from the British and French. The kingdom was able to defend itself against European colonization; indeed, Thailand was never colonized. In 1932, a revolution forced the king to accept a constitutional monarchy, but the monarchy has retained its prestige and has considerable influence, especially in rural areas. Since the 1950s, Thailand has had a range of governments from military juntas to elected democracies, but the monarchy has provided stability throughout. In recent years, greater degrees of political instability have affected Thailand, culminating in a 2006 military coup (which, interestingly, was justified in part as a means to protect the monarchy). A new constitution calling for democratic elections was ratified in 2007, and elections were held at the end of that year. Despite ongoing political scandals and the Constitutional Court's removal of the sitting Prime Minister in 2008, the Thai monarchy has been remarkably stable over the past 150 years, and indeed, over the 700 years since its emergence.

The focal time for Korea is 1947, just before the beginning of the Korean War. One hundred years earlier, Korea was ruled by the Joseon dynasty, which had been in place since the fifteenth century. In the middle of the nineteenth century, Korea had closed its borders to trade with all nations except China, and by the end of the century Russia, Japan, and the United States were putting enormous pressure on Korea to open its markets to foreign trade. In 1897, the last Joseon king, Gojong, declared himself emperor of Korea to bolster his authority in the face of the Japanese occupation of parts of Korea following the Sino-Japanese War. The attempt failed, and in 1910, Japan annexed Korea. Korea remained under Japanese rule until 1945. Korea was divided into North and South following World War II, and the division intensified following the Korean War. Since 1953, North

Korea (where the focal community for the case is located) has been a communist dictatorship with a hereditary leader from the Kim family. In the last 150 years, Korea has seen the collapse of a five-century dynasty, conquest, and civil war. The polity remains, but is a divided entity and cannot be termed entirely stable.

The focal time period for Amhara, the largest and most politically powerful ethnic group in Ethiopia, is 1953. One hundred years earlier, in 1853, civil unrest fostered by European colonial efforts and the crumbling of the ancient Solomonid dynasty led to the emergence of Tewodros (crowned emperor in 1855) who sought to unite Ethiopia under his rule. Tewodros ultimately failed, and the political disruption that followed his suicide in 1868 provided the opportunity for Muslim insurgents to wreak havoc on the largely Christian country. At the same time an heir to the Solomonid dynasty, Menelik II, emerged and regained power for the Solomonids, moving the capital from Gonder (which had been destroyed by Muslim insurgents) to Addis Ababa, where it remains. Menelik's heir, Haile Selassie, was crowned emperor in 1930, just before the focal time for the case. Ethiopia was invaded by Italy in 1936, but Haile Selassie was able to take control of the country once again following Italy's defeat in 1941. He remained emperor until 1974, when he was deposed by a military junta. In the years that followed, Ethiopia was wracked by civil wars and famine. In 1994, a constitution defining a parliamentary democracy was ratified, and the nation has remained relatively stable under this new government. The last 150 years have not been stable ones for Ethiopia or the Amhara people. The Solomonid dynasty fell and rose again, the nation was conquered and liberated by Europeans, and in recent years the nation has suffered through multiple periods of civil war and unrest.

Considering these three case studies, it does appear that corporate, volunteeristic, and profane strategies are more stable than network, terroristic, and sacred ones. The most corporate-, volunteeristic-, and profane-oriented polity (Central Thai) appears to have been the most stable over the past 150 years, and is the only one that has not suffered at least one major foreign invasion or a civil war. The other two polities have both been conquered by external polities, and both have experienced at least one civil war. The hypothesis that there are more stable constellations of political strategies that might differentially survive over time does seem to be supported.

Differential survival over time can lead to evolutionary change, and this gets us to the final point of this chapter: the multidimensional approach to typology I have described here is also an approach to understanding cultural evolution. It is an approach that is similar to but more nuanced than the approach behind neoevolutionary typologies. Pragmatically, the multidimensional approach provides a way for variation within "types" to be discerned and perhaps explained. It also allows for exploration and perhaps explanation of variation in other aspects of society. Philosophically, the multidimensional approach moves away from the unilineal evolutionary trajectories inherent in neoevolutionary typologies, and allows for particular forms of political strategy to vary and evolve in different ways. Although I have hypothesized (and provided some support for) a general evolutionary trend toward greater stability, it is clear from the case studies that this is not unilineal, but rather multilineal and multidimensional. It involves historical circumstances, and it takes place in the context of both domination and resistance, a context in which domination and resistance both play active roles in stability and change.

Summary and Conclusions

I assume that the past is more complex than the archaeological record makes it appear. From this basic assumption it follows that neoevolutionary typologies are unsatisfactory, as a basic problem with the typological approach is that it masks variation within defined types. Because the past is always more complex than the archaeological record makes it appear, no typology can accurately reflect the past, as we cannot know what range of variation we have captured, and what we have missed. What I have suggested here is that we consider political formations from a multidimensional perspective, focusing on variation and ranges of variation rather than on traits and their presence or absence.

I presented three dimensions of political strategy: the corporate-network dimension, which represents strategies for the construction of power; the terroristic-volunteeristic dimension, which represents strategies for the implementation of power; and the sacred-profane dimension, which represents strategies for the legitimation of power. These three dimensions are useful descriptors, but they can also be used to explain variation in other aspects of culture. These dimensions are also correlated with established neoevolutionary typologies because the strategies leaders employ to create and maintain power have impact on many other aspects of culture. And because political strategies impact other aspects of culture, change in political strategy can cause change in other aspects of culture.

Following this logic, I proposed a specific model of cultural evolution. First, I assumed that maintaining power is the basic, underlying goal of political actions, and that power was under constant threat from legitimation crises. Second, I assumed that leaders facing a potential crisis will adopt strategies of containment that they can implement without much social endorsement; that is, ones they can implement largely by themselves. I then hypothesized that there are different "costs" associated with implementing different strategies and that some are more difficult to maintain, and demonstrated support for this hypothesis. Next, I hypothesized that less costly, more stable formations of these strategies will survive longer than more costly, less stable ones. Again, I demonstrated support for this hypothesis.

To conclude, I suggest that a multidimensional approach provides important insights into the past, overcomes problems inherent in neoevolutionary approaches, and provides a useful theory of cultural evolution. In line with suggestions in Chapters 2 (Smith and Peregrine) and 12 (Smith), I hope others will join me in pursuing this approach.

Appendix: Data and Coding Information

Table 8.7. Codebook and data

1. Society name
2. Standard cross-cultural sample number
3. Corporate-network dimension (Bramm 2001)
    1 = Most corporate
    2 = Corporate
    3 = Intermediate
    4 = Network
    5 = Most network
4. Terroristic-volunteeristic dimension (Bramm 2001)
    1 = Most terroristic
    2 = Terroristic
    3 = Intermediate
    4 = Volunteeristic
    5 = Most volunteeristic
5. Sacred-profane dimension (Bramm 2001)
    1 = Most sacred
    2 = Sacred
    3 = Intermediate
    4 = Profane
    5 = Most profane
6. Service's neoevolutionary typology (Bramm 2001)
    1 = Band
    2 = Tribe
    3 = Chiefdom
    4 = State

7. Fried's neoevolutionary typology (Bramm 2001)
  1 = Egalitarian
  2 = Ranked
  3 = Stratified
8. Conflict (Social or Political) in the Local Community (Ross 1982)
  1 = Endemic: a reality of daily existence (e.g., physical violence, feuding, bitter factionalism)
  2 = High: Conflict present but not a pervasive aspect of daily life
  3 = Moderate: Disagreements and differences do not result in high violence or severe disruption
  4 = Mild or rare
9. Descent: Membership in Corporate Kinship Groups (Murdock and Wilson 1972)
  1 = Matrilineal – through female line
  2 = Double descent – separate groups through male and female lines
  3 = Patrilineal – through male line
  4 = Ambilineal – through one parent in each generation
  5 = Bilateral – not a corporate kin group
10. Enforcement Specialists (e.g., Police, Tax Collectors) (Ross 1983)
  1 = Present
  2 = Not specialized but done by leaders who do other things as well
  3 = Absent, or carried out by social pressure of wider community
11. Family Size (Murdock and Wilson 1972)
  1 = Nuclear Monogamous
  2 = Nuclear Polygynous
  3 = Stem Family
  4 = Small extended
  5 = Large extended
12. Food Stress or Hunger (Sanday 1985)
  1 = food constant
  2 = occasional hunger or famine
  3 = periodic or chronic hunger
  4 = starvation or evidence of protein deficiency
13. Household Form (Murdock and Wilson 1972)
  1 = Large communal structures
  2 = Multi-family dwellings
  3 = Single family dwellings
  4 = Family homestead
  5 = Multi-dwelling households, each with married pair
  6 = Multi-dwelling households, husband rotates among wives
  7 = Mother-child households, husbands separate
  8 = Multi-dwelling households, each dwelling occupied by individual married man or woman

(continued)

Table 8.7. (*continued*)

14. Jurisdictional Hierarchy beyond Local Community (Murdock 1962–1971)
    1 = No levels (no political authority beyond community)
    2 = One level (e.g., petty chiefdoms)
    3 = Two levels (e.g., larger chiefdoms)
    4 = Three levels (e.g., states)
    5 = Four levels (e.g., large states)
15. Perceptions of Political Leaders' Benevolence as seen by Society (Ross 1983)
    1 = Capricious and arbitrary, power used to further own interests
    2 = Neither particularly malevolent nor benevolent in use of power
    3 = Basically benevolent, working in interest of entire community
16. Political Role Differentiation: Full-Time Specialists and Their Differentiation
    from Others in the Society (Ross 1983)
    1 = Highly differentiated by wealth, special titles, or lifestyle
    2 = Moderately differentiated
    3 = Somewhat wealthier but share much of lifestyle by age, gender
    4 = Same lifestyle, may be older and have somewhat more prestige
    5 = Few exist but leadership roles present, wealthier than others
    6 = Few exist but leadership roles present, same lifestyle (as #4)
    7 = None exist, no permanent leadership roles
17. Taxation Paid to Community (e.g., in agricultural produce, labor, finished
    goods) (Ross 1983)
    1 = Regular and nonnegligible taxes to community
    2 = Only in special situations or Modest level
    3 = None
18. Unstable Political Power Index (Paige and Paige 1981)
    1 = All three variables – ritual warfare, achieved leadership, and social
        indebtedness – have a score of 0
    2 = Only one of the three variables has a score of 1; the other two score 0
    3 = Two of the variables have a score of 1; the other has a score of 0
    4 = All three variables have a score of 1

Table 8.8. Coding criteria for the dimensions of political strategy variables (from Bramm 2001:59)

How do leaders behave?				
Corporate (1)	(2)	(3)	(4)	(5) Network
"First among equals" Position is more important than the person.	Some differentiation between leaders and others.	Marked differentiation between leaders and others.	Marked differentiation between leaders; special privileges and identity.	"True elites" Person is the power holder, not the position.
No individual leader identity.	Leaders have some privileges. Identity of leader clearly defined.	Leaders have special privileges such as housing or access to goods.	Leaders expected to consume and display wealth, authority, etc.	Individual aggrandizement and cult of leader.

How do leaders behave?				
Corporate (1)	(2)	(3)	(4)	(5) Network
Powers of the leader are circumscribed or restricted. Number of leadership positions available is not limited. Emphasis on group solidarity and survival of the group.		Leadership is clearly defined with recognizable symbols of power and special behavior.	Leaders identified by personal name instead of title; person is more important than position. Patronage and nepotism may be common.	Conspicuous consumption and display of wealth, authority, etc. Problems of succession are characteristic. Number of leadership positions is limited. Prestige goods systems common.

(*continued*)

Table 8.8. (*continued*)

How do leaders legitimate their authority?				
Sacred (1)	(2)	(3)	(4)	(5) Profane
Divine ruler. Authority comes through supernatural ability and/or because of favor by supernatural being.	Leadership predicated on kinship ties, but ritual training, taboos, supernatural ability, or knowledge of / interaction with the supernatural are vital to maintaining authority.	Leadership predicated on kinship ties.	Leadership predicated on kinship ties, but group acknowledgment and natural abilities are vital to maintaining authority.	Leaders chosen by group based on the individual's abilities. Popular support is necessary to maintain authority.

How to leaders exercise authority?				
(1) Terroristic	(2)	(3)	(4)	(5) Volunteeristic
Leaders exercise power using force/coercion, military, police. Leader may exercise power without popular support or the consent of the people governed.	Leaders may use force as constrained by formal laws, often written. Offenses are punishable by death or imprisonment; physical harm may be done.	Leaders may use force as constrained by tradition; may or may not be written laws. Punishments are formal and usually fines; physical harm usually not done.	Offenses are handled on an individual basis and are adjudicated situationally. Punishment is informal; physical harm is not used.	No formal control over individual behavior. Leaders exercise authority by convincing others or appealing to the common good. Shame, guilt, or ostracism are common forms of punishment.

Table 8.9. Outline of coding criteria for Band, Tribe, Chiefdom, State variable (from Bramm 2001:61)

Exchange		
I	2.5	5
reciprocal exchange no control over resources	mostly reciprocal exchange, but some distribution/ redistribution	controlled access to resources

Subsistence		
I	2	3
hunter/gatherer low population density	pastoral horticultural	agricultural high population density

Specialization		
I	2	3
no specialization division of labor by age/sex only duties of subsistence come first everyone possesses the same skills	some specialization some groups with more access to particular skills	high degree of specialization division of labor into discrete skill groups

Integration		
I	2.5	5
family is the primary sociopolitical unit	pan-tribal sodalities kin-based units primary	non-kin units predominant sociopolitical units presence of chief or other preeminent leader

Coding is determined by the sum of these variables, according to the following formula:
Sum = 1 to 4 = Band
4.5 to 7.5 = Tribe
8 to 13.5 = Chiefdom
14 to 16 = State

References Cited

Blanton, Richard 1998 Beyond Centralization: Steps towards a Theory of Egalitarian Behavior in Archaic States. In *Archaic States*, edited by G. Feinman and J. Marcus, pp. 135–172. School of American Research Press, Santa Fe, NM.

Blanton, Richard, Gary Feinman, Stephen Kowalewski, and Peter N. Peregrine 1996 A Dual-Processual Theory for the Evolution of Mesoamerican Civilization. *Current Anthropology* 37(1):1–14.

Bloch, Marc 1953 *The Historian's Craft*. Vintage, New York.

Bramm, Adam 2001 Cross-Cultural Evaluation of the Corporate-Network Strategy: A Study of Human Sociopolitical Organization. Honors Thesis, on file at the Seeley G. Mudd Library, Lawrence University, Appleton, Wisconsin.

Ember, Carol R. and Melvin Ember 2009 *Cross-Cultural Research Methods*, Second Edition. AltaMira Press, Lanham, MD.

Ember, Melvin 1973 An Archaeological Indicator of Matrilocal versus Patrilocal Residence. *American Antiquity* 38:177–82.

Flannery, Kent 1972 Cultural Evolution of Civilizations. *Annual Review of Ecology and Systematics* 3:399–426.

―――.1998 The Ground Plans of Archaic States. In *Archaic States*, edited by G. M. Feinman and J. Marcus, pp. 15–57. School of American Research, Santa Fe.

Foucault, Michel 1977 *Discipline and Punish: The Birth of the Prison*. Pantheon, New York.

Fried, Morton 1967 *The Evolution of Political Society*. Random House, New York.

Habermas, Jurgen 1973 *Legitimation Crisis*. Beacon Press, Boston.

Jameson, Fredric 1981 *The Political Unconscious*. Cornell University Press, Ithaca, NY.

King, Adam 2006 Leadership Strategies and the Nature of Mississippian Chiefdoms in Northern Georgia. In B. M. Butler and P. D. Welch, eds., *Leadership and Polity in Mississippian Society*, pp. 73–90. Southern Illinois University Press, Carbondale.

Machiavelli, Niccolò 1513 (1998) *Il Principe* [The Prince], translated by H. Mansfield. University of Chicago Press, Chicago.

Matthiae, Paolo 1981 *Ebla: An Empire Rediscovered*. Doubleday, Garden City, NY.

Murdock, George P. 1962–71 Ethnographic Atlas. Twenty-six installments in *Ethnology* (1–10).

Murdock, George P. and Suzanne F. Wilson 1972 Settlement Patterns and Community Organization. *Ethnology* 11:254–95.

Paige, Karen and Jeffrey Paige 1981 *The Politics of Reproductive Rituals*. University of California Press, Berkeley.

Peregrine, Peter N. 1999 Legitimation Crises in Prehistoric Worlds. In P. N. Kardulias, ed., *World-Systems Theory in Practice*, pp. 37–52. Rowman and Littlefield, Lanham, MD.

―――.2001 Matrilocality, Corporate Strategy, and the Organization of Production in the Chacoan World. *American Antiquity* 66:36–46.

Pettinato, Giovanni 1991 *Ebla: A New Look at History*. Johns Hopkins University Press, Baltimore.

Ross, Marc 1982 Political Decision Making and Conflict: Additional Cross-Cultural Codes and Scales. *Ethnology* 22:169–92.

Sanday, Peggy 1985 Female Power and Male Dominance. *World Cultures* 1(4).

Service, Elman 1962 *Primitive Social Organization: An Evolutionary Perspective.* Random House, New York.

Toulmin, Stephen 1990 *Cosmopolis: The Hidden Agenda of Modernity.* University of Chicago Press, Chicago.

Wilkinson, Tony 1994 The Structure and Dynamics of Dry Farming States in Northern Mesopotamia. *Current Anthropology* 35(5):483–520.

Wright, Henry and Greg Johnson 1975 Population, Exchange, and Early State Formation in Southwestern Iran. *American Anthropologist* 77:267–89.

Yoffee, Norman 2005 *Myths of the Archaic State: Evolution of the Earliest Cities, States, and Civilizations.* Cambridge University Press, New York.

CHAPTER 9

THE STRATEGIES OF PROVINCIALS IN EMPIRES

Barbara L. Stark and John K. Chance

Empires, with their varied histories and characteristics, have been subjected to considerable scholarly scrutiny to detect recurrent imperial problems and their attempted solutions. Not so the provinces. Provincial people also face new challenges and opportunities in empires, but they have seldom been accorded the same degree of comparative study. This chapter is one way station in that effort.

In the intensive versus systematic spectrum of comparative approaches noted by Smith and Peregrine (Chapter 2), our effort began intensively for Stark in an attempt to understand archaeological data in an Aztec province (Skoglund et al. 2006). Four Aztec provincials' strategies were identified that accounted for those data. Subsequently, our collaboration addressed Aztec provincials' strategies more widely (data from other provinces) and, importantly, compared them with those in Colonial New Spain, Chance's specialty. This widened perspective gave us two imperial cases, and we identified five additional strategies (Chance and Stark 2007). Clearly the expansion of the comparative base was crucial for understanding the range of provincials' strategies.

For this chapter we expanded our scope again, considering data from colonial archaeology and adding the cases of the Inka and Colonial Spain in the Andes, affording a chance to assess variations in the Spanish Empire. Would we continue to find empirical support for previously identified strategies, would there be others not yet detected, or would we need to substantially revise our ideas about any of them? There were revisions in our approach, but they were not revolutionary. One strategy ("assertion") did not yield additional supporting data and was folded into another ("appropriation"). Another ("exodus") was substantially modified to include internal population movement because the Andes afforded much more information on its importance. Despite these changes, our modified set of eight

Table 9.1. List of strategies of provincials in empires

Strategy	Definition
1. Bolstering	Elites and rulers collaborate politically with significant imperial others to guarantee their own position locally and within the empire.
2. Emulation	Elites and others in the province employ a prestigious style or practices associated with imperial elites.
3. Resistance	Provincial peoples seek to reduce or overthrow imperial control of local affairs.
4. Exodus and internal population movement	Commoners or disaffected provincial elites move to escape imperial boundaries or policies, or to otherwise improve their life chances.
5. Information control	Provincial peoples seek to control or conceal to their own advantage information sought by the imperial government.
6. Appropriation	Provincial peoples selectively adopt or modify imperial procedures and institutions and use them to further local ends.
7. Complicity	Elites and sometimes commoners in the province collaborate economically with significant imperial others to further their own interests.
8. Assimilation	Elites or commoners in the province, as individuals or groups, seek varying degrees of social, economic, or identity integration with the dominant society.

strategies held up well against the new Inka case and the addition of another part of the Spanish Empire (Table 9.1). There were earlier archaeological empires in the New World that we have not addressed, as we deliberately sought a combination of archaeological and documentary data so that the exploratory identification of strategies would have particularly rich sources of information.

The intensive versus systematic scale does not easily fit this history of research – our cases remain few, but even a single empire has many and varied provinces encompassing considerable social variation. Thus, each "case" we consider presents a great variety of provincial examples, leading us to be uncomfortable with the idea that we have achieved an intensive study of any one empire. Our framework represents generalizations about what provincials were up to – in a sense, it explains particular actions in terms of broader structural considerations. At the same time, we establish some of the coherence of provincial activities that in turn were part of the circumstances confronted by imperial governments, potentially strengthening or weakening empires. Inherently these provincial actions are less well documented, explicated, and justified compared to those of central authorities, who often differentially controlled many media and records. Thus, provincials' strategies are harder to detect, sometimes better revealed by documents than archaeology and sometimes vice versa. Not every province provides the same record or displays the same strategies. The strategies we define were affected by geographic distance and environmental factors, duration of imperial rule, social class, and differences in the economic and social integration of subject populations.

Our emphasis is on recurrent kinds of actions that shaped the success of provincials in the empire, or, sometimes, in evading imperial authority. Certainly many additional empires have a rich potential to modify and add to our ideas about provincials' strategies.

Empires

We define empires as expansionist states that incorporate diverse societies well beyond immediate neighbors (see Schreiber 1992:3). The predominant focus in understanding empires has been central government and associated elites, with provinces usually employed to identify the challenges for and variety of central imperial endeavors (e.g., for the Aztecs, Berdan et al. 1996). Doyle's (1986) analysis of the histories of empires uses "metropole and periphery" concepts but nevertheless is not focused on peripheral strategies. Robinson (1972), however, stresses the role of local collaborators for successful imperial control. Scott (1998) and Eisenstadt (1993) provide particularly comprehensive treatments of state and imperial strategies. Eisenstadt's (1993 [1963]) emphasis on internal contradictions within bureaucratic empires focuses on multiple social interests, a perspective shared with our attention to provincials' strategies (see also Brumfiel 1992; Stein 2002:903–04; Yoffee 2005:15, 113–15). Goldstein (2005:7–28) provides a concise and wide-ranging summary of centrist versus agency perspectives on state dynamics and expansion, and much of our discussion has an agency emphasis (see also Peregrine, Chapter 8).

To a considerable extent, as Doyle (1986:118–19, 353) recognizes, successful imperial strategies have depended on a "coevolutionary" interface with provincial strategies. As state-imperial societies increase in scale, so do the number of interest groups, along with the bases around which actions can be organized, such as economic specializations or local political authority. Taintor (1988:198, 200) notes that either the "peasantry" or provinces may, at some point, find the larger society too costly and defect through direct action (or inaction to defend it).

Fundamentally, we are reversing the perspective about empires – instead of the core as the focus, we emphasize the provinces (see also Morrison 2001). This reversal of perspective is akin to Scott's (1985, 1990) efforts to better understand the coherence and logic of subordinates' actions in the face of varied forms of social domination. Our emphasis in elaborating ideas about provincials' strategies is grounded in a combination of an agency and institutional or group perspective. Our stance implies a complex of dynamic adjustments for analysis rather than a classificatory effort, but this initial effort is devoted to identifying and illustrating a spectrum of provincial strategies. Occasionally we elaborate concerning strategies with examples outside the areas of focus, but mainly stick to our cases to draw better upon our own scholarly backgrounds.

The time frames considered are the late pre-Hispanic era, including for Mesoamerica the Late Postclassic period (A.D. 1350–1521), when the Aztec Empire developed, and for the Andes the Late Horizon[1] and its immediate antecedents (A.D. 1438–1532), when the Inka Empire developed (D'Altroy 2002:45–47, 312). For the Spanish Empire we consider the Colonial period (A.D. 1521–1821 in Mesoamerica and 1532–1821 for the Andes).

For both the Andes and Mesoamerica, ethnohistory has played a major role in our understanding of the last native empires; archaeological work has focused more on imperial sites or on the imperial core than distant provinces (e.g., D'Altroy 2001b:336). For the Aztecs, we rely heavily on archaeological research in Morelos adjacent to the Basin of Mexico where the Aztec capitals were located (Smith 1986, 1994; Smith and Heath-Smith 1996) and in the Cuexcatlan province in south-central Veracruz (Garraty and Stark 2002; Ohnersorgen 2001, 2006; Skoglund et al. 2006). Morelos and south-central Veracruz involve an inner and an outer tributary province, respectively (see Berdan et al. 1996). For the Inka, we draw heavily on archaeological research in the Mantaro Valley (e.g., Costin and Earle 1989; D'Altroy 2002) because of the explicit concern with comparison before and after the Inka gained control, but we use supplements from archaeology and ethnohistory elsewhere. For the Colonial period, we rely primarily on documentary studies because appropriate historical archaeology is not abundant. All of the data sources pose biases that impede analyses of provincials' strategies to a greater extent than imperial strategies.

Among our imperial contexts the extent of direct administration varies. The Aztec Empire employed a mix of more direct administration in the

Basin of Mexico and indirect measures in more distant provinces (Berdan et al. 1996; Hodge 1984). A mosaic of actions and investments is characteristic, however, as is typical in empires (Menzel 1959; Ohnersorgen 2006; Schreiber 1992). The Inka engaged in varied practices according to local situations, distance, and time (e.g., Frye 2005; Grosboll 1993; Lynch 1993; Malpass and Alconini 2010; Salomon 1986; Schreiber 1993; Stanish 1997, 2001). Incorporation of Colonial information provides a useful comparison to both pre-Hispanic situations because the colonies soon involved substantial direct administration and eventually a marked degree of bureaucratic integration with insular Spain (Doyle 1986:117–18). Importantly, the Colonial situation provides a longer chronological perspective. Of course, Andean and Mesoamerican Spanish administrations were not identical, but for our purposes broadly similar.

To further our goals, we consider the notion of strategies and how several factors affect them: geographic distance and imperial duration, differences in the economic and social integration of subject populations, the role of certain environmental characteristics, and organizing features of provincial social life, such as class. Spanish Colonial administration truncated larger pre-Hispanic units and relied heavily on the level of towns or *municipios*, which provide the counterpart of provincial information under the Aztecs and Inka. Despite this terminological and organizational difference, the Colonial community setting presents a relevant level of information. The subject of provincial- (and community-) level strategies is potentially enormous, and we address only part of it. In particular, we do not address issues related to provinces that were not hierarchically organized prior to incorporation, or were scarcely so organized (see Doyle 1986:162–97; Schreiber 1992:22–25).

Concepts Concerning Strategies

The term "strategy" has been applied in a variety of ways with respect to "statecraft," by which we mean the methods (tactics and techniques) by which state (and imperial) governments and ruling classes or authorities maintain or enhance central power and assure its longevity, as well as the social and economic success of the individuals holding power. Because empires are an outgrowth of state expansion, statecraft is an appropriate term for imperial contexts as well. Strategies contribute toward those goals through specific policies or actions. Because individuals in key governmental positions can exercise power and render decisions affecting others, there is often a well-developed element of conscious planning that enters into strategies, but there often are unplanned effects as well; ultimately we treat strategies as an analytical generalization.

There is no general agreement about how broadly to define strategies and which procedures or policies can be viewed more specifically as tactics or techniques. In the case of recent analysis of the Aztecs, some imperial strategies were labeled broadly in categories that virtually constitute domains of social life, for example, economic and political strategies (Berdan et al. 1996). In contrast, the Aztec elite and frontier strategies reflected narrower concerns, the former restricted by class and the latter by geopolitical factors. Decisions about these "levels" of analysis are largely matters of convenience, but where possible we opt for a more restricted level for strategy concepts to maintain a sharper focus. Broad domains, such as the economy, are ways to group strategies.

We recognize that the provincial strategies we discuss may have implications for states as well as empires, but we do not address these issues. States themselves usually involve subordinate communities (they are hierarchical societies, among other key features), but at minimum the subordinate communities may involve only rural hamlets or populations in the surrounding support zone. As we note later in the chapter, there are some dimensions affecting provincial strategies that are sensitive to the greater scale and diversity of empires compared to states, such as geographic distance. In our cases the provinces or parts of them had prior state histories, and such initial conditions result in a complex and partly overlapping set of provincial versus imperial strategies. We do not organize our discussion according to types of imperial administration, such as direct versus indirect rule, although we note some effects of these differences. The empires examined, at least at the outset, relied to a varying extent on indirect rule, which magnifies the effects of preexisting organization and the potential overlap of strategies between province and empire.

Observations on Statecraft and Strategies

The methods of statecraft include achieving compliance from subjects through ideological and coercive techniques, garnering and giving resources, and designing and executing "foreign" policies, including waging wars. State-imperial strategies often comprise overlapping and sometimes mutually antagonistic endeavors that may shift over time. Many efforts have unforeseen consequences that require compensating actions. Many plans walk a tightrope in achieving some ends and minimizing other undesired effects. A variety of decisions and actions may emanate from different officials with varying spheres of authority and may be at odds with decisions or policies that others pursue.

Because power is relative in a governmental hierarchy, some statecraft may have utility and be exercised at various decision-making levels, down to the provincial level. Thus some strategies are *pervasive*. This action of authority at different levels makes it unwarranted to expect uniquely provincial strategies. One example is elite intermarriage, which may serve the central authority and provincial elites alike. Some provincial marital alliances may be pursued laterally with elites in other provinces or communities rather than hierarchically with royals or the ruling class.

Some provincials' strategies are inverses of state strategies. For example, if rulers in states or empires seek key information through uniform measures – censuses for taxation, or maps to improve planning and access to resources, as Scott (1998:47–49) argues – then the *inverse* strategy of provincial rulers/governors or peasants is to conceal select resource information through underestimation or misinformation. Another form of inverse strategy concerns the exodus of groups from one state who seek accommodation in another, with the latter accepting incomers as part of a strategy of augmenting loyal clients, perhaps for agricultural production or warfare (e.g., Hicks 1982:243). Thus, the analysis of provincials' strategies is best conducted with a close eye toward statecraft at a broader level and with considerable attention to the overall context and history of a province.

Distant provinces require considerable state or imperial expenditures of effort and personnel to maintain administrative contacts and apply force; such distant provinces have more opportunities for independent action than provinces close to hand that permit frequent visits and exchange of personnel. Resource mobilization is also sensitive to distance costs in transport (D'Altroy 1992:81–93; Drennan 1984; Hassig 1985:28–40; Malville 2001). Distance has figured into analyses of imperial foreign colonies, interaction, and trade (Stein 1999:62–64), military conduct (D'Altroy 1992:81–93), and the ways that states function within their territories (Cowgill 1988:264–65). Consequently, more geographically distant provinces may be taxed differently or assigned tasks differently than nearby ones. The Aztec frontier strategy identified by Berdan et al. (1996) is an excellent example because some provinces were located at the edge of imperial control confronting imperial enemies (and often simultaneously their own traditional enemies). Although core-periphery concepts linked to World Systems Theory speak to a combination of geographic and economic differentiation, we prefer to discuss geographic considerations independently of any particular theoretical interpretation.

Closely bound with distance is an environmental factor. If physical access to populations is difficult because of vegetation or broken topography ("nonstate spaces" in Scott 1998:187), then central government confronts challenges in obtaining information and resources in the face of "resistance" (which, of course, may be viewed locally simply as competing goals).

We underscore the importance of actor perspectives in provincials' strategies and differences in provincials' strategies according to class or other factional or identity concerns. Although imperial strategies necessarily emanate from central governmental authorities and closely respond to elite- or ruling-class concerns, provincial strategies may more readily expose independent actions and concerns across a social spectrum that includes commoners or subsidiary communities. Archaeological data in particular offer opportunities to assess practices of everyday life and the actions of commoners or others poorly represented in documents.

Strategies may display important variation according to early and late imperial rule. Temporal distinctions accommodate the fact that statecraft and strategies necessarily undergo revision as circumstances change. Colonial practices reflect both the long history of the Spanish state and, as the Colonial period unfolds, 300 years of imperial rule. This contrasts markedly with the short imperial timeline for the Aztecs and Inka, not quite a century.

We discuss eight provincial strategies (Table 9.1). In the discussion of each strategy, if possible we provide late pre-Hispanic and Colonial examples. Predictably, the two sources of data, archaeology and documents, are quite differentially useful. Each at times plays a unique role, sometimes they harmonize, and sometimes they offer opposed information. For each strategy, we attempt to distinguish the cross-cutting issues of geography, time, and social actors. We also remark on strategies as pervasive or inverse. Importantly, the eight strategies are not mutually exclusive, even if some imply contradictory efforts. More than one can be pursued simultaneously, and more than one can be pursued by the same people at different times or in different social contexts.

Provincials' Strategies

Bolstering. Bolstering refers to the efforts of provincial elites and especially local provincial rulers to collaborate politically with significant imperial others to guarantee their own position locally and within the empire (some of Robinson's [1972] collaborators). It subsumes a range of considerations that Berdan (2006) teases apart for the Aztecs as acquiescence and accommodation, self-interested cooperation, and intermarriage and other

exchanges (feasting, gifts). Bolstering is a pervasive strategy because imperial officials and the ruling class also implement this strategy. As part of their
discussion of Aztec imperial elite cooptation, Berdan and Smith (1996:215)
comment on the benefits of the empire for local conquered rulers, who
were backed up by the empire and therefore less vulnerable to local factionalism and meddling or attack by neighboring polities. Local rulers may
have capitulated to imperial incorporation because it would help them com-
bat rivals in their region. If once defiant, rulers and elites may have become
cooperative imperial subjects for the same reasons. Imperial officials wanted
to sustain compliant clients, a convergence of strategies.

   A common tactic in bolstering is elite marital alliances, which can be
pursued both as an element of internal strategies and external foreign
policy (Berdan 2006; Patterson 1991:102; Rivera Casanovas 2010:157–58;
Rostworowski de Diez Canseco 1960:424; Rowe 1946:204; Spores 1974;
Wernke 2006:180). Emulation, discussed later, helps bolster provincial
elites through participation in or use of select imperial practices and symbolic items. This tactic draws on the prestige of imperial ritual, material
symbols, or other cultural traits (e.g., Berdan [2006:161] suggests use of
Nahuatl as a lingua franca for the Aztec realm). Emulation underscores the
importance of local elites and communicates active connections to imperial power. If emulation or some forms of it are pursued only by provincial
elites and not more widely in the population, then it becomes an aspect
of bolstering. Because this class limitation is not always the case, we treat
emulation as a separate strategy.

   Late Pre-Hispanic Period. Berdan (2006:156) provides examples of marital
alliances antedating Aztec rule and argues that such horizontal ties continued to be important for provinces after incorporation into the empire even
though they are not well documented. Hicks (1994) observed that sometimes polities acquiesced peacefully to Aztec rule when an internal faction
sought imperial support, rendering those that gained local office particularly dependent on the empire. Berdan (2006:162; Berdan et al. 1996:279,
286) notes instances in which a city-state's population deposed their unpop-
ular rulers with Aztec support, but we do not know to what extent these
were commoner political uprisings versus ones mobilized by internal elite
factions.

   Aztec ethnohistoric records indicate important provincial leaders and
even enemy leaders were invited to witness key ceremonies in the Aztec
capital (Berdan and Smith 1996:215); this was also part of coercive efforts
to show the scale of Aztec sacrifice of prisoners and the scale of imperial
resources. Although such trips are not recoverable archaeologically, such

social interactions provided provincial elites opportunities to see imperial symbolic items in use and observe imperial rituals. In addition to some gifts to provincial leaders, trade probably brought imperial heartland objects to distant provinces, where they may have served as models for local emulation, such as decorated Aztec III Black-on-Orange serving vessels (Skoglund et al. 2006).

In the lower Blanco area of the Cuetlaxtlan tributary province, Garraty and Stark (2002:28) observed that Aztec III-style Black-on-orange vessels might have served as local tokens of legitimacy as part of the cooptation of local elites. Garraty and Stark (2002:28) also found that the Lower Blanco area showed greater concentration of wealth at the local center of Callejón del Horno than at the earlier Middle Postclassic center of El Sauce (prior to the Aztec Empire), suggesting local elites were advantaged through their relationship with the imperial regime. This result contrasts with Morelos where Smith and Heath-Smith (1994) found lower-ranking elites were disadvantaged under imperial rule.

In the Andes, Mantaro Valley researchers showed that the local or regionally obtained decorated vessels that had been consumed disproportionately by local elites before Inka conquest (Costin and Earle 1989:707) became more accessible to commoners in local society. Inka-style vessels, controlled through state production, substantially supplanted local decorated wares and become mainly (not exclusively) the purview of local elites – now dependent on imperial largesse for a ware important in social displays (Costin and Earle 1989:700, 707; D'Altroy 2002:196–214; Earle 2001:309). In the distant Yampara area, local elites in a frontier context were bolstered by Inka control but with fewer consequences for the local economy than in the Mantaro Valley (Alconini 2010:104–06). Ethnohistoric records indicate many instances of differential manipulation of local elites (e.g., for Chimor; Rowe 1948:45; see review in Stanish 2001), but the Mantaro Valley work is especially important in showing an archaeological signature of such efforts. In the Inka realm, selective reinforcement of local elites came at a considerable cost of imperial surveillance and control, with important local rulers required to spend part of the year at the imperial capital, Cuzco, and heirs either held there continuously or educated there (Rowe 1982:95). These sojourns provided additional opportunities to see and adopt Inka-style material culture and may have contributed to emulation because local versions of Inka styles were elaborated in some regions (discussed later).

Colonial Period. Bolstering was a widespread strategy among Mesoamerican and Andean elites during the Colonial period. After the conquest, the lot of indigenous peoples in most regions changed for the worse as population levels declined drastically. The death of many of their subjects left local elites struggling to find new ways to maintain their position, and selective cooperation with Spanish individuals or with the Spanish regime was often the best way to do so. The Spanish sought Indian labor and tribute and were quick to recognize and cultivate local rulers (Katz 1988:79; Schroeder 1998:xiii).

Indigenous rulers and their descendants, *caciques* in Spanish or *kurakas* in Quechua, found it in their interest to cooperate on many levels. Caciques were among the first Indians to be baptized, and in many regions they assumed Christian names. In Colonial Mexico, they successfully sought the top office of *gobernador* in the newly introduced town councils (*cabildos*). In later years, the political role of cacique descendants declined in many areas of Mesoamerica, but cabildo service itself became an avenue of local power and prestige (Chance 1989:132–46; Ouweneel 1995).

In the Andes, the office of gobernador was absent, and the powers and responsibilities of recognized kurakas were correspondingly greater. In the sixteenth century, Andean *corregidores* (Spanish officials in charge of local or regional districts) needed the kurakas to obtain access to Indian labor, and the indigenous rulers gained some autonomy by cooperating (Saignes 1999:77–78). In early colonial Peru, Spanish *encomenderos* (holders of grants of Indians) routinely appointed kurakas who would carry out their instructions and replaced those who did not deliver (Ramírez 1996:26, 33–34).

Caciques in both colonies effectively bolstered their positions by becoming cultural brokers between Indian commoners and Spaniards. Many learned the Spanish language and rapidly adopted aspects of Spanish material culture (see Emulation, later in the chapter). By late Colonial times, Andean kurakas drew authority from identification with the Spanish Crown. Aymara chieftains in the La Paz region acquired coats of arms and enumerated their military merits, adopting a Hispanic vision of history (Thomson 2002:36–40).

Intermarriage with members of the dominant imperial elite, a prevalent aspect of bolstering in pre-Hispanic times, was much less common in the sixteenth century, as Spanish racial and cultural prejudices worked against the practice. Limited formal intermarriage in these early years was primarily between Spanish men and Indian women of the highest levels in indigenous society, a practice that bolstered the prestige of the brides' families (Carrasco Pizana 1991:12–13, 16; Stern 1982:170–71). Intermarriage of caciques with non-Indians continued into the late Colonial period and will be discussed later under the heading of Assimilation.

Emulation. Emulation refers to efforts in the province to employ a prestigious style or practices associated with the empire. Emulation may be a pervasive strategy, as the imperial authorities conceivably could cloak themselves and their government in valuable symbols adopted from geographically or temporally distant prestigious societies (such as neoclassical architecture in Washington, DC) (Helms 1993). The Aztecs claimed descent from Toltec society and imitated Toltec practices, lionizing the Toltecs (as did many neighbors) as icons of a cultured past, which can be traced in material evidence such as carved monuments (Umberger 2008).

Emulation can be expressed in very durable material culture, such as monuments or architecture, as well as through less well-preserved practices involving claims about descent, dress, or personal accoutrements. An emulation strategy is likely to be pervasive in empires, applying to both the imperial core and provinces, and likely more prominent early in imperial history than later because of the initial push to establish legitimacy. Provincial elites are the leading sector in emulation during the earliest stage of imperial rule through a combination of self-interest and coercion. Eventually emulation may involve a range of practices for multiple social classes and yield to assimilation (discussed later), but this does not necessarily imply abandonment of all aspects of local identities and practices.

Late Pre-Hispanic Period. The Aztec and Inka empires show a considerable mosaic of provincial histories and material culture, and we do not attempt to examine all possible expressions of emulation. Each must be carefully analyzed because empires also relocate people and communities for purposes such as obtaining information, assuring resources, and inserting loyal subjects in rebellious areas. Thus, some distant occurrences of imperial styles may reflect colonists, not emulation. There is considerable variation in the expressions of emulation according to the nature of imperial administration, whether direct or indirect, and whether provinces are accessible or quite distant.

Under the Aztecs at Cuetlaxtlan, as in the nearby lower Blanco area, a reasonably broad range of consumers used imperial styles, but sites or areas connected to local elites and imperial personnel yielded greater quantities of such items (Garraty and Stark 2002; Ohnersorgen 2006). Documentation of local production both at Cuetlaxtlan and along the lower Blanco of Aztec III-style Black-on-orange bowls and Texcoco Molded censers suggests changes in local production and relatively extensive consumption geared to exogenous styles (Skoglund et al. 2006). This selective use of imperial styles is unlikely to have been because of acts of imperial policy at locations as small and subsidiary as Callejón del Horno along the Blanco

River. Documentation of local production assures us that most of the vessels did not arrive via imperial merchants.

Thus, unless prevented by sumptuary rules, a range of people across social classes could emulate imperial serving bowls and small censers in locally fabricated vessels, even if other, more costly avenues of emulation were beyond their direct knowledge or means. In this line of reasoning, local producers responded to local social demand, perhaps expressed as market demand. Emulation was not restricted to elites in the lower Blanco area, but elite-restricted archaeological data of other kinds emerge from a provincial center, like Cuetlaxtlan (Ohnersorgen 2006).

In the Inka Empire, state-sponsored production and a predilection for a greater degree of direct administration and reorganization of local economies makes it difficult to detect local emulation because elaborate Inka-style vessels and sometimes blended Inka-local styles (Acuto 2010:137–39) were produced and distributed under imperial control. Acuto (2010) notes among sites in the northern Calchaquí Valley, northwest Argentina, a rare residence with Inka-style architecture (including Inka construction techniques) but a few residences with a mix of Inka and local construction, while most residences still follow local styles. Acuto (2010:133) proposes that a combination of imperial restrictions concerning imitations and local emulation was at work. In the Mantaro Valley, local people, usually elites but sometimes commoners, used valuable Inka vessels especially for hospitality and social displays (Costin 2001; D'Altroy 2001c). In such cases, emulation and coercion both may have figured in local decisions. The benefits to commoners of resettlement on fertile Mantaro Valley bottom lands (D'Altroy 2002:147) suggest they may have been willing appreciators of Inka styles. In the Mantaro Valley, Inka vessels were mainly used by elites (the bolstering strategy previously discussed) but also reached commoners, yet in the Huanuco area, as with many others, such vessels are mainly restricted to imperial administrative sites as an aspect of bolstering (see review in D'Altroy 2001a:336–38). In some provinces, blended imitation styles also appeared that were connected to local elites, such as in the Ica Valley (Menzel 1959, 1960). Thus, a mosaic of imperial practices is indicated, and it is difficult to disentangle local actions versus imposed practices. The Mantaro Valley was profoundly affected by Inka direct administration, and a mix of bolstering, emulation, and complicity (see later section) appear to have been at work with distinct local effects.

Colonial Period. Emulation of Spanish styles and practices was a frequent Indian strategy in Colonial Mesoamerica and Peru. Caciques and *principales* (members of the lower nobility) built their houses in Spanish

Colonial styles and adopted Spanish furnishings and other material items (e.g., Chance 1997, 2009; Spores 1967:170, 241–44). They used the Spanish honorifics *don* and *doña*, and many learned to read and write Spanish and took Christianity seriously (Gibson 1964:156; Ramírez 1996:40; Spalding 1984:223; Stern 1982:167–69). Commoners and native elites alike used maiolica pottery, even in distant communities in Tehuantepec and the Soconusco (Gasco 1989:319; Zeitlin 2005:154–60), showing commoner emulation not unlike the pre-Hispanic Cuetlaxtlan case.

Thus, even if emulation was most visible among Indian elites, it was also practiced by socially mobile commoners (Stern 1982:167). For the early years of the colony, it is sometimes difficult to disentangle Indian emulation from Spanish coercion. Thus commoners were pressured to abandon indigenous for European dress, and caciques were told they should be baptized first to set an example for the commoners. For example, small ceramic figurines used in indigenous domestic rituals in parts of the Basin of Mexico changed during Colonial times to show European costumes while pre-Hispanic deities disappeared from the repertoire (Charlton et al. 2005). A mix of emulation of clothing styles and religious coercion favoring Catholicism was likely responsible.

Resistance. Resistance is the effort by provincials to reduce or overthrow imperial control of local affairs and may be expressed in diverse forms. Although rebellion and physical resistance may spring to mind first, Scott (1985, 1990) has emphasized that many less obvious forms of resistance to exploitation operate at various levels, and Adas (1981, 1986) analyzes related peasant tactics in Southeast Asia. One facet of resistance is movement to avoid imperial control, addressed later under "Exodus and Population Movement." Local cultural traditions may be upheld to maintain local loyalties and solidarity, or gossip and private communications may ridicule or expose weaknesses (ideological or otherwise) of dominant authorities. Scott stresses that both public and "hidden" expressions may operate as resistance. Although Scott focused on resistance by the downtrodden, provincial elites or leaders may be among the most active in shirking imperial taxation or other obligations (Cowgill 1988:260; Kaufman 1988:227–29), placing self-interest or local interests ahead of those of the central authority.

Many covert expressions of resistance may not be recoverable from either documentary or archaeological sources. Documents favor expressions of dominant classes and authorities (Adas 1986), and archaeology is confined to the material record, which may be ambiguous on many subtle topics. Persistence of local styles in the material record in the face of close imperial connections may signify local independent action that maintains a cultural distinction, however. In a related argument, Spencer and Redmond (2006) interpret contrasts in archaeological architecture and pottery in the San Martín Tilcajete area of Oaxaca, Mexico, compared to Monte Albán during the period 500 B.C.–A.D. 100, as part of an active resistance to the powerful expansionist neighboring polity. When Monte Albán finally incorporated the area, public architecture and ceramics shifted to a general adherence to state canons (Elson 2006).

Physical resistance is documented ethnohistorically, as elites and especially rulers often sought to reduce or overthrow Inka and Aztec imperial control, and rebellions are recorded in Colonial times. Therefore, "provincial" may be a fluctuating status, becoming more cemented with time as imperial consolidation advances both bureaucratically and geographically (in part so that no independent neighbors remain with whom to ally and connive).

Late Pre-Hispanic Period. In Mesoamerica, the Gulf Cuetlaxtlan province under Aztec rule illustrates that conflicting strategies occur. In contrast to the archaeological data from the nearby lower Blanco that suggest pursuit of a compliant bolstering strategy by local elites and rulers, documents mention rebellions at Cuetlaxtlan (Kelly and Palerm 1952:264–317). The mix of Cuetlaxtlan rebellions and some evidence of bolstering in a dependency or lower-order settlement likely are signs of the complexity of tactics and decisions among different segments of the local population as well as shifts over time. From the documents we can recognize a "resistance strategy" operating violently (at least episodically).

As yet no archaeological data document the Cuetlaxtlan rebellions, but other forms of resistance may be expressed materially. Miller (2006) identifies hair (or headdress) styles and ornaments on figurines in the lower Blanco area that appeared prior to Aztec rule in the Middle Postclassic period (A.D. 1200–1350) and continued despite a variety of imperial interactions and the occasional presence of figurine styles like those typical in the Basin of Mexico. Mesoamerican figurine headdress and ornamentation are particularly promising as a basis to discern communications about local identity because they are personal attributes, and figurines in domestic ritual may reflect frequent local practice. Other artifacts might have played a role in active expressions of local identity under imperial rule, such as local versions of stamped-base serving bowls (Fondo Sellado) that also had their inception prior to Aztec rule and continued during the Late Postclassic period in the face of wide access to local imitations of a few Aztec vessel styles.

Patterson (1991:98–128) views rebellions against Inka rule as an outgrowth of the efforts of local elites and commoners alike to resist imperial intrusions and controls. Local resentment could be catalyzed into open rebellion particularly at times when royal succession was at issue or imperial forces were occupied in distant regions. The northern borders of expanding imperial rule afford one set of examples. Another set involves the Colla in the Late Titicaca basin as the Inka expanded control into that area. The Colla, eventually incorporated, revolted forty years later for a protracted period of resistance. Commoners were allied with their local leaders in both the northern and Titicaca cases, but Patterson (1991:119) notes that commoners shook off local leaders who cooperated with Inka authorities in the Inka Valley at the time of Spanish intervention when Inka rule therefore became vulnerable (see Jennings 2003:453 for the Cotahuasi Valley). A protracted war of Inka succession, mentioned later in the chapter, shortly antedated the Spanish intrusion and afforded a prime opportunity for local leaders and provinces to throw their support to one of the factions, opposing the faction viewed as less desirable. Revolts and allegiance were two sides of a political coin.

Ceramic data from one Andean valley suggest local commoner resistance to the Inka and their ceramic style even though elites embraced it. These data derive from the Ica Valley on the south coast where Menzel (1959, 1960) notes local production of Inka-style vessels, a local Inka–Ica style that was an innovative blend, and a continuation of local styles of decoration. The last styles characterized commoner contexts, with the two others confined to administrative centers and local elites. With the end of Inka rule, the Inka-related styles disappeared and the local tradition continued in full force. Patterson (1991:105) considers this a likely case of commoner resistance. Acuto (2010:141) interprets widespread access to Inka-style pottery at Cortaderas in the Calchaquí Valley, Argentina, coupled with avoidance of Inka vessels among grave goods, as resistance that kept local rituals intact.

Other valleys did not imitate or use much Inka-style pottery in local society (Grosboll 1993:60; Julien 1993:227–29; Lynch 1993:133; Malpass 1993:236–37; Schreiber 1993:91). We do not yet have a basis to understand such wide variation in provincial actions. Strict sumptuary restrictions for imperial styles are an alternate explanation to resistance that could account for class differences, as Acuto (2010:133) proposed for provincial imitation of Inka architecture. A concerted reexamination of archaeological ceramic sequences and contexts for Mesoamerica and the Andes holds promise for more examples of stylistic postures related to social classes and resistance.

Colonial Period. Resistance was ubiquitous under the Colonial regime and seriously impeded Spanish plans for political and economic control and religious conversion. It took many forms, and at a minimum it is necessary to distinguish between active, overt forms such as revolt, rebellion, and litigation, and the semi-covert forms that involved various kinds of foot-dragging and noncompliance (Scott 1985).

Uprisings have drawn much scholarly attention, especially in the Andes, where Colonial rebellions were more extensive and profound than in Mesoamerica. Both colonies encountered rebellions along their frontiers, in Mexico in the north and among southern Maya groups; and in the Andes to the south and southeast of the Charcas, in Chile, and in the "cordillera" of the Chiriguanos (Katz 1988:77; Wachtel 1984:237, 240).

In Peru, however, there were also early large revolts that gained adherents in the core provinces. Manco Inka besieged Cuzco in A.D. 1536–1537 before taking refuge in the inaccessible mountains of Vilcabamba where he restored a "neo–Inka" state. His descendants continued to challenge Spanish hegemony until Tupac Amaru, the last Inka of Vilcabamba, was publicly beheaded in Cuzco in 1572. Another early major uprising was the Taqui Onqoy millenarian movement, influential in the central Andes in the 1560s (Stern 1982:51–71; Wachtel 1984:237–40). In contrast, once the Spanish regime gained control of the core provinces of Mexico, the sixteenth century was relatively peaceful (Spores 1998:46).

The pattern of rebellions in Mexico and Peru also differed notably as the colonies matured in the eighteenth century. Late colonial uprisings in the Mesoamerican core areas of central Mexico and Oaxaca, most of them after 1760, were highly localized, spontaneous, short-lived, and aimed at agents of the state (often at their abuse of power) rather than overthrow of the Colonial government (Coatsworth 1988:32; Katz 1988:80; Taylor 1979:114–16). In the Andes, too, the number of village uprisings increased after 1760 (Coatsworth 1988:32), but far more significant were the popular challenges to Spanish authority in the 1780s led by Tupac Amaru II in southern Peru and Tomás Katari in Bolivia. More than 100,000 people died in this loosely coordinated series of regional conflagrations, during a civil war with revolutionary aims (Stern 1987:34).

Space does not permit an exploration of the causes of the greater scope and significance of rebellion in the Andes, but several factors have been adduced, including the different modes of political integration of the Inka and Mesoamerican states and the differential impact of the eighteenth-century Bourbon reforms in Mexico and the Andes (Coatsworth 1988:26, 32, 49, 53–54, 58; Katz 1988:80; Wachtel 1984:219).

Although violent rebellions in both colonies rarely achieved their goals, semi-covert forms of resistance were ever-present and arguably more effective in alleviating suffering. The withholding of labor and tribute were the most common varieties, and these forms of foot-dragging seriously distorted the government's plans (Schroeder 1998: xiv; Spalding 1984:225; Spores 1998:46; Stern 1982:63). Kepecs (2005:133) argues there are archaeological traces of Yucatecan illegal native trade outside controlled markets shown by native incense burners similar to those to the south in refuge zones but recovered at northern sites. While these might reflect population movement instead of illegal trade, in either case resistance is indicated. Resistance was also expressed through indigenous Christian organizations or rituals or token missionization, even though there was extensive accommodation and reinterpretation of Christianity as well, and religious change was uneven and unpredictable (Mills 1997:3–5; Taylor 1994:153–55).

Exodus and Internal Population Movement. We use the term "exodus" to refer to relocations effectively beyond imperial administration and the phrase "internal population movement" to refer to relocations within administered areas. Because the term "migration" has been used with reference to both types of relocations, we do not apply it here. Both exodus and internal relocations may be impermanent, as individuals or groups reconsider options or as circumstances change; they may return to their prior home locations where they retain social ties; thus, part of what we discuss can be considered "population circulation" (see discussion in Schachner 2007:17–31).

Exodus allows people to escape imperial boundaries or at least readily administered areas (e.g., Scott [1998:185, 395] for Southeast Asia, Europe after the Black Death, pre–Civil War United States, and Czarist Russia). Exodus is likely to be especially attractive to oppressed commoners (Brumfiel 1983:269) but also disaffected local elites or cadet royal lines. Physical relocation avoids tribute demands, rebukes, punishment, or other disagreeable consequences of imperial rule. Although exodus forfeits a local position, it may have been viewed as a temporary measure that could be reversed (as local social claims could be reinstated) and may have operated along preexisting social networks that offered havens or opportunities. In many instances, exodus will involve small groups and may fail to be readily observable archaeologically, but wholesale peasant flight may occur (Adas 1986:73).

Exodus that was pivotal in political history may become enshrined in migration accounts (e.g., Ufipa in east-central Africa, see Willis 1981).

Earlier in our discussion of resistance, we noted Inka who fled to inaccessible mountainous regions for nearly a half century of opposition to Spanish rule, a special case of a "government in exile."

An important element in an exodus strategy is the nature of the refuge. An independent polity may shelter disaffected individuals or groups. Naturally difficult terrain may provide adequate cover. Scott (1998:187) recognizes the role of natural topography in concealment and refuges.

Internal population movements can reflect two elements in decision-making: repulsion or attraction. Individuals or families may be drawn to economic or social opportunities attendant on imperial structure – such as employment in growing imperial centers or related to other aspects of the economy (e.g., transshipment, ranching, mining). Switching clientage or joining religious or communal groups can be part of avoiding demands and may involve relocation. The tactic of local "patron swapping" operates at multiple levels, from commoners to lower-level elites (Adas 1981:227, 243; 1986:73; Alexander 2004:51, 155). Social opportunities also may arise in which people relocate to redefine their social status. But if some imperial contexts offer opportunities, others repel allegiance and encourage actions to evade onerous or dangerous conditions. Documents generally greatly underestimate the efforts of people to flee to other locations because such evasive maneuvers seek to elude administrative records, but remarks on problems fulfilling labor demands give an inkling (e.g., Morrison 2001:260, 271, 272 for Vijayanagara, India).

Late Pre-Hispanic Period. Most exodus or population movement is likely to be nearly invisible archaeologically if individuals or small groups negotiated movement to socially allied neighbors, although isotopic analyses of skeletons may reveal movements, depending on the geographic conditions. Deposed rulers may seek exile, perhaps accompanied by retainers. For example, Brumfiel (1983:272–73) compiled documentary data about eight instances of flights of defeated rulers during the Late Postclassic period in the Basin of Mexico, prior to the Aztec Empire. Legendary accounts about Tula in Mexico include the idea of a governmental crisis and migration of members of one faction. These Tula accounts are subject to quite diverse interpretations (Gillespie 1989:123–207), but in turbulent Postclassic Mexico the idea of contested succession and exodus is an expectable cultural preoccupation.

Other exodus may involve commoners escaping harsh political conditions (Hicks 1982:243). According to historical records, some Matlazinca and Otomí communities in the Toluca area fled onerous Aztec control and were received and settled in enemy Tarascan territory, usually with both leaders and subjects relocating (García Castro 1999:66–67; Herrejón Peredo 1978:28–29; Quezada Ramírez 1972:43–44; Zorita 1994 [1963]:266). Another series of flights from Aztec control involved Otomí from the Basin of Mexico and nearby who went eastward to enemy Tlaxcala areas (Carrasco Pizana 1950:280–81). In cases such as this, relocation of sizable groups might be recognizable as an intrusive community, enclave, or refugee camp, but we cannot point to any clear-cut archaeological examples with current evidence. It is not enough to document migrations; migrations must be tied back to a political context to identify an exodus strategy.

We have not located pre-Hispanic Andean exodus information (other than the Inka exile government mentioned earlier), but internal population movement is posited as a strong element of both local community arrangements to address diverse resource zones, usually organized by altitude, and it is known to have been important in Inka imperial strategies of political control and resource and labor management (D'Altroy 2001b:214–18; 2002:147–84; D'Altroy and Earle 1985; Rowe 1982; Salomon 1986:143–86; Stanish 1997). Murra (1972) proposed a vertical archipelago model for Andean communities, suggesting that some members would operate in distinct resource zones to provide a division of labor and greater economic security to the community as a whole. The political and defensive practicality of the more extensive aspects of this arrangement prior to Inka expansion has been justifiably questioned (D'Altroy 2002:148), but it seems likely that the much greater Inka effort to relocate colonies (*mitmaqkuna*) compared to the Aztecs built upon a long-standing set of cultural practices involving population movement. Andeanists are assessing possible colonies or laborers (or finding against them) using skeletal measurements (Haun and Cock Carrasco 2010), dental measurements (Sutter 2000), pottery and architectural styles (Covey 2000; Rivera Casanovas 2010), skeletal isotopic values (Mackey 2010), and styles of burial goods (Salazar 2007).

Population movement under Aztec rule is not as prominent an element of state activity compared to the Inka, but it occurred (e.g., Herrera y Tordesillas 1952:211–12; Hicks 1982:243). As with the Andes, however, we have few indications of movements undertaken independently of state arrangements. During a drought in the Basin of Mexico, families sold children into servitude in the agriculturally productive Gulf lowlands (Hassig 1981), an unusual example of population movement likely involving commoners and one likely to be difficult to observe archaeologically because of the individual scale of arrangements.

Colonial Period. Flight, as studied by Colonial historians, could take the form of either exodus or internal population movement. Permanent or temporary exodus, like armed resistance, was most common in peripheral zones where there were long traditions of migration and Spanish political control was weak or nonexistent. The best-known cases come from the Yucatan peninsula, where Maya could escape Spanish dominion by fleeing into the unpacified regions to the east and south (e.g., Alexander 2005:176; Farriss 1984; Kepecs 2005:132; Palka 2005).

Opportunities for exodus were more limited in more densely popu-lated regions where Spanish control was stronger, but population move-ment was nonetheless a significant strategy in Oaxaca, much of central and western Mexico, and doubtless other regions as well (Schroeder 1998:xiv; Spores 1998:46; Taylor 1996:364–66). Internal population movement was sometimes a strategy of semi-covert resistance and sometimes a product of fear. It could also be a potent negotiating tool, as evidenced by threats to abandon pueblos altogether, depriving the government of tribute, unless abusive Spanish officials were removed. Population movement could take the form of a public gesture or it could be mainly avoidance of abusive offi-cials, priests, labor practices, or hacendados. D'Altroy (1992:85) notes that the conquistador Francisco Pizarro remarked that one reason for moving the Spanish capital from Jauja to Lima was that local people had moved away to avoid being drafted for onerous service as burden bearers. In and around the Basin of Mexico, escapes were less often to the moun-tains than to Mexico City, where people could hide in urban anonymity and more easily seek judicial remedies for exploitation (Taylor 1996:364–65).

Other forms of internal population movement that did not involve con-cealment were even more common, whether in permanent, cyclical, or temporary guises. Colonial relocation was sometimes undertaken to avoid specific types of exploitation like tribute or labor drafts (thus resistance), but it could also be a more open-ended attempt to better life chances, such as moving to a Spanish city or hacienda to engage in wage labor. These kinds of movement were of course not mutually exclusive. In Yucatan and Chiapas, Mexico, regular movements of populations about the country-side proceeded unchecked except in times of extreme disorder (Farriss 1978:187–216; Watson 1990:277). Alexander's (2004) archaeological work at the Maya settlement of Yaxcabá shows effects of seasonal dispersal to outlying plots and the process that Farriss (1978; 1984:199–214) terms "drift," that is, longer-term relocation to outlying smaller settlements that helped avoid Spanish exploitation. There are many indications of exten-sive movements in other areas and periods, ranging from Nueva Galicia in the seventeenth century to central Guatemala in the eighteenth (Sherman 1970; Taylor 1996:364; Watson 1990:240).

Internal population movements were strongly evident in the Andes, and have attracted considerable attention from historians. The greatest population flow – basically male – was to the major mining centers, especially Potosí, but there was also substantial movement to other Spanish cities and haciendas. Population movement was seasonal and permanent, forced and voluntary, and the destinations ranged from a few kilometers distant for agricultural labor to 1,000 kilometers away for *mita* labor service in the mines (Cook 1981:248–51). We have seen how the Andean archipelago settlement pattern in Inka times involved exchange, transhumance, and seasonal movement across sometimes distant ecological zones (Spalding 1984:175), and this predisposition to move distinguished the Andean highlands from the Mesoamerican ones.

The fluid nature of Andean settlement played havoc with Spanish efforts to concentrate people in settled villages (*reducciones*) where they could be more easily controlled. Bandy and Janusek (2005:285–87), using Titicaca archaeological settlement data, show that population declined in encomienda areas but augmented beyond natural increase in an area administered less oppressively by the crown. Finally, following Albarracin-Jordan (1992:329), they raise the possibility that augmentation of colonial occupation in some high elevation areas suited to camelid herding was not simply a subsistence option but also one that increased mobility and remoteness from Spanish control (Bandy and Janusek 2005:268).

Of even greater import in Colonial Peru was the legal category of *forastero* (literally, foreigner), which had no counterpart in Mexico or Guatemala. Technically, forasteros were Indians living outside their reducciones, and who were therefore exempt from the mita, the system of forced labor that channeled from one-seventh to one-fifth of the Andean population at any given time to feed the labor demands of the mines and Spanish cities, a system so onerous that virtually all Indians subject to it protested (Powers 1995a:7; Stavig 2000:529). Legally, forasteros remained members of their home communities where they were still liable for tribute, but in practice many avoided payment (Wightman 1990a:19–20).

The numbers of forasteros were staggering. By the end of the seventeenth century, between one-third and two-thirds of all Andeans were forasteros, depending on the region. For the Audiencia of Quito in the sixteenth and seventeenth centuries, Powers (1995a:107; 1995b:34, 56) has argued that not only did movement lead to the emergence of new ethnic identities, but that it subverted the Colonial order, undermined the forced labor system, and threatened elite hegemony (for treatments of forasteros and movement in other Andean regions, see Larson 1998; Saignes 1985, 1995; Spalding 1984; Stern 1982).

Information Control. In information control, provincial people seek to control or conceal to their advantage information sought by the imperial government. As noted earlier, information control is an inverse strategy, also pursued by imperial governments. Some aspects of state information control may not be broadly directed, but focused instead on inner government circles, such as concealment of a ruler's illness or death while the process of succession is arranged to the benefit of particular factions (Goody 1966:10; Rostworowski de Diez Canseco 1960:421). Broadly directed state information controls lead to the inverse aspects of this strategy for provinces. Scott (1998:80) underscores the "project of legibility" that lies behind state efforts to codify names, conduct censuses, make accurate maps, and secure uniform measures, all undertaken to simplify and order information reliably for state purposes, but subordinates may tend to conceal some of this information or distort it for their own advantage. Much depends on the degree of cooptation of local elites and the different social levels involved in information concealment. Commoners may resist providing certain types of demographic or economic information to their local rulers.

Provincial information control, predictably, is seldom recorded. Nor is it likely to be observable archaeologically, but, as we noted concerning Colonial population movement mentioned earlier, some relocation and dispersal may be intimately tied to information control. It is likely that the brevity of Aztec and Inka expansion truncated systematization of information along with any provincial counterploys. In any case, we have only a few indications of state information management.

Late Pre-Hispanic Period. Aztec-era long-distance merchants (*pochteca*) served as spies to acquire information about distant regions both inside and outside the empire (Townsend 1992:188). Certainly Aztec tribute rolls constituted steps toward systematic recordkeeping, and the Inka conducted censuses. Despite nascent Aztec efforts in information control, provincial information concealment is not obvious archaeologically or in documents. Morris and Covey (2006:148) remark on a coastal Inka province where reportedly workers were hidden from census takers. Patterson (1991:103) notes that severe penalties were prescribed for those who lied to census takers or people who traveled without permission (among other crimes); harsh penalties for information and communication infractions hint that locals at times evaded Inka dictates.

Colonial Period. Although Indian communities were left to their own devices in many spheres of life where local custom posed no threat to Spanish norms, the Colonial regimes of Mexico and Peru sought to impose their will in bureaucratic fashion in three areas: the exploitation of labor, collection of tribute, and conversion to the Catholic religion. All three provided ample incentives for local information control, as it was in the communities' interest to minimize their economic exploitation and preserve beliefs and rituals that were important to them.

The Spanish state administered its Indian subjects not as individuals, but as members of Indian communities. Labor and tribute quotas were set according to population, and Spanish officials kept tribute rolls for each community. Predictably, tribute counts were prime occasions for local forms of information control. In Mesoamerica, local Indian gobernadores, who were responsible for tribute collections, could hide people by claiming they had moved away or by misrepresenting their age or health. Minimizing tribute counts also alleviated the burden of *repartimiento* labor drafts, common in New Spain in the seventeenth century. As brokers, the gobernadores were in a position to control information flows between the community and the state, and they sometimes abused their power and exploited villagers for personal gain (Chance 1989:135–36).

In the Andes, the masters of information control were the kurakas, who were responsible for both tribute collections and labor drafts. Engaged in a tug-of-war with Spanish officials, many kurakas were able to conceal large numbers of tributaries as their personal retainers, and hence exempt from the mita (Wightman 1990a:23). Some reported false deaths and absences (Powers 1995a:82–83; Stern 1982:123–28).

The other arena where communities practiced information control concerned religious life. Catholicism quickly became a state religion, but, as is well known, local religious beliefs and practices varied enormously. Much religious change was gradual and virtually unconscious, yet in the Andes by the early eighteenth century there was a "guarded silence" in which indigenous communities kept their religious beliefs to themselves to minimize external interference (Mills 1997:4, 113, 247, 252, 284). Communities sometimes went to great lengths to shield prohibited ritual observances from Spanish eyes. In the Yucatan peninsula, population mobility and rural rancherias afforded a measure of geographic insulation from Spanish observation of traditional ceremonies.

Information control often involved high stakes. In the northern sierra of Oaxaca, Mexico, for example, two Indian *fiscales*, later canonized as the Venerable Martyrs of Cajonos, were killed by fellow villagers for revealing an indigenous household ceremony to Dominican friars. The ensuing civil and ecclesiastic crackdown snuffed out most indigenous public rituals in the region and ushered in a new period of heightened syncretism (Chance 1989:164–68, 173).

Appropriation. In appropriation, provincials selectively adopt or modify imperial practices and institutions and use them to further local ends. Provincials may capitulate to or be forced into use of imperial institutions to protect their own interests. An important point, however, is that they may do so actively in pursuit of their own ends. Appropriation may take advantage of fissures in authority and purposes within an empire. For example, during Colonial times, indigenous caciques used Spanish courts to protect or enlarge their rights, and pueblos used them for protection against exploitative taxation or labor demands. An appropriation strategy relates to the length of rule because imperial institutions must be established, and provincial people have to have an adequate opportunity to learn about them. In time, an appropriative provincial strategy becomes a pervasive strategy that integrates an empire through its institutions because imperial core members or ruling-class members attempt to use institutions for self-promotion and protection as well.

Late Pre-Hispanic Period. For the Aztec situation, we cannot readily disentangle appropriation in the material record because we have insufficient detail to distinguish it from imperial investments, bolstering, emulation, and complicity for most provinces. In any case, appropriation will be challenging for archaeology. The documentary record for Aztec times is sufficiently biased toward the core area and affected by the Early Colonial period that Aztec-era provincial appropriation is unlikely to be clearly attested. It is unlikely in the brief span of the Aztec Empire – with its considerable reliance on indirect rule – that much appropriation had occurred. In the Andes, judgments about appropriation are equally difficult, and documentary data are considerably affected by the first chaotic decades of Spanish rule and the Inka exile government, with past Inka times reinterpreted more favorably by native leaders (Patterson 1991:136–51; Rowe 1982:111–14).

Colonial Period. The appropriation of imperial mechanisms for local ends is easier to detect in many aspects of Colonial Indian life. Indian elites, such as those of Huamanga, Peru, in the seventeenth century, drew on strategies and relationships from the dominant Spanish society to further their own ends (Stern 1982:166). A widespread tactic of kurakas, who were under pressure to meet Spanish labor and tribute demands, was to privatize, in European fashion, their ownership of formerly communal lands vacated by out-migrating forasteros. At the same time, they coopted the labor of in-migrating forasteros seeking shelter. In this way, the more successful kurakas composed private work forces on their own lands, managing to fulfill Spanish demands while retaining enough resources to operate their own and their communities' enterprises (Powers 1995a:109–10; Spalding

1984:229). This combination of European-style individual property owner-ship with local Andean labor practices ultimately strengthened the kurakas' position relative to their communities (Powers 1998:200).

Indians also used the Spanish courts extensively to carry on disputes over land, status, and many other relationships. They were quick to realize that they could challenge decisions made by Spanish officials, dispute land grants and boundaries, and sue private persons or corporate entities for damages (Borah 1983:40; Serulnikov 2003:34–35, 122–23; Stavig 1999:83–85; Stern 1982:115).

The goal of appropriation strategies was often a conservative one, and instances could be multiplied almost indefinitely. In sixteenth-century Peru, indigenous noblewomen, who were entitled to land under native inheri-tance rules, manipulated Spanish law (which classified them as legal minors) to preserve their rights by conducting transactions through their male affines (Silverblatt 1987:121–22). Another example comes from the north-ern sierra of Oaxaca, Mexico, where late colonial Zapotec villagers turned to the Spanish district court to validate their claims to the noble status of *principal*. This strategy was so effective that by the late eighteenth century, more than one-third of the inhabitants of these small pueblos held *principal* status, illustrating how appropriation could also stimulate significant social change (Chance 1989:137–48).

Finally, we call attention to the substrategy of assertion, an especially strong form of appropriation that also entails *changing* the appropriated mechanism and persuading the imperial government or elites to accept the innovation. Originally, we treated assertion as a separate strategy (Chance and Stark 2007:221), but our inability to locate additional clear examples leads us to subsume it under appropriation, a possibility we debated orig-inally. One clear instance of assertion from late Colonial Mexico was the stretching of the legal identity of "cacique." By law in New Spain, a cacique was an heir of a pre-conquest ruler who was the sole possessor of a *cacicazgo* estate. Yet in Santiago Tecali in the Valley of Puebla in the mid-eighteenth century, more than one hundred individuals were recognized as caciques and consequently exempt from royal tribute. In effect, by asserting their own prerogatives, these nobles successfully redefined the legal parameters of cacique status and persuaded Spanish officials – in the immediate region, at least – to validate their claims (Chance 1996:490, 500).

Complicity. Whereas bolstering was discussed earlier as an essentially political strategy to strengthen the power base of a local ruler or elites vis-à-vis the empire, we define complicity as a strategy of economic cooperation of local elites or commoners with significant imperial others. Certainly political and economic power normally had to be combined, but specific endeavors may be more readily ascribed to political versus economic benefits. Most of our evidence points to elite complicity because commoner documentary coverage on this score is meager, but archaeological data from Andean households led us to discard our initial definition of this strategy as involving *only* elites. Household archaeology across a social spectrum has the advantage of revealing some of the economic and other conditions of everyday life (see Earle and Smith, Chapter 10). Complicity was used in situations where elites or commoners and outsiders shared certain economic interests and actively collaborated in enterprises; when elites were involved, complicity sometimes worked to the disadvantage of the commoners.

Late Pre-Hispanic Period. In the discussion of bolstering in the Aztec Cuetlaxtlan province, one example was the concentration of wealth signaled by decorated serving bowls in and near the local town of Callejón del Horno, suggesting that local elites benefited under Aztec rule. Decorated serving vessels may have been used in feasting and other social negotiations important for crafting local political power, but, if marketing was present, as seems likely (Garraty 2009), these vessels also imply use of an imperial style to express wealth. Nevertheless, this observation falls short of delineating a complicit connection between local elites and imperial personnel. Such subtle arrangements may be exceedingly difficult to define with material evidence.

Documents indicate some provincial rulers benefited economically from Aztec rule. Berdan (2006:159) notes that the imperial demand to participate in wars yielded lands and tribute for some rulers of conquered Basin of Mexico city-states. Similar sharing of gains from warfare is not recorded for distant provinces more recently incorporated in the empire. This disparity is one indication of differences due to geographic distance and the duration of provincial status. Distant provinces, more recently conquered, were typically less profoundly affected by Aztec rule compared to city-states in the Basin of Mexico and nearby, which experienced more meddling in offices, officeholders, and markets, along with establishment of competing hierarchies for tribute collection and marketing, cross-cutting traditional political units (Blanton 1996; Hodge 1984).

Smith (1986:81–82; 1994:340) suggests that Aztec provincial rulers in general were not inconvenienced economically by the empire, as there was no interference with their tribute collection, and they may even have been able to increase their own tribute because of stabilization of their rule. Lesser nobles, on the other hand, may not have fared as well, but commoners probably suffered the most because of the imposition of an imperial level of tribute on top of their traditional quotas. Finally, provincial rulers in some cases expanded their own tributary domain under Aztec rule, as they were not prohibited from such undertakings, or at least this was the case for Morelos provinces located adjacent to the Basin of Mexico. Smith (1986:81) summarizes Morelos evidence indicating that states that had been expansionist before the Aztecs had even greater success after entry into the empire; more subject towns and people meant more tribute. Whether a distant province, such as Cuetlaxtlan in the Gulf lowlands, could enjoy such expansion is unknown. The Morelos Cuauhnahuac dynasty had intermarried at various times with the Mexica dynasty and may have had opportunities different from distant provinces.

Mantaro Valley research in Peru shows that local elites who acquiesced to Inka rule enjoyed an elevated supply of imperial-style decorated ceramics, but they also lost much of their access to distant luxury items obtained through exchange, as discussed earlier for the emulation strategy. One of the most important findings of Mantaro research concerns the lot of commoner households under Inka rule. Under Inka authority, population was moved from higher elevation locations (more easily defended during the contentious pre-Inka period) to valley bottom locations more suited to maize cultivation. Although this reflects a state strategy to promote maize cultivation, it seems to have led to improved commoner economic prosperity to judge from evidence of more consumption of maize and meat, slightly more access to valuables, such as bronze and shell, and even modest access to Inka-style storage jars (Costin and Earle 1989; Earle 2001:309, 311; Owen 2001:289).

Certainly no Mantaro plebian paradise ensued, but the prospect of access to better lands and improved economic opportunities may well have made commoners complicit in Inka rule. As often remarked in discussions of Inka imperial strategies, the Inka state had to curtail the traditional authority and independent resources of local elites who otherwise could serve as foci of resistance or rebellion. A degree of alliance of the imperial state and commoner sectors at the expense of traditional authorities would take place most successfully where commoners were complicit in the changed conditions. The Inka state relied heavily on "internal revenues" of labor and staple finance (although external warfare built up resources) and conforms to Fargher and Blanton's (2007) contention that states reliant on internal revenues make important concessions to and provide more services for commoner segments. A possibility exists that at least some colonists who were moved by state decree benefited from lands assigned to them compared to their original conditions of life.

Colonial Period. Complicity was a common economic strategy pursued by many Colonial Andean and Mesoamerican elites. From the very beginning, caciques especially were thrust into brokerage positions where economic cooperation with Spaniards with regard to the provisioning of labor, tribute, and other resources was desirable, and often necessary. In early Peru, kurakas also formed business relationships with Spanish entrepreneurs and used their positions to amass European-style private wealth (Spalding 1973:585–87, 589, 591).

Additional forms of complicity appeared in later years as the Colonial economies matured. A common practice of provincial Spanish officials in both Mexico and Peru in the seventeenth and eighteenth centuries was the *repartimiento de efectos.* This was a coercive trading mechanism in which Indian villagers were forced to purchase goods (cattle, for example) at high prices or to produce goods (such as cotton cloth) and sell them back to the official at low prices. In parts of Mexico, Spanish *alcaldes mayores* enlisted the help of Indian cabildos to distribute goods and collect payments, and native officials found ways to profit economically from these activities (Chance 1989:147). In other regions, such as Mexico's Valley of Puebla, caciques participated in joint business ventures with the alcaldes mayores, often as investors (Chance 1996:487). Similar practices were common in the Andes, where kurakas were frequently wealthier and more powerful than their Mesoamerican counterparts (Garrett 2005:123; Serulnikov 2003:56; Stern 1982:164).

Another common strategy of many caciques was the sale or rental of land – private or communal – to Spaniards. In late Colonial Tecali, Mexico, caciques preferred to rent their lands to Spanish and mestizo farmers because they were more reliable in their payments than were Indian commoners or pueblos (Chance 2003:38–40). Similar complicit land deals involving Spaniards and Indian elites existed in the Andes (Spalding 1984:230).

Assimilation. In assimilation, provincial elites or commoners, as individuals or groups, seek varying degrees of social, economic, or identity integration with the dominant society. Assimilation is perhaps the most complex of the eight strategies we have delineated and the most difficult to observe directly in the archaeological and historical records. This is partly because it is so multifaceted and therefore difficult to define precisely. In some respects, it can be an outgrowth of bolstering and emulation. We view assimilation as a process that sometimes achieved completion, but more often than not stopped short of an absorption of one population into another so thorough that cultural and any biological differences give way to a new condition without such differences. Social and economic assimilation, we believe, were frequent strategies in both late pre-Hispanic and Colonial Mesoamerican contexts and could be accomplished, to a degree, within a single generation. But total absorption – complete assimilation – of an individual or group implies a change in identity of the persons involved, and this was certainly less common. Where it occurred, it likely took more than one generation and was a strategy pursued by offspring of intermarriage – children of marriages where the partners represented both imperial and provincial spheres. As we show with Colonial data, assimilation varied according to wealth and status, with highly differential results. The Spanish Colonial situation was complicated by the arrival of an exogenous population that brought new racial and cultural principles for ordering social relations. Racial distinctions per se did not exist prior to the arrival of the Spanish.

Late Pre-Hispanic Period. Much of our perspective on assimilation in the Aztec Empire relies on evidence of elite cooptation under the empire, discussed earlier under bolstering and emulation, and more broadly, the claim that an elite class shared a cultural orientation and values across Central Mexico (Berdan and Smith 1996:210–11; see review in Voorhies and Gasco 2004:177–82). This proposed elite cultural assimilation had roots earlier in the Postclassic period through elite intermarriage and expanding marketing and luxury trade that integrated elites across polities. For example, Boone (1996) provides detailed evidence that Aztecs modified widespread pictorial manuscript styles in Central Mexico to forge an imperial version. Smith (2008:31, 95) shows that some practices in architecture and city planning were shared in city-states prior to Aztec expansion, likely also symptomatic of elite interactions.

To further establish the prior Mesoamerican formation of an elite class with a shared set of cultural conventions and practices, many forms of material evidence must be examined in more detail in multiple regions prior to the spread of the empire. This issue of elite cultural and economic assimilation raises the question of whether assimilation proceeds at different rates according to class position. This issue also highlights how key imperial practices may modify processes that antedate the empire and were generated through the actions of elites or others in what *were to become* provincial societies. In several respects, the provincial assimilation strategy suggests a necessary extension of our diachronic observations for "pre-provincial" societies. In this respect, the late pre-Hispanic and Colonial situations differ because Colonial society broke sharply with pre-Columbian elite cultural practices.

Inka assimilation, as analyzed by Rowe (1982), did not enjoy great success; meanwhile, other Inka policies sought to maintain local identities. At Machu Picchu, retainers (*yanaconas*), including craft specialists (*camayocs*) and possibly colonists (*mitimaes*) were drawn from at least four different localities as indicated by burials (osteology and grave goods); they retained distinctive material culture but adopted Inka burial practices (Salazar 2007). Homeland identities of these subordinates do not seem to have been suppressed, and assimilation is evident only in burial forms, a more public context than the use of pottery and other items in homes that also were included as grave goods. The rapidity with which many provincial groups broke ranks with the two warring sides of the Inka succession and aided the Spanish, as well as the tumultuous decades that followed, suggest that assimilation was not a prominent feature of the Inka realm during its brief history.

Colonial Period. Indian assimilation in the Colonial context could mean becoming familiar and comfortable with the conventions of Hispanic society, being socially accepted to some degree by members of Hispanic society (not necessarily as one of them, but as a socially acceptable other), having a Spanish artisan or commercial occupation and working alongside members of Hispanic society, and ultimately exchanging an Indian for a mestizo or Spanish creole identity. In practice, therefore, assimilation was not an all-or-nothing proposition, but a gradual process that could take different forms and had built into it various stopping points along the way. It was further complicated by a situational aspect: a person who was an Indian in the village could be regarded as a mestizo (or in the Andes a *cholo*, a person of one-quarter European ancestry with one Spanish grandparent) in the city. Assimilation of individuals was sometimes a conscious strategy, but in other cases is best viewed as an end result of a series of smaller, less momentous life decisions.

Moving to a Spanish city was often a first step toward assimilation, but cities developed their own urban Indian sectors that could absorb migrants and insulate them from full integration – involving a change in identity – with the Hispanic sector. Perhaps the surest route to assimilation after a move to the city was through marriage to a Spanish creole, mestizo, or mulatto. In the case of the city of Oaxaca, Mexico, Indian commoners comprised a bounded ethnic segment, yet in social and economic terms, Indians had assimilated to city life and were not in any sense marginal: they often attended the same churches, held similar jobs, and worked in the same shops as non-Indians (Chance 1978:112–24, 151–55).

Indians also assimilated into the lower ranks of Spanish urban society in the Andean cities of Lima, Cuzco, and Cochabamba (Larson 1998:101; Wightman 1990a:111–12; 1990b:91, 111). By 1612, Lima had more than 500 skilled Indian artisans, and by the eighteenth century, separate Indian craft guilds. Lima's Indian artisans lived, dressed, and worked much like members of Hispanic society and participated fully in the Colonial monetarized economy. Yet there were also limits to assimilation: in the mid-eighteenth century, the city's Indian artisans still lacked full access to the honors and careers open to members of European society, and some of them participated in a conspiracy against the government in 1750 (Spalding 1984:280–81). In all these cities and others, there was a degree of intermarriage and various opportunities to pass as cholos or mestizos, although these trends as yet cannot be quantified (Larson 1998:101, 111; Saignes 1985:24).

The assimilative strategies of Indian elites were even more heterogeneous, as were the elite groups themselves. Some nobles who lost their wealth and the esteem of their commoner subjects assimilated to the Indian masses, whereas others, through strategic marriage choices, attempted to enter Hispanic society in the cities (Spalding 1984:230). At the highest levels, Mesoamerican and Andean caciques merged with the Hispanic elite of Mexico City, Lima, Cuzco, and even cities in Spain (Chipman 2005; Spalding 1984:230), although shedding a cacique identity completely usually took more than one generation. At lower levels, caciques that retained significant status and wealth tended to distance themselves from Indian commoners, even if they continued to reside in their home communities. Many such nobles took Spanish spouses, a trend that, in Mexico at least, became more common in the late Colonial period (Chance 2009; Garrett 2005:100).

Summary and Discussion

The information examined involves comparisons on two levels – among the empires, and among provinces in them. At times a third level comes into play, as social segments within provinces are addressed. Different social classes and identities proved crucial in examination of provincials' strategies. As we expanded the number of imperial cases or contexts to include the Inka and the Colonial Andes, the initial set of strategies underwent some modifications, as noted previously. On the whole, however, the strategies held up well as a basis to conceptualize and organize a variety of indications of provincial efforts. We also repositioned our discussion to place greater stress on a diachronic perspective that can reveal important variation in initial conditions confronted by imperial administrators and provincials alike. A diachronic perspective is important in other ways. For the Aztecs, we noted that elite interactions underway among "pre-provincial" societies may have affected assimilation.

For assimilation and integration at the other end of imperial timelines, the empires show important variation. Doyle (1986:118–19, 353) stresses that longevity of empires depends on decreasing asymmetry in economic and political relationships between the imperial core and subsidiary areas; an increasing range of opportunities for "peripheral" imperial groups is crucial. He attributes the greater longevity of the Spanish Empire in the New World, compared to England's, to such differences. We have to consider imperial "life histories" among our cases. In many respects, the Aztec and Inka involved empires with a beginning, scarcely any "middle," but with an abrupt end. The numerous adjustments indicated by the strategies evident during the brief span of Aztec and Inka imperial administration (e.g., Blanton 1996; Brumfiel 1983; Hodge 1984, 1996:41; Patterson 1991:72–97) should alert us that Smith's (1986:70) rhetorical question about the Aztecs – "an empire with no provincial infrastructure?" – could be rephrased as "an empire truncated before imperial infrastructure?" He suggests Aztec integration not so much through military force or provincial infrastructure but through elite cooptation, later also emphasizing market integration (Berdan et al. 1996; Smith 1986).

Inka integration was variable, but featured a more direct state incursion into the economic realm via state labor demands, resettlement, and state staple and wealth finance (D'Altroy and Earle 1985). Yet Inka emphases on local identities and community relocation contrast with the Aztecs because such practices reduced assimilation in the Inka Empire and likely increased the potential for fission, perhaps contributing to more Andean turbulence under Colonial administration compared to Colonial Mesoamerica. Provincials' strategies reflect important historical contingencies, and variation in emphases among strategies should be expected.

In Colonial contexts, as institutional integration was increasingly effected through direct rule, provincials became involved in a world of shared legal and administrative procedures with the imperial government. Complicity and assimilation are examples of provincials' strategies that played a marked role in Colonial times once imperial integration was well advanced.

The investigation of eight provincial strategies has shown a marked difference in evidence for strategies according to sources of information. Colonial documents provide very specific records, such as the litigation of individuals and families or their possessions, descent, and titles – important for evaluation of appropriation, which proved indistinct through archaeology. We have much less archaeological work for Colonial times to document material expressions of provincials' strategies, but settlement patterns and household consumption provide important information about commoner movements and market participation. Likewise, for the late pre-Hispanic period, archaeological work has lagged compared to the use of documents about the Aztec and Inka empires. Often archaeology shows better than documents the divergent tendencies of commoner populations, allowing us to see ways in which economic advantages accrued to them in cooperation with imperial policies, how they lost ground, and ways in which local innovations took advantage of imperial models.

We detected geographic effects. Indirect rule tends to be more characteristic for distant provinces in pre-Hispanic times, at least in Mesoamerica. The distant Aztec Cuetlaxtlan province likely engaged in emulation of imperial styles across social strata, reflecting decisions that employed locally produced versions of imperial items for local ends. Closer provinces may have engaged in trade with the Basin of Mexico that brought objects and styles associated with the imperial core into broad use both before and after conquest (Smith and Heath-Smith 1994). Rebellions and opposition were a nearly continuous feature of Inka attempts to expand on the far north. Ethnohistoric Aztec data and records from the Colonial administration provide examples of rebellions and exodus, but whether rebellions tend to occur more frequently in distant provinces is uncertain. Smith (1986:79) notes that just outside the Basin of Mexico, the polity of Cuauhnahuac, Morelos, after incorporation, continued to prosper through conquests of its own neighbors; he suggests that rulers eventually felt sufficiently strong and prosperous to rebel (although they were then re-conquered). Consequently, individual provincial histories and political and economic resources require assessment. The economic and political benefits of bolstering strategies may eventually give way to resistance irrespective of geographic distance.

Perhaps the most important conclusion we offer is the importance of examining provincials' strategies in their own right – not independent of their imperial context but, rather, as foci of actions that affect the social, economic, and cultural trajectory of empires. Certainly imperial governments that ignore or misapprehend provincials' strategies become more susceptible to internal competition, external alliances, and fracture along many cleavage lines. Doyle (1986:367–69) notes that even within a well-integrated empire, provincial elites and wealthy merchants may eventually reject exploitative relations and seek separation, an ingredient in the cost–benefit calculations that Taintor (1988) proposes. The recurrent interest in how empires originate, succeed, and fail must be as much an investigation of provincials' strategies as imperial ones (see Robinson 1972).

Although our discussion is cast in terms of provincials' strategies, the theoretical posture and attention to local conditions and strategies has implications for a variety of areas "peripheral" to major states or empires as well, especially as states or empires expand. Strategies of bolstering, emulation, exodus, and others have applicability for peripheral allied or independent polities that are busy defending themselves from neighbors, from an expanding major state or empire, or that are taking advantage of opportunities conditioned by their powerful neighbor (see discussion of the northern Inka borders by Patterson [1991:107–16]).

We have demonstrated a wealth of possibilities for understanding the active role of people in provincial (or peripheral) societies using both archaeological and ethnohistoric data. Many of the sources of information show how archaeologists or historians can pursue these issues in other provinces (or empires) and redress the spottiness of relevant information. By expanding our range of cases, we found evidence of commoner complicity, for example, and we detected the importance of both exodus and internal population movement, whereas previously we emphasized exodus. In fact, internal population movement proved to be much more widely practiced than we had initially anticipated; it is also underappreciated by researchers, at least for pre-Hispanic times in Mesoamerica, whereas in the Andes, analyses of state-sponsored resettlement predominate compared to moves initiated by communities or groups. We will not be surprised if further research in Mesoamerica reveals more internal population movement than commonly has been discussed. Thus a comparative stance can alert researchers to issues warranting reexamination, and the eight provincials' strategies establish a comparative structure to appreciate variation and its bases.

We have established some of the complexity of provincial strategies that redress the ample core-centric documentation of imperial strategies. We noted some chronological emphases in strategies between early imperial rule and later rule (if there is any), with appropriation and assimilation becoming more prominent later, but bolstering and emulation more significant earlier. Nevertheless, we have not adequately captured all the important dimensions of provincials' strategies. For example, demographic change is another cross-cutting factor that affects provincials' strategies, like class. Adas (1986:76, 78) observes that population growth and declining land reserves reduce the opportunities for exodus and internal movement, as does increasingly bureaucratic direct administration. The utility of exodus and movement can therefore vary geographically, reflecting demography and land access, as its prominence in the Colonial Yucatan peninsula demonstrates. Another relevant issue we have not explored is the analytic balance between survival and provincials' strategies. At times, provincial people may have few or no options if they wish to survive oppression, threats, or force. We have written in a way that recognizes provincials' actions without the level of contextual detail required to distinguish survival necessities, but this is an important issue. We expect a wealth of additional comparative work on provincials' strategies. Provincial people, usually "outgunned" by imperial power, nevertheless profoundly conditioned imperial rule.

Acknowledgments

Archaeological data from the lower Blanco area were made possible with support from the National Science Foundation (BNS 85–19167, BNS 87–41867, and SBR–9804738), the National Geographic Society, and Arizona State University, with permission from the Instituto Nacional de Antropología e Historia. This expansion of our original study benefited greatly from comments by Rani Alexander, Elizabeth Brumfiel, Katharina Schreiber, Michael Smith, and Emily Umberger, but they are not responsible for our decisions about the content or blunders of interpretation. They provided more ideas for improvement than we were able to act upon. Likewise the conference participants provided a number of suggestions for expansion to other imperial contexts that we are unable to address here. We thank Michael E. Smith for the invitation to expand our investigations for his comparative conference "Settlement, Economy, and Power in Deep History: Towards a New Comparative Synthesis."

Bibliography

Acuto, Félix A. 2010 Living Under the Imperial Thumb in the Northern Calchaquí Valley, Argentina. In *Distant Provinces in the Inka Empire: Toward a Deeper Understanding of Inka Imperialism*, edited by Michael A. Malpass and Sonia Alconini, pp. 108–50. University of Iowa Press, Iowa City.

Adas, Michael 1981 From Avoidance to Confrontation: Peasant Protest in Precolonial and Colonial Southeast Asia. *Comparative Studies in Society and History* 23:217–47.

———. 1986 From Footdragging to Flight: The Evasive History of Peasant Avoidance Protest in South and Southeast Asia. *Journal of Peasant Studies* 12(2):64–86.

Albarracin-Jordan, Juan 1992 Prehispanic and Early Settlement Patterns in the Lower Tiwanaku Valley, Bolivia. Ph.D. dissertation, Department of Anthropology, Southern Methodist University, Dallas. University Microfilms, Ann Arbor.

Alconini, Sonia 2010 Yampara Households and Communal Evolution in the South-eastern Inka Peripheries. In *Distant Provinces in the Inka Empire: Toward a Deeper Understanding of Inka Imperialism*, edited by Michael A. Malpass and Sonia Alconini, pp. 75–107. University of Iowa Press, Iowa City.

Alexander, Rani T. 2004 *Yaxcabá and the Caste War of Yucatán: An Archaeological Perspective*. University of New Mexico Press, Albuquerque.

———. 2005 Isla Cilvituk and the Difficulties of Spanish Colonization in South-western Campeche. In *The Postclassic to Spanish-Era Transition in Mesoamerica: Archaeological Perspectives*, edited by Susan Kepecs and Rani T. Alexander, pp. 161–81. University of New Mexico Press, Albuquerque.

Bandy, Matthew S., and John W. Janusek 2005 Settlement Patterns, Administrative Boundaries, and Internal Migration in the Early Colonial Period. In *Advances in Titicaca Basin Archaeology–1*, edited by Charles Stanish, Amanda B. Cohen, and Mark S. Aldenderfer, pp. 267–88. Cotsen Institute of Archaeology at UCLA, Los Angeles, California.

Berdan, Frances F. 2006 The Role of Provincial Elites in the Aztec Empire. In *Intermediate Elites in Pre-Columbian States and Empires*, edited by Christina M. Elson and R. Alan Covey, pp. 154–65. University of Arizona Press, Tucson.

Berdan, Frances F., and Michael E. Smith 1996 Imperial Strategies and Core-Periphery Relations. In *Aztec Imperial Strategies*, by Frances F. Berdan, Richard E. Blanton, Elizabeth H. Boone, Mary G. Hodge, Michael E. Smith, and Emily Umberger, pp. 209–17. Dumbarton Oaks Research Library and Collection, Washington, DC.

Berdan, Frances F., Richard E. Blanton, Elizabeth H. Boone, Mary G. Hodge, Michael E. Smith, and Emily Umberger 1996 *Aztec Imperial Strategies*. Dumbarton Oaks Research Library and Collection, Washington, DC.

Blanton, Richard E. 1996 The Basin of Mexico Market System and the Growth of Empire. In *Aztec Imperial Strategies*, by Francis F. Berdan, Richard E. Blanton, Elizabeth H. Boone, Mary G. Hodge, Michael E. Smith, and Emily Umberger, pp. 47–84. Dumbarton Oaks Research Library and Collection, Washington, DC.

Boone, Elizabeth Hill 1996 Manuscript Painting in Service of Imperial Ideology. In *Aztec Imperial Strategies*, by Francis F. Berdan, Richard E. Blanton, Elizabeth H. Boone, Mary G. Hodge, Michael E. Smith, and Emily Umberger, pp. 181–206. Dumbarton Oaks Research Library and Collection, Washington, DC.

Borah, Woodrow 1983 *Justice by Insurance: The General Indian Court of Colonial Mexico and the Legal Aides of the Half-Real*. University of California Press, Berkeley.

Brumfiel, Elizabeth 1983 Aztec State Making: Ecology, Structure, and the Origin of the State. *American Anthropologist* 85:261–84.

———. 1992 Distinguished Lecture in Archeology: Breaking and Entering the Ecosystem: Gender, Class, and Faction Steal the Show. *American Anthropologist* 94:551–67.

Carrasco Pizana, Pedro 1950 *Los Otomíes: Cultura e historia prehispánicas de los pueblos mesoamericanos de habla otomiana*. Universidad Nacional Autónoma de México, Mexico City.

———. 1991 Matrimonios hispano–indios en el primer siglo de la colonia. In *Familia y poder en Nueva España: Memoria del tercer simposio de historia de las mentalidades*, pp. 11–21. Instituto Nacional de Antropología e Historia, Mexico City.

Chance, John K. 1978 *Race and Class in Colonial Oaxaca*. Stanford University Press, Stanford.

———. 1989 *Conquest of the Sierra: Spaniards and Indians in Colonial Oaxaca*. University of Oklahoma Press, Norman.

———. 1996 The Caciques of Tecali: Class and Ethnic Identity in Late Colonial Mexico. *Hispanic American Historical Review* 76:475–502.

———. 1997 The Mixtec Nobility under Colonial Rule. In *Codices, Caciques, y Comunidades*, edited by Maarten Jansen y Luis Reyes, pp. 161–78. Asociación de Historiadores Latinoamericanistas Europeos, Leiden. Cuadernos de Historia Latinoamericana, no. 5.

———. 2003 Haciendas, Ranchos, and Indian Towns: A Case from the Late Colonial Valley of Puebla. *Ethnohistory* 50:15–45.

———. 2009 Marriage Alliances among Colonial Mixtec Elites: The Villagómez Caciques of Acatlan–Petlalcingo. *Ethnohistory* 56:91–123.

Chance, John K., and Barbara L. Stark 2007 Estrategias empleadas en las provincias imperiales: perspectivas prehispánicas y coloniales en Mesoamérica. *Revista Española de Antropología Americana* 37:203–33.

Charlton, Thomas H., Cynthia L. Otis Charlton, and Patricia Forunier García 2005 The Basin of Mexico A.D. 1450–1620: Archaeological Dimensions. In *The Postclassic to Spanish-Era Transition in Mesoamerica; Archaeological Perspectives*, edited by Susan Kepecs and Rani T. Alexander, pp. 49–63. University of New Mexico Press, Albuquerque.

Chipman, Donald E. 2005 *Moctezuma's Children: Aztec Royalty under Spanish Rule, 1520–1700*. University of Texas Press, Austin.

Coatsworth, John H. 1988 Patterns of Rural Rebellion in Latin America: Mexico in Comparative Perspective. In *Riot, Rebellion, and Revolution: Rural Social Conflict in Mexico*, edited by Friedrich Katz, pp. 21–62. Princeton University Press, Princeton.

Cook, Noble David 1981 *Demographic Collapse: Indian Peru, 1520–1620*. Cambridge University Press, Cambridge.

Costin, Cathy Lynne 2001 Production and Exchange of Ceramics. In *Empire and Domestic Economy*, edited by Terence N. D'Altroy, Christine A. Hastorf, and Associates, pp. 203–42. Kluwer Academic/Plenum Publishers, New York.

Costin, Cathy Lynne, and Timothy Earle 1989 Status Distinction and Legitimation of Power as Reflected in Changing Patterns of Consumption in Late Prehispanic Peru. *American Antiquity* 54:691–714.

Covey, R. Alan 2000 Inka Administration of the Far South Coast of Peru. *Latin American Antiquity* 11:119–38.

Cowgill, George L. 1988 Onward and Upward with Collapse. In *The Collapse of Ancient States and Civilizations*, edited by Norman Yoffee and George L. Cowgill, pp. 244–76. University of Arizona Press, Tucson.

D'Altroy, Terence N. 1992 *Provincial Power in the Inca Empire*. Smithsonian Institution Press, Washington, DC.

———. 2001a From Autonomous to Imperial Rule. In *Empire and Domestic Economy*, edited by Terence N. D'Altroy, Christine A. Hastorf, and Associates, pp. 325–39. Kluwer Academic/Plenum Publishers, New York.

———. 2001b Politics, Resources, and Blood in the Inka Empire. In *Empires: Perspectives from Archaeology and History*, edited by Susan E. Alcock, Terence N. D'Altroy, Kathleen D. Morrison, and Carla M. Sinopoli, pp. 201–26. Cambridge University Press, Cambridge.

———. 2001c State Goods in the Domestic Economy: The Inka Ceramic Assemblage. In *Empire and Domestic Economy*, edited by Terence N. D'Altroy, Christine A. Hastorf, and Associates, pp. 243–64. Kluwer Academic/Plenum Publishers, New York.

———. 2002 *Provincial Power in the Inka Empire*. Smithsonian Institution Press, Washington, DC.

D'Altroy, Terence N., and Timothy K. Earle 1985 Staple Finance, Wealth Finance, and Storage in the Inka Political Economy. *Current Anthropology* 26:187–206.

Doyle, Michael W. 1986 *Empires*. Cornell University Press, Ithaca.

Drennan, Robert D. 1984 Long-distance Transport Costs in Pre-Hispanic Mesoamerica. *American Anthropologist* 86:105–12.

Earle, Timothy K. 1985 Commodity Exchange and Markets in the Inca State: Recent Archaeological Evidence. In *Markets and Marketing*, edited by Stuart Plattner, pp. 369–97. Monographs in Economic Anthropology No. 4. Society for Economic Anthropology, Lanham, New York.

———. 2001 Exchange and Social Stratification in the Andes: The Xauxa Case. In *Empire and Domestic Economy*, edited by Terence N. D'Altroy, Christine A. Hastorf, and Associates, pp. 297–314. Kluwer Academic/Plenum Publishers, New York.

Eisenstadt, Shmuel Noah 1993 [1963] *The Political Systems of Empires*. Transaction Publishers, New Brunswick.

Elson, Christina M. 2006 Intermediate Elites and the Political Landscape of the Early Zapotec State. In *Intermediate Elites in Pre-Columbian States and Empires*, edited by Christina M. Elson and R. Alan Covey, pp. 44–67. University of Arizona Press, Tucson.

Fargher, Lane F., and Richard E. Blanton 2007 Revenue, Voice, and Public Goods in Three Pre-Modern States. *Comparative Studies in Society and History* 49:848–82.

Farriss, Nancy 1978 Nucleation versus Dispersal: The Dynamics of Population Movement in Colonial Yucatan. *Hispanic American Historical Review* 58:187–216.

———. 1984 *Maya Society under Colonial Rule*. Princeton University Press, Princeton.

Frye, Kira L. 2005 The Inca Occupation of the Lake Titicaca Region. In *Advances in Titicaca Basin Archaeology–1*, edited by Charles Stanish, Amanda B. Cohen, and Mark S. Aldenderfer, pp. 197–208. Cotsen Institute of Archaeology at UCLA, Los Angeles, California.

García Castro, René 1999 *Indios, territorio y poder en la provincia matlatzinca: La negociación del espacio político de los pueblos otomianos, siglos XV–XII*. CIESAS, Instituto Nacional de Antropología e Historia and El Colegio Mexiquense, Mexico City and Toluca.

Garraty, Christopher P. 2009 Evaluating the Distributional Approach to Inferring Marketplace Exchange: A Test Case from the Mexican Gulf Lowlands. *Latin American Antiquity* 20:157–74.

Garraty, Christopher P., and Barbara L. Stark 2002 Imperial and Social Relations in Postclassic South-central Veracruz, Mexico. *Latin American Antiquity* 13:3–33.

Garrett, David T. 2005 *Shadows of Empire: The Indian Nobility of Cusco, 1750–1825.* Cambridge University Press, Cambridge.

Gasco, Janine 1989 Economic History of Ocelocalco, a Colonial Soconusco Town. In *Ancient Trade and Tribute: Economies of the Soconusco Region of Mesoamerica,* edited by Barbara Voorhies, pp. 304–25. University of Utah Press, Salt Lake City.

Gibson, Charles 1964 *The Aztecs under Spanish Rule.* Stanford University Press, Stanford.

Gillespie, Susan D. 1989 *The Aztec Kings: The Construction of Rulership in Mexica History.* University of Arizona Press, Tucson.

Goldstein, Paul S. 2005 *Andean Diaspora: The Tiwanaku Colonies and the Origins of South American Empire.* University Press of Florida, Gainesville.

Goody, Jack 1966 Introduction. In *Succession to High Office,* edited by Jack Goody, pp. 1–181. Cambridge Papers in Social Anthropology 4. Cambridge University Press, Cambridge.

Grosboll, Sue 1993 ... And He Said in the Time of the Ynga, They Paid Tribute and Served the Ynga. In *Provincial Inca: Archaeological and Ethnohistorical Assessment of the Impact of the Inca State,* edited by Michael A. Malpass, pp. 44–76. University of Iowa Press, Iowa City.

Hassig, Ross 1981 The Famine of One Rabbit: Ecological Causes and Social Consequences of a Pre-Columbian Calamity. *Journal of Anthropological Research* 37:172–82.

———. 1985 *Trade, Tribute, and Transportation: The Sixteenth-century Political Economy of the Basin of Mexico.* University of Oklahoma Press, Norman.

Haun, Susan J., and Gillermo Cock Carrasco 2010 A Bioarchaeological Approach to the Search for Mitmaqkuna. In *Distant Provinces in the Inka Empire: Toward a Deeper Understanding of Inka Imperialism,* edited by Michael A. Malpass and Sonia Alconini, pp. 193–220. University of Iowa Press, Iowa City.

Helms, Mary W. 1993 *Craft and the Kingly Ideal: Art, Trade, and Power.* University of Texas Press, Austin.

Herrera y Tordesillas, Antonio de 1952 *Historia General de los Hechos de los Castellanos en las Islas y Terrafirme del Mar Océano,* vol. 9 (Década Cuarta, Libro Séptimo). Imprento Real de Nicolas Rodiguea Franco, Madrid. (originally published 1730).

Herrejón Peredo, Carlos 1978 La pugna entre mexicas y tarascos. *Cuadernos de Historia (Toluca)* 1:11–47.

Hicks, Frederic 1982 Tetzcoco in the Early 16th Century: The State, the City and the Calpolli. *American Ethnologist* 9:230–49.

———. 1994 Alliance and Intervention in Aztec Imperial Expansion. In *Factional Competition and Political Development in the New World,* edited by Elizabeth M. Brumfiel and John W. Fox, pp. 111–16. Cambridge University Press, Cambridge.

Hodge, Mary G. 1984 *Aztec City-States.* Memoirs of the Museum of Anthropology, 18. University of Michigan, Ann Arbor.

———. 1996 Political Organization of the Central Provinces. In *Aztec Imperial Strategies,* by Frances F. Berdan, Richard E. Blanton, Elizabeth H. Boone, Mary

G. Hodge, Michael E. Smith, and Emily, Umberger pp. 17–45. Dumbarton Oaks Research Library and Collection, Washington, DC.

Jennings, Justin 2003 Inca Imperialism, Ritual Change, and Cosmological Continuity in the Cotahuasi Valley of Peru. *Journal of Anthropological Research* 59:433–62.

Julien, Catherine J. 1993 Finding a Fit: Archaeology and Ethnohistory of the Incas. In *Provincial Inca: Archaeological and Ethnohistorical Assessment of the Impact of the Inca State*, edited by Michael A. Malpass, pp. 177–233. University of Iowa Press, Iowa City.

Katz, Friedrich 1988 Rural Uprisings in Preconquest and Colonial Mexico. In *Riot, Rebellion, and Revolution: Rural Social Conflict in Mexico*, edited by Friedrich Katz, pp. 65–94. Princeton University Press, Princeton.

Kaufman, Herbert 1988 The Collapse of Ancient States and Civilizations as an Organizational Problem. In *The Collapse of Ancient States and Civilizations*, edited by Norman Yoffee and George L. Cowgill, pp. 219–35. University of Arizona Press, Tucson.

Kelly, Isabel, and Angel Palerm 1952 *The Tajin Totonac, Part I. History, Subsistence, Shelter, and Technology*. Institute of Social Anthropology Publication No. 13. Smithsonian Institution, Washington, DC.

Kepecs, Susan 2005 Mayas, Spaniards, and Salt: World Systems Shifts in Sixteenth-Century Yucatán. In *The Postclassic to Spanish-Era Transition in Mesoamerica; Archaeological Perspectives*, edited by Susan Kepecs and Rani T. Alexander, pp. 117–37. University of New Mexico Press, Albuquerque.

Larson, Brooke 1998 *Cochabamba, 1550–1900: Colonialism and Agrarian Transformation in Bolivia*. Expanded Edition. Duke University Press, Durham.

Lynch, Thomas F. 1993 The Identification of Inca Posts and Roads from Catarpe to Río Frio, Chile. In *Provincial Inca: Archaeological and Ethnohistorical Assessment of the Impact of the Inca State*, edited by Michael A. Malpass, pp. 117–42. University of Iowa Press, Iowa City.

Mackey, Carol 2010 The Socioeconomic and Ideological Transformation of Farfán under Inka Rule. In *Distant Provinces in the Inka Empire: Toward a Deeper Understanding of Inka Imperialism*, edited by Michael A. Malpass and Sonia Alconini, pp. 221–59. University of Iowa Press, Iowa City.

Malpass, Michael A. 1993 Variability in the Inca State: Embracing a Wider Perspective. In *Provincial Inca: Archaeological and Ethnohistorical Assessment of the Impact of the Inca State*, edited by Michael A. Malpass, pp. 234–44. University of Iowa Press, Iowa City.

Malpass, Michael A., and Sonia Alconini (editors) 2010 *Distant Provinces in the Inka Empire: Toward a Deeper Understanding of Inka Imperialism*. University of Iowa Press, Iowa City.

Malville, Nancy J. 2001 Long-distance Transport of Bulk Goods in the Pre-Hispanic American Southwest. *Journal of Anthropological Archaeology* 20:230–43.

Menzel, Dorothy 1959 The Inca Occupation of the South Coast of Peru. *Southwestern Journal of Anthropology* 15:125–42.

———. 1960 Archaism and Revival on the South Coast of Peru. In *Men and Cultures, Selected Papers of the Fifth International Congress of Anthropological and Ethnological*

Sciences, Philadelphia, September 1–9, 1956, edited by Anthony F. C. Wallace, pp. 596–600. University of Pennsylvania Press, Philadelphia.

Miller, Roberta Neil 2006 Figurines and Middle to Late Postclassic Changes in the Western Lower Papaloapan Basin (A.D. 1200–1521). Master's Paper, School of Human Evolution and Social Change, Arizona State University, Tempe, Arizona.

Mills, Kenneth 1997 *Idolatry and Its Enemies: Colonial Andean Religion and Its Extirpation, 1640–1750*. Princeton University Press, Princeton.

Morris, Craig, and R. Alan Covey 2006 The Management of Scale or the Creation of Scale: Administrative Processes in Two Inka Provinces. In *Intermediate Elites in Pre-Columbian States and Empires*, edited by Christina M. Elson and R. Alan Covey, pp. 136–53. University of Arizona Press, Tucson.

Morrison, Kathleen D. 2001 Coercion, Resistance, and Hierarchy: Local Processes and Imperial Strategies in the Vijayanagara Empire. In *Empires: Perspectives from Archaeology and History*, edited by Susan E. Alcock, Terence N. D'Altroy, Kathleen D. Morrison, and Carla M. Sinopoli, pp. 252–78. Cambridge University Press, Cambridge.

Murra, John V. 1972 El control vertical de un máximo de pisos ecológicos en la economía de las sociedades Andinas. In *Visita de la provincia de León de Huánuco en 1562*, Tomo 2, edited by John V. Murra, pp. 429–76. Universidad Nacional Hermilio Valdizán, Huánuco, Peru.

Ohnersorgen, Michael Anthony 2001 Social and Economic Organization of Cotaxtla in the Postclassic Gulf Lowlands. Ph.D. Dissertation, Department of Anthropology, Arizona State University, Tempe, AZ. University Microfilms, Ann Arbor.

————. 2006 Aztec Provincial Administration at Cuetlaxtlan, Veracruz. *Journal of Anthropological Archaeology* 25:1–32.

Ouweneel, Arij 1995 From Tlahtocayotl to Gobernadoryotl: A Critical Examination of Indigenous Rule in Eighteenth-Century Central Mexico. *American Ethnologist* 22:756–85.

Owen, Bruce 2001 The Economy of Metal and Shell Wealth Goods. In *Empire and Domestic Economy*, edited by Terence N. D'Altroy, Christine A. Hastorf, and Associates, pp. 265–93. Kluwer Academic/Plenum Publishers, New York.

Palka, Joel W. 2005 Postcolonial Conquest of the Southern Maya Lowlands, Cross-Cultural Interaction, and Lacandon Maya Culture Change. In *The Postclassic to Spanish-Era Transition in Mesoamerica: Archaeological Perspectives*, edited by Susan Kepecs and Rani T. Alexander, pp. 183–201. University of New Mexico Press, Albuquerque.

Patterson, Thomas C. 1991 *The Inca Empire: The Formation and Disintegration of a Pre-Capitalist State*. Berg, New York.

Powers, Karen Vieira 1995a *Andean Journeys: Migration, Ethnogenesis, and the State in Colonial Quito*. University of New Mexico Press, Albuquerque.

————. 1995b The Battle for Bodies and Souls in the Colonial North Andes: Intraecclesiastical Struggles and the Politics of Migration. *Hispanic American Historical Review* 75:31–56.

————. 1998 A Battle of Wills: Inventing Chiefly Legitimacy in the Colonial North Andes. In *Dead Giveaways: Indigenous Testaments of Colonial Mesoamerica and the*

Andes, edited by Susan Kellogg and Matthew Restall, pp. 183–213. University of Utah Press, Salt Lake City.

Quezada Ramírez, María Noemí 1972 *Los matlatzincas: Época prehispánica y época Colonial hasta 1650*. Serie Investigaciones 22, Departamento de Investigaciones Históricas, Instituto Nacional de Antropología e Historia, Mexico City.

Ramírez, Susan E. 1996 *The World Upside Down: Cross-Cultural Contact and Conflict in Sixteenth-Century Peru*. Stanford University Press, Stanford.

Rivera Casanovas, Claudia 2010 Forms of Imperial Control and the Negotiation of Local Autonomy in the Cinti Valley of Bolivia. In *Distant Provinces in the Inka Empire: Toward a Deeper Understanding of Inka Imperialism*, edited by Michael A. Malpass and Sonia Alconini, pp. 151–72. University of Iowa Press, Iowa City.

Robinson, Ronald 1972 Non-European Foundations of European Imperialism: Sketch for a Theory of Collaboration. In *Studies of the Theory of Imperialism*, edited by Roger Owen and Bob Sutcliffe, pp. 117–42. Longman Group Ltd, London.

Rostworowski de Diez Canseco, María 1960 Succession, Cooption to Kingship, and Royal Incest among the Inca. *Southwestern Journal of Anthropology* 16:417–27.

Rowe, John Howland 1946 Inca Culture at the Time of the Spanish Conquest. In *Handbook of South American Indians, Volume 2, The Andean Civilizations*, edited by Julian H. Steward, pp. 183–330. Smithsonian Institution, Washington, DC.

————. 1948 The Kingdom of Chimor. *Acta Americana* 6:26–59.

————. 1982 Inca Policies and Institutions Relation to the Cultural Unification of the Empire. In *The Inca and Aztec States 1400–1800*, edited by George A. Collier, Renato I. Rosaldo, and John D. Wirth, pp. 93–118. Academic Press, New York.

Saignes, Thierry 1985 *Caciques, Tribute, and Migration in the Southern Andes: Indian Society and the 17th-Century Colonial Order (Audiencia de Charcas)*. Institute of Latin American Studies, University of London, London.

————. 1995 Indian Migration and Social Change in Seventeenth-Century Charcas. In *Ethnicity, Markets, and Migration in the Andes: At the Crossroads of History and Anthropology*, edited by Brooke Larson, Olivia Harris, with Enrique Tandeter, pp. 167–95. Duke University Press, Durham.

————. 1999 The Colonial Condition in the Quechua-Aymara Heartland (1570–1780). In *The Cambridge History of the Native Peoples of the Americas*, Vol. 3, Part 2, edited by Frank Salomon and Stuart B. Schwartz, pp. 59–137. Cambridge University Press, Cambridge.

Salazar, Lucy C. 2007 Machu Picchu's Silent Majority: A Consideration of the Inka Cemeteries. In *Variations in the Expression of Inka Power: A Symposium at Dumbarton Oaks 18 and 19 October 1997*, edited by Richard L. Burger, Craig Morris, and Ramiro Matos Mendieta, pp 165–83. Dumbarton Oaks Research Library and Collection, Washington, DC.

Salomon, Frank 1986 *Native Lords of Quito in the Age of the Incas: The Political Economy of North Andean Chiefdoms*. Cambridge University Press, Cambridge.

Schachner, Gregson 2007 Population Circulation and the Transformation of Ancient Cibola Communities. Ph.D. dissertation, School of Human Evolution and Social Change, Arizona State University. University Microfilms, Ann Arbor.

Schreiber, Katharina J. 1992 *Wari Imperialism in Middle Horizon Peru*. Anthropological Papers No. 87, Museum of Anthropology, University of Michigan, Ann Arbor.

———. 1993 The Inca Occupation of the Province of Andamarca Lucanas, Peru. In *Provincial Inca: Archaeological and Ethnohistorical Assessment of the Impact of the Inca State*, edited by Michael A. Malpass, pp. 77–116. University of Iowa Press, Iowa City.

Schroeder, Susan 1998 Introduction. In *Native Resistance and the Pax Colonial in New Spain*, edited by Susan Schroeder, pp. xi–xxiii. University of Nebraska Press, Lincoln.

Scott, James C. 1985 *Weapons of the Weak: Everyday Forms of Peasant Resistance*. Yale University Press, New Haven.

———. 1990 *Domination and the Arts of Resistance: Hidden Transcripts*. Yale University Press, New Haven.

———. 1998 *Seeing Like a State: How Certain Schemes to Improve the Human Condition Have Failed*. Yale University Press, New Haven.

Serulnikov, Sergio 2003 *Subverting Colonial Authority: Challenges to Spanish Rule in Eighteenth-Century Southern Andes*. Duke University Press, Durham.

Sherman, William 1970 Tlaxcalans in Postconquest Guatemala. *Tlalocan* 6:124–39.

Silverblatt, Irene 1987 *Moon, Sun, and Witches: Gender Ideology and Class in Inca and Colonial Peru*. Princeton University Press, Princeton.

Skoglund, Thanet, Barbara L. Stark, Hector Neff, and Michael D. Glascock 2006 Compositional and Stylistic Analysis of Aztec-Era Ceramics: Provincial Strategies at the Edge of Empire, South-central Veracruz, Mexico. *Latin American Antiquity* 17:541–59.

Smith, Michael E. 1986 The Role of Social Stratification in the Aztec Empire: A View from the Provinces. *American Anthropologist* 88:70–91.

———. 1994 Economies and Polities in Aztec-Period Morelos: Ethnohistoric Overview. In *Economies and Polities in the Aztec Realm*, edited by Mary G. Hodge and Michael E. Smith, pp. 313–48. Studies on Culture and Society, volume 6. Institute for Mesoamerican Studies, The University at Albany, State University of New York, Albany, New York.

———. 2008 *Aztec City-State Capitals*. University Press of Florida, Gainesville, Florida.

Smith, Michael E., and Cynthia Heath-Smith 1994 Rural Economy in Late Postclassic Morelos. In *Economies and Polities in the Aztec Realm*, edited by Mary G. Hodge and Michael E. Smith, pp. 349–76. Studies on Culture and Society, volume 6. Institute for Mesoamerican Studies, The University at Albany, State University of New York, Albany, New York:

Spalding, Karen 1973 Kurakas and Commerce: A Chapter in the Evolution of Andean Society. *Hispanic American Historical Review* 53:581–99.

———. 1984 *Huarochirí: An Andean Society under Inca and Spanish Rule*. Stanford University Press, Stanford.

Spencer, Charles S., and Elsa M. Redmond 2006 Resistance Strategies and Early State Formation in Oaxaca, Mexico. In *Intermediate Elites in Pre-Columbian States and Empires*, edited by Christina M. Elson and R. Alan Covey, pp. 21–43. University of Arizona Press, Tucson.

Spores, Ronald 1967 *The Mixtec Kings and Their People*. University of Oklahoma Press, Norman.

———. 1974 Marital Alliances in the Political Integration of Mixtec Kingdoms. *American Anthropologist* 76:297–311.

———. 1998 Differential Response to Colonial Control among the Mixtecs and Zapotecs of Oaxaca. In *Native Resistance and the Pax Colonial in New Spain*, edited by Susan Schroeder, pp. 30–46. University of Nebraska Press, Lincoln.

Stanish, Charles 1997 Nonmarket Imperialism in the Prehispanic Americas: The Inka Occupation of the Titicaca Basin. *Latin American Antiquity* 8:195–216.

———. 2001 Regional Research on the Inca. *Journal of Archaeological Research* 9: 213–41.

Stavig, Ward 1999 *The World of Túpac Amaru: Conflict, Community, and Identity in Colonial Peru*. University of Nebraska Press, Lincoln.

———. 2000 Continuing the Bleeding of These Pueblos Will Shortly Make Them Cadavers: The Potosí Mita, Cultural Identity, and Communal Survival in Colonial Peru. *The Americas* 56:529–62.

Stein, Gil J. 1999 *Rethinking World-systems: Diasporas, Colonies, and Interaction in Uruk Mesopotamia*. University of Arizona Press, Tucson.

———. 2002 From Passive Periphery to Active Agents: Emerging Perspectives in the Archaeology of Interregional Interaction. *American Anthropologist* 104: 903–16.

Stern, Steve J. 1982 *Peru's Indian Peoples and the Challenge of Spanish Conquest: Huamanga to 1640*. University of Wisconsin Press, Madison.

———. 1987 The Age of Andean Insurrection, 1742–1782: A Reappraisal. In *Resistance, Rebellion, and Consciousness in the Andean Peasant World, 18th to 20th Centuries*, edited by Steve J. Stern, pp. 34–93. University of Wisconsin Press, Madison.

Sutter, Richard C. 2000 Prehistoric Genetic and Cultural Change: A Bioarchaeological Search for Pre-Inka Altiplano Colonies in the Coastal Valleys of Moquegua, Peru, and Azapa, Chile. *Latin American Antiquity* 11:43–70.

Taintor, Joseph A. 1988 *The Collapse of Complex Societies*. Cambridge University Press, Cambridge.

Taylor, William B. 1979 *Drinking, Homicide, and Rebellion in Colonial Mexican Villages*. Stanford University Press, Stanford.

———. 1994 Santiago's Horse: Christianity and Colonial Indian Resistance in the Heartland of New Spain. In *Violence, Resistance, and Survival in the Americas: Native Americans and the Legacy of Conquest*, edited by William B. Taylor and Franklin Pease G.Y., pp. 153–89. Smithsonian Institution Press, Washington, DC.

———. 1996 *Magistrates of the Sacred: Priests and Parishioners in Eighteenth-Century Mexico*. Stanford University Press, Stanford.

Thomson, Sinclair 2002 *We Alone Will Rule: Native Andean Politics in the Age of Insurgency*. University of Wisconsin Press, Madison.

Townsend, Richard F. 1992 *The Aztecs*. Thames and Hudson, Ltd, London.

Umberger, Emily 2008 Ethnicity and Other Identities in the Sculptures of Tenochtitlan. In *Ethnic Identity in Nahua Mesoamerica: The View from Archaeology, Art History, Ethnohistory, and Contemporary Ethnography*, by Frances F. Berdan,

John K. Chance, Alan Sandstrom, Barbara L. Stark, James Taggart, and Emily Umberger, pp. 64–104. University of Utah Press, Salt Lake City.

Voorhies, Barbara, and Janine Gasco 2004 *Postclassic Soconusco Society: The Late Prehistory of the Coast of Chiapas, Mexico*. Monograph 14. Institute for Mesoamerican Studies, University at Albany, Albany, New York. (Distributed by the University of Texas Press.)

Wachtel, Nathan 1984 The Indian and the Spanish Conquest. In *The Cambridge History of Latin America*, Vol. 1, edited by Leslie Bethell, pp. 207–48. Cambridge University Press, Cambridge.

Watson, Rodney 1990 Informal Settlement and Fugitive Migration amongst the Indians of Late-Colonial Chiapas, Mexico. In *Migration in Colonial Spanish America*, edited by David J. Robinson, pp. 238–78. Cambridge University Press, Cambridge.

Wernke, Steven A. 2006 The Politics of Community and Inka Statecraft in the Colca Valley, Peru. *Latin American Antiquity* 17:177–208.

Wightman, Ann M. 1990a *Indigenous Migration and Social Change: The Forasteros of Cuzco, 1570–1720*. Duke University Press, Durham.

————. 1990b 'Residente en esa ciudad . . .': Urban Migrants in Colonial Cuzco. In *Migration in Colonial Spanish America*, edited by David J. Robinson, pp. 86–111. Cambridge University Press, Cambridge.

Willey, Gordon R. 1971 *An Introduction to American Archaeology*, volume two, South America. Prentice-Hall, Inc., Englewood Cliffs, New Jersey.

Willis, Roy 1981 *A State in the Making: Myth, History, and Social Transformation in Precolonial Ufipa*. Indiana University Press, Bloomington.

Yoffee, Norman 2005 *Myths of the Archaic State: Evolution of the Earliest Cities, States, and Civilizations*. Cambridge University Press, Cambridge.

Zeitlin, Judith Francis 2005 *Cultural Politics in Colonial Tehuantepec: Community and State among the Isthmus Zapotec, 1500–1750*. Stanford University Press, Stanford.

Zorita, Alonso de 1994 [1963] *Life and Labor in Ancient Mexico: The Brief and Summary Relation of the Lords of New Spain*. Translated and with an introduction by Benjamin Keen. University of Oklahoma Press, Norman.

Note

1 The Late Horizon (A.D. 1476–1534) refers to the peak of Inka expansion and is a major period in traditional Peruvian studies (Willey 1971:82–86), but the inception of Inka expansion is slightly earlier.

CHAPTER 10

HOUSEHOLD ECONOMIES UNDER THE AZTEC AND INKA EMPIRES

A COMPARISON

Timothy Earle and Michael E. Smith

How were household economies organized in prehistory? In most stateless societies, households dominate much of everyday life, including making a living, sociability, and ritual. A family produced much of what it consumed and exchanged reciprocally with neighboring households. Some specialization and exchange existed certainly, but they were apparently concentrated on special tools and social valuables. With the emergence of political and market economies, households adjusted, but the scope, tempo, and reasons for these adjustments are not well understood.

Premodern economies were composed of four intertwined sectors, involving household subsistence, social relationships among neighbors, political mobilizing for finance, and mercantile trading. We focus here on the household as the nexus of these economic sectors, creating a field of necessities and opportunities that varied temporally and cross-culturally. All human societies have intimate household-size units, which typically are primary constituents in decision making, production and consumption, and childrearing (Johnson and Earle 2000). Because households vary greatly in composition and activities (D'Altroy and Hastorf 2001; Netting et al. 1984), they are good social units for cross-cultural comparison. Households are typically tethered to a house or a residential compound, which allows archaeologists to study the material remains of their activities and social conditions (Allison 1999; D'Altroy and Hastorf 2001; Hendon 1996; Wilk and Rathje 1982).

As materialists, we model variation among households in economic terms. Foremost, the household was concerned with subsistence. In traditional societies, much of household work involved direct maintenance. Households produced for themselves many goods (especially foods) and simple technologies that they consume. This pattern is sometimes called the Domestic Mode of Production (Sahlins 1972). All households, however, are organized within a social community, and inter-household exchanges provided special products and helped build community relationships. Households became imbedded within larger political economies of local chiefdoms, city-states, and empires that mobilize resources from their underlying economies for finance (Earle 2002a). And self-organizing systems of exchange often created broad marketing systems, through which trade offered new goods and economic strategies to households (Smith 2004). Households participated in these economic sectors, and their strategic engagement with each created the conditions that we can observe archaeologically.

We describe similar and contrasting patterns of consumption, specialized production, and trade across two time periods to investigate how the political economies of the pre-Hispanic Inka and the Aztec empires were bound to their underlying household economies. Despite many similarities in chronology, technology, subsistence, scale, and environment, these empires were structured differently both politically and economically (Berdan et al. 1996; D'Altroy 1992; Murra 1980); we hope to describe how these differences were internalized into the everyday life of households, using excavated data from the Mantaro Valley, Perú, and Morelos, Mexico.

Our working hypothesis is that the state and imperial political economies adjusted systems of mobilization to fit existing economic relations. Tensions existed between the necessities of households to meet their subsistence requirements and social aspirations and of states to mobilize surplus to finance expanding operations. The balance among household, community, and political strategies was dynamic and changing, and we believe that investigating the household helps understand how households affected and reacted to state economies. Unlike some who might propose that household economies were fundamentally transformed by imperial manipulation, we propose that preexisting conditions of commercialization and regional political economies structured the nature and opportunities for imperial expansion and finance. Prior to imperial expansion, the underlying household economies were fundamentally different between our two cases, and perhaps surprisingly, they changed in only limited ways to adjust to demands for surplus mobilization.

Dimensions of Comparison

We propose that states engage households with quite different strategies reflecting contrasting political economies. We single out two dimensions of variation in state-level economies that have important implications:

imperial control and commercialization. As known from the historical record, the Inka and Aztec empires differed sharply in these interrelated dimensions, and their differences should be linked to the household activities. Our approach to comparison is contextualized within archaeological comparative methods by Smith and Peregrine (Chapter 2). By focusing on provincial households, this study is closely linked to the processes of provincial strategies discussed by Stark and Chance (Chapter 9).

Imperial Control. Ancient empires differed in their control over provincial areas. Of the many dimensions of imperial control and organization that have been discussed by comparative historians (Alcock et al. 2001; Doyle 1986; Luttwak 1976; Morris and Scheidel 2009), the Inka and Aztec empires present a particularly interesting contrast in two related dimensions: the directness of rule of provincial areas and the nature of state finance. The Inka Empire was an example of a "territorial empire," one with considerable direct control over provincial areas (D'Altroy 1992), whereas the Aztec Empire exemplifies a "hegemonic empire," in which control was more indirect (Berdan et al. 1996). The clearest manifestation of this contrast is the extent of imperial infrastructure in provincial areas. The Inka Empire, for example, built cities, roads, bridges, agricultural terraces, and other architectural features throughout its zone of control, whereas the Aztec Empire did not engage at all in such infrastructural elaboration.

Although the material infrastructural distinction between territorial and hegemonic empires was dramatic and highly visible archaeologically, the differences between territorial and hegemonic empires may prove less significant at the household level. In the territorially based Inka Empire, control over the hinterland required direct mobilization of surplus to support state institutions there. The levels of household extraction were probably high and should be visible archaeologically in domestic remains. The Aztec case, in contrast, is best categorized as a city-state economy, with a hegemonic imperial overlay in the final pre-Hispanic period. Although the lack of direct imperial presence in provincial areas might be expected to require less extraction, indirect imperial exploitation was imposed on top of existing local institutions of mobilization. Thus the combined impact of the local polity and the imperial superstructure on the household level may be quite similar to that of territorial empires.

D'Altroy and Earle (1985) identified two strategies of state funding, staple and wealth finance, which link in part to these different imperial strategies. In staple finance systems, rulers extract payments in food and utilitarian items to finance largely dispersed imperial activities, whereas wealth finance systems involve payments in money and/or luxury goods that support an urban administrative core. In systems of staple finance, production within the household should be little changed after imperial conquest. States required foods, clothing, and other items normally produced by households; mobilization of a surplus should translate into intensification of commoner household budgets. The effects of wealth finance on commoner households can be quite similar to staple finance; in both cases, commoners increased agricultural and craft production to meet state and elite demands. For example, in dominated local polities, staples extracted from household production were used to support attached specialists producing wealth items used internally or as tribute and taxes. Elite households should show increasing production by attached specialists of wealth objects used in tributary exchanges. In the case of the Aztecs, the production of high-value luxury goods by attached specialists is well attested in the documentary record, but this practice has yet to be identified archaeologically outside of the imperial capital. Domestic production of cotton textiles was linked to taxation at both the city-state and imperial levels, although it may be difficult to distinguish production for taxes from production for markets.

Staple and wealth finance were not alternative types of taxation; rather they were different strategies to mobilize and control the flows of surplus used to support ruling institutions. Thus the real impact on the households may prove to be quite unexpected, and the comparison that we seek should provide contrasting cases of the implication of finance on the everyday lives of households. Because empires require the mobilization of a surplus for finance, a central question is whether imperial conquest and incorporation helps or hurts household lifestyles. Based on our comparison, the effects of imperial conquest on the household are mixed, resulting from the nature of finance and the relationships between the state and its people.

Degree of Commercialization. The degree of commercialization refers to the prevalence of markets, money, credit, and entrepreneurship in an economy (Smith 2004). The Inka and Aztec cases present a strong contrast along this dimension. Markets, money, and merchants were crucial to the Aztec economy, both before and during the imperial period (Smith 2003a:chapter 5), whereas these institutions were largely absent from most of the Andes in the Inka period. As illustrated by archaeological research in Mesoamerica, commercial exchanges could become a central element of state finance, at the same time that it impacted households (Feinman and Nicholas 2004; Garraty 2010; Hirth 1998; Smith 2004). One material correlate is a high frequency of imported goods, particularly among commoner households. One would expect more imports in a commercial economy than in an economy more strongly regulated by the state.

Another implication of commercial exchange is that both commoners and elites should obtain relatively high-value goods, particularly imports. The expectation is that in a less commercialized economy most luxury goods will be exchanged among elites, with fewer or no luxuries finding their way to commoner houses (Hirth 1998). Although reasonable, Hirth's model has yet to be tested with household data from contrasting commercial and noncommercial economies. Consumers should also have more options in purchasing commodities from merchants or in markets, resulting in more varied domestic inventories. Our chapter can be considered a test of this model, as we contrast the state-administered exchange of the Inka with commercial exchange of the Aztec. Our results provide partial support for Hirth's hypothesis, while suggesting some additional complexities that influence domestic inventories in noncommercial economies.

The Inka and Aztec Empires

The Inka Empire. Our cross-continental comparison contrasts a territorial empire (the Inka) based on staple finance and little commercialization with a hegemonic empire (the Aztec) based largely on wealth finance with tribute and taxation and considerable commercialization. Assembled by military conquest, the Inka Empire contained a territory of nearly 1,000,000 km^2 and a population probably more than 8,000,000 dispersed among a thousand or so formally independent polities that ranged in size from small-scale chiefdoms to impressive states. Across the empire, the subsistence economy was highly variable, incorporating everything from the coastal desert to the high Andes to the tropical forests. Centralized mobilization and redistribution of food, textiles, and other craft goods functioned as a means of staple finance, and some objects of significance (especially metals, textiles, and imperial ceramics) were manufactured and distributed by the state. The empire asserted ownership over all lands through right of conquest, and returned them to local communities for their subsistence in return for obligatory corvée labor given to state administrative, religious, and military bodies.

The Inka political economy mobilized staples through household labor and supported specialized production of prestige goods for redistribution. State operations were distributed broadly through the empire, and each region's activities were supported locally by its staple finance. Goods were generally not moved over long distances, and the imposition of

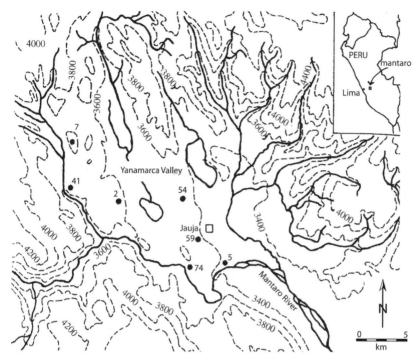

Figure 10.1. Map of the Mantaro region of the Inka Empire.

broad-scale political integration did not result in increased movement of goods or the development of markets (Earle 2002b). An Inka provincial administrative center, such as Hatun Xauxa in the Mantaro Valley (Figure 10.1, site 5), received workers from local communities, which were assigned annual corvée obligations. The Wanka, the local population in the Upper Mantaro, then farmed extensive state lands to fill the center's massive storage complexes (D'Altroy 1992).

Provincial peoples also constructed state roads and buildings and provided specialists to manufacture special cloth, pottery, and other items. The mobilized staples were stored in massive state warehouses and distributed to support state administrators, military personnel, religious specialists, crafters, and local laborers. Specialists attached to state institutions manufactured the symbolically charged objects. The expected changes to the household economy resulting from state imperial mobilization are relatively minor in consumption, production, and exchange. Each household would simply work harder to provide corvée labor and produce surpluses to support the state. Unexpectedly, the lifestyle of commoners appears to have improved significantly as the power of local leaders was undercut.

To study Inka impact on local conquered populations, the Upper Mantaro Archaeological Research Project excavated several dense Wanka settlements (D'Altroy and Hastorf 2001; Earle et al. 1987). The Upper Mantaro region is in the high Andes of Perú, about 430 km north of the Inka capital of Cuzco. This was a fertile area of irrigated farming for some maize, extensive dry land farming of potatoes and quinoa, and animal herding. Wanka settlements were built of local stone along high limestone ridges, and the architecture was often remarkably well preserved. Before imperial conquest, the Wanka were organized into several large chiefly polities with populations estimated to have been more than ten thousand each (Earle 2005). After conquest, the region became an imperial district administered from Hatun Xauxa, but the population remained dispersed in settlements much like those from the pre-conquest period (D'Altroy 1992).

Following a full settlement survey of the Upper Mantaro region by Jeffrey Parsons (Earle et al. 1980), the six excavated sites were Hatunmarca (5), Tunanmarca (7), Umpamalca (41), Marca (54), Chucchus (74), and Huaca de la Cruz (59). These represented different size categories in the settlement hierarchy for the pre-Inka Period A (the Wanka II phase, 1250–1460) and imperial Period B (Wanka III phase, 1460–1532). Pre-Inka settlements included: Tunanmarca, a central place located high on a limestone ridge with surrounding fortification walls that enclosed more than two thousand house structures and a central plaza; and Umpamalca, a town-size settlement, located on a small knoll with a surrounded wall that enclosed more than one thousand house structures. Inka-period settlements included: Marca, a town-size settlement located on a broad hill with more than one thousand house structures; and Chucchus and Huaca de la Cruz, large villages, located on high ground, each with more than three hundred house structures. Hatunmarca was a large settlement occupied in both periods. In pre-Inka times, it was a major center with more than two thousand house structures, located high on a limestone ridge with surrounding fortification walls. In the Inka period, settlement size decreased to a town-size settlement with more than one thousand house structures.

Working from air photographs of the settlements, we mapped individual house structures (usually circular and occasionally rectangular) arranged into patio groups (DeMarrais 2001). An individual patio group consisted of one to seven structures facing inward on a common patio; walls with only narrow entrances defined the patio space (Figure 10.2). For sampling purposes, we stratified patio groups into elite versus commoner based on the quality of masonry, location (central vs. peripheral to the settlement's

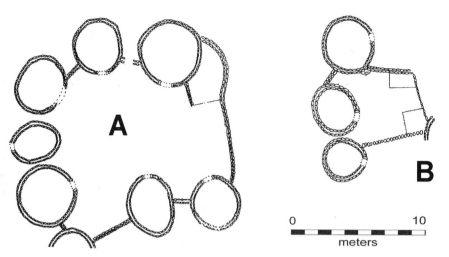

Figure 10.2. Elite (A) and commoner (B) residential compounds at the Wanka II site of Tunanmarca.

central precinct), and size of roofed space and work area. To define the distribution of features and midden, we began by excavating all of several groups. Individual houses were residential, containing hearths with evidence of cooking. Patio areas were probably primary workspaces, and refuse associated with house-holding was packed against the walls. We believed that the patio group contained a household with one or more nuclear families. Analyses of the domestic artifacts from these households are available in articles, books, and dissertations (Costin 1986, 1993, 2001; Costin and Earle 1989; D'Altroy 1992; D'Altroy and Hastorf 2001; Hastorf and Johannessen 1991; Hastorf 1990, 2001; Russell 1988; Sandefur 1988, 2001).

The Aztec Empire. In Aztec central Mexico, a network of city-states (*altepetl*) created a densely populated, politically fragmented but culturally integrated world that corresponds to Hansen's (2000) concept of city-state culture. Allying three city-states in 1428, the Triple Alliance formed the Aztec Empire. Over the next ninety years, it conquered 170,000 km^2 with a population on the order of six million. Rulers of most conquered city-states remained in place but paid tax and tribute to the empire. There was little effort to interfere in internal city-state operations. This was a hegemonic empire, based on indirect provincial control. City-states remained important units of local administration, indeed into the Spanish period (Lockhart 1992). The continued importance of city-states under imperial rule makes it difficult to disentangle direct and indirect effects on household economies.

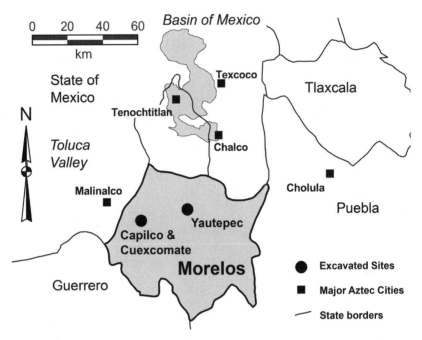

Figure 10.3. Map of the Morelos region of the Aztec Empire.

Both local city-states and the imperial overlay impinged on the lives of provincial peoples.

Aztec imperialism established a system of regular tribute and taxes, and it promoted commercial exchange (Berdan et al. 1996). In the core area of the Basin of Mexico, the imperial rulers meddled in the internal affairs of polities, designing tributary provinces to cross-cut city-state boundaries. Outside the Basin, the empire created client states, giving provincial rulers privileges and incentives to cooperate with the empire. The expansion of markets and commercial exchange occurred in most of Mesoamerica during the Middle and Late Postclassic periods (Smith and Berdan 2003). Markets were critical for provisioning households. Commoners obtained many commodities through the markets, and kings, nobles, priests, or public institutions apparently provided few if any goods directly to commoner households. Nobles received gifts from the emperor and from one another, and they received rents (in money and goods) and labor service from commoners. Nobles could then sell these products in markets to provision their households and to support attached specialists producing wealth goods used in tribute and tax payments.

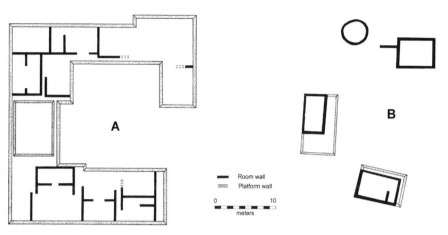

Figure 10.4. Elite (A) and commoner (B) residential compounds at the Aztec site of Cuexcomate.

Aztec imperial strategies are analyzed here with data from domestic middens at three sites (Capilco, Cuexcomate, and Yautepec), representing different size categories in the settlement system in Morelos (Figure 10.3), the Mexican state located across the Ajusco mountains and just south of the Basin of Mexico (the Aztec imperial core). Much of Morelos is hilly, and agricultural terraces were built here in the Aztec period. Several rivers run through the state, and irrigation systems were constructed to water maize and cotton.

In western Morelos, Capilco was a small village of circa 20 similar houses, and Cuexcomate was a nearby town site with circa 150 houses and a small central area with two elite compounds, a temple, and a public plaza. Stone foundation walls were visible on the surface at these sites, and random sampling was used to select houses for testing. A number of houses were completely excavated. All excavations emphasized domestic midden, located by soil phosphate testing. These excavations are described in Smith (1992), and the artifact analyses will be published in Smith (n.d.–a). Yautepec was a city-state capital in north-central Morelos, excavated with similar methods. Because house remains were not evident on the surface, fewer houses were located. Clearing defined house architecture, and midden were excavated and collections analyzed (Smith n.d.–b). These three sites show similarities that aid comparative analysis. The great majority of houses were classified as commoner; their structures were small (ca. 20–30 m²) with simple stone bases for adobe-brick walls. Many were organized into patio groups of two to four structures facing a common open area. Each house probably served a single household (Figure 10.4). Rich middens were adjacent to nearly all structures. At the larger settlements of Cuexcomate and Yautepec, elite residences were distinguished on the basis of their superior architecture.

Morelos was the first area to be conquered when the Aztec Empire began its program of expansion in the 1430s. The sites analyzed are located some 70–80 km from Tenochtitlan, the imperial capital. The contexts described here come from two time periods: Period A is the first half of the Late Postclassic period (ca. A.D. 1300–1440); it corresponds to the Early Cuauhnahuac phase in western Morelos and the Atlan phase at Yautepec. This was a time of population growth, agricultural intensification, and commercial expansion. Period B, the imperial period, is the second half of the Late Postclassic period (ca. A.D. 1440–1520); this includes the Late Cuauhnahuac phase in western Morelos at the Molotla phase in Yautepec. Analyses of the domestic artifacts can be found in Smith (Smith 1997, 2001, 2002, 2003b; Smith and Heath-Smith 1994); other studies include three dissertations (Fauman-Fichman 1999; Norris 2002; Olson 2001).

Contrasting Household Economies

We identify three axes of comparison for changing household economies under the Inka and Aztec empires: (1) domestic inventories to monitor consumption and mobilization; (2) household production debris and association artifacts to monitor specialization; and (3) distance of goods from their source to monitor trade. The goal is to assess household production and consumption as a means to establish the nexus of economic sectors. We want to know how the economies were organized prior to imperial expansion and how expanding the political economies changed household consumption, production, and exchange. A goal is to assess the nature, extent, and significance of state-administered distribution, social exchanges, and commercialization under the contrasting patterns of imperial finance and control seen in the Inka and Aztec empires.

Analyses involve artifact inventories recovered archaeologically from dated contexts, usually midden, assignable to individual households. Each case uses a fairly large sample of households (thirty from the Mantaro Valley; forty-three from Morelos), which can reasonably be said to represent each region's households. For the Mantaro Valley, excavated sites varied across the spectrum of settlement sizes, and the patio groups (households) excavated ranged across the spectrum of social differentiation (D'Altroy and Hastorf 2001). Households included six elite and nine common

Table 10.1. Excavated contexts discussed in this chapter

	Phase A (preconquest)		Phase B (postconquest)	
Site	Phase	No. contexts	Phase	No. contexts
Aztec Sites:				
Yautepec	Atlan	9 houses	Molotla	7 houses
Cuexcomate	Early Cuauhnahuac	3 houses	Late Cuauhnahuac	11 houses
Capilco	Early Cuauhnahuac	3 houses	Late Cuauhnahuac	5 houses
Inka Sites:				
Hatunmarca	Wanka II	3 patio groups	Wanka III	5 patio groups
Tunanmarca	Wanka II	8 patio groups		
Umpamalca	Wanka II	6 patio groups		
Marca			Wanka III	7 patio groups
Chucchus			Wanka III	1 patio group
Huaca de la Cruz			Wanka III	2 patio groups

compounds from each the pre-Inka (Period A) and Inka (Period B) periods. In both periods, elite houses were limited to central places and town-sized settlements. With the exception of Hatunmarca, sites were single component, and well-preserved architecture made sampling and excavations quite straightforward. For Morelos, sites include a village, a small town, and a city-state capital, each with representation before (Period A) and after (Period B) Aztec conquest. Because the two projects directed by Earle (Inka) and Smith (Aztec) employed different samples and analytical techniques, we recompiled the domestic artifact databases to produce comparable measurements. Data are based on artifact counts from well-dated household contexts, mostly from patio midden. The result is a four-way comparison between households occupied immediately before and after imperial conquest from provincial areas in the Inka and Aztec empires. Table 10.1 lists the sites and contexts analyzed in this chapter.

Household Inventories and Patterns of Consumption

Household inventories help describe the balance between the objectives of consumption, reflecting maintenance (food, housing, clothing, and related technologies) and of social display (social identification and networking).

Objects always combine elements of both maintenance and social identity, but the relative balance, we believe, can be roughly measured by stylistic elaboration in the artifact categories. Thus, elaborately decorated pottery or clothing were more likely to have served for social display than simpler forms. This balance in consumption goods then reflects the relative orientation of household activities toward subsistence versus social strategizing. The degree to which this balance contrasts between elite and commoner households can help test Hirth's hypothesis that different amounts of display items and the contrast between elite and commoner households in these items link to the extent of commercialization.

Inka Case. Among the Wanka of Peru, for whom commercial exchanges were unavailable, household consumption was quite restrained and oriented primarily toward maintenance, evidently not meant to be particularly conspicuous. The dominant objects recovered in household excavations were subsistence items, with relatively little symbolic elaboration or ritual contexts. Trash associated with each household included food products and ceramic and stone tools used in food preparation and serving. Objects with display significance include ceramic vessels with elaborated forms and decoration evidently used in feasting and rare items used for bodily decoration, such as occasional metal disks and pins, semiprecious stone beads, and some bone items. Prior to Inka conquest, these were rare and concentrated in elite households. Special ritual contexts were rare, limited primarily to burials placed in subfloors. The consumption patterns were quite similar across the spectrum of Wanka households, mainly self-supporting and subsistence-oriented (Hastorf 2001). In the following presentation, artifact frequencies are presented as percentage (by piece) of assemblages to provide data comparable to the Aztec case. Quantitative patterns represent total assemblages, combining elite and commoner data for the period before and under Inka domination. "Elite" households were distinguished, but differences were fairly subtle and quantitative; in a separate article, Costin and Earle (1989) describe the changing elite and common assemblages that resulted from imperial conquest. In terms of access to high-end consumption items (special foods and symbolic items), the social differentiation between elite and commoner households narrowed considerably. The symbolically charged items continued to be of the same forms, but increased in frequency, shifting toward items that the Inka state probably distributed to reward those working for them (Costin and Earle 1989). Overall, living standards were raised by Inka conquest.

Food items were common in all household middens. They were almost exclusively local, presumably mostly from household production, and most food consumption involved simple maintenance. Although food production and consumption would have had great significance in the everyday life of households, this significance was apparently only selectively used in inter-household context, although this was admittedly not a focus of our research. These food data are not presented in detail here because differences in preservation, recovery methods, and analysis make comparison difficult with Morelos. The primary source of food was domesticated plants (Hastorf 1993, 2001). Prior to imperial conquest, the rank order in plant prevalence is quinoa, maize, potato, and legumes, after conquest shifting to maize as the most common crop. The preferred Andean food was maize. It was quite restricted to elite households prior to conquest and then became more generally consumed.

A direct comparison is available for Hatunmarca, our single site occupied in both pre-Inka and Inka periods. Prior to conquest, maize was recovered in 79 percent of flotation samples from elite households in contrast to 17 percent from commoner contexts; following conquest, it was in 80 percent elite samples versus 56 percent commoner. As calculated from bone remains, meat was also important in the diet, increasing from 160 to 172 kg/m^3 following conquest (Sandefur 2001). In both periods, domesticated llama was the primary meat source (89 percent), followed in order by wild deer, domesticated guinea pig, and dog. Llama meat was more common in elite contexts prior to conquest, but jumped dramatically in commoner context following conquest (pre-Inka, 137 kg/m^3 in elite context vs. 118 kg/m^3 in commoner context; Inka, 130 kg/m^3, elite vs. 147 kg/m^3, commoner). Diet improved following Inka conquest, especially among commoner households, and correspondingly health improved as measured by a significant drop in mortality (Earle et al. 1987).

Some food consumption related to feasting, involving special foods, cooking, and presentation. In the pre-Inka period, evidence for feasting was concentrated in elite households, where it presumably served for display. Maize and meat were then more restricted to elite contexts. These items were probably prepared and served as a special, feasting cuisine. The frequency of burnt bone, indicative of roasting, concentrated in elite households especially in Wanka II. After imperial conquest, the concentrations of the specialty food items in elite households lessened, as maize and meat became more widely available. Under the Inka, staples, mobilized regionally as part of state finance, would have supported feasting associate with corvée labor on imperial projects; some probably returned to the households.

Table 10.2. Lithic tools at Inka sites

Period	Hoe	Sickle	Flake tools	Food prep.	Ground stone	Weapons	Display	N
Period A	2.0	12.2	50.1	23.6	10.6	0.7	0.7	1,742
Period B	16.3	9.0	35.8	20.1	17.5	0.7	0.6	1,853

Food preparation and serving items of stone and ceramics were common in all household midden deposits. Used largely in maintenance activities involving food procurement, stone artifacts were common in household consumption. The stone tool assemblage shows little elaboration not
involved in the specific utilitarian activities including agriculture (soil preparation and crop harvesting), food processing (plant and meat processing),
and a wide range of small-scale productive activities involving wood, hides,
textiles, ceramics, and stone (Table 10.2; Russell 1988). Most tools were
made from modified flakes, blades, cobbles, and the like. Much stone tool
production was quite opportunistic, manufactured quickly from local chert
and meta-volcanic stone; more formal agricultural tools include the sickles
and hoes that together make up 14 to 25 percent of the tool assemblage.
The blades (roughly 8 cm long and 3 cm wide) typically show silica gloss,
resulting from plant harvesting.

Used for cultivation, hoes (roughly 15 cm long by 11 cm wide) have a haft-
ing shaft and a broad blade often with substantial wear and re-sharpening.
An assortment of modified flakes and other informal tools would have been
used opportunistically for butchering, cutting, abrading, drilling, and the
like. Manufactured from local and regional materials, ground stone tools
represented 34 to 37 percent of the assemblage, included a wide range of
activities, but especially grinding platforms and grinding stones used in food
preparation. The distribution of both flaked and ground stone tools shows
a generalized range of household processing and manufacturing activities,
but especially the preparation of food. The distribution suggests a range of
generalized and nonconspicuous maintenance activities.

As seen in Table 10.2, overall the stone tool assemblage shows only
specific changes from pre-Inka to Inka periods. The character of general
house-holding activities appears little changed by imperial conquest. Two
broad changes are, however, evident. First, the shift in locations of settlements to lower elevations (toward the east) changed stone availability based
on distance to sources, making access to the chert used in flaking more
costly and the phyllite used for ground stone less costly. Because secondary

Table 10.3. Ceramic forms at Inka sites

Period	Cooking/ storage jar	Bowls/ other serving	Indeterminate	N
Period A	59	35	6	7,362
Period B	58	34	8	6,145

modification of chert tools are easier to recognize and phyllite less easy to recognize, this is probably represented in a decrease in our ability to recognize flake tools (rather than unmodified flakes) and food preparation tools (rather than other ground stone) in the archaeological record for Wanka III in comparison with Wanka II. This appears to have resulted in a decrease in the flake tools, and a shift from food preparation to other ground stone.

The second change was a dramatic increase in the frequency of hoes from 2 percent of the assemblage in pre-Inka times to 16 percent in Inka times. Ethnographically in the Andes, hoes are used for weeding, mounding, and water channeling, activities that intensify agriculture by added work. The rapid and profound increase in hoes in Wanka III contrasts dramatically to the overall continuity in other stone tool uses. The change in hoes appears to document an intensification of agriculture probably geared to the mobilization of staple surpluses demand by the Inka state (Russell 1988).

By far the most common artifacts recovered from the Xauxa households were ceramics used for food preparation, storage, and serving. In these uses, ceramics provided both maintenance and social positioning (Costin 2001). Our artifact collections included more than 300,000 ceramic sherds. Working with rim sherds, Costin (1986) classified ceramics into various forms, including jars (used primarily for cooking and storage), bowls (used primarily for serving), and a very small number of special Inka forms used in serving. The basic pattern of ceramic forms in pre-Inka and Inka contexts was unchanged (Table 10.3).

Ceramics were also classified into four distinctive wares that reflected a gradation in the amount of decorative elaboration, probably reflecting the relative amount of maintenance versus social significance in vessels' uses. The local Micaceous Self-slip vessels were almost undecorated. They were low-necked globular jars, used for cooking. The local Xauxa Ware vessels were simply decorated with white or red slips and/or rapidly applied "straight, undulation, or cross-hatched lines on vessel neck, collar, or body" (Costin 2001:208). These vessels included high-necked and low-necked jars and globular bowls, probably used interchangeably for storage, cooking, and

Table 10.4. Ceramic wares at Inka sites

Period	Xauxa wares	Micaceous wares	Andesite ware	Inka wares	N
Period A	67	29	4	0	118,997
Period B	58	27	5	10	100,213

serving. Although most vessels were likely important primarily in household maintenance, more elaborate vessels certainly were socially important for local identity and display. Andesite and Inka Wares were the most elaborate in terms of decoration and fine finishing, and they probably had more significance socially. The regional Andesite-tempered Wares (especially Base Roja) were either slipped a deep red or polished and then painted with patterned designs, most dramatically large face necked vessels that probably served especially for liquid storage (Costin 2001:209). The regional Inka Wares were distinctive, made in special imperial forms, finishing, and decorative motifs that required considerable labor investments (D'Altroy 2001). These Inka Wares included especially the large "aryballoid" jars and a variety of other forms, such as enclosed bowls, pedestal dishes, and an occasional plate, an assemblage associated with liquid storage and serving.

With less decoration, the Micaceous and Xauxa Wares heavily dominated the assemblages, but they decreased significantly from pre-Inka (96 percent) to Inka (85 percent) times (Table 10.4). These were used for basic household maintenance activities involving food preparation, storage, and serving, and the more elaborate vessels would probably have also served for household-based feasting. With more decoration, the Andesite and Inka Wares increased from 4 to 15 percent of the Assemblage. As discussed later, both of these wares were produced outside the local area. Andesites were never common, being only 4 to 5 percent of the assemblage. The elaborately decorated Inka Wares were found only in Wanka III assemblages, where they represented 10 percent of the household assemblage. From Wanka II to III, Inka ceramics partially replaced the less decorated, local Xauxa wares. Costin and Earle (1989) show that the density of decorated ceramics (g/m³) were overall much higher in elite household assemblage in both period; 5.6 times greater in Wanka II, decreasing to only 1.4 times greater in Wanka III. Overall, percentage of the elaborately decorated wares increased dramatically. The conspicuousness of consumption reflects the replacement of local Xauxa wares with Inka Wares, and, by controlling production and distribution, highly decorated ceramics, the Inka Empire could partially

Table 10.5. Metal objects at Inka sites

Period	Display	Utilitarian	Weaponry	N
Period A	71.5	17.1	11.4	35
Period B	71.4	23.8	4.2	42

control information systems in household contexts. This patterned change represented a strong concentration of socially significant feasting in elite household prior to the Inka conquest, but a dramatic weakening of that pattern with the introduction of decorated Inka ceramics that were unexpectedly common in commoner households.

Objects of personal decoration and ritual use include a scattering of beads, disks, pins, pendants, figurines, and other objects representing a wide range of local and foreign materials including bone, stone, crystals, metal, and shell. These objects were simple in form and frequencies were low, representing a low investment in household objects carrying obvious symbolic information. The objects of bone, stone, and ceramic were all simple. The odd bone artifacts included a few beads and pendants. Stone objects included some beads, pendants, figurines, and unmodified crystals. Fifteen small (less than 7 cm), simple ceramic animal or human figures were also found in household contexts.

Display object of metal (71 percent of metal artifacts) were made of copper/bronze, silver, and occasionally gold, but these items were found mostly in burials, with relatively few examples in domestic contexts (Table 10.5). These display objects included simple pins, disks, and pendants of small size. Two pins with molded heads (llama and human), occasional simple engraving, one large bronze *tumi* pendant, and a large (92 g) *tupu* pin were exceptions. Metal display objects were concentrated in elite households in both periods, but distribution changes significantly (Owen 2001). Frequency of metal display items tripled under the Inka, and equalized (8.5 times greater in elite contexts in pre-Inka times vs. 3.4 times greater in Inka times). Following Inka conquest, all copper objects were alloyed with tin to create a true bronze. The use of tin required long-distance imports, presumably controlled by the empire. Made of both marine and land species, thirty-six shell items (beads and cut ornaments) were recovered from both periods, but the numbers changed little. All display objects were found in both burials and as stray finds; they appear to have been part of dress, showing some distinctions in status. Although objects of wealth clearly concentrated in elite households, except for silver pins, no metal display objects were exclusive to elite households (Owen 2001). Overall patterns of consumption improved and equalized following Inka imperial conquest.

Surprising perhaps, weapons were rare in household contexts and show no change in frequency from pre-Inka to Inka times. The most frequent weapons were stone discoids, clubs made from rounded cobbles modified to create a uniform, circular, and flat object with a biconically drilled central hole (Russell 1988). Although sometimes called "digging-stick weights," these discoids show wear along the central hole and minimal battering along the edges; the wear pattern makes everyday agricultural work highly unlikely. Two discoids were distinctive star-shaped clubs. Other weapons include a few projectile points and bola stones, both of which could have been used in hunting. Most weapons were of stone, representing less than 1 percent of the household stone assemblage. The counts of stone weapons were identical for the fifteen households from pre-Inka and Inka periods: each period had fourteen discoids (one star discoid), nine projective points, and six bolas! Six small lead bola weights were probably too light for fighting. Despite clear evidence for warfare in the defensive architecture of Wanka II settlements (Earle 2005), weaponry was not a substantial part of household inventories. In Wanka II times, we surmise that military strategy depended primarily on defensive architecture with weapons cached near to defenses. Because of our household-based excavation strategy, such caches were not recovered in the Mantaro settlement, although they have been described elsewhere. In Wanka III, the Inka state may have tried to restrict access to weapons, but the observed household pattern suggest that any prohibition was ineffective.

Aztec Case. In terms of material types, domestic inventories excavated from Aztec houses are dominated by ceramics, and considerable functional and stylistic variation existed. Most chipped stone tools and other objects were made of obsidian. Chert is rare at Yautepec and Capilco, and somewhat more common at Cuexcomate. Ground stone tools of basalt and andesite were recovered at most houses. Other artifact categories are numerically rare, although they are important for social and economic reconstruction; these include bone tools, tools and jewelry of bronze, pieces of quartz, pigments, imported greenstone ("jade"), and small stone balls. Botanical remains are quite rare due to poor preservation. Faunal remains are somewhat more frequent.

Although little direct botanical evidence exists for diet, ethnohistoric sources suggest that diet was based on maize. Tortilla griddles (*comals*) are abundant ceramic vessels in all houses, confirming the importance of maize, consumed as tortillas. The faunal assemblages are dominated by the domesticated species – dog and turkey – with rabbit, deer, reptiles, and other birds also present. Food preparation items of stone are mostly blades and flakes of obsidian and chert, with a few minor chipped stone tool types. Ground stone artifacts include a variety of tool types, particularly manos, metates, mortars, and pestles. The quantities of these items at the Aztec houses do not change greatly with imperial conquest (Table 10.6). There are few changes at Yautepec, and the rural sites show minor adjustments in the frequencies of tool types. Table 10.6 also summarizes the types of lithic materials found at the sites. Green obsidian, from the Cerrro de las Navajas source area north of the Basin of Mexico, dominates all domestic assemblages in Morelos. The category of gray obsidian includes several geological sources. As in the case of tool types, Yautepec lithic materials manifest few changes with imperial conquest, while the rural sites show some minor changes in frequencies.

Turning to ceramics, the most abundant functional category is plain ceramic food preparation and storage vessels (Table 10.7). Sherds from jars (cooking and storage jars could not be distinguished) make up the majority of this category, followed in quantitative order by comals, basins, and a number of minor specialized vessels. Painted jars and ceramic tripod grater bowls (*molcajetes*) are rare but a consistent part of most inventories. The abundance of decorated ceramic serving vessels, including many that were imported (see later), is one of the distinctive features of the Morelos household assemblages. As shown in Table 10.7, such serving vessels make up some 10 to 12 percent of most domestic inventories. Most are bowls, but painted cups and pitchers are also common.

Each region of Morelos in Aztec times had one or two abundant and distinctive polychrome ceramic types, along with a larger number of rarer decorated types. Most of these types conform to a broad pattern of red and black decoration on a white background called the "Tlahuica polychrome style" (Smith n.d.–c). The individual ceramic types are distinguished by the layout of their decorative fields and the use of design elements. The spatial distribution of the overall Tlahuica polychrome style corresponds almost precisely with the distribution of the Tlahuica ethnic group (one of the Nahuatl-speaking Aztec groups) as described in ethnohistoric sources (Smith n.d.–c:chapter 16). Most of the individual types within the Tlahuica style had limited spatial and temporal distributions whose patterning can be traced to changing dynamics of city-states and market systems (Smith 2010 a). Other common decorated ceramic types include polished redwares,

Table 10.6. Lithic tools at Aztec sites

Phase	Tool type				Material type				Total lithics	Obsidian: sherd ratio	No. houses
	Blade	Flake	Other flaked	Ground stone	Green obsidian	Gray obsidian	Chert	Other			
Yautepec:											
Period A	81.1	14.9	2.3	1.8	91.3	3.1	3.8	1.8	1,906	2.6	9
Period B	81.7	13.9	2.4	2.0	92.3	2.2	3.5	2.0	2,421	2.4	7
Cuexcomate:											
Period A	70.9	22.7	6.4	0.0	69.0	6.8	18.2	6.0	324	3.4	3
Period B	77.5	17.1	3.1	2.3	76.4	5.9	14.2	3.5	1,189	3.2	11
Capilco:											
Period A	88.6	4.4	2.2	4.8	82.6	3.6	3.8	10.0	281	1.8	3
Period B	86.5	8.0	3.7	1.7	84.7	4.3	8.4	2.6	287	1.9	5

Note: The obsidian:sherd ratio is expressed as pieces of obsidian per 100 ceramic sherds.

Table 10.7. Ceramic forms at Aztec sites

Phase	Food preparation				Food serving				Ritual	Other	Total sherds
	Painted	Plain	Eroded	Total	Painted	Plain	Eroded	Total			
Yautepec:											
Period A	0.6	56.4	13.8	70.8	10.3	12.7	4.1	27.1	1.1	1.0	68,819
Period B	0.5	58.2	10.1	68.8	10.8	11.1	7.0	28.9	1.0	1.3	96,775
Cuexcomate:											
Period A	0.4	48.6	16.7	65.8	11.8	14.7	3.5	30.0	3.2	1.0	7,209
Period B	0.1	42.0	26.9	69.0	6.4	14.0	7.7	28.1	1.3	1.5	30,553
Capilco:											
Period A	0.7	62.8	2.9	66.3	16.0	13.7	0.7	30.4	1.5	1.8	13,636
Period B	0.5	60.9	5.4	66.8	11.7	16.3	1.8	29.7	1.6	1.9	13,675

Table 10.8. Ceramic wares at Aztec sites

Phase	Local/regional	Guinda	Imported
Yautepec:			
Period A	91.0	3.4	5.6
Period B	94.2	2.5	3.3
Cuexcomate:			
Period A	92.7	3.9	3.4
Period B	94.6	2.8	2.6
Capilco:			
Period A	94.6	2.2	3.3
Period B	95.9	1.7	2.3

known as the "guinda," and Aztec orangewares imported from the Basin of Mexico.

Most domestic inventories have many sherds from one or two types of decorated serving vessels, plus a smaller number of sherds from many local and imported types. The specific types present at each house, however, vary widely. It seems clear that people in Aztec-period Morelos obtained decorated serving bowls in great abundance and variety. Although the concept of the "ceramic ware" is not used among researchers on Aztec-period ceramics, Table 10.8 shows the frequencies of three broad categories resembling the ware categories described earlier for the Mantaro ceramics. The local/regional categories include all ceramics produced within Morelos except for guinda, and the imported category includes imports from the Basin of Mexico and other areas (but not including guinda). The highly polished and decorated guinda ceramics are a distinctive category of fine serving vessel, including bowls, plates, pitchers, cups, and some minor special-purpose types. These vessels are commonly found in burials and special offerings as well as in domestic middens. Chemical sourcing analysis shows that some of the guinda ceramics from Yautepec were produced locally (30 percent), some were imported from other parts of Morelos (19 percent), and about half (51 percent) were imported from the Basin of Mexico. Guinda cups and pitchers were probably used in feasting (Smith et al. 2003). Special offerings of these objects, most likely the remains of key ceremonial means, have been recovered in public architectural contexts at sites in Morelos. It is not possible, however, to distinguish feasting from other domestic consumption behavior at the houses described in this chapter (Smith et al. 2003).

Although the magnitudes are not great, guinda and imported ceramics declined at all sites with Aztec conquest (Table 10.8); furthermore, the frequencies of painted serving wares declined markedly at the rural sites (although note that these categories are not independent of one another). These declines were more dramatic at commoner households than at elite households, suggesting that a broad reduction in standards of living and an increased social differentiation among Morelos households following Aztec conquest. This decline in the economic well-being of households was probably due to increased taxation – at both the imperial and city-state levels – after imperial conquest, which limited the options of commoner households in purchasing high-value (decorated and imported) ceramic vessels.

Items used in domestic ritual are found in all domestic inventories, with an average frequency around 1 to 2 percent. Most are ceramic goods: censers, figurines, musical instruments, stamps, and a variety of rare and sometimes enigmatic objects such as stamps, pipes, and tiny vessels; quartz crystals were also probably used in domestic ritual. These objects point to two possibly distinct realms of domestic ritual (Smith 2002). Some goods (e.g., long-handled censers and musical instruments) duplicate ritual objects used by priests in public state ceremonies, suggesting a linkage between state and domestic ritual. Other goods (particularly ceramic figurines) were not a part of public or state ceremony and point to a domestic realm or women's ritual separate from Aztec public religion. Nearly all houses have artifacts from both categories.

Other items in domestic inventories are quite rare. The only possible weapons are a few projectile points, and these could have been used in hunting. Items of bodily decoration include ceramic beads and earspools, beads, earspools and labrets of greenstone, obsidian and rock crystal, and bronze bells and tweezers. Except for the ceramic items, these are all imported goods that represent the most costly or valuable items recovered in domestic excavations. Their rarity makes them difficult to analyze quantitatively, but existing examples were recovered from a variety of domestic contexts, with greater representation in commoner houses than elite houses (see later discussion). Finally, there are a number of rare enigmatic specialized goods whose uses are not known; these include stone balls, odd basalt objects, and several unidentified but distinctive ceramic forms. Small ceramic balls were probably blowgun pellets used in hunting.

The overall impression of these inventories is one of abundance and diversity. This characterization applies to both elite and commoner contexts. These two settings can be distinguished on the basis of their artifact inventories (Olson 2001), but the differences are quantitative, not qualitative in nature. That is, commoner households have the same kinds of goods found in elite households, but they have differing frequencies of some key types, particularly decorated and imported serving ware. This is a modification of Hirth's (1998) expectations for household inventories in commercial economies. Hirth initially argued that under commercial exchange, elites and commoners should have the same quantities of valuable and imported goods. In a comment on Hirth's paper, Smith (1999) cited ethnographic data (Smith 1987) to the effect that elites and commoners should have the same *types* of valuable goods, but with *higher frequencies* at elite houses. He presented data from Period A at Cuexcomate that conform to this pattern (Smith 1999).

The transition from Period A to Period B was marked by two distinct patterns in well-being or standard of living at the sites in Morelos. First, the levels of well-being declined for both commoners and elites as measured by a wealth index constructed from frequencies of valuable ceramic types. As noted earlier, local and regional painted ceramics and imported ceramics declined at the sites, resulting in reductions of circa 25 percent in the wealth index (Olson 2001). Second, the distinction between elites and commoners in residential architecture, at Cuexcomate at least, declined with imperial conquest. The reduction in the elite-commoner gap is manifest in both an energetic measure of house construction as measured by the Gini index, and a symbolic measure of distinction based on architectural style and elaboration (Smith 1992:359–67; 1994b). These two changes most likely were consequences of imperial conquest and the resulting higher levels of taxation. Provincial peoples (both nobles and commoners) not only had to pay the new imperial taxes, but they were also subject to higher levels of taxation at the hands of their local city-state king (Smith 1986, 1994a). Although provincial elites at powerful capitals such as Cuauhnahuac may have benefited from the opportunities created by imperial conquest, elites and commoners at smaller provincial cities and in rural areas bore the brunt of increased imperial and city-state exploitation in Period B.

Comparison. In many ways, the Mantaro and Morelos consumption appear quite similar, reflecting basic subsistence orientations in households among provincial populations. Particulars of the local ecology and history created some differences between Mantaro and Morelos households, but much of these differences reflect contrasting patterns of commercialization and state-administered economies. Prior to conquest, the Mantaro and Morelos households differed in the extent of conspicuous consumption. Morelos households had more decorated ceramics and higher-value objects of everyday life, evidently obtained through market exchange. The marketless Mantaro households had simpler, less decorated ceramics, and depended on locally available food and stone, often of lesser quality. Imperial conquests, however, affected household consumption quite differently and perhaps unexpectedly. Without markets, the Inka appear to have provided important goods. Increases in specialty foods (maize and meat), highly decorated state ceramics, and items of bodily decoration suggest improved lifestyles, probably resulting from state payments for services provided to the state. Essentially, the surpluses mobilized by the state were balanced to some measure by return flows in items not previously available or available only to elite households. In contrast, the Morelos households may have been negatively affected by Aztec conquest, as increasing stress of tax demands may have strained local populations suffering deteriorating agricultural conditions. Let us summarize the evidence.

The subsistence base was different between the Mantaro and Morelos. The Mantaro was much higher in elevation, maize was marginal, and cotton could not be grown. Raised on the high-elevation grasslands, domestic llamas and alpacas were common, providing pack animals, meat in the diet, and wool for home weave. Following conquest, the overall diet quality improved, probably a result of imposed peace and access to state foods, especially maize, grown in new agricultural complexes. Diets equalized across elite and commoner households, probably representing greater mobility for herding as war ceased and access to maize and other crops in compensation for corvée labor. Health improved dramatically. This took place despite the intensification of agriculture and mobilization of substantial surpluses by the state. In Morelos, the lower elevation allowed for irrigated farming of both maize and cotton, although domesticated animals were of little importance. People were already engaged in intensive production of maize and cotton, which they probably traded actively through the local markets. Following Aztec conquest, conditions appear to have worsened. Although the Aztec imperial authorities had little reason to interfere with an already successful production-distribution system, their additional demands may have impoverished households. Overall, the Andean household improved as the Mesoamerican household lost ground.

In terms of consumption goods, the contrast was initially quite profound. In Morelos, higher commercialization appears to have created much broader access to a wide variety of utilitarian and display goods in households. A good contrast is the use of relatively low-quality local stone in the Mantaro versus the broad access of Morelos' households to obsidian, a preferred material from which to make cutting tools, but available only at a distance (Smith et al. 2007). In ceramics a similar contrast exists. In Morelos, high-quality decorated pottery, produced by regional specialists represented 15 percent of the assemblage; ceramics were evidently distributed through markets. In the Mantaro, ceramics were originally much simpler in forms and decoration, with only 4 percent of the assemblage produced by regional specialists. With Inka conquest, high-quality ceramics increased substantially to the same 15 percent as seen in Morelos, representing state distribution of a high-end pottery that augmented the much smaller-scale regional ceramic tradition. Display items, which were used for personal dress and ritual events, were rare and simple, but they increased following Inka conquest. With the absence of commercialization, Inka imperial conquest created a broadening and equalizing of access to consumer items.

Rather than marked differences in imperial strategies, the consumption data from Inka and Aztec provincial households seems to document considerable differences in pre-conquest conditions that set up contrasting means for state extraction and control of conquered territories. Without preexisting market systems, the Inka asserted direct territorial control over the Mantaro region. They mobilized a substantial agricultural surplus by demanding farmers to work harder, creating new agricultural facilities. Significantly, an imperial presence created direct relationships between local commoners and the state, giving opportunities that without markets had not existed previously. The power of the local lords to control flows of valued materials appears to have been undercut, probably an imperial strategy to weaken the powerful local leaders. The Aztecs, on the other hand, were able to take advantage of preexisting systems of extraction and control at the city-state level, and preexisting regional market systems. As a result, the effect of imperial conquest on provincial households was less dramatic. The imposition of imperial taxes would have increased the tax burden on individual households, but only to a limited extent; imperial taxes averaged less than one piece of cloth per household per year in Morelos (Smith 1994a). Perhaps most importantly, the power of local leaders may well have increased as conduits for Aztec rule (Smith 1986).

Our data provide partial support for Hirth's hypothesis that commercialization increases access to long-distance goods and equalizes access among elites and commoners to high-value items. During Period A, the greater commercialization in Morelos, in comparison to the Mantaro, created more ready access to distant (as discussed later) and high-value items, and this access was spread broadly across the social spectrum. Households had access to a diversity of consumer forms, showing the many commodity chains that a market gave access to. In contrast, Mantaro commoners had far fewer imports and valuable goods, and the contrast with elite inventories was greater.

After imperial conquest (during Period B), the configuration of valuable goods in the Aztec households did not change dramatically. The Period A pattern of commoner access to valuables, but at slightly lower frequencies than in elite contexts, continued and this provides another case conforming to the expectations of the modified Hirth model. But in the Inka case, commoners gained greater access to valuable goods after imperial conquest. The Inka state, as part of its direct local rule, provided an alternative mechanism for access to goods. This produced domestic inventories more closely resembling the Morelos households, but in the absence of commercial exchange. It appears that in the absence of markets in the Mantaro case the state could build closer bonds with its conquered population. Hirth's hypothesis seems to be confirmed for our comparison of the regions in Period A, prior to imperial expansion, but during Period B the state's role evidently made the material contrast between the economic systems less clear.

Craft Production and Household Specialization

Each household is involved in production of food and crafts for both its own use and for exchange with other households and institutions. The key question is to what degree are households self-reliant, producing the items that they consume? Or alternatively, to what degree are households specialized, producing goods for use by others? These questions can be answered by studying the comparative amounts of production debris and production tools in households in correspondence with extent of consumption in the products.

Inka Case. In the Mantaro, manufacture was geared heavily toward meeting immediate household consumption needs, but some household activities were specialized, producing goods for local exchange that evidently created a reciprocal interdependence among local populations. Manufacture is best documented for four classes of objects – chert blades, ceramics, textiles, and metals. In most cases, the best measure of production was the ratio between finished objects and debris; with the exception of the spindle whorls and needles used for textile production, production tools were highly generalized in form and hard to identify. Households in settlements positioned close to limited and localized resources, like stone and clay sources and local grasslands to graze alpaca for wool, were partly specialized in the production of some tools, utensils, and clothing.

Specialized production of chert blades is well documented for households in the settlements closest to the primary chert source, the Pomacancha quarry. Although small deposits of chert were probably distributed across the region's limestone formations, this quarry was the source for the best chert used for blades. The site is littered with dense blade-core reduction debris. Although these blades were widely used for plant harvesting in all local households, the secondary stage of blade manufacture was strongly concentrated in two sites located nearest the source (Russell 1988). In Wanka II, households at Umpamalca had a much higher ratio of manufacturing debris to finished blades. The simplest ratio is blade cores (manufacturing debris) versus blades (the consumer item); in Umpamalca, that ratio is about 1:12; in other settlements, that ratio is nearly 1:500. Some production took place in all settlements, but it was highest in the settlement nearest the quarry. During Wanka III, the pattern of a single-producing settlement continued; following the abandonment of Umpamalca, production shifted to Hatunmarca, then the nearest settlement to the quarry.

Ceramic manufacture was also specialized, presumably tied to the distribution of clay sources (Costin 1986, 2001). Production can be documented by the distribution of wasters, the overfired ceramic pieces that would have had no value in exchange. Based on ethnographic parallels, wasters probably served primarily as "furniture," supporting the arrangement of ceramic pieces in the firing process. The ratio of wasters to normal sherds for any ceramic group can indicate the extent and location of specialized ceramic manufacture. In Wanka II, the primary ceramic-producing site for the Wanka-decorated types was Umpamalca. Here the ratio was 1 waster to 350 Wanka ware sherds, as opposed to all other settlements with a ratio of 1:1,450. Among Wanka settlements and their households, the distribution of wasters was highly patterned, with specific villages (and only certain households within those villages) being partly specialized in pottery production for distribution to neighboring communities. After the abandonment of Umpamalca, the Wanka III settlement of Marca became the main ceramic-producing site within the region. Here the ratio of wasters to all ceramics sherds in the Wanka styles was 1:100, as opposed to all other settlements with a ratio of 1:1,350. Probably all settlements had some ceramic production, but a few had significantly higher levels of production. Costin (2001) refers to this as settlement specialization.

No production debris was recovered for either the Andesite or Inka wares. They involved distinctive fabrics that suggest separate locales of production. The primary change was the Inka state imposition of specialized production for its highly decorated ceramics that permitted direct administrative control over production and distribution of objects of high symbolic value linking ideologically the local population to the state. No production data exist for the Inka ceramics, which used distinctive clays from the local ceramics (D'Altroy and Bishop 1990).

Cloth manufacture also shows settlement specialization related to available wool harvested from domesticated alpaca. Spinning was a routine activity across households, and a few spindle whorls, made from recycled sherds, were normal to all households. These whorls were used to spin relatively coarse thread for common cloth; the amount of rough cloth needed per capita within a household should have been roughly similar. Degree of household specialization can then be documented by the ratio of the whorls – indicating spinning – to 100 jar rims – indicating normal household activities of cooking and storage (Costin 1993). During Wanka II times, this ratio is fairly strongly patterned with settlement elevation, ranging from a low of 1:50 at Hatunmarca (3800 m) to a high of 1:17 at Chawín (4000 m). A strong linear correlation existed between the frequencies of whorls and the elevation of settlements. The frequency of spinning in households probably increased with elevation, closely associated with decreasing agricultural productivity and increasing availability of puna grasses and greater alpaca herding. Higher elevation settlements appear thus to have produced several times more thread than lower elevation sites, presumably trading the thread or finished textiles for food from the lower settlements.

During the Inka period, the overall frequency of spindle whorls more than doubles from around 1:25 in Wanka II to 1:10 in Wanka III. This increase in spinning under the Inka probably reflects state demands for surplus production of cloth as part of staple finance. The relationship between spinning and elevation ceased following imperial conquest; regardless of elevation all settlements were involved in spinning, apparently required by the state.

In addition to part-time specialization of everyday goods for households, some production of display goods appears to have been concentrated in elite households, illustrating minor attached specialization. Production of higher-quality textiles may be documented by fine copper/bronze needles. In Wanka II, four of the five metal needles were recovered from elite households; in Wanka III, this distribution equalized to four of eight. Evidence for metals production (small amounts of recycled waste, slag, and ores) is

Table 10.9. Craft production artifacts at Aztec sites

Phase	N	Textiles	Ceramic	Pounding	Paper	Paint	Total artifacts
Yautepec:							
Period A	9	0.571	0.138	0.024		0.005	70,745
Period B	7	0.721	0.173	0.024	0.005	0.036	99,221
Cuexcomate:							
Period A	3	0.835				0.049	7,536
Period B	11	1.295	0.053		0.008	0.081	31,745
Capilco:							
Period A	3	1.656	0.065	0.030			13,926
Period B	5	1.620	0.025		0.057	0.057	13,964

very limited (only twenty-three items total), but this scattered debris concentrated (70 percent) in elite households. The concentration decreased from 75 to 67 percent in Wanka II to Wanka III. Attached specialization of wealth items appears to have been of little significance, but Inka conquest lessened elite domination of these industries.

All specialization was part-time. Debris was found in households accompanying the full range of subsistence-related activities involving agriculture, animal herding, food preparation, and the like. The impression is that specialized production was small scale and organized only a small part of the overall local economy. Unexpectedly, Inka imposition of a regional peace, which we had originally expected to have increased access to distant exchange, had no impact on the unchanging patterns of specialization.

Aztec Case. Morelos households engaged in the production of a variety of goods (Table 10.9). By far the most important craft product – quantitatively, economically, and socially – was cotton textiles. Standardized lengths of cotton cloth served as money in Aztec central Mexico and as such cotton textiles played a central role in the economy. In addition they were used for clothing and a variety of other domestic and ritual purposes (Hicks 1994). Textile production was an important component of female gender identity, and written sources say that all Aztec women – from nobles to slaves – spun and wove cloth. The Basin of Mexico is at too high an elevation (more than 2,000 m) to grow cotton, and Morelos is the area closest to the Basin where cotton was cultivated (Yautepec is at 1,200 m). The production of cotton was therefore of great interest to the rulers of the Aztec Empire.

Table 10.10. Households engaged in obsidian tool production at Aztec sites

Phase	N	Lack of production	Core-blade production	Intensive core-blade production	Lapidary production
Yautepec:					
Period A	10	5	3	1	1
Period B	12	7	4	0	1
Cuexcomate:					
Period A	5	5	0	0	0
Period B	10	10	0	0	0
Capilco:					
Period A	2	2	0	0	0
Period B	3	3	0	0	0

Abundant ethnohistoric documents describe the irrigated production of cotton in Morelos.

All Aztec-period sites in Morelos have spindle whorls and spinning bowls, the major tools used in spinning cotton thread, and these are the most abundant categories of craft production evidence at the excavated sites (Table 10.9). Bronze needles and bone tools (awls and picks) are rare tools also used in textile production. The frequencies of textile production items are much higher at the rural sites than at Yautepec. The transition from Period A to Period B saw increased production of textiles at Yautepec and Cuexcomate, with little change at the village of Capilco. At Cuexcomate and Capilco, an inverse association existed between textile production items and wealth at the household level (Smith and Heath-Smith 1994). There is a cross-cultural association between the intensity of rural household craft production and poverty; peasants with insufficient land frequently take up part-time craft production to make ends meet (Arnold 1985:171–96; Kellenbenz 1974; Tambunan 1995). Following this line of argument, the lowering of standards of living after imperial conquest provides one of two likely explanations for the increase in textile production at that time; the other relates to the need to intensify cloth production to meet increased tax and rent demands.

The production of obsidian tools was a common domestic activity at Yautepec but not at the rural sites (Table 10.10). Several households were engaged in significant levels of core-blade production at Yautepec in both periods, in contrast to Cuexcomate and Capilco, where there is virtually no evidence for such production activities (Norris n.d.). An Aztec-period production center at the site of El Ciruelo was located just a few kilometers from these sites, however, and their residents probably obtained blades from that site.

Yautepec and Capilco show evidence for low levels of ceramic production (Table 10.9), including ceramic molds for figurines and spindle whorls, sherd polishers, and polishing stones. All houses at Yautepec in all phases yielded some ceramic production items, and the frequencies are much higher than at Capilco or Cuexcomate. Several types of ground stone tools are included in the category of pounding items: hammer stones, anvils, and hafted tools. These may have been used in some production activities that went beyond normal domestic activities. These objects are rare but consistent parts of household inventories at Yautepec, but they are nearly absent at the western sites.

Stone bark beaters used to produce paper from the wild amate tree were recovered in several contexts. This is a case where many of the excavated items are from contexts not included in this sample. Nevertheless, these data do show that paper production was most common at Capilco. Paint stones (graphite, hematite, and limonite) were recovered in small quantities at a number of houses, and these show a concentration, together with bark beaters, at the Phase B elite compound at Cuexcomate and at the closest commoner patio group (group 10). It is possible that bark paper was being produced by and for the elites, and that the paints were used by scribes to produce painted manuscripts (most likely economic or ritual codices).

The major patterns of craft production at these sites are: (1) widespread and fairly intense production of cotton textiles at all houses, with some potentially significant differences; (2) intensive production of obsidian tools at several houses in Yautepec coupled with virtually no production at other houses and other sites; (3) scattered low-level production of ceramics and other objects at many houses; and (4) potential production of codices at Cuexcomate in Period B.

Comparison. Textile production was common in all household contexts. In the Mantaro region, the intensity of wool spinning (as measured by the frequency of spindle whorls) varied with elevation, whereas in Morelos the intensity of cotton spinning varied along a rural-to-urban dimension. After imperial conquest, households in both regions increased their production of textiles, presumably a result of tax collection. This increase was quite dramatic in the Inka case, as compared to a more modest growth at the Aztec sites. The regional configuration of craft production differs between the two cases. In the Mantaro area, spatial variation in craft production mapped onto the distribution of resources: chert production near the quarry, textile manufacture at higher elevations where farming was less effective, and ceramic production at most sites. In Morelos, on the other hand, spatial variation in craft activities was less strongly related to environmental conditions. Obsidian, imported from long distances, was worked at urban Yautepec but not at the rural sites, and at Yautepec obsidian production was specialized by household. Although good clay for ceramics was widespread, none of the excavated sites were involved in the manufacture of ceramic vessels; production must have taken place at other settlements.

These differences in household craft production relate to the economic and political difference between the Inka and Aztec cases. The system of regional markets that operated in Aztec central Mexico led to higher levels of regional and long-distance exchange (see later in the chapter). As a result, households in Morelos had readier access to goods from near and far, and specialists could operate effectively at a wider range of places in the regional economy. Presumably because of easier access to markets, the production of obsidian tools, ceramic objects, and probably other goods was more intensive in urban contexts (Yautepec) than at rural settlements. Textiles, in contrast, were produced more heavily in rural areas. As a domestic industry practiced by all women in Aztec households, the intensification of textile production may have been especially responsive to local economic conditions, such as declining rural agricultural yields (Smith and Heath-Smith 1994).

Distance of Procurement and Exchange Mechanisms

We compare the amount of exchange largely by the distance to the sources for materials (compare Earle 2001). Objects found in household contexts are classified as local (<15 km), regional (15–50 km), and long-distance (>50 km). Likely mechanisms of exchange vary with the amount of commercialization and the distances that goods were moving. In the Mantaro case, local goods were probably obtained either directly by the households for their own use or by reciprocal exchanges between households. Goods obtained regionally and at long distances could have been obtained through interpersonal gift exchanges (mainly between elites) or administered trade by the state. In contrast, in the Morelos case, much of the distribution at all scales would have involved market exchanges. Households would certainly have produced goods locally for themselves and obtained goods from neighbors, but many moved regionally and long distances in markets and as taxes and tribute delivered to local nobles and the state.

Table 10.11. Import distances at Inka sites

Material	Local	Regional	Distant
PLANTS:			
Period A	100	0	0
Period B	80	20	0
ANIMALS:			
Period A	91	9	0
Period B	90	10	0
LITHICS:			
Period A	100	trace	trace
Period B	97	3	trace
GROUND STONE:			
Period A	85	15	0
Period B	91	9	0
CERAMICS:			
Period A	95	4	1
Period B	85	15	trace
METALS:			
Period A	0	100	0
Period B	0	98	2
MARINE SHELL:			
Period A	0	0	100
Period B	0	0	100

The Inka Case. Among the Wanka, the volume of exchange was quite limited and specific (Earle 2001); see Table 10.11. For food goods, the vast majority of both plants (80–100 percent) and animals (90 percent) were local in origin and presumably produced by households for their own consumption. Households consumed foods that they produced; this is documented clearly by variations from settlement to settlement reflecting specific site catchment areas associated with individual sites (Hastorf 1993). Households at higher elevations have more quinoa and potatoes, and those at lower elevations, more maize.

In terms of craft goods, the pattern of local availability and limited trade appears to be fairly stable across the political transformations accompanying imperial conquest, except for the introduction of a regionally administered ceramics. For lithics and ground stone, relatively minor changes in materials traded reflect only shifting settlement location and resulting accessibility to stone resources (Earle 2001). As documented from the pattern of specialized production for the chert blades, some stone was evidently exchanged locally, probably reciprocally between households and communities. For ceramics, the general pattern of local production and exchange is quite similar to the chert blades. Prior to Inka conquest, the bulk of ceramics (95 percent) were of local origin. The area of our research was divided into two chiefdoms, and most ceramics moved within the territories of each chiefdom (Costin 2001). A small percent of the ceramics (4–5 percent) were the more decorated Andesite vessels: they were produced in the main Mantaro Valley, about 40 km to the south. These vessels were especially large liquid storage vessels probably for the ceremonial preparation and serving of chiche (corn beer); they concentrated in elite households probably for feasts. These special ceramic vessels likely moved as regional gift exchanges among elites. Additionally, a small amount of ceramics (1 percent) was non-Wanka styles that appear to represent long-distance exchange.

The primary change in craft goods involved the addition of imperial ceramics. Following Inka conquest, Inka ceramics appear in varying amounts on all settlements; overall they come to represent 10 percent of the ceramic assemblage. Their techniques of manufacture, the materials used in their clay bodies, and the absence of Inka wasters on Wanka III sites argue that Inka Wares were produced by specialized crafters, who were probably directly attached to the Inka state. Their production and distribution would thus have been state-administered and probably associated with ceremonial events linked to state ideology.

The third class of objects was the special goods used especially for bodily decoration and some ritual. Although never common, these items were routinely recovered in small numbers from all households. Items of shell, crystal, stone, bone, and metal were shaped into beads, disks, pins, and pendants sown onto clothing, used to fasten dress, and worn suspended around the neck. They would have helped present a person's identity, and often were buried with a person at death. Special objects, especially those of metal and shell, were concentrated differentially in elite households. Some of the materials used for special objects were locally available, but the typical display objects were derived from local bone and stone, stone and metals mined regionally, and from shell and tin that came from long distances.

During Wanka II, metal objects were made of regional silver and copper. We estimate that 100 percent of metals were regional in their sources. During Wanka III, a significant change was noted in the copper objects, as they consistently incorporate tin to create a true bronze alloy. The Late Horizon has been called "the bronze horizon," as tin was added systematically to coppers across the empire (Lechtman 1979). Because the tin was apparently found only in Chile, its use as an alloy required distant procurement. Although the tin represented a small overall percentage of the metal (perhaps 2 percent), its addition was quite significant. Most of the copper was used decoratively; the addition of tin would change the color (and look) but not its properties of use. The addition of tin had the apparent result of increasing, in a very targeted way, the long-distance movement of material, thus creating the opportunity for the Inka state to administer this trade along its road systems and so control the production of local significant display objects.

Marine shells were also imported from more than 100 km away, the distance to the Pacific coast. During Wanka III, the overall abundance of special objects shows little change from the period prior to Inka conquest. Inka peace and large-scale political integration did not result in increased commercialization and movement of such special objects. The inventory of metals, however, shifted to include more items of copper and fewer of silver; we believe that this shift reflected the Inka state's extraction of silver as tribute (Costin and Earle 1989).

The Aztec Case. In contrast to the Mantaro, the Morelos inventories are notable for the abundance of imported items. Table 10.12 shows the frequencies of lithics and ceramics from various distances.[1] For lithics, the local category includes ground stone tools at all sites, and chert tools at Cuexcomate and Capilco. At Yautepec, chert is a regional good. All obsidian was obtained from distant sources; items from the Otumba source area (95 km from Yautepec) are indicated under the Basin of Mexico, and all other obsidian is listed under the Distant category. The most notable feature of these data (Table 10.12) is that the vast majority of the lithic tools come from distant areas. The dominant Cerro de las Navajas obsidian source is 140 km from Yautepec, and the other obsidian sources vary from 140 to 200 km distant. The heavy reliance on obsidian for cutting tools, with only minor use of chert, was a widespread pattern in central Mexico from the Formative period through the early Colonial period. Aztec conquest had little effect on the patterns of imported lithic tools.

Most ceramic vessels and objects were probably obtained locally. Our understanding is hampered by the fact that, outside of minor production of special-purpose ceramic items, we do not know where most of the ceramics were made. The regions of origin of a number of ceramic types have been established from chemical characterization (Smith et al. n.d.), and in most cases the sourcing results matched earlier assumptions based on the principle of abundance. A number of ceramic types were imported from the Basin of Mexico; again this interpretation is based on typological interpretations tested with chemical characterization. The Distant category

Table 10.12. Import distances at Aztec sites

Phase	Local	Regional	Basin of Mex	Distant
LITHICS:				
Yautepec:				
Period A	1.9	3.8	1.6	92.7
Period B	2.0	3.6	1.1	93.4
Cuexcomate:				
Period A	24.2	0.0	3.5	72.3
Period B	17.8	0.0	3.1	79.1
Capilco:				
Period A	13.8	0.0	2.4	83.8
Period B	11.0	0.0	2.6	86.4
CERAMICS:				
Yautepec:				
LP-A	94.8	1.6	3.5	0.1
LP-B	96.3	1.0	2.6	0.1
Cuexcomate:				
LP-A	92.5	1.5	5.9	0.1
LP-B	95.3	0.7	4.0	0.0
Capilco:				
Period A	94.2	1.4	4.1	0.3
Period B	96.1	0.6	3.0	0.2

for ceramics includes items imported from other areas, primarily adjacent parts of central Mexico such as Guerrero, Toluca, and Puebla/Tlaxcala.

Copper-bronze objects and exotic stone ornaments are rare but consistent components of household inventories in both periods at all of the Morelos sites. Bronze items were imported from Tarascan territory in western Mexico, and rock crystal and greenstone jewelry were probably imported from southern Mesoamerica. With Aztec conquest, the quantities of bronze objects declined at Capilco and increased at the other two sites, whereas the quantities of exotic stone jewelry declined at all three sites. These objects are too rare to provide social interpretations of these changes, however.

The data on imports (Table 10.12) document several points. First, imports were abundant at all sites in all phases. From the start of the Aztec epoch through the Spanish conquest (and into the colonial period), Morelos households had ready access to a large quantity and wide variety of imported goods coming from numerous places of origin. Second, the Basin of Mexico predominated as a source for more distant ceramic imports, while non-Basin obsidian sources (particularly Cerro de las Navajas) dominated inventories in all periods. Third, the abundance of Basin of Mexico goods – both ceramics and obsidian – declined with conquest in most contexts. Fourth, the lack of dramatic shifts in the frequencies or places of origin of imported goods suggests that imperialism had relatively little effect on the movement of these goods. Exchange took place largely through channels that were not closely linked to the imperial polities or practices. Commercial factors were responsible for moving imports around central Mexico both before and after the expansion of the Aztec Empire.

Comparison. Not surprisingly, most goods used by households in all four contexts originated in their local area (Tables 10.11, 10.12). These were stable agrarian societies, well adapted to their local and regional settings. Nevertheless, the dominant artifacts categories – lithics and ceramics – show striking contrasts between the Inka and Aztec households. Most Mantaro lithics are local in origin, whereas most Morelos lithics consist of obsidian, imported from distances of 100 to 200 km. The Morelos households had ready access to obsidian, which occurred at all households, typically in frequencies of 1 to 2 pieces per 100 sherds. In both the Mantaro region and Morelos, local ceramic wares comprise more than 85 percent of the total ceramic inventories, but in Morelos, most of the remainder were vessels imported from the Basin of Mexico and other areas more than 50 km distant, whereas most of the nonlocal wares at the Mantaro sites were from places within the region.

After imperial conquests, an increase in regional ceramics in the Mantaro came only from administered trade in state ceramics. In the Mantaro, we had originally predicted that the imposition of regional peace would lower transaction costs and result in a jump in trade. Trade, however, remained largely unchanged from the pre-imperial levels. The state appears to have limited trade that it did not control. Again, the distinctions between the Aztec and Inka cases arise from different political and market economies. Imperial conquest had some impact on the patterns of imports in each area, but this did not obscure the roles of economic processes in structuring the access of households to imported goods.

Conclusions

We present data comparing the changing patterns of household economies in provincial areas of the Inka and Aztec empires. Our primary goal is to show how and why these household patterns developed differently under two imperial regimes. To what degree were changes top-down, induced by the state, versus bottom-up, induced by household adaptation to new conditions brought by the empire? Our conclusions are that changes were state-induced to the degree that new requirements for mobilization and order were brought in, but that the households and their communities changed in rather specific adjustments to imperial rule.

In the Mantaro Valley, the structure of the economy prior to Inka imperial conquest was distinctive in that commercialization was remarkably low. No evidence exists for markets, and the extent of both specialization and trade was low for a complex society. Most goods consumed by the household were local, and the household probably produced for itself much of the food and everyday items that it used. Household objects were fairly simple and utilitarian in form with little elaboration in information carrying decoration. Community specialization did exist, with part-time household specialists in particular communities involved in the production of blades, ceramics, and textiles for nearby exchanges with neighboring households and communities. Regional and long-distance trade was very limited to a few largely display items, significance in ritual and dress. These items included elaborated ceramics and items of dress, such as metal pins and pendants, but also a few elite-related utilitarian objects including copper needles and bolas. Concentrated heavily in elite households, such items were probably traded person to person through a regional network of elite persons.

With Inka imperial conquest, patterns changed subtly (Costin and Earle 1989; Earle et al. 1987), despite an extraordinary state-building program and presumed local presence with a major administrative center, a road system, extensive storage silo complexes, and probably new agricultural complexes (D'Altroy 1992). Similarity in overall pattern of household economy before and after imperial conquest suggests that household independence in economic activities continued. Production did intensify in goods mandated by the state. Agricultural production intensified, documented by a dramatic increase in hoes used to manipulate soils, and spinning doubled as production increased across all communities and household. Counter to original expectations, patterns of specialization and trade remained remarkably unchanged.

Overall, however, patterns of consumption improved, especially in commoner households, which now had access to better foods and more highly decorated ceramics. The Inka state provided specialty ceramics, elaborately decorated in imperial styles that were by far the most ornamented consumer objects in household use. Provided by state distribution, these noticeable serving pieces partially replaced locally produced ceramics. Elite control over decorated ceramics and the statuses that they displayed significantly decreased. Additionally, metal objects increased in frequency and equalized somewhat in distribution. With a shift toward copper alloyed with distant tin, the state was able to assert control over these display items. Strategically, the more display-related objects came under some imperial control, allowing an extension of the state ideology into ceremonial feasting and dress that identified local society with the state superstructure. The broadening of access to goods controlled by the administered state economy effectively undercut elite domination and created a direct relationship between the state and the commoners working on its many projects. Local commoner household lifestyles improved, presumably from the imposition of peace, from access to goods through direct involvement with the state, and from increased freedom from local elite extractions.

In the Aztec case, archaeological fieldwork shows that society in Morelos prior to Aztec imperial conquest in the 1430s was remarkably similar to the situation described in ethnohistoric documents when the Spaniards arrived in 1519. Numerous small city-states were characterized by high regional population densities, intensive agricultural practices (irrigation and terracing), and extensive commercial exchange involving merchants, money, and marketplaces. Although most ceramic vessels were local in origin, significant numbers were imported from regional and distant areas and all households had access to these imports. The majority of the lithic tools were made from imported obsidian, with only a minor role for local chert resources. All households engaged in the production of textiles from locally grown cotton. Exotic long-distance imports, including bronze objects and greenstone jewelry, are rare but consistent components of household inventories of both elite and commoners.

The conquest of Morelos polities by the Aztec Empire had a minimal effect on local households. Most categories of goods showed little change from Periods A to B. Households still imported most of their lithic tools as obsidian blades, domestic textile production continued at a high level, and household goods found in middens remained relatively constant. Only a few trends can be identified at multiple sites, and all are manifest in modest quantitative changes. First, the quantities of several high-value categories declined: decorated ceramics, imported ceramics, and rare exotic goods. A decline in standards of living at the rural sites was concomitant with Aztec conquest (Smith and Heath-Smith 1994), and the data presented here suggest a similar process of economic decline at the urban settlement of Yautepec. Second, the frequencies of textile production tools increased at Yautepec and Cuexcomate, but remained constant at the village Capilco.

Although it is tempting to attribute this growth to an augmented demand for textiles to pay imperial taxes, in fact the rate of imperial taxation was quite modest on the household level (Smith 1994a, 2010b). Other factors that could have generated more demand for textiles include augmented taxation at the city-state level as well as the desire of households to improve their economic conditions through market exchange.

In the four-case comparison of imperial conquest in the Mantaro and Morelos, the importance of preexisting conditions appears clear. With a very low level of commercialization (market development), the Inka state relied on the mobilization of staple goods (seen most clearly in food and everyday cloth). The direct Inka imperial presence, with a strong military component, was an important factor in provincial dynamics. For households, several key display items used in feasting (Inka ceramics) and dress (bronze items) suggest an imperial concern with direct control over household-symbolizing activities. Prior to imperial conquest, these activities were of little importance outside of some elite households. With the much higher level of commercialization in highland Mexico, including Morelos, imperial conquest had a more indirect and subtle impact on the households. Aztec authorities were able to tap into existing political and economic structures and extract taxes using established channels and mechanisms. Households made no radical changes to accommodate imperial incorporation. Given the system of city-states with their highly commercialized and productive economies, the Aztec Empire needed to do little locally and thus built few facilities and stationed few state personnel in this provincial area. It could rule "lightly," relying on indirect administration through the provincial city-states, the leaders of which remained in control.

In contrast, without commercialization and the means to convert wealth objects into staples, the Inka ruled heavily with substantial demands for surplus production and considerable imposition of state ideology. The obvious question is why the Inka did not impose a market system that would have logically lowered costs of administration and tax collection. Without previous experience with markets, this was not attempted, although there was an evident increase in wealth finance that had some of the same outcomes (D'Altroy and Earle 1985). With extensive knowledge of market and finance in both Europe and Mexico, the conquering Spanish Empire was quick to introduce market systems, which caught on rapidly to accomplish local provisioning of urban and mining specialists while incorporating elements of traditional Andean state finance.

References Cited

Alcock, Susan E., Terence N. D'Altroy, Kathleen D. Morrison, and Carla M. Sinopoli (editors) 2001 *Empires: Perspectives from Archaeology and History*. Cambridge University Press, New York.

Allison, Penelope M. (editor) 1999 *The Archaeology of Household Activities*. Routledge, New York.

Arnold, Dean 1985 *Ceramic Theory and Cultural Processes*. Cambridge University Press, New York.

Berdan, Frances F., Richard E. Blanton, Elizabeth H. Boone, Mary G. Hodge, Michael E. Smith, and Emily Umberger 1996 *Aztec Imperial Strategies*. Dumbarton Oaks, Washington, DC.

Costin, Cathy L. 1986 *From Chiefdom to Empire State: Ceramic Economy among the Prehispanic Wanka of Highland Peru*. Ph.D. dissertation, Department of University of California, Los Angeles.

———. 1993 Textiles, Women, and Political Economy in Late Prehispanic Peru. *Research in Economic Anthropology* 3:3–28.

———. 2001 Production and Exchange of Ceramics. In *Empire and Domestic Economy*, edited by Terence N. D'Altroy and Christine A. Hastorf, pp. 203–42. Plenum, New York.

Costin, Cathy Lynne and Timothy K. Earle 1989 Status Distinction and Legitimation of Power as Reflected in Changing Patterns of Consumption in Late Prehispanic Peru. *American Antiquity* 54:691–714.

D'Altroy, Terence N. 1992 *Provincial Power in the Inka Empire*. Smithsonian Institution Press, Washington, DC.

———. 2001 State Goods in the Domestic Economy: The Inka Ceramic Assemblage. In *Empire and Domestic Economy*, edited by Terence N. D'Altroy and Christine A. Hastorf, pp. 243–64. Plenum, New York.

D'Altroy, Terence N. and Ronald L. Bishop 1990 The Provincial Organization of Inka Ceramic Production. *American Antiquity* 55:120–38.

D'Altroy, Terence N. and Timothy Earle 1985 Staple Finance, Wealth Finance, and Storage in the Inka Political Economy. *Current Anthropology* 26:187–206.

D'Altroy, Terence N. and Christine A. Hastorf (editors) 2001 *Empire and Domestic Economy*. Plenum, New York.

DeMarrais, Elizabeth 2001 The Architecture and Organization of Xauxa Settlements. In *Empire and Domestic Economy*, edited by Terence N. D'Altroy and Christine A. Hastorf, pp. 115–53. Plenum, New York.

Doyle, Michael W. 1986 *Empires*. Cornell University Press, Ithaca.

Earle, Timothy 2001 Exchange and Social Stratification in the Andes: The Xauxa Case. In *Empire and Domestic Economy*, edited by Terence N. D'Altroy and Christine A. Hastorf, pp. 297–314. Plenum, New York.

———. 2002a *Bronze Age Economics: The Beginnings of Political Economies*. Westview Press, Boulder, CO.

———. 2002b Commodity Flows and the Evolution of Complex Societies. In *Theory in Economic Anthropology*, edited by Jean Ensminger, pp. 81–104. Society for Economic Anthropology Monographs, vol. 18. Altamira Press, Walnut Creek, CA.

————. 2005 The Tunanmarca Polity of Highland Peru and Its Settlement System (A.D. 1350–1450). In *Settlement, Subsistence, and Social Complexity: Essays Honoring the Legacy of Jeffrey Parsons*, edited by Richard E. Blanton, pp. 89–118. Cotsen Institute of Archaeology, UCLA, Los Angeles.

Earle, Timothy, Terence D'Altroy, Christine A. Hastorf, C. Scott, and Terry Y. LeVine 1980 Changing Settlement Patterns in the Upper Mantaro Valley, Peru. *Journal of New World Archaeology* (special issue), vol. 4 (1). University of California, Los Angeles.

Earle, Timothy, Terence N. D'Altroy, Christine A. Hastorf, C. Scott, C. Costin, Glenn Russell, and E. Sandefur 1987 *Archaeological Field Research in the Upper Mantaro, Peru, 1982–1983: Investigations of Inka Expansion and Exchange*. University of California at Los Angeles, Institute of Archaeology, Los Angeles.

Fauman-Fichman, Ruth 1999 Postclassic Craft Production in Morelos, Mexico: The Cotton Thread Industry in the Provinces. Ph.D. dissertation, Department of Anthropology, University of Pittsburgh.

Feinman, Gary M. and Linda M. Nicholas 2004 Unraveling the Prehispanic Highland Mesoamerican Economy: Production, Exchange, and Consumption in the Classic Period Valley of Oaxaca. In *Archaeological Perspectives on Political Economies*, edited by Gary M. Feinman and Linda M. Nicholas, pp. 167–88. University of Utah Press, Salt Lake City.

Garraty, Christopher P. 2010 Investigating Market Exchange in Ancient Societies: A Theoretical Review. In *Archaeological Approaches to Market Exchange in Ancient Societies*, edited by Christopher P. Garraty and Barbara L. Stark, pp. 3-32. University Press of Colorado, Boulder.

Hansen, Mogens Herman 2000 Introduction: The Concepts of City-State and City-State Culture. In *A Comparative Study of Thirty City-State Cultures*, edited by Mogens Herman Hansen, pp. 11–34. The Royal Danish Academy of Sciences and Letters, Copenhagen.

Hastorf, Christine A., and Sissel Johannessen 1991 Understanding Changing People/Plant Relationships in the Prehispanic Andes. In *Processual and Post–Processual Archaeologies: Multiple Ways of Knowing the Past*, edited by Robert Preucel, pp. 140–55. Southern Illinois University Press, Carbondale.

Hastorf, Christine A. 1990 The Effects of the Inka State on Sausa Agriculture Production and Crop Consumption. *American Antiquity* 55:262–90.

————. 1993 *Agriculture and the Onset of Political Inequality Before the Inka*. New York, Cambridge University Press.

————. 2001 Agricultural Production and Consumption. In *Empire and Domestic Economy*, edited by Terence N. D'Altroy and Christine A. Hastorf, pp. 155–78. Plenum, New York.

Hendon, Julia A. 1996 Archaeological Approaches to the Organization of Domestic Labor: Household Practices and Domestic Relations. *Annual Review of Anthropology* 25:45–61.

Hicks, Frederic 1994 Cloth in the Political Economy of the Aztec State. In *Economies and Polities in the Aztec Realm*, edited by Mary G. Hodge and Michael E. Smith, pp. 89–111. Institute for Mesoamerican Studies, Albany.

Hirth, Kenneth G. 1998 The Distributional Approach: A New Way to Identify Marketplace Exchange in the Archaeological Record. *Current Anthropology* 39:451–76.

Johnson, Allen W. and Timothy K. Earle 2000 *The Evolution of Human Societies: From Foraging Group to Agrarian State*. 2nd ed. Stanford University Press, Stanford.

Kellenbenz, Hermann 1974 Rural Industries in the West from the End of the Middle Ages to the 18th Century. In *Essays in European Economic History, 1500–1800*, edited by Peter Earle, pp. 45–88. Clarendon Press, Oxford.

Lechtman, Heather 1979 Issues in Andean Metallurgy. In *Precolumbian Metallurgy of South America*, edited by Elizabeth P. Benson, pp. 1–40. Dumbarton Oaks, Washington, DC.

Lockhart, James 1992 *The Nahuas After the Conquest: A Social and Cultural History of the Indians of Central Mexico, Sixteenth Through Eighteenth Centuries*. Stanford University Press, Stanford.

Luttwak, Edward N. 1976 *The Grand Strategy of the Roman Empire from the First Century A.D. to the Third*. Johns Hopkins University Press, Baltimore.

Minc, Leah D. n.d. La cerámica guinda de Yautepec: composición oligoelemental por activación neutrónica. In *Excavaciones de casas en la ciudad azteca de Yautepec, Morelos, México/Residential Excavations in the Aztec-Period City of Yautepec, Morelos, Mexico*, edited by Michael E. Smith. University of Pittsburgh Memoirs in Latin American Archaeology. University of Pittsburgh (in press), Pittsburgh.

Morris, Ian and Walter Scheidel (editors) 2009 *The Dynamics of Ancient Empires: State Power from Assyria to Byzantium*. Oxford University Press, Oxford.

Murra, John V. 1980 *The Economic Organization of the Inka State*. JAI Press, Greenwich, CT.

Netting, Robert McC., Richard R. Wilk, and Eric J. Arnould (editors) 1984 *Households: Comparative and Historical Studies of the Domestic Group*. University of California Press, Berkeley.

Norris, Susan 2002 Political Economy of the Aztec Empire: A Regional Analysis of Obsidian Craft Production in the Provinces of Huaxtepec and Cuauhnahuac, Mexico. Ph.D. dissertation, Department of Anthropology, Harvard University.

———. n.d. *Lítica tallada*. In *Excavaciones de casas en la ciudad azteca de Yautepec, Morelos, México/Residential Excavations in the Aztec-Period City of Yautepec, Morelos, Mexico*, edited by Michael E. Smith. University of Pittsburgh Memoirs in Latin American Archaeology. University of Pittsburgh (in press), Pittsburgh.

Olson, Jan Marie 2001 Unequal Consumption: A Study of Domestic Wealth Differentials in Three Late Postclassic Mexican Communities. Ph.D. dissertation, Department of Anthropology, University at Albany, SUNY.

Owen, Bruce D. 2001 The Economy of Metal and Shell Wealth Goods. In *Empire and Domestic Economy*, edited by Terence N. D'Altroy and Christine A. Hastorf, pp. 265–93. Plenum, New York.

Russell, Glenn S. 1988 The Impact of Inka Policy on the Domestic Economy of the Wanka, Peru: Stone Tool Production and Use. Ph.D. dissertation, Department of Anthropology, University of California, Los Angeles.

Sahlins, Marshall 1972 *Stone-Age Economics*. Aldine, Chicago.

Sandefur, Elsie C. 1988 Andean Zooarchaeology: Animal Use and the Inka Conquest of the Upper Mantaro Valley. Ph.D. dissertation, Department of Archaeology Program, Institute of Archaeology, University of California, Los Angeles.

———. 2001 Animal Husbandry and Meat Consumption. In *Empire and Domestic Economy*, edited by Terence N. D'Altroy and Christine A. Hastorf, pp. 179–202. Plenum, New York.

Smith, Michael E. 1986 The Role of Social Stratification in the Aztec Empire: A View From the Provinces. *American Anthropologist* 88:70–91.

———. 1987 Household Possessions and Wealth in Agrarian States: Implications for Archaeology. *Journal of Anthropological Archaeology* 6:297–335.

———. 1992 *Archaeological Research at Aztec-Period Rural Sites in Morelos, Mexico*. Volume 1, Excavations and Architecture/Investigaciones Arqueológicas en Sitios Rurales de la Época Azteca en Morelos, Tomo 1, Excavaciones y Arquitectura. University of Pittsburgh Memoirs in Latin American Archaeology, vol. 4. University of Pittsburgh, Pittsburgh.

———. 1994a Economies and Polities in Aztec-Period Morelos: Ethnohistoric Introduction. In *Economies and Polities in the Aztec Realm*, edited by Mary G. Hodge and Michael E. Smith, pp. 313–48. Institute for Mesoamerican Studies, Albany.

———. 1994b Social Complexity in the Aztec Countryside. In *Archaeological Views from the Countryside: Village Communities in Early Complex Societies*, edited by Glenn Schwartz and Steven Falconer, pp. 143–59. Smithsonian Institution Press, Washington, DC.

———. 1997 Life in the Provinces of the Aztec Empire. *Scientific American* 277(3):56–63.

———. 1999 Comment on Hirth's "Distribution Approach." *Current Anthropology* 40:528–30.

———. 2001 The Aztec Empire and the Mesoamerican World System. In *Empires: Perspectives from Archaeology and History*, edited by Susan E. Alcock, Terence N. D'Altroy, Kathleen D. Morrison, and Carla M. Sinopoli, pp. 128–54. Cambridge University Press, New York.

———. 2002 Domestic Ritual at Aztec Provincial Sites in Morelos. In *Domestic Ritual in Ancient Mesoamerica*, edited by Patricia Plunket, pp. 93–114. Monograph, vol. 46. Cotsen Institute of Archaeology, UCLA, Los Angeles.

———. 2003a *The Aztecs*. 2nd ed. Blackwell Publishers, Oxford.

———. 2003b Economic Change in Morelos Households. In *The Postclassic Mesoamerican World*, edited by Michael E. Smith and Frances F. Berdan, pp. 249–58. University of Utah Press, Salt Lake City.

———. 2004 The Archaeology of Ancient State Economies. *Annual Review of Anthropology* 33:73–102.

———. 2010a Regional and Local Market Systems in Aztec-Period Morelos. In *Archaeological Approaches to Market Exchange in Ancient Societies*, edited by Christopher P. Garraty and Barbara L. Stark, pp. 161-182. University Press of Colorado, Boulder.

———. 2010b Aztec Taxation at the City-State and Imperial Levels. Paper presented at the conference, The Fiscal Regimes of Early States, Stanford University.

———. n.d.–a *Archaeological Research at Aztec-Period Rural Sites in Morelos, Mexico*. Volume 2, Artifacts and Chronology/Investigaciones arqueológicas en sitios rurales de la época azteca en Morelos, Tomo 2, artefactos y cronología. University of Pittsburgh Memoirs in Latin American Archaeology. University of Pittsburgh (in press), Pittsburgh.

———. n.d.–b *Residential Excavations in the Aztec-Period City of Yautepec, Morelos, Mexico*/Excavaciones de casas en la ciudad azteca de Yautepec, Morelos, México.

University of Pittsburgh Memoirs in Latin American Archaeology. University of Pittsburgh (in press), Pittsburgh.

———. n.d.–c *Tlahuica Ceramics: The Aztec-Period Ceramics of Morelos, Mexico*. IMS Monographs, vol. 15. Institute for Mesoamerican Studies, Albany.

Smith, Michael E. and Frances F. Berdan (editors) 2003 *The Postclassic Mesoamerican World*. University of Utah Press, Salt Lake City.

Smith, Michael E., Adrian Burke, Timothy S. Hare, and Michael D. Glascock 2007 Sources of Imported Obsidian at Postclassic Sites in the Yautepec Valley, Morelos: A Characterization Study Using XRF and INAA. *Latin American Antiquity* 18:429–50.

Smith, Michael E. and Cynthia Heath-Smith 1994 Rural Economy in Late Postclassic Morelos: An Archaeological Study. In *Economies and Polities in the Aztec Realm*, edited by Mary G. Hodge and Michael E. Smith, pp. 349–76. Institute for Mesoamerican Studies, Albany.

Smith, Michael E., Hector Neff, and Ruth Fauman-Fichman n.d. Ceramic Imports at Yautepec and Their Implications for Aztec Exchange Systems. In *The Archaeology of Production, Distribution, and Consumption in Postclassic Central and Western Mexico: Contributions from Materials Composition Analysis*, edited by Thomas H. Charlton, Deborah L. Nichols, and Hector A. Neff (book in preparation).

Smith, Michael E., Jennifer Wharton, and Jan Marie Olson 2003 Aztec Feasts, Rituals, and Markets: Political Uses of Ceramic Vessels in a Commercial Economy. In *The Archaeology and Politics of Food and Feasting in Early States and Empires*, edited by Tamara L. Bray, pp. 235–68. Kluwer Publishers, New York.

Tambunan, Tulus 1995 Forces Behind the Growth of Rural Industries in Developing Countries. A Survey of Literature and a Case Study from Indonesia. *Journal of Rural Studies* 11:203–15.

Wilk, Richard R. and William L. Rathje (editors) 1982 Archaeology of the Household: Building a Prehistory of Domestic Life. *Special Issue of American Behavioral Scientist*, vol. 25:6.

Note

1. For lithics in Table 10.12, the Basin of Mexico category consists of obsidian from the Otumba source area. For Yautepec, the percentage of sourced gray obsidian from Otumba (Smith et al. 2007) was applied to the total count of gray obsidian for each context. No comparable sourcing study was done for the other sites, and we use an estimated constant of 50% (of the gray obsidian) for Otumba. In both cases, counts of green obsidian (Pachuca source area) are used. For ceramics, imported types from other parts of Morelos form the regional category. The guinda ceramics from each context were apportioned among the local, regional, and Basin of Mexico categories according to the corresponding frequencies in a sample of sourced guinda from Yautepec (Minc n.d.); those frequencies are 30.1% (local), 18.7% (regional), and 51.2% (Basin of Mexico).

CHAPTER 11

LOW-DENSITY, AGRARIAN-BASED URBANISM

SCALE, POWER, AND ECOLOGY

Roland Fletcher

The significance of low-density urbanism was articulated for both the industrial and the preindustrial world in the 1950s and 1960s. Jean Gottman defined the industrial megalopolis in his famous analysis of the low-density conurbation along East Coast of the United States of America (Figure 11.1) while Gordon Willey and the pioneering settlement archaeologists who studied the Maya in Lowland Mesoamerica showed that their great ritual centers, such as Tikal, had raised roadways or *sacbe* and were located within extensive settlements of dispersed housemounds, and plazas (Figure 11.2). Low-density urbanism has now been studied and affirmed for nearly half a century (Sharer and Traxler 2005; Morrill 2006). Settlement pattern studies have "done more to change archaeologists' views of the Maya than any single new procedure" (Sabloff 1990:68). And Morrill honors Gottman, remarking that the term *megalopolis* referring to "a string of closely interconnected metropolises was logical and inspired and has become part of the language" (Morrill 2006:155).

Low-density urbanism is, therefore, a vital part of how we understand our social world. It plays a profound role in industrialization, vividly apparent in the conurbations (Hall 1977) of the Ruhr in Germany and the Midlands in the United Kingdom in the early twentieth century as interconnected network of cities and industries enclosing patches of rural land; these are the precursors of the megalopolis as defined by Gottman (1961). Megalopoli proliferate worldwide. In the industrializing societies of Southern and Eastern Asia researchers have, since the 1970s, defined the extensive *desakota* ("ruralurban") of urban expansion in the region (see McGee 1991; Davis 2006:9–11). Urban growth occurs rapidly along communication routes and encapsulates the rural world in the mesh of the urban network. Hinterland is incorporated in the urban fabric. Low-density urbanism in the industrial world is recognizably and unavoidably present and highly problematic.

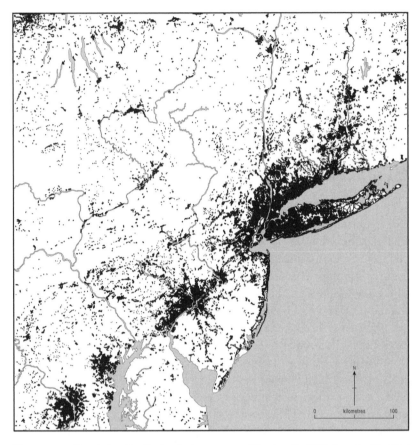

Figure 11.1. Population distribution in the east coast Megalopolis, USA, in 1963. Modified after Doxiadis (1968:81).

Even defining the extent of a low-density urban settlement is an issue for administrators, urban planners, the national census, and theoreticians of industrial urbanism, as illustrated by papers such as "The Edgeless City" (Lang and LeFurgy 2003).

The existence of industrial, low-density urbanism is not in doubt. Therefore, it is now untenable to define urban as a term restricted to compact and clearly bounded settlements, whether in industrial, industrializing, or agrarian-based societies. Agrarian-based urbanism incorporating large amounts of open space is therefore unproblematic. Furthermore, every major category of socioeconomic organization used by humans has created and sustained low-density settlements (Fletcher 1991). They have contained hunter-gatherer communities (Watanabe 1973; Fletcher 1991:399;

Figure 11.2. Tikal, Guatemala, ninth century A.D. Modified after Coe (1967).

O'Connell 1998), pastoralists such as the Mongols (Fletcher 1991:412–13), agro-hunters (Fletcher 1991:402), farmers (Netting 1968), and also mobile urban communities (Gleichen 1898:157; Sinopoli 1994) as well as industrial populations. The most parsimonious and least radical argument is therefore that low-density, agrarian-based urban communities have existed across a wide range of settlement sizes and that this is consistent with the behaviors of human beings who use and have used them in other major socioeconomic ways of life (see also Kolb, Chapter 7).

Agrarian-Based, Low-Density Urbanism

In the 1950s and early 1960s, Michael Coe (1957, 1961, 2003) pointed out the equivalence between the great temple centers of the Maya and the Khmer. It is now apparent that the equivalence extends far beyond the monumental centers to include extensive suburbs. Just as the Mesoamerican archaeologists were starting to focus on Maya urbanism, a landscape survey had started at Angkor in Cambodia in the 1960s under the direction of B.-P. Groslier to map in detail the area beyond central monuments. Tragically, it was halted by increasing conflict, but the insight of Groslier into Angkor as a hydraulic city of suburbs bound together by a water management network was in print by 1979 in French in the Bulletin of the École Française d'Extrême-Orient (Figure 11.3). By 1978, Bennet Bronson was extending the comparison of tropical forest cultures to include Anuradhapura, one of the medieval Buddhist capitals of Sri Lanka. Although Anuradhapura and Bagan in Myanmar and Angkor have been consistently referred to as urban since the early mid-twentieth century, they were viewed, even in the 1990s, in terms of their walled central enclosures (labeled the city or sometimes the citadel), using a standard Western, medieval model of compact preindustrial urbanism.

Surveys at Anuradhapura (Coningham et al. 2007) and Bagan (Hudson 2004) and more recently at Angkor (Fletcher et al. 2003; and see Evans et al. 2007 for the new standard map) are transforming our understanding of these urban centers. They now need to be considered in terms of low-density residence patterns, just as happened with the analysis of Maya settlements from the 1950s and 1960s onwards. In the context of Southern Asia, these great urban centers have been placed in a larger comparative framework by Miksic (2000) in his discussion of a continuum between orthogenetic and heterarchical cities. The former were large and usually organized on a spatial layout such as a partial grid, and operated as the locus of ritual state power, as at Angkor. The latter were more commonly small, with compact, variegated spatial layouts and a strong mercantile function. The former were more common in mainland Southeast Asia and the latter in island Southeast Asia (although the 100 km² site of Truwalen on Java appears to be a low-density complex with mercantile and substantial ritual functions). The extensive scatter of shrines, from Borobudur to Prambanan, around the flanks of Mount Merapi, suggests a strong role for the orthogenetic form in island Southeast Asia prior to the ninth century A.D. Stark (2006) has recently reviewed the first millennium A.D. contexts in Southeast Asia in which urbanism began to develop and has made clear that the tangled history of maritime trade and inland states based on rice wealth is yet to be unraveled. An entire suite of urban settlements of a distinctive low-density form needs to be investigated in Southern Asia. These include places like Khahajuro (950–1050 A.D.) in India; My Son, the great Cham center of

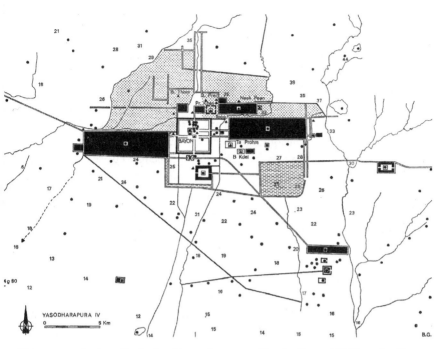

Figure 11.3. Angkor, Cambodia, thirteenth century. Plan by Bernard-Philippe Groslier; courtesy l'École Française d'Extrême-Orient.

the fourth to thirteenth centuries A.D. in the Hoi An valley of Vietnam; and Sukhothai, a capital in Thailand from 1238–1438 A.D. in the northern Chao Praya basin. This urban tradition needs to be brought into comparison with the rapidly expanding data from the Maya and other Mesoamerican cities.

Of special significance is the demise of low-density urbanism in the Maya world, in Sri Lanka and in central Cambodia. The eventual demise of these great urban centers seems to have led to the almost total disappearance of any significant urbanism in the former heartlands of their civilizations. Indeed, the decline in occupation in these regions was sufficient that terms such as "abandonment" are used to describe what European visitors found in the nineteenth century. No large, agrarian-based, low-density urbanized settlement has existed during the past five hundred years. Except on brief, rare occasions in the sixteenth century A.D., when a deteriorating example may have been observed, no case of such a city was encountered (or at least reported) by a European until the African literate examples of Ouagadougou (Skinner 1964:31–59) and Addis Ababa (Gleichen 1898), which came into being in the nineteenth century. And prior to the sixteenth century we have relatively few outsider reports of visits to such cities comparable to the Chinese diplomats and monks who visited Southeast Asian cities between the seventh and fourteenth centuries (e.g., Harris 2007). This scarcity of reports by members of the other great civilizations, which habitually created compact urban settlements, has no doubt contributed to a professional sense of unease among present-day scholars about the existence of the general class of low-density, agrarian-based cities. But it might perhaps warn us to be curious, not about whether or not that category exists, but why if they did exist they had ceased to be occupied by the seventeenth century and why we do not find them as long-lasting settlements in the well-known, old primary regions of urban development. That they might, therefore, have been almost entirely secondary urban formations and also displayed a capacity for irreversible decline within the first fifteen hundred years of the Common Era is a matter of some concern.

The iconic case is, of course, the Classic Maya of Lowland Mesoamerica who have been generally regarded, since the 1960s, as possessing low-density urban centers and are considered to have experienced a "collapse" of their civilization in the late ninth and tenth centuries. In the nineteenth century, Europeans, such as Catherwood and Stephens (Bahn 1996:111–12), began to encounter these cities abandoned in the forest (Figure 11.4A), adding them to the repertoire of cases demonstrating the "Fall of Civilization" – a peculiarly European post-Roman fixation. The identification of similar places in Sri Lanka and Cambodia began to provide a somewhat worrying list of "lost" civilizations, suggesting that such demise was not perhaps rare and is a matter to be taken seriously. The great sites of Anuradhapura and Pollonnaruwa were found and reported in the early nineteenth century, by British colonial administrators and soldiers, overgrown and abandoned in the Dry Zone (see Murphey 1957; Figure 11.4B). Then in the 1860s, at Angkor, in the dense forests of the heart of Cambodia, Belgian and French missionaries and explorers, respectively, reported the same kind of great monuments and sophisticated art, covered with forest (Dagens 1995) in regions occupied predominantly by small farming communities (Figure 11.4C).

We are left with the possibility that not only were these cases a similar kind of moral experience for Europeans in the nineteenth century, they were also, in their own time, similar kinds of places, characterized by massive central clusters of spectacular monuments surrounded by a vast penumbra of occupation sites and numerous small ritual monuments scattered around features of massive engineering in the form of embankments, water control systems, and modified landscapes. Their existence and demise are disturbing

Figure 11.4. Low-density agrarian cities today. A: Tikal (courtesy Michael Smith); B: Anuradhapura (courtesy Damian Evans); C: Angkor (courtesy Roland Fletcher).

because they were places of immense beauty and magnificence, even in ruins, as portrayed in the nineteenth-century drawings of Maya and Khmer cities. The key issues are where and when did low-density agrarian urbanism exist on the planet; how extensive could such urban settlements become; on what staple crop economies did they function; and how and why did they cease to function?

Case Studies

To assess the nature of agrarian-based, low-density urbanism requires an overview of settlements of different sizes in different regions worldwide. My aim is to offer a comparative perspective on the variety and the differences among the case studies in their size, form, staple economy, and operation, and to provide a basis for discussing common issues and logical problems. Five cases – ranging from Copan in Honduras with an area of about 25 km² up to Angkor in Cambodia, with a total area for the Greater Angkor urban complex of about 900 to 1,000 km² – provide the size range. See Smith and Peregrine (Chapter 2) for a contextual discussion of this and other approaches to comparative analysis.

Copan has been meticulously surveyed and intensively dated. Bagan, in Mynmar, is also well surveyed and covers about 90 km². Of consequence for the analysis is the significant factor that Bagan's staple food supply of rice was not primarily grown at Bagan but instead was produced in several valleys 100 to 200 km away upstream and downstream on tributaries of the Ayeyarwady River. This is of some relevance when assessing the apparent impact of low-density cities on their production landscapes. Tikal is included because it is one of the most intensively studied and reported sites in Mesoamerica and, with an area of somewhere between 100 and 200 km² (Webster et al. 2007), it is the largest Maya center for which there is a current comprehensive map. Anuradhapura in Sri Lanka has been included because it appears to cover a larger extent than the 100–200 km² of Tikal. Over the past twenty to thirty years Anuradhapura has also been the subject of intensive research by Sri Lankan and international scholars on its extent, its archaeology, and its epigraphic history. Finally, Angkor is included because it is now the largest known case of a low-density preindustrial urban complex at circa 1,000 km² and may indicate the general suite of factors that stopped this entire class of settlements from continuing to grow.

The Maya. In the lowlands of Mesoamerica and the adjacent southern hill ranges, centers with large monuments, built roadways and scattered surrounding residential occupation began to develop after 1000 B.C. By 300 A.D., the lowlands were the setting for massive centers such as El Mirador, the oldest Maya capital (Coe 1999:76), with its famous El Tigre and Danta pyramids that were 50–70 m high. El Tigre had a built volume of 380,000 m³ (Evans 2008:321). Dirt was also shifted to create reservoirs and canals as at Edzna where two million m³ of deposit was removed to make twenty-seven reservoirs (Evans 2008:233). By 300 A.D., seven major sites dominated the southern half of the peninsula, growing to around twenty centers in the period 600–900 A.D. Among the most comprehensively studied are Tikal, Copan, and Caracol.

In the Classic period (600–900 A.D.), Copan covered an area of about 25 km² (Figure 11.5) with its center close to the river and residential occupation scattered evenly along the river flats and even more dispersed on the hillslopes. Houses were built of timber and daub with thatched roofs. The most conspicuous occupation feature is the low masonry mounds on which houses were located. Similar sized housing units are spread across the landscape. Farming occurred around the housing and there are indications of forest clearance and erosion (Webster, Freter, and Gonlin 2000:118–19).

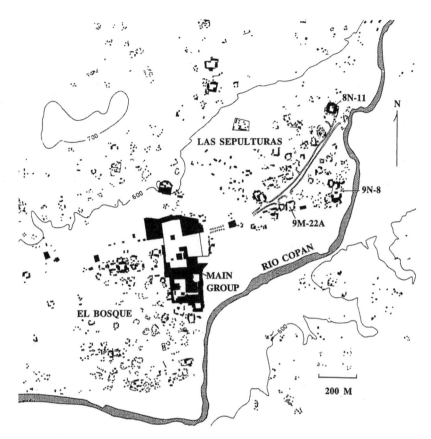

Figure 11.5. Copan, Honduras, core zone, ninth century A.D. Courtesy David Webster.

The center of Tikal is located on a shallow hill that rises between several *aguadas*, or seasonal ponds (Figure 11.2). There was occupation in higher areas by the Middle Formative (900–600 B.C.). Uaxactun, about 19 km to the north, had pyramid structures in the Late Formative (300 B.C. to early A.D.) and by the third century A.D., pyramid clusters were being built at Tikal. Tikal rapidly reached its maximum extent and absorbed Uaxactun around 378 A.D. (Sharer and Traxler 2005:185). The major temples (I to IV) were built in the seventh and eighth centuries. Surrounding the massive mounds, great causeways and water tanks of Tikal was a widely distributed pattern of masonry-built housemounds whose occurrence gradually decreased away from the center. Tikal had outlier subcenters, some of which became late autonomous centers. Tikal's last royal stela was emplaced in 869 A.D. Puleston (1983) estimated Tikal's areal extent as about 100–120 km², but

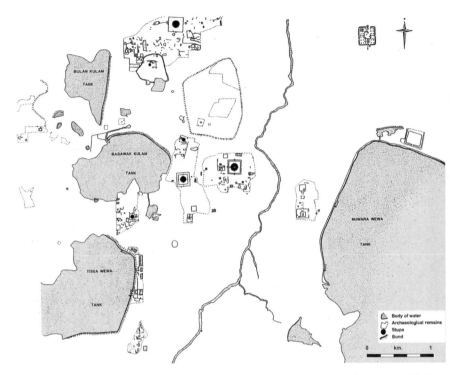

Figure 11.6. Anuradhapura, Sri Lanka, twelfth century A.D. Central urban area. Modified after Coningham (1999:29).

Webster and colleague's recent survey (2007) has shown that the discontinuous sectors of the various "moats" form a partial boundary to an area of about 200 km². These "moats" somewhat resemble the partial boundary banks and ditches of the later Yoruba "towns" in Nigeria (Mabongunje 1962; Kusimba et al. 2006). Exactly what this fragmented edge constituted is not clear and contiguous low-density occupation may well have extended beyond it, well out toward the *aguadas*. Such ambiguous edges are a feature of low-density cities. Surveys of Maya centers between the 1960s and 1980s showed that residential densities were on the order of about 6 p/ha (Sharer and Traxler 2005:688).

Sri Lanka. The development of urban centers commenced in Sri Lanka in the first millennium B.C. with textual evidence from Anuradhapura around 500 B.C. and then structural evidence and imported items from the third century onwards (Bandaranayake 2003). The city has a walled center surrounded by massive monastic establishments (Figure 11.6) and a wide skirt

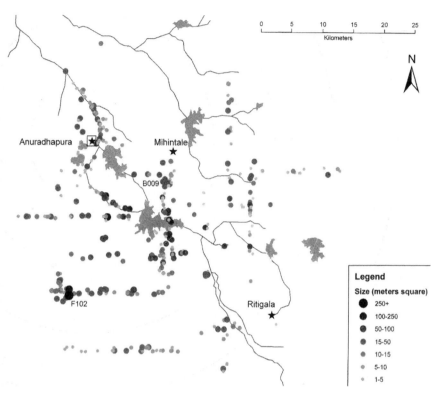

Figure 11.7. Anuradhapura, twelfth century A.D. Dispersed occupation. Courtesy Robin Coningham.

of ritual sites extending out for about 14 km to monasteries, such as Mihintale on the hills to the east. Numerous occupation loci of relatively similar size and superficial form are scattered across the intervening landscape (Coningham et al. 2007; Figure 11.7). Ordinary domestic houses appear to have been flimsy timber and thatch structures. The multi-foci, urban complex is wrapped around several huge water tanks, such as the Tissavava, which was extended in the third century B.C. (Coningham 1999:23), and numerous reconfigured rivers whose water was shunted into adjacent bunded fields. The landscape has been substantially modified and is dotted with numerous smaller water tanks. In addition, a network of roads marked by bridged crossing points, extended out from the central enclosure. At its peak in the ninth and early tenth centuries, Anuradhapura's central zone covered 40 km² (Bandaranayake 2003:4). In the late tenth century, it was abandoned with some partial reoccupation and monument restoration into the late twelfth century (Seneviratna 1994:34–35). Pollon-naruwa, which had a similar spatial configuration, was established as the formal capital in the eleventh century (Seneviratna 1998:91), was sacked in 1196, and abandoned after several brief revivals in the thirteenth and early fourteenth centuries (Murphey 1957:187–88; Seneviratna 1998:222; and see Paranavithana 1960).

Southeast Asia. Urbanism began to develop in Southeast Asia in the late first millennium B.C. in Ayurawaddy basin (O'Reilly 2007:13–31) and in the vicinity of the Mekong delta in first half of the first millennium A.D. (Higham 2002:236–43). The western centers (Pyu or Tircul towns, such as Beikthano and Sri Ksetra) were as much as 9 to 19 km² in extent and were enclosed by moats and walls. They incorporated substantial water management features such as tanks. In the east the urban sites of Oc Eo and Angkor Borei (Stark 2006:417–19), with areas of about 3 to 5 km², were both in use in the first half of the first millennium A.D. They were enclosed by ramparts and moats with water channels and large interconnecting canals. As in the Pyu sites, brick shrines and structures are present.

From the sixth century onward, settlements such as Sambor Prei Kuk (Tranet 1995; Ichita et al. 1999) emerged with a more dispersed pattern of occupation with large enclosures, widely separate shrines, and substantial water management features. The pattern of dispersed, low-density urbanism became a distinctive feature of medieval states in mainland Southeast Asia. Both the diversity and the varied histories of this class of urban complex are illustrated by one of the smaller examples, Bagan at circa 90 km², and by Angkor at about 1,000 km², the largest known preindustrial case of this kind of settlement worldwide.

Bagan (Figure 11.8) had a long ancestry (Hudson 2001). A major capital was established there in the eleventh century on the east bank of the Ayurawaddy River and was replaced as the capital by Pinya and then Awa, near what is now Mandalay, in the early fourteenth century (Stadner 2005:22–26). At its center is a walled enclosure containing the brick foundations of what are referred to as palaces. Surrounding the center are numerous massive Buddhist shrines. These form an arc along the edge of the river and also extend away from it over a total area of about 80 km², interspersed with monasteries and the debris of domestic life (Hudson 2001:48). These shrines and monasteries had support and servicing staff who would have lived nearby. A large shrine, the Dhammayangi, had a recorded service staff of about 130 people in 1165; and a dedication of 1,000 slaves is mentioned for another major stupa (Luce 1969:111–12 and 70–73).

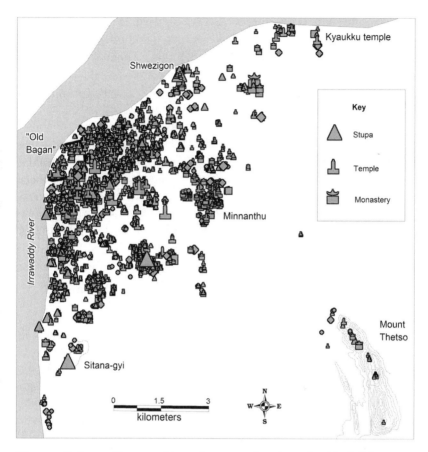

Figure 11.8. Bagan, Myanmar, thirteenth century. Locations of public buildings, A.D. Courtesy Bob Hudson.

Early Angkor, in the eighth and early ninth centuries, consisted of two centers: one around Ak Yum dating from the seventh century, under what is now the western end of the West Baray; and the other, Hariharalaya, from the eighth century, at what is now called Roluos in Southeast Angkor. Both centers were unbounded and apparently low-density settlements (Pottier 2006). Hariharalaya in the ninth century already had a large baray or reservoir, the Indratataka. In the late ninth century, the center was moved to Phnom Bakheng and the East Baray was built. This capital, named Yasodharapura, was also unbounded (Pottier 2000) and incorporated both Hariharalya and Ak Yum to form Greater Angkor (Figure 11.9). Thereafter until the late twelfth and early thirteenth centuries, the locations of administrative centers and palaces moved around within the network of the urban complex. Only in the late twelfth century, with the construction of the walled and moated central enclosure of Angkor Thom, did the practice of relocating the administrative center cease. Thereafter, the Bayon, the central temple of Angkor Thom, also became the permanent state temple of Angkor. The urban complex consists of a complex network of channels and embankments that tied together the sprawling, almost monotonously self-similar suburbs of scattered housemound clusters and their associated shrines (*prasat*) and water tanks (*trapeang*) (Figure 11.10). The population lived along the embankments, on the housemounds and within enclosures, some of which also contained major temples (Fletcher et al. 2003:109–10). Rice fields occur right in the heart of Angkor, for example immediately to the west of Angkor Wat, and may also have been present within Angkor Thom.

The Ecology of Agrarian-Based, Low-Density Urbanism: Behavior, Landscape, and Economics

The settlements under discussion here range very considerably in size. The resource regions that supported the settlements also differed markedly in extent, as did the water management systems and the staple crops. My aim is to compare their staple crop economies based on Smith's (2004) comparative analysis of the economies of early states. At this stage I am not going to attempt highly specific comparisons because that would require levels of detail that I either do not possess or are not yet available. The critical contrast is between the Mesoamerican and the Southern Asian cases. The staple crop differences are well known. In Mesoamerica, the primary crop is maize with the associated beans and squash assemblage. There were no large, quadrupedal domesticants. Southern Asia has numerous bovids, and the staple crop is rice. A critical factor is that the yields from rice production can be drastically enhanced by basic crop-production procedures. In Sri Lanka, for example, dry-field agriculture produces circa 70–100 kg of rice per ha while bunded rice field production yields of circa 1,030 kg per ha (Coningham 1999:24). Southern Asia also has substantial stocks of domesticated quadrupeds, especially cattle and buffalo, and people make substantial use of fish for protein.

It is important to note, however, that both regions have a "monsoonal" seasonality that provides substantial quantities of rainwater for several months whereas the remainder of the year, usually four to five months,

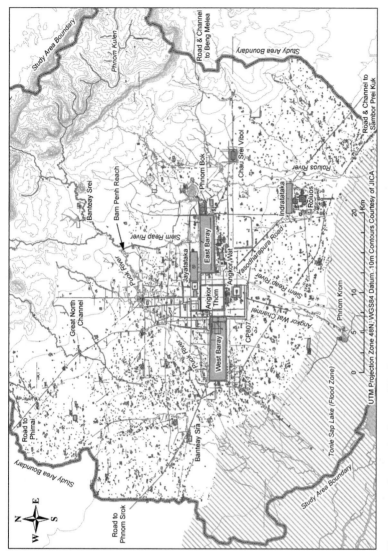

Figure 11.9. Greater Angkor, twelfth–thirteenth century A.D. Courtesy Damian Evans and Christophe Pottier.

is completely dry. The Mesoamerican settlements generally received far less water than the South and Southeast Asian sites. Copan, on the southern edge of the lowlands, received only 1,400 mm of rainfall annually. The water in the adjacent river was undrinkable in the dry season (see Lucero 2006:155). Tikal featured constructed reservoirs in the center among the main monuments and around the periphery of the central area that could hold about 568,000 m³ of water at one time and more than 900,000 m³ during the course of a year (Scarborough and Gallopin 1991:661). By contrast, the West Baray at Angkor could hold more than 50 million m³ of water at one time and covered 16 km² (Fletcher et al. 2008). In Anuradhapura, the Kalavava tank covers 18 km² (Coningham 1999:10).

Clearly the South Asian settlements operated on a far larger spatial scale than the Mesoamerican ones. Nor were the Mesoamerican support regions as large. Most Maya centers were relatively close together, with circa 20–30 km between them (Sharer and Traxler 2005:705), about the same as the radius of Greater Angkor. Larger Maya centers dominated bigger areas. For example, Calakmul and Tikal are reckoned to have effectively controlled regions of about 8,000 km² each, perhaps with total populations in their polities of as many as 425,000 people (see Folan et al. 1995). Dos Pilas, which was much smaller, apparently controlled around 4,000 km² at one time. By contrast, Bagan controlled more than 18,000 km² of irrigated land carrying about 16,000 km² of rice fields (Aung Thwin 1990:52–57). At its peak Bagan claimed control of much of what is now Myanmar with a population in its empire estimated at around 2.5 million in the lowlands (Aung Thwin 1990:54–55). Anuradhapura, to varying degrees, controlled about half of Sri Lanka for much of the period from the fourth to the twelfth centuries and occasionally dominated the whole island – circa 65,610 km² (Perera 2001:34–44). Populations were considerable. Two monasteries at Anuradhapura, the Abhayagiri and the Mahavihara, had 5,000 and 3,000 monks, respectively, according to Fa-Hsien (Seneviratna 1994:27).

Angkor, largest of all the agrarian low-density urban sites, controlled a core area of 70,000 to 100,000 km² under Suryavarman I (early eleventh century), Survayarman II (early twelfth century), and Jayavarman VII (late twelfth to early thirteenth centuries) (Hendrickson 2010) and periodically laid claim to an empire that extended into modern Thailand, Laos, and Vietnam with an area as great as 420,000 km². With a fluctuating but persistent political dominance that extended from the ninth to the fourteenth centuries, it is hardly surprising that Angkor could build a temple enclosure (Angkor Wat) the size of central Tikal

Figure 11.10. Greater Angkor. Dispersed occupation and field systems. Courtesy Scott Hawken.

1) and create a low-density urban complex with a water man-
work that spread across nearly 1,000 km² of intermeshed
...n landscape. That landscape could have fed between 300,000
and 750,000 human beings (see Fletcher et al. 2003:117 for assessment
by Lustig). An inscription at the Ta Prohm temple in the late twelfth
century listed categories of people who made up its workforce of 12,640
people, and notes that 66,625 farmers were indentured to support it, presumably by delivering rice as tax and tithe (Kapur and Sahai 2007:52–
56). Note that another late twelfth-century temple in Angkor, the Preah
Khan, also has a dedicatory stela, which enumerates that 97,840 farmers
in 5,324 "communities" had to support it (see Face C, stanzas LXXIII to
LXXVII in Coedès 1941). So the Preah Khan and the Ta Prohm temples
alone absorbed the rice yield of about 150,000 farmers in the late twelfth
century – and hence a far larger total population if all family members are
included. Given the costs of transporting grain, these people were presumably both within and close to the overall area of Greater Angkor. In
addition, numerous other temples had to be supplied, including at least one
giant – the late twelfth-century Bayon in the center of Angkor Thom.

By contrast, the residential population of Copan at its peak between
600 and 800 A.D. is given as 18,000–25,000 people by Sharer and Traxler
(2005:307) and Rice (2006:364). Tikal's population has recently been given
as circa 60,000 with another 30,000 in a rural periphery (Valdés and Fahsen
2005:156). The issue, of course, is deciding the extent of Tikal – a discussion that is greatly complicated for conventional categories by the incorporation of "hinterland" within the urban area of a low-density city. Perhaps
the estimated 90,000 is more like the population of Greater Tikal. But
debate continues on this topic for Maya settlements. Anuradhapura and
Bagan have uncertain populations.

What is clear is that agrarian-based, low-density urbanism could create settlements of highly varied size and form, characterized by extremely
homogenous spatial patterns spread over vast areas. The distribution of
residence units in Copan and Tikal suggests considerable self-similarity
between different parts of the same settlement. For Anuradhapura and
Angkor, the similarity has been quantified. In both sites the residential
loci are either very similar in size or are very consistently distributed across
the landscape (Coningham et al. 2007). In the case of Angkor, for which
we have the most detail, the settlement pattern is self-similar across a
3,000 km² catchment area and was apparently invariant from the eighth
to the late sixteenth centuries (Pottier 2006; Evans et al. 2007). This is a
disturbing degree of homogeneity, suggesting a profound lack of variety in
daily praxis. These large low-density urban complexes apparently did not

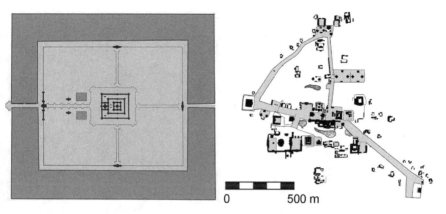

0   500 m

Figure 11.11. Angkor Wat compared to central Tikal.

contain much operational variability that could have offered a basis for new ways of adjusting to changing circumstances *in situ*.

These urban centers had two other characteristics that likely placed them at risk when circumstances began to change: a commitment to infrastructure and a tendency toward extensive modification of the landscape for agriculture. We are greatly impressed today by the massive structures and engineering they contain. The Dhammarajika in Bagan, built in the twelfth century, contained about six million bricks (Aung Thwin 1990:55–58). The four great temple pyramids of Tikal rear 60–70m into the air and the North Acropolis is a pile of masonry covering 1.5 ha that was raised in stages over several centuries (Coe 1965). This capacity also created massive infrastructure that would have exerted considerable inertia while binding the population to the facilities it provided. In Anuradhapura, the Padiwaya tank has 13 million cubic meters of earthworks (Murphey 1957:185). The banks of the West Baray in Angkor contain about 20 million cubic meters of soil. A canal nearly 25 km long runs down from north to south at a very shallow gradient to the *baray* and another channel, more than 40 km long, runs away from the West Baray to the southeast on a shallow gradient across the slope of the land. As Lucero (2002) noted for the water reservoirs in Maya cities such as Tikal and Copan, such infrastructure generates a risk that the population may become dependent on it. But because the infrastructure only works under a limited set of conditions and cannot be readily re-geared to deal with change such as extremely high or severely reduced rainfall, this infrastructural inertia and dependency opens the possibility that an altered, anthropogenic landscape combined with climate change could create irreversible operational failures that would cascade through the fabric of the dependent community.

(terraces not mapped)

Figure 11.12. Caracol, Belize, ninth century A.D. Section of the city showing extensive agricultural and residential terraces. From Chase and Chase (1998:68), reproduced with permission.

In addition, the low-density cities engaged in extensive modification of the landscape for food production. It is now apparent that the Maya had substantially modified the landscape through the construction of raised fields and terraces. In the 1980s, the evidence for more intensive and regulated agriculture began to be reported and discussed (Fedick 1996). We now know that drained swamps, raised fields, hydraulics, and terracing provided an economic base for larger populations; for example, see Chase and Chase (1998) and Chase et al. (2010) for terracing at Caracol (Figure 11.12). Previously pollen analyses have been considered to show that substantial deforestation was occurring (Rice 1996). Recent studies (e.g., Mueller et al. 2010) identify that soil erosion decreased and forests recovered over periods of 80-280 years after the end of the Classic period, which raises the possibility that the population had perhaps overexploited its landscape

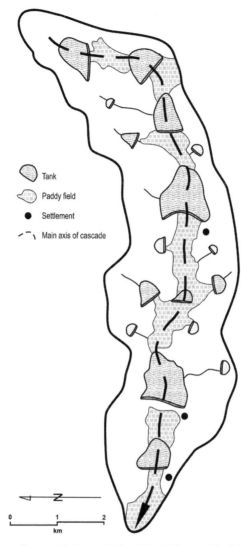

Figure 11.13. Anuradhapura. Tank cascade from Diwul Wewa to Tumbira Wewa. Modified after Brohier (2006).

and that the biodiversity of the landscape had been reduced by focusing on the maize-squash-beans triad and economic trees. In the Dry Zone of Sri Lanka, a quick observation makes it clear that most of the main rivers flowing northwest, north, and northeast were modified with off-takes, major tanks, and cascades of minor tanks (Dhanasekara and Maddumabandara 2004; Figure 11.13). As now, the shallow valleys would have been taken over by bunded rice fields where an anthropogenic wetland could be created to deliver high rice yields. Similarly, in the Angkor region we can now see, on the basis of satellite images, aerial photographs, and radar, that the regional landscape was converted to an anthropogenic wetland (Figure 11.10). The forest cover was removed even up into the lower slopes of the Kulen and Khror hills that lie north of Angkor (Fletcher et al. 2003:118–19). The landscape was converted to extensive area of bunded rice fields, with a cultivated woodland of economic trees around the houses. In Sri Lanka, the entire northern third of the island was modified for agriculture to such a degree that when the British administrators entered the area in the nineteenth century, they recognized the huge, abandoned water systems and instituted a policy of reconstruction and recolonization from the south to resurrect the irrigation systems and the rice yields they could offer (Parker 1909; Murphey 1957; De Silva 2005:378–87).

These large low-density settlements are apparently associated with extensification of land use. Such extensive landscape modification in regions that are liable to extreme dry seasons opened up the risk that forest clearance and climate change could combine to severely damage the economy. Forest clearance affects the degree to which water can be retained in the soil, creating problems that are well known from Brazil and other South American countries where deforestation has led to severe soil erosion off hill slopes. This would have affected landscapes with shallow gradients on slopes leading down into major regions of low-lying ground, such as the *aguada* in Mesoamerica, the great open plains around the Tonle Sap in Cambodia, and the shallow valleys of Sri Lanka that debouch into the Indian Ocean. These regions also experience periodic severe climatic fluctuations that affected their annual cycle with occasions of extremely poor rainfall and drought followed by intensely heavy rains. As a result, the water management networks, dams, field banks, and terraces would have been subject to extreme variation in water flow, sedimentation, and erosion. Ominously, landscape-management agendas that seem to have been predicated on achieving regional economic stability through consistent, repetitious self-similarity would themselves have generated circumstances that could create severe ecological stress. Population accumulated on the landscape, creating delicately balanced, anthropogenic environments that could be destabilized by long-term fluctuations in rainfall.

Two further factors have to be considered that do not at first appear to be problematic but together would proliferate long-term ecological damage across the regional landscape. In Sri Lanka (see Brohier 1934; Murphey 1957:190, 192; Siriweera 1990:143–45; Brohier 2006:803) and in the

Maya area (Fedick 1996; and see Faust 1998 for the recent past), swidden agriculture with short-term clearance of forest by burning to grow a crop for three to five years, coexisted with long-term agricultural practices that created features such as bunded fields and terracing. It is less well known that this combination coexists in Cambodia even today and occurred in the nineteenth century (see Delvert 1961; Boulbet 1979). The Angkorian inscriptions and Zhou Daguan refer to "hill people" as different from the lowlanders (Harris 2007:61), suggesting that the contrast between present-day food economies in the lowland and the hills may have a long ancestry. On the Kulen range, northwest of Angkor, swidden agriculture is used today to grow rice in dry fields within 3 to 5 kilometers of landscapes covered with hundreds of square kilometers of bunded rice fields. Even more consequential is the fact that swidden agriculture is regularly practiced on the slopes above the higher-yield fields and their water networks. In Sri Lanka the two activities are interdigitated, with swidden on the shallow ridges between the broad shallow river valleys where bunded rice was grown (Senanayake 1982; Seneviratna 1989). Inscriptions indicate that irrigated rice may not even have been the most extensive activity. Parakamabahu I, a late–twelfth-century ruler at Polonnawura, notes that "there are many paddy lands that are watered chiefly by water from rain clouds, but the fields that depend on a perpetual supply of water from rivers and tanks are verily few in number ... " (Murphey 1957:197). The occurrence of transient swidden upslope, but close to, permanent fields is strongly indicated in the Belize River Archaeological Settlement Survey (BRASS) surveys and in the descriptions of Maya agriculture (Fedick 1996).

Here the second factor becomes relevant. Increasingly, the Mayanist researchers are emphasizing that the urban farmers would have been seasonally mobile, relocating to field houses at various times of year on distributed landholdings that gave them some security of crop return in unpredictable rainfall conditions (Lucero 2006:35). Interviews with farmers in the Angkor region today make it clear that families have distributed landholdings in several different localities as a risk management strategy. One would expect such a policy to have become prevalent quite quickly in regions with marked seasonal rainfall and fluctuating intensity of rainfall over several years and would surely have been a standard feature of Angkor from the ninth to the sixteenth centuries. Inscriptions indicate that owners could hold numerous separate patches of land (for elite owners, see Finot et al. 2000:75–76). If this was a prevalent pattern in the great low-density cities, then rapid urban population increase, especially at the peak of a state's power, could produce a potentially dangerous development. Land would already have been substantially taken up in the capital area but with continuing population influx and growth an increasingly large, marginal urban population would develop in a landscape where seasonally mobile residence and swidden agriculture were practiced. They would have available to them a ready means to obtain crops by extensifying the region where swidden was carried out. This is also a practice that preindustrial states would not have had a mechanism to manage or prevent. In Cambodia a similar process occurs within 50 to 100 km of the provincial capital of Siem Reap and the lush tourist hotels.

In medieval Sri Lanka, this process may have been of especial significance because it is generally considered that significant expansion of agriculture in the central hills, upstream from the managed water systems of Anuradhapura and Pollonnaruwa, did not occur until after the cities were abandoned. The alternative now needs to be investigated that extensive and rapidly expanding swidden in those areas was contemporary with the pinnacle of growth in each city. If so, then this would have seriously increased the downstream flow of sediment and increased the amount and rate of runoff. The British engineers in the nineteenth and early twentieth centuries remarked on the degree to which the dams for tanks that they were repairing displayed repeated old repairs (e.g., Brohier 1934, Part II:8) indicating that the dams of the water tanks were quite vulnerable to damage by increased water flow. A breach could lead to a cascade of dam failure down a channel (Brohier 2006:18). If we find that there was actually a rapid increase in swidden agriculture south of Anuradhapura in the ninth and tenth centuries (before its collapse) and southwest of Polunnaruwa in the century before its demise in the thirteenth century A.D., then the impact of an uncontrolled increase in short-term swiddening may be a process that we need to incorporate into our models of the demise of the low-density cities of the Classic Maya, Medieval Sri Lanka, and the Khmer Empire.

One key implication of the swidden expansion model is that not only would the crop-production infrastructure fail in varied and erratic ways, but the impact of the swidden pattern would be long-lasting. The key effect would be that a far smaller population than was sustained by the infrastructure could have a drastic impact over a much larger area for far longer. As the crop supply for the cities declined, an increasing population would have sought to move away to exploit swidden agriculture, creating a ripple effect until the gradually dispersing population itself began to decrease. The dispersing population would be liable to cause further reduction of forests and longer recovery times as swidden periodicity was, for a while, reduced. The environmental signature of such a dispersal should therefore be a substantial delay in the recovery of the primary forest long after the

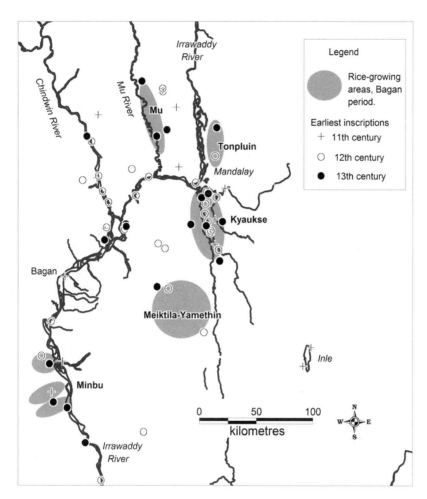

Figure 11.14. Bagan region. Locations of rice production areas of the Bagan period in relation to the earliest dated inscriptions. Courtesy Bob Hudson.

breakdown began. Interestingly, at Copan the last stela was erected in 822 A.D., residence declined but continued until at least 1000 A.D. and forest recovery was only really visible by 1200 A.D. In Angkor, Dan Penny and colleague's analyses (2007:392) of cores taken from the large moats and reservoirs indicate that around the Sras Srang in central Angkor even into the eighteenth century, the landscape was similar to the present one.

Bagan is a valuable control case because its rice production areas were between 50 and 200 km away from the city (Aung Thwin 1990:68; Figure 11.14). The region around Bagan is poor for rice production and the adjacent hills on the east are steep and intractable for swidden agriculture. In addition, the major rice production valleys, which are some distance away from Bagan, are fed by massive monsoonal rainfall in high hill country that delivers enough water to cause local flooding before the water flows from the tributaries into the main river channels of the Ayeyarwady River. These rice production regions are therefore somewhat buffered from decadal changes in the monsoon. Crucially, the capitals of the Burmese kingdoms, with the brief exception of Pegu, are all located within 150 km of each other in central-upper Burma (Aung Thwin 1990:1). After the collapse of Bagan in the late thirteenth century, in conjunction with political chaos in central Burma, the capital moved northwards to the Mandalay area but there was no sustained abandonment of central Burma. The long-term shift to the south and to the coastal areas around Rangoon was a very late process in the eighteenth century, occurring only shortly before the British began to infiltrate the region. The strong implication is that the separation of the capital – Bagan – from its rice production areas, and the use of water transport to deliver the rice, created a system in which ecological instability apparently did not cumulate.

Demise

The most striking similarity in the histories of the low-density cities from Mesoamerica, Sri Lanka, and Cambodia is that they are associated with famous cases of severe "collapse" that did not occur in quite the ways that Western analysts at first supposed. Recent research has shown that the processes of "collapse" were not as straightforward as was envisaged in the late nineteenth and early twentieth centuries. But archaeologists have identified significant similarities as well as specific regionally unique phenomena. The key points are that the "collapses" were more protracted than expected, the occupations of urban areas continued after the elites were gone, and may have led to a long, slow process of reforestation rather than a quick recovery of the forest.

Since the 1980s, the Maya collapse has been reappraised as a complex, protracted process (Webster 2002) that involved climate change (Petersen and Haug 2005). Elite practices disappeared rapidly in the Peten region between about 800 and 880 A.D. New centers developed further north in the Puuc but these too were largely abandoned by the eleventh century A.D. as was Chichen Itza (Andrews et al. 2003). It is important to note, however, that the great Classic sites like Tikal (Valdés and Fahsen 2005), Caracol (Chase and Chase 2000), and Copan (Webster 2002:310) retained a declining population for over a century after the last stelae were carved (see

Webster et al. 1992). The overall character of the society also continued. The final phase of Maya urbanism in the Postclassic period moved toward the formation of small, more compact towns, such as Mayapan, Lamanai, and Tayasal (Masson 2000).

What is of relevance to this study is the fact that a region of about 40,000 km² became devoid of large low-density cities and even small compact towns. We need to exercise care in calling the interior of the peninsula abandoned. Outside of compact towns like Tayasal, settlements are difficult to identify. Johnston's work (2004) at Itzan in the Peten shows that Maya house sites were not necessarily on housemounds, suggesting that there may have been more people in the preceding centuries than the desolate nineteenth-century forests might imply. The Maya "collapse" cannot, therefore, be understood simply as a demographic disaster. It may have been, but its key characteristic is that it was the permanent termination of large low-density cities. None were present to be seen by the Spanish in the sixteenth century. Indeed, Cortes marched close by Tikal in the earlier part of the sixteenth century and makes no reference even to its ruins (Webster 2002:83–84).

The decline and disappearance of low-density urbanism did not mark the disappearance of a tradition of social life. Although the practices of the Maya elite were largely extinguished by the 880s, the continuity of social life is readily apparent (Masson 2000). What we are therefore seeing is the eventual decoupling of that world of social action from the material framework that had encased it since at least the late first millennium B.C. The process took several hundred years. There were fewer and fewer low-density cities and few were large. The extent of the occupation around the center of Chichen Itza would be a valuable piece of data because it may be the one late example larger than about 20 km².

At first, in the late ninth and tenth centuries, the Maya sought to reconstitute their urban world in the Puuc, although on a smaller scale (Carmean et al. 2004). If low-density urbanism was the problem, the populace was apparently not able to shake itself free of the encumbrance, repeating the progressive deterioration over several centuries until only smaller settlements, such as Mayapan, were left to prevail for a while. There appear to have been more than two vulnerabilities in Maya society – first, the costly elite and its associated water storage infrastructure, second, the crop economy, and third, the low-density settlement pattern. Each played out its failure over differing timespans – the reason presumably why the "collapse" is not quite what it once seemed when a holistic viewpoint dominated interpretation.

In Sri Lanka between 1017 and 1285, the low-density urban world of the Dry Zone disintegrated and the successive capitals of the Rajarata state moved back up into the wet highlands and toward the coasts of the island. Although the specific demise of Anuradhapura in 1017 A.D. and of Pollonnaruwa in 1214 A.D. is ascribed to conquest by foreigners, it is striking that although the foreigners were driven out, attempts by the Sinhalese rulers to repair and reoccupy the cities failed (e.g., 1287–93 at Pollonnaruwa and 1270–72 at Anuradhapura; De Silva 2005:110–11, and 132). In addition, the outside invaders and the Tamils at the northern end of the island also did not successfully reoccupy the Dry Zone (see De Silva 2005:132). The Sinhalese rulers moved up to the edge of the hills (e.g., at Dambudeniya) and then gradually shifted toward living in compact, small cities away from the Dry Zone (e.g., Gampola in the fourteenth century). They then moved down to the Kotte area on the west coast near Colombo in the fifteenth century and eventually back up to Kandy in the Highlands where they stayed when the Portuguese arrived in the early sixteenth century. The Dry Zone was left largely abandoned; the population density in Pollonnaruwa province in 1871, for example, was less than 2 persons per km² over more than 3,000 km² (Murphey 1957:198). Only after the mid-nineteenth century was the Dry Zone reoccupied under the direction of the British Colonial administration.

The relationship between the abandonment of the Dry Zone and climate change is suggestive but problematic. The great period of stability and wealth for Anuradhapura in the eighth and ninth centuries coincides with the two periods of poor monsoons (Sinha et al. 2007). Then Anuradhapura was sacked shortly after the very substantial tenth-century temperature rise that marked the start of the Medieval Warm Phase. Pollonnaruwa was sacked during the stable period of warmer than average temperatures in the twelfth and thirteenth centuries. The abandonment of the Dry Zone seems to have become permanent during the thirteenth century and before the plunge into the low temperatures of the start of the Little Ice Age in the subcontinental peninsula in the fourteenth century and the extreme variability of the first half of the fifteenth century (Sinha et al. 2007). If anything, the relationship between the urban histories and the climate is that the Dry Zone cities were generally doing better when the temperatures were lower in part of the eighth century, part of the ninth century, and in the middle of the eleventh century. This perhaps suggests that the Dry Zone tank irrigation system worked better on relatively low water-flow rates from weaker monsoons and was adversely affected by higher flow rates, as is suggested by the repeated repairs to the big bunds.

For Angkor, the conventional explanation has been that the city was sacked by the Thai in 1431 and was then abandoned by its Khmer rulers. This has been called into question for many years by Vickery (1977) and is now being questioned by other historians, including Claude Jacques (2007:42–43). The various chronicles of Ayuthaya do not say that Angkor was sacked – only that it was "taken" – and they differ in their specifics (Vickery 2004:20–21). One mentions that the son of the ruler of Ayuthaya was on the throne in Angkor (Nakhon Luang) in 1441 and refers to conflict "between two mixed Ayutthayan-Cambodian factions" (Vickery 2004:21). The last Sanskrit inscription was carved in Angkor in the first half of the fourteenth century (Snellgrove 2004:176). We know little of the history of the fourteenth and fifteenth centuries, and the Khmer chronicles are primarily eighteenth- and nineteenth-century court documents created in the eastern Khmer capitals, in particular Phnom Penh, with a specific political agenda in mind (Vickery 1977). The archaeological record is more informative (Jacques 2007:43). Elaborate construction was occurring on the Elephant Terrace in front of the palace in the sixteenth century, as shown by Pottier's reconstruction work reported in 1998. Massive Buddhist constructions were being erected at the Baphuon and on Phnom Bakheng and around the Bayon from the fifteenth to the seventeenth centuries. The carving of the bas-reliefs in the northeastern corridors of Angkor Wat was finished in the late sixteenth century.

Ming pottery of the sixteenth century and Thai and Vietnamese wares of the fifteenth century are now being reported around the Royal Plaza by the JASA team (Nakagawa 2005:87, 106, 117–20). Analysis of the deposits in some of the great moats indicates that activity to clean them out – a considerable task – was continuing into the seventeenth and eighteenth centuries (Penny et al. 2007:391). A parallel, disturbing note is, however, that the complete and terminal fill of the major canals in southern Angkor consisted of relatively coarse-grained, cross-bedded sand (Fletcher et al. 2008:668; Sam Player, personal communication). The main river now runs 5–8 m lower than its Angkorian ground surface. The story of the end of Angkor is far more protracted and more convoluted than expected. And environmental factors also appear to play a role (Stone 2009).

By the seventeenth century, the urban focus of the region lay far to the east around the junction of the Tonle and Bassac rivers with the Mekong, in a peripheral zone south and southwest of the Tonle Sap, and far to the north along the Dangrek mountains. By the eighteenth and nineteenth centuries, the region that had been the heartland of the Khmer Empire was largely devoid of towns and substantially reforested, reverting to a landscape of forest scattered with small villages and open patches of rice fields.

Conclusions

Agrarian low-density urbanism appears to be a conservative mode of settlement organization that creates highly repetitious spatial pattern over vast regions, locks itself into massive infrastructure that has high inertia, and affects the natural landscape in a variety of ways through economic extensification of the staple crop. These factors make the society that occupies the settlement peculiarly vulnerable to the impact of alterations in external circumstances, such as human-induced changes to local ecology. The lack of capacity to adjust to circumstances coincides with a tendency for their agrarian activity to cause potentially severe alterations in the local ecology. In addition, the degree of mobility and the use of distributed landholdings and several levels of crop production could have led to severe impacts on the environment when burgeoning urban populations tried to gain access to additional food resources through low-grade swidden agriculture. When, on top of this, severe climate change occurred, these societies were placed at severe risk. In Mesoamerica in the ninth and tenth centuries, rising planetary temperatures led to climatic fluctuations, whereas South Asia (Sinha et al. 2007) and Southeast Asia experienced similar climatic instability during the fourteenth and fifteenth centuries as temperatures declined (Stone 2009). But we must avoid too quick a slide from correlation to explanation because the oscillations in climate are not straightforward, the correlations are not simple, small settlements survived better than very large ones, and issues of lag, resistance, and inertia must be taken into account. That low-density urbanism has some tendency to internal disintegration with serious regional consequences is a matter to take seriously, however, especially in our era of ecological sensitivity and global warming. The case of Bagan demonstrates, however, that regional particulars are important and that cross-comparison is not about creating blanket generalizations that homogenize diverse cases. Rather, we need to construct operational models that can be tested against the varied scenarios of diverse human history across the planet.

Acknowledgments

My special thanks first to Mike Smith and to the Amerind Foundation for the wonderful meeting at Dragoon that formed the basis for this book and to Robin Coningham and Tony Wilkinson at Durham University for the Fellowship at the Institute of Advanced Study, which enabled me to carry out the basic research for this chapter.

The research on Angkor, which forms the basis for the chapter, is the result of an international collaboration with the APSARA National Authority; the Cambodian agency, which manages Angkor; and with the École Française d'Extrême-Orient (EFEO). I and the University of Sydney team of the Greater Angkor Project are deeply grateful to our Cambodian and French colleagues for many years of fruitful collaboration, help, and goodwill. I am especially grateful to Christophe Pottier and the staff of the EFEO and to Ros Borath and the staff of the Department for Conservation of Monuments and Preventive Archaeology in APSARA.

At the University of Sydney, my particular thanks to Dan Penny, Martin King, and Damian Evans for all their support and for their work in the Greater Angkor Project, the management of the Angkor Research Program Facility in the University of Sydney, and the University's Robert Christie Research Centre in Siem Reap. Their support and the work of the staff and researchers of the program, as well as our many volunteers over the past decade, have been essential to the success of the University's work at Angkor.

The Greater Angkor Project is supported by the Australian Research Council and by the University of Sydney.

References Cited

Andrews, Anthony P., E. Wyllys Andrews, and Fernando Robles Castellanos 2003 The Northern Maya Collapse and Its Aftermath. *Ancient Mesoamerica* 14:151–56.

Aung Thwin, Michael 1990 Irrigation in the Heartland of Burma. Foundations of the Pre-Colonial Burmese State. Occasional Paper 15. Monograph Series. Center for Southeast Asian Studies. Northern Illinois University, Dekalb.

Bahn, Paul G. 1996 *The Cambridge Illustrated History of Archaeology*. Cambridge University Press, Cambridge.

Bandaranayake, Senake 2003 The Pre-Modern City in Sri Lanka: The "First" and "Second" Urbanisation. In *The Development of Urbanism from a Global Perspective*, edited by Paul J. J. Sinclair. Uppsala University, Uppsala. Available at http://www.arkeologi.uu.se/digitalAssets/9/9377_bandaranayake.pdf.

Boulbet, Jean 1979 *Le Phnom Kulen et sa région. (Collection de Textes et Documents sur l'Indochine, Vol. XII)*. École Française d'Extrême-Orient, Paris.

Brohier, Richard Leslie 1934 *Ancient Irrigation Works in Ceylon*. Government Press, Colombo.

———. 2006 *The Story of Water Management in Sri Lanka down the Ages*. Sooriya Publications, Colombo.

Bronson, Bennet 1978 Angkor, Anuradhapura, Prambanan, Tikal: Maya Subsistence in an Asian Perspective. In *Pre-Hispanic Maya Agriculture*, edited by Peter

D. Harrison and B. L. Turner, pp. 255–300. University of New Mexico Press, Albuquerque.

Carmean, Kelli, Nicholas Dunning, and Jeff K. Kowalski 2004 High Times in the Hill Country: A Perspective from the Terminal Classic Puuc Region. In *The Terminal Classic in the Maya Lowlands: Collapse, Transition, and Transformation*, edited by Arthur A. Demarest, Prudence M. Rice, and Don S. Rice, pp. 424–49. University Press of Colorado, Boulder.

Chase, Arlen F. and Diane Z. Chase 1998 Scale and Intensity in Classic-Period Maya Agriculture: Terracing and Settlement at the "Garden City" of Caracol, Belize. *Culture and Agriculture* 20(2/3):60–77.

———. 2000 Inferences about Abandonment: Maya Household Archaeology and Caracol, Belize. *Mayab* 13:67–77.

Chase, Arlen F., Diane Z. Chase, John F. Weishampel, Jason B. Drake, Ramesh L. Shrestha, K. Clint Slatton, Jaime J. Awe, and William E. Carter 2010 Airborne LiDAR, Archaeology, and the Ancient Maya Landscape at Caracol, Belize. *Journal of Archaeological Science* 37:387–98.

Coe, Michael D. 1957 The Khmer Settlement Pattern: A Possible Analogy with That of the Maya. *American Antiquity* 22:409–10.

———. 1961 Social Typology and the Tropical Forest Civilizations. *Comparative Studies in Society and History* 4:65–85.

———. 1999 *The Maya*. Thames and Hudson, London.

———. 2003 *Angkor and Khmer Civilisation*. Thames and Hudson, London.

Coe, William R. 1965 Tikal, Guatemala, and the Emergent Maya Civilization. *Science* 147:1401–19.

———. 1967 *Tikal: A Handbook of the Ancient Maya Ruins. University Museum*, University of Pennsylvania, Philadelphia.

Coedès, George 1941 La stèle du Práh Khàn d'Ankor. *Bulletin de l'École Française d'Extrême-Orient* 41:255–302.

Coningham, Robin 1999 Anuradhapura: The British-Sri Lankan Excavations at Anuradhapura Salgaha Watta 2. *British Archaeological Reports*, International Series 824. Archaeopress Press, Oxford.

Coningham, Robin, Prishanta Gunawardhana, Mark Manuel, Gamini Adikari, Mangala Katugampola, Ruth Young, Armin Schmidt, K. Krishnan, Ian A. Simpson, Gerry McDonnell, and Cathy Batt 2007 The State of Theocracy: Defining an Early Medieval Hinterland in Sri Lanka. *Antiquity* 81:699–719.

Dagens, Bruno 1995 *Angkor, Heart of an Asian Empire*. Thames and Hudson, London.

Davis, Mike 2006 *Planet of Slums*. Verso, London.

Delvert, Jean 1961 *Le Paysan Cambodgien*. Mouton and Co, Paris.

De Silva, K. M. 2005 *A History of Sri Lanka*. Penguin Books: New Delhi.

Dhanasekara, D. M. and C. M. Maddumabandara 2004 Relationship with Land and Water Management for Agricultural Production of a Tank Cascade in the Dry Zone of Sri Lanka, *Water Resources Research in Sri Lanka*:13–23.

Doxiadis, Constantinos A. 1968 *Ekistics: An Introduction to the Science of Human Settlements*. Oxford University Press, New York.

Evans, Damian, Christophe Pottier, Roland Fletcher, Scott Hensley, Ian Tapley, Anthony Milne, and Michael Barbetti 2007 A Comprehensive Archaeological

Map of the World's Largest Preindustrial Settlement Complex at Angkor, Cambodia. *Proceedings of the National Academy of Sciences* 104:14277–82.

Evans, Susan Toby 2008 *Ancient Mexico and Central America. Archaeology and Culture History*. Thames and Hudson, London.

Faust, Betty Bernice 1998 *Mexican Rural Development and the Plumed Serpent: Technology and Cosmology in the Tropical Forest of Campeche*. Bergin and Garvey, Westport.

Fedick, Scott L. (editor) 1996 *The Managed Mosaic: Ancient Maya Agriculture and Resource Use*. University of Utah Press, Salt Lake City.

Fletcher, Roland J. 1991 Very Large Mobile Communities: Interaction Stress and Residential Dispersal. In *Ethnoarchaeological Approaches to Mobile Campsites: Hunter-Gatherer and Pastoralist Case-studies*, edited by Clive S. Gamble and William A. Boismer, pp. 395–420. Ethnoarchaeological Series 1. International Monographs in Prehistory, Ann Arbor.

Fletcher, Roland J., Damian Evans, Mike Barbetti, Dan Penny, Heng Than, Im Sokrithy, Khieu Chan, Tous Somaneath, and Christophe Pottier 2003 Redefining Angkor: Structure and Environment in the Largest, Low-Density Urban Complex of the Pre-Industrial *World. UDAYA* 4:107–21.

Fletcher, Roland, J., Dan Penny, Damian Evans, Christophe Pottier, Mike Barbetti, Matti Kummu, Terry Lustig and Authority for the Protection and Management of Angkor and the Region of Siem Reap (APSARA) Department of Monuments and Archaeology Team 2008 The Water Management Network of Angkor, Cambodia. *Antiquity* 82:658–70.

Finot, Louis, Henri Parmentier, and Victor Goloubew 2000 *A Guide to the Tempe of Banteay Srei at Angkor*. White Lotus, Bangkok.

Folan, William J., Joyce Marcus, Sophia Pincemin, María del Rosario Domínguez Carrasco, Laraine Fletcher, and Abel Morales Lopez 1995 Calakmul: New Data from an Ancient Maya Capital in Campeche, Mexico. *Latin American Antiquity* 6:310–34.

Gleichen, A. Edward W. 1898 *With the Mission to Menelik*. Edwin Arnold, London.

Gottman, Jean 1961 *Megalopolis: The Urbanized Northeastern Seaboard of the United States*. Twentieth Century Fund, New York.

Hall, Peter 1977 *World Cities*. Weidenfeld and Nicholson, London.

Harris, Peter 2007 *A Record of Cambodia. The Land and Its People. By Zhou Daguan*. Silkworm Books, Chiang Mai.

Hendrickson, Mitch 2010 Historic Routes to Angkor: Development of the Khmer Road System (Ninth to Thirteenth Centuries A.D.) in Mainland Southeast Asia. *Antiquity* 84:480–96.

Higham, Charles 2002 *Early Cultures of Mainland Southeast Asia*. River Books, Bangkok.

Hudson, Bob 2001 The Origins of Bagan: New Dates and Old Inhabitants. *Asian Perspectives* 40:48–74.

——. 2004 *The Origins of Bagan. The Archaeological Landscape of Upper Burma to A.D. 1300*. Unpublished Ph.D. Thesis, University of Sydney, Sydney.

Ichita, Shimoda, Nakagawa Takeshi, and Tsuchiya Takeshi 1999 Preliminary Report on the Survey of Sambor Prei Kuk Monuments. A Study on Khmer Architecture in Pre-Angkor Period. (I). Summaries of Technical Papers of Annual

Meeting Architectural Institute of Japan. F-2. *History and Theory of Architecture*: 187–88.

Jacques, Claude 2007 The Historical Development of Khmer Culture from the Death of Suryavarman II to the 16th Century. In *Bayon: New Perspectives*, edited by Joyce Clark, pp. 28–49. River Books, Bangkok.

Johnston, Kevin J. 2004 The "Invisible" Maya: Minimally Mounded Residential Settlements at Itzán, Petén, Guatemala. *Latin American Antiquity* 15:145–75.

Kapur, Pradeep Kumar and Sachidanand Sahai 2007 *Ta Prohm. A Glorious Era in Angkor Civilisation*. White Lotus, Bangkok.

Kusimba, Chapurukha, Sibel Barut Kusimba, and Babatunde Agbaje-Williams 2006 Precolonial African Cities: Size and Density. In *Urbanism in the Preindustrial World: Cross-Cultural Approaches*, edited by Glenn R. Storey, pp. 145–58. University of Alabama Press, Tuscaloosa.

Lang, Robert E. and Jennifer LeFurgy 2003 Edgeless Cities: Examining the Non-centered Metropolis. *Housing Policy Debate* 14:427–60.

Luce, Gordon H. 1969 *Old Burma: Early Pagan* Volume 1. Artibus Asiae Supplimentum 25. New York University, New York.

Lucero, Lisa J. 2002 The Collapse of the Classic Maya: A Case for the Role of Water Control. *American Anthropologist* 104:814–23.

———. 2006 *Water and Ritual. The Rise and Fall of Classic Maya Rulers*. University of Texas Press, Austin.

Mabongunje, A. Lloyd 1962 *Yoruba Towns*. Ibadan University Press, Ibadan.

Masson, Marilyn A. 2000 *In the Realm of Nachan Kan: Postclassic Maya Archaeology at Laguna de On, Belize*. University Press of Colorado, Boulder.

McGee, T. G. 1991 The Emergence of Desa Kota Regions in Asia: Expanding an Hypothesis. In *The Extended Metropolis: Settlement Transition in Asia*, edited by Norton Ginsburg, Bruce Koppel, and T. G. McGee, pp. 3–26. University of Hawaii Press, Honolulu.

Miksic, John 2000 Heterogenetic Cities in Premodern Southeast Asia. *World Archaeology* 32:106–20.

Morrill, Richard 2006 Classic Map Revisited: The Growth of Megalopolis. *The Professional Geographer* 58:155–60.

Mueller, Andreas, Gerald Islebe, Flavio Anselmetti, Daniel Ariztegui, Mark Brenner, David Hodell, Irka Hajdas, Yvonne Hamann, Gerald Haug, and Douglas Kennett 2010 Recovery of the forest ecosystem in the tropical lowlands of northern Guatemala after disintegration of Classic Maya polities. *Geology* 38(6):523–26.

Murphey, Rhoads 1957 The Ruin of Ancient Ceylon. *The Journal of Asian Studies* 16:181–200.

Nakagawa, Takeshi (editor) 2005 Report on the Conservation and Restoration Work of the Prasat Suor Prat Tower. *Japanese Government Team for Safeguarding Angkor*. JICE, Tokyo.

Netting, Robert McC. 1968 *Hill Farmers of Nigeria: Cultural Ecology of the Kofyar of the Jos Plateau*. University of Washington Press, Seattle.

O'Connell, James F. 1998 Alyawara Site Structure and its Implications. *American Antiquity* 52:74–108.

O'Reilly, Dougald J. W. 2007 *Early Civilizations of Southeast Asia*. Alta Mira Press, New York.

Paranavithana, S. 1960 *The Withdrawal of Sinhalese from the Ancient Capitals. History of Ceylon*, Vol. 1. University of Ceylon, Peradeniya.

Parker, Henry 1909 *Ancient Ceylon*. Asian Educational Services, New Delhi.

Penny, Dan, Quan Hua, Christophe Pottier, Roland Fletcher, and Mike Barbetti 2007 The Use of AMS 14C Dating to Explore Issues of Occupation and Demise at the Medieval City of Angkor, Cambodia. *Nuclear Instruments and Methods in Physics Research B* 259:338–94.

Perera, Lakman Susantha 2001 *The Institutions of Ancient Ceylon from Inscriptions (From the 3rd Century to 830 A.D.)* Volume 1. International Centre for Ethnic Studies, Kandy.

Petersen, Larry and Gerald Haug 2005 Climate and the Collapse of Maya Civilization. *American Scientist* 93:322–28.

Pottier, Christophe 1998 Quelques découvertes récentes au perron nord de la Terrasse des Eléphants (Angkor Thom). In *La Khmérologie: Connaissance du passé et contribution au renouveau du Cambodge*. Vol. 1, edited by Sorn Samnang, pp. 513–29. Phnom Penh.

———. 2000 A la recherché de Goloupura. Melanges du Centenaire de l'EFEO. *Bulletin de l'École Française d'Extrême-Orient* 87:79–107.

———. 2006 Early Urban Settlements in Angkor. In *Reassessing East Asia in the Light of Urban and Architectural History*, edited by ReEA, pp. 133–40. International Conference on East Asian Architectural Culture, Kyoto.

Puleston, Dennis E. 1983 *Settlement Survey of Tikal*. Tikal Report No. 13. University Museum. University of Pennsylvania, Philadelphia.

Rice, Don S. 1996 Paleolimnological Analysis in the Central Peten, Guatemala. In *The Managed Mosaic: Ancient Maya Agriculture and Resource Use*, edited by Scott L. Fedick, pp. 193–206. University of Utah Press, Salt Lake City.

———. 2006 Late Classic Maya Population: Characteristics and Implications. In *Urbanism in the Preindustrial World: Cross-cultural Approaches*, edited by Glenn R. Storey, pp. 252–76. University of Alabama Press, Tuscaloosa.

Sabloff, Jeremy A. 1990 *The New Archaeology and the Ancient Maya*. Freeman, New York.

Scarborough, Vernon L. and Gary G. Gallopin 1991 A Water Storage Adaptation in the Maya Lowlands. *Science* 251:658–62.

Senanayake, Upalli 1982 Traditional Agriculture in Sri Lanka. *The Ecologist* 12:215.

Seneviratna, Anuradha 1989 *The Springs of Sinhala Civilization: An Illustrated Survey of the Ancient Irrigation System of Sri Lanka*. Navrang, New Delhi.

———. 1994 *Ancient Anuradhapura. The Monastic City*. Archaeological Survey Department, Colombo.

———. 1998 *Pollonnaruwa. Medieval Capital of Sri Lanka*. Archaeological Survey Department, Colombo.

Sharer, Robert and Loa P. Traxler 2005 *The Ancient Maya*. Stanford University Press, Stanford.

Sinha, Ashish, Kevin G. Cannariato, Lowell D. Stott, Hai Cheng, R. Lawrence Edwards, Madhusudan G. Yadava, R. Ramesh, and Indra B. Singh 2007 A 900-year (600 to 1500 A.D.) Record of the Indian Summer Monsoon Precipitation from the Core Monsoon Zone of India. *Geophysical Research Letters* 34:L16707.

Sinopoli, Carla M. 1994 Monumentality and Mobility in Mughal Capitals. *Asian Perspectives* 33:293–308.

Siriweera, W. I. 1990 Farming Systems in the Ancient Dry Zone. In *The Settlement Archaeology of the Sirigiya-Dambulla Region*, edited by Senaka Bandaranayake, Mats Mogren, and Seneviratne Epitawatte, pp. 143–48. Postgraduate Institute of Archaeology, University of Leaniya, Kelaniya.

Skinner, Elliot P. 1964 *The Mossi of Upper Volta*. Stanford University Press, Stanford.

Smith, Michael E. 2004 The Archaeology of Ancient State Economies. *Annual Review of Anthropology* 33:73–102.

Snellgrove, David 2004 *Angkor Before and After. A Cultural History of the Khmers*. Orchid Press, Bangkok.

Stadner, Donald Martin 2005 *Ancient Pagan. Buddhist Plain of Merit*. River Books, Bangkok.

Stark, Miriam 2006 Early Mainland Southeast Asian Landscapes in the First Millennium B.C. *Annual Review of Anthropology* 35:407–32.

Stone, Richard 2009 Tree Rings Tell the Story of Angkor's Dying Days. *Science* 323:999.

Tranet, Michel 1995–96 Sambaur-Prei-Kuk, Monuments d'Içanavarma 1er (615–628 A.D.), vol. 1, Phnom Penh.; 1996–97 Sambaur-Prei-Kuk, Monuments d'Içanavarma 1er (615–628 A.D.), vol.2. Phnom Penh.; 1997–98 Sambaur-Prei-Kuk, Monuments d'Içanavarma 1er (615–628 A.D.) et ses environs, vol. 3, Phnom Penh.; Maspéro, H. 1904 L'empire Khmer, Phnom Penh.

Valdés, Juan Antonio and Federico Fahsen 2005 Disaster in Sight: The Terminal Classic at Tikal and Uaxactun. In *The Terminal Classic in the Maya Lowlands: Collapse, Transition, and Transformation*, edited by Arthur A. Demarest, Prudence M. Rice, and Don S. Rice, pp. 162–94. University of Colorado Press, Boulder.

Vickery, Michael 1977 *Cambodia after Angkor, the Chronicular Evidence for the Fourteenth to the Sixteenth Centuries*. Yale University, Ph.D. dissertation, University Microfilms, Ann Arbor.

———. 2004 Cambodia and Its Neighbors in the 15th Century. ARI Working Paper 27.

Watanabe, Hitoshi 1973 *The Ainu Ecosystem: Environment and Group Structure*. University of Washington Press, Seattle.

Webster, David L. 2002 *The Fall of the Ancient Maya*. Thames and Hudson, London.

Webster, David L., William T. Sanders, and Peter van Rossum 1992 A Simulation of Copan Population History and Its Implications. *Ancient Mesoamerica* 3:185–97.

Webster, David L., Timothy Murtha, Kirk Straight, Jay Silverstein, Horacio Martinez, Richard Terry, and Richard Burnett 2007 The Great Tikal Earthwork Revisited. *Journal of Field Archaeology* 32:41–64.

Webster, David L., Ann Corinne Freter, and Nancy Gonlin 2000 *Copan: The Rise and Fall of an Ancient Maya Kingdom*. Harcourt College Publishers, Fort Worth.

CHAPTER 12

ARCHAEOLOGY, EARLY COMPLEX SOCIETIES, AND COMPARATIVE SOCIAL SCIENCE HISTORY

Michael E. Smith

The chapters in this volume focus on what may appear to be a narrow domain: comparative studies of early complex societies using archaeological data. But this topic is a crucial part of a broad and far-reaching theme in the human sciences. Many institutions of modern society were largely created by the Urban Revolution; that is, by the transformations of farming villages into agrarian states many millennia ago. Chronologically myopic scholars who think that Medieval Europe constituted the deep, dark, and ancient past of modern society may disagree with this claim, but anthropologists and historians who examine the broad sweep of human history will recognize its value. For when we consider that 99 percent of human history was taken up by small hunting bands and tribal farming villages, the Urban Revolution emerges as the single most momentous social transition on the road to the modern era of states, empires, and global processes (M. E. Smith 2009).

Research on the origins of early complex societies – chiefdoms and states – has long been a staple of fieldwork and comparative analysis within anthropological archaeology (e.g., Adams 1966; Childe 1950; Liu 2009; Wright 1977). Nevertheless, the results of this research have had relatively little impact on thinking in comparative history and the social sciences outside of archaeology and anthropology. Indeed, some economists and political scientists, recognizing the importance of the Urban Revolution for human history, have felt free to construct theoretical models of the process unencumbered by empirical data (e.g., Barzel 2002). Not surprisingly, these models tend to be at odds with the archaeological and historical data on early chiefdoms and states.

By the first decade of the twenty-first century, archaeological data on early chiefdoms and states have become quite abundant, but much of the information remains locked up in technical fieldwork reports, specialized regional publications, and other corners of the scholarly literature in archaeology. To make sense out of the plethora of new data, many archaeologists are convinced that careful comparative analysis is required. The chapters in this volume showcase some of the more productive comparative methods and approaches for archaeological data. These studies advance our understanding of the origins of and changes within early complex societies, and we hope they will contribute to a broader, transarchaeological understanding of the social, economic, and political processes that shaped human societies before the modern era.

Archaeology and Comparative Social Science History

Scholars outside of archaeology have been slow to acknowledge and incorporate archaeological findings into general theoretical and comparative models about chiefdoms, states, and empires. There are several reasons for this state of affairs, many of them originating in the nature of archaeological data and the discipline of archaeology. Much archaeological research on early states simply has not produced the kinds of data that illuminate processes of social change. The archaeological study of early complex societies began in the eighteenth century with the excavation of temples, tombs, and palaces. Although carrying off luxurious objects for museums has been greatly reduced in recent decades, much archaeology in ancient states today continues the emphasis on monumental and spectacular finds that excite public interest. Such research contributes relatively little to a social understanding of historical processes, yet for many nonarchaeologists this is their dominant view of the discipline.

In recent decades, fieldwork on settlement patterns, households, communities, and economic processes has burgeoned and many archaeologists have adopted a comparative social science perspective on early complex societies (Robin 2001). We now have the data, methods, and concepts to begin to model processes such as the origins of social inequality, trajectories of urbanization, the political strategies of kings, the operation of commercial and noncommercial economies, and the dynamics of ancient imperial expansion. The preceding chapters illustrate some of the best of this new comparative social research, and it is our hope that these and other studies will have an impact on comparative social science research outside of anthropology.

Similarly, we invite archaeologists to consider external theory and case studies to elucidate and contextualize their findings. Productive ties between archaeological research on complex societies – as exemplified by the chapters in this volume – and comparative social science history should be encouraged in both directions. Archaeological findings can inform on broader issues addressed by social historians and comparative social scientists. At the same time, concepts and methods from that literature have great potential for improving the analysis and understanding of the past within archaeology. Although it seems that few archaeologists currently engage the literature in comparative social science history, much current work in the latter field addresses themes such as long-term change, political economy, and practice that are staples of comparative archaeology (Hoffman 2006; Kiser and Kane 2007; Steckel 2007).

A notable recent example of the archaeological value of work in historical social science is Blanton and Fargher's (2008) use of collective action theory from political science to illuminate preindustrial state dynamics. Although not a specifically archaeological study, the concepts they explore have great potential for archaeologists (e.g., M. E. Smith 2008:chapter 8). Models and concepts from economic history and comparative political economy are increasingly being used to illuminate ancient state dynamics. Economists, for example, have used the tools of their trade to model the operations of ancient economies, from the origins of agriculture in Egypt (Allen 1997) to the Roman Empire (Temin 2006). A new wave of comparative historical and archaeological scholarship on Ancient Rome and Greece is using economic models and concepts to study topics ranging from commerce (Bang 2008) to standard of living (Scheidel 2010) to economic growth (Morris 2004).

I would like to suggest in this context that archaeology could benefit not only from the models and comparative data of the historical social sciences, but also from some of the approaches to causality and explanation that are being developed in fields such as sociology and political science. Within anthropology and much of archaeology, postmodern scholarship has led to an emphasis on high-level social theory, or what might be called "Theory-with-a-capital-T." But theory exists on numerous levels (Ellen 2010), and much archaeological research engages theory at a lower, more empirically based level than abstract social theory. Nevertheless, there are few discussions of theory, causality, or explanation in recent archaeology that acknowledge this lower level of theoretical engagement; for many archaeologists, Theory still tends to be capitalized (Johnson 2010). But in sociology and political science, there is an active and productive engagement with lower levels of social theory and archaeologists can learn from this literature.

Much of this work in sociology and political science can be categorized as what sociologist Robert Merton (1968) termed "middle-range theory."[1] In the words of Peter Hedström and Lars Udéhn, middle-range theory is:

> a clear, precise, and simple type of theory which can be used for partially explaining a range of different phenomena, but which makes no pretense of being able to explain all social phenomena, and which is not founded upon any form of extreme reductionism in terms of its explanans [the factors invoked to explain a phenomenon]. It is a vision of sociological theory as a toolbox of semigeneral theories each of which is adequate for explaining a limited range or type of phenomena. (Hedström and Udéhn 2009:31)

An active area of middle-range research in sociology and political science today focuses on the concept of "mechanisms," which can be defined as "the pathway or process by which an effect is produced or a purpose is accomplished" (Gerring 2007:178). "Mechanisms consist of entities (with their properties) and the activities that these entities engage in, either by themselves or in concert with other entities. These activities bring about change, and the type of change brought about depends on the properties of the entities and how the entities are organized spatially and temporally" (Hedström and Ylikoski 2010:51). In other words, mechanisms are the ways in which actors, processes, and structural constraints interact to bring about particular situations or changes; they are not universal forces or causes but context-specific explanations of social dynamics and change. One of the few anthropologists who has focused explicitly on causal mechanisms is Andrew Vayda (Vayda 2008; Walters and Vayda 2009).

Most of the chapters in this volume discuss the mechanisms that most likely accounted for changes and dynamics in past social systems, although the authors do not use the phrase "mechanism." Peregrine's alternative strategies of rulers (Chapter 8), for example, or the processes of market exchange, local political dynamics, imperial conquest, and household production analyzed by Earle and Smith (Chapter 10), or the social competition that generated monumental constructions as discussed by Kolb (Chapter 7) are all examples of causal mechanisms that brought about the changes documented in the archaeological record. One of the few explicit applications of this approach to ancient complex societies is the philosopher of science Benoît Dubreuil's (2010) wide-ranging analysis of the evolution of hierarchy and inequality in human societies. Discussion of the role of middle-range theory and mechanisms in archaeological explanation would improve the conceptual precision of our models of the past and at the same time improve communication between archaeologists and other comparative historical social scientists. For further discussion of the potential of Mertonian middle-range theory in archaeology, see M. E. Smith (2011).

Methods and Approaches

The central message of this book is that a comparative approach can greatly advance understanding of social processes in the complex societies of the past. Some scholars might think that what is needed is a manual of methods or a description of best practices. In our discussions at the symposium, however, we decided to avoid such an approach in favor of a series of exemplary case studies. The reasons for this are simple: compared to most data in the historical social sciences, archaeological data are quite refractory, varied, and resistant to standardization. The authors of these chapters are in agreement that there is no single best method for comparative analysis of archaeological data. The varieties of comparisons employed in the preceding chapters are discussed in Chapter 2.

The units of comparison and analysis vary widely among these studies. Monica L. Smith (Chapter 4) focuses on the actions of individuals in a comparison of three very different world regions, whereas Earle and Michael Smith (Chapter 10) focus on households to compare two early empires. Peterson and Drennan (Chapters 5 and 6) compare regional settlement trajectories in a number of world regions, while Kolb (Chapter 7) uses monuments to compare chiefdoms around the world. Fletcher (Chapter 11) compares examples of a particular type of ancient city, whereas Peregrine (Chapter 8) compares a variety of nonwestern polities. Finally, Stark and Chance (Chapter 9) compare several New World empires – Pre-Hispanic and Spanish – to explore the variation in provincial strategies.

The kinds of archaeological data employed in the chapters are equally diverse, ranging from counts of domestic artifacts to sizes of stone monuments and cities, to measures of settlement distribution. Some chapters make considerable use of documentary data (see especially Stark and Chance, Chapter 9), whereas Peregrine (Chapter 8) compares standardized ethnographic data to draw archaeologically relevant conclusions. Some authors (e.g., Feinman, Chapter 3) argue for a larger role for theory in our comparisons, while Drennan and Peterson (Chapter 5) argue that before we can generate useful theory we must understand the empirical archaeological record in more detail and in more locations.

Given this great diversity in data, methods, questions, and concepts, it is reasonable to ask what these chapters have in common. I see two important commonalities running through the case studies described here: a scientific approach to the past, and an emphasis on the use of primary data. First, there is a commitment to a scientific understanding of the past. Notably, all authors employ some kind of methodological uniformitarianism, the notion that processes and conditions are consistent in operation through space and time (Gould 1986). For anthropology and other social sciences, methodological uniformitarianism produces the assumption that the processes we model operated among numerous human societies throughout the world and throughout history (and prehistory).

Second, the authors in this volume are committed to the analysis of primary archaeological data. As discussed most fully by Drennan and Peterson (Chapter 5), the common practice of comparing the interpretations of diverse archaeologists incorporates too much bias and error. These can be greatly reduced by focusing on the analysis and comparison of primary data – the actual measurements of the archaeological record, rather than the second-level interpretations of diverse scholars. This is not an easy task: Drennan and Peterson spent countless hours determining which archaeological survey data they could use for their comparisons, and Earle and Smith had to make major efforts to get their archaeological data into a basic and standardized format for comparison. But the investment in effort pays off in terms of the empirical results obtained.

Archaeological Comparative Analysis into the Future

By the end of the twentieth century, comparative analysis in archaeology had declined greatly from its midcentury peak. Postmodern scholarship frowned on scientific approaches to explanation and on rigorous comparisons; in the words of geographer Jan Nijman (2007:1), "Comparative methodologies largely disappeared from view" (see also Ward 2009:6). For many, "comparative analysis" consisted of assembling a group of case studies by divergent authors within a single symposium or edited volume, often with little or no systematic evaluation of similarities and differences (for discussion of some of the problems with this procedure, see Kantor and Savitch 2005; M. E. Smith 2006). For others, comparison consisted of the haphazard use of comparative tidbits to illustrate an argument (e.g., Rykwert 1976), a trend that continues today. In discussing James Scott's book, *The Art of Not Being Governed* (Scott 2009), Frederik Barth comments, "His conclusions seem weakened because of a failure of comparative method...I felt overwhelmed by a spate of brief comparisons and one-liners about much of the world...If we are to draw useful conclusions, we need features to be systematized and the connections among them to be illuminated" (Barth 2010:175).

Nevertheless, a number of archaeologists have managed to maintain a systematic approach to comparison. In another paper I single out Bruce Trigger's massive *Understanding Early Civilizations* (Trigger 2003) and Adam T. Smith's *The Political Landscape* (A. T. Smith 2003) as contrasting examples of work in this area by a senior and a junior scholar (M. E. Smith 2006). Several of the authors represented in the current book – particularly Robert Drennan, Timothy Earle, Gary Feinman, and Roland Fletcher – have made significant contributions to the comparative analysis of archaeological data over the years.

The essays in the preceding chapters join a growing number of rigorous comparative studies of ancient complex societies by scholars in a number of disciplines, including archaeology (Blanton and Fargher 2008; Feinman and Garraty 2010; Peregrine et al. 2007), classics or ancient history (Bang 2008; Morris and Scheidel 2009), cultural anthropology (Ember and Ember 2001; Hunt 2007), and even biologists-turned-historians (Diamond and Robinson 2010; Turchin 2003, 2008). This body of work is now illuminating some of the most important historical transformations in human society – from the initial rise of social complexity to the changes brought about by imperialism or commercial exchange – using models based on actual archaeological and historical data in place of the speculative accounts of earlier scholars.

Acknowledgments

I thank Cynthia Heath-Smith, Monica Smith, and Barbara Stark for helpful comments on an earlier draft of this chapter.

References Cited

Adams, Robert McC. 1966 *The Evolution of Urban Society: Early Mesopotamia and Prehispanic Mexico*. Aldine, Chicago.
Allen, Robert C. 1997 Agriculture and the Origins of the State in Ancient Egypt. *Explorations in Economic History* 34:134–54.
Bang, Peter F. 2008 *The Roman Bazaar: A Comparative Study of Trade and Markets in a Tributary Empire*. Cambridge University Press, New York.
Barth, Frederik 2010 Steering Clear of State Control: Review of *The Art of Not Being Governed* by James C. Scott. *Science* 328:175.
Barzel, Yoram 2002 *A Theory of the State: Economic Rights, Labor Rights, and the Scope of the State*. Cambridge University Press, New York.
Blanton, Richard E. and Lane F. Fargher 2008 *Collective Action in the Formation of Pre-Modern States*. Springer, New York.

Childe, V. Gordon 1950 The Urban Revolution. *Town Planning Review* 21:3–17.

Diamond, Jared and James A. Robinson (editors) 2010 *Natural Experiments of History*. Harvard University Press, Cambridge.

Dubreuil, Benoît 2010 *Human Evolution and the Origins of Hierarchies: The State of Nature*. Cambridge University Press, New York.

Ellen, Roy 2010 Theories in Anthropology and "Anthropological Theory." *Journal of the Royal Anthropological Institute* 16:387–404.

Ember, Carol R. and Melvin Ember 2001 *Cross-Cultural Research Methods*. AltaMira, Walnut Creek, CA.

Feinman, Gary M. and Christopher P. Garraty 2010 Preindustrial Markets and Marketing: Archaeological Perspectives. *Annual Review of Anthropology* 39:167–91.

Gerring, John 2007 Review Article: The Mechanistic Worldview: Thinking Inside the Box. *British Journal of Political Science* 38:161–79.

Gould, Stephen Jay 1986 Evolution and the Triumph of Homology, or Why History Matters. *American Scientist* 74:60–69.

Hedström, Peter and Lars Udéhn 2009 Analytical Sociology and Theories of the Middle Range. In *The Oxford Handbook of Analytical Sociology*, edited by Peter Hedström and Peter Bearman, pp. 25–49. Oxford University Press, New York.

Hedström, Peter and Petri Ylikoski 2010 Causal Mechanisms in the Social Sciences. *Annual Review of Sociology* 36:49–67.

Hoffman, Philip T. 2006 Opening Our Eyes: History and the Social Sciences. *Journal of the Historical Society* 6:93–117.

Hunt, Robert C. 2007 *Beyond Relativism: Comparability in Cultural Anthropology*. Altamira Press, Lanham.

Johnson, Matthew 2010 *Archaeological Theory: An Introduction*. 2nd ed. Blackwell, Oxford.

Kantor, Paul and H. V. Savitch 2005 How to Study Comparative Urban Development Politics: A Research Note. *International Journal of Urban and Regional Research* 29:135–51.

Kiser, Edgar and Denielle Kane 2007 The Perils of Privatization: How the Characteristics of Principals Affected Tax Farming in the Roman Republic and Empire. *Social Science History* 31:191–212.

Liu, Li 2009 State Emergence in Early China. *Annual Review of Anthropology* 38:217–32.

Merton, Robert K. 1968 *Social Theory and Social Structure*. 3rd ed. Free Press, New York.

Morris, Ian 2004 Economic Growth in Ancient Greece. *Journal of Institutional and Theoretical Economics* 160:709–42.

Morris, Ian and Walter Scheidel (editors) 2009 *The Dynamics of Ancient Empires: State Power from Assyria to Byzantium*. Oxford University Press, Oxford.

Nijman, Jan 2007 Introduction: Comparative Urbanism. *Urban Geography* 28:1–6.

Peregrine, Peter N., Carol R. Ember, and Melvin Ember 2007 Modeling State Origins Using Cross-Cultural Data. *Cross-Cultural Research* 41:75–86.

Raab, L. Mark and Albert C. Goodyear 1984 Middle-Range Theory in Archaeology: A Critical Review of Origins and Applications. *American Antiquity* 49:255–68.

Robin, Cynthia 2001 Peopling the Past: New Perspectives on the Ancient Maya. *Proceedings of the National Academy of Sciences* 98:18–21.

Rykwert, Joseph 1976 *The Idea of a Town: The Anthropology of Urban Form in Rome, Italy, and the Ancient World*. Princeton University Press, Princeton.

Scheidel, Walter 2010 Real Wages in Early Economies: Evidence for Living Standards from 1800 BCE to 1300 CE. *Journal of the Economic and Social History of the Orient* 53(3):425–62.

Scott, James C. 2009 *The Art of Not Being Governed: An Anarchist History of Upland Southeast Asia*. Yale University Press, New Haven.

Smith, Adam T. 2003 *The Political Landscape: Constellations of Authority in Early Complex Polities*. University of California Press, Berkeley.

Smith, Michael E. 2006 How Do Archaeologists Compare Early States? Book Review Essay on Bruce Trigger and Adam T. Smith. *Reviews in Anthropology* 35:5–35.

_____. 2008 *Aztec City-State Capitals*. University Press of Florida, Gainesville.

_____. 2009 V. Gordon Childe and the Urban Revolution: An Historical Perspective on a Revolution in Urban Studies. *Town Planning Review* 80:3–29.

_____. 2011 Empirical Urban Theory for Archaeologists. *Journal of Archaeological Method and Theory* 18 (in press).

Steckel, Richard H. 2007 Big Social Science History. *Social Science History* 31:1–34.

Temin, Peter 2006 The Economy of the Early Roman Empire. *Journal of Economic Perspectives* 20:133–51.

Trigger, Bruce G. 2003 *Understanding Early Civilizations: A Comparative Study*. Cambridge University Press, New York.

Turchin, Peter 2003 *Historical Dynamics: Why States Rise and Fall*. Princeton University Press, Princeton.

_____. 2008 Arise "Cliodynamics." *Nature* 454:34–35.

Vayda, Andrew P. 2008 Causal Explanation as a Research Goal: A Pragmatic View. In *Against the Grain: The Vayda Tradition in Human Ecology and Ecological Anthropology*, edited by Bradley B. Walters, Bonnie J. MacKay, Paige West, and Susan Lees, pp. 317–67. AltaMira, Lanham, MD.

Walters, Bradley B. and Andrew P. Vayda 2009 Event Ecology, Causal Historical Analysis, and Human-Environment Research. *Annals of the Association of American Geographers* 99(3):534–53.

Ward, Kevin 2009 Towards a Relational Comparative Approach to the Study of Cities. *Progress in Human Geography* 33:1–17.

Wright, Henry T. 1977 Recent Research on the Origin of the State. *Annual Review of Anthropology* 6:379–97.

Note

1 Robert Merton's concept of middle-range theory should not be confused with the unrelated archaeological concept that was labeled middle-range theory by Lewis Binford to refer to archaeological formation processes. See discussion in Raab and Goodyear (1984).

INDEX

abandonment of settlements, 108–110, 289.
  See also collapse of civilizations
Adams, Robert McC., 11, 106, 152, 195–227
Addis Ababa (Ethiopia), 289
agricultural intensification, 253, 303–306
agriculture, 48–49, 250–251, 263, 298–300
  swidden, 306–307
alliances, marriage, 200
Amhara (Ethiopia), 182
ancestor worship, 142, 143
ancestral pueblo culture, 32
ancient-modern comparisons, 15–16,
  322–325
Angkor (Cambodia), 296–298, 314
Angkor Borei (Cambodia), 296
Anuradhapura (Sri Lanka), 294–296,
  298–314
appropriation, provincial strategy, 215–217
archaeology and other disciplines, 23,
  35–36, 322–325, 327
assertion, strategy of. *See* appropriation,
  provincial strategy
assimilation, provincial strategy, 220–223
Aztec pottery, 201, 203–204
Aztecs, 238–247

Bagan (Myanmar), 296–297, 298–314
Balearic Islands, 146
ballcourts, 97
Basin of Mexico (Mexico), 82–83, 100–104,
  116–133, 245–247
Black Warrior Valley (Alabama), 114–116,
  133
bolstering, provincial strategy, 199–203
Borobudur (Java), 288
Briggs, Xavier de Souza, 11

Brochtorff Circle (Gozo), 149
burials, 50, 52, 68–69, 144, 150

caciques, indigenous rulers, 202
Calchaquí Valley (Argentina), 204
Callejón del Horno, 201
Capilco (Mexico), 246–248
capitalism, 177–178
Catholicism, conversion to, 215
causality, 9, 323
cemeteries, 150
centralization, community, 73–74
ceramics, 253–255, 257–261, 266–267,
  269–270, 272–273, 274–275
ceremonies, imperial, 200
Chaco Canyon (New Mexico), 55
chert. *See* lithics
Chichen Itza (Mexico), 311
chiefdoms, 64–66, 90–129, 321, 323
Chifeng. *See* Liao Valley, Western (China)
Childe, V. Gordon, 6
Chucchus (Peru), 243–245
circumscription, 155–156
cities. *See* urbanism
city-states, 29, 245–246
classics, scholarly discipline, 8, 23
climate change, 306, 312–313
cloth, 267, 268–269
cocktail napkins, 89, 127, 129
cognitive capacity, 45, 56, 58
Colla peoples, 207
collapse of civilizations, 290, 310–314
collective action, 34–35, 323
colonies, imperial, 211
commercialization, 241–242. *See also*
  markets

community growth, 116–121
community structure, 72–73
comparative analysis, 1–3, 226, 314–315
　methods, 7–16, 138–139, 193, 248–249,
　　298, 325–326
　synchronic vs. diachronic, 13, 80
competition, social, 156–158
complicity, provincial strategy, 217–220
conflict. *See* warfare
consumption, household, 249–265
containment strategy, 178
cooperation, 31
Copan (Honduras), 292–294, 298–314
corporate-network framework, 31–32, 65,
　　156–157, 167–168
corregidor, Spanish official, 202
costly signaling, 57
craft production, 78–79, 265–271
Crete, 150–153, 154–158
cross-cultural research. *See* holocultural
　　analysis
Cuetlaxtlan (Mexico), 199–223
Cuexcomate (Mexico), 246–248
Cuicuilco (Mexico), 102
cultural evolution, 1–2, 5–7, 21–22, 27–28,
　　62–64, 182–183. *See also*
　　neo-evolutionary approach
Cuzco (Peru), 201

data threads, 71–72
decision making, 46–47, 56, 58
desakota, Southeast Asian urban settlements,
　　285–286
Dholavira (India), 53
disposal of trash, 50–51
domestic mode of production, 238–239

Easter Island. *See* Rapa Nui
Ebla. *See* Tell Mardikh (Syria)
economic history, scholarly discipline, 23
economic organization, 78–79, 155–156,
　　241–242, 248–276, 303–306
economics, scholarly discipline, 321
Edzna (Mexico), 292
El Sauce, 201
empires, 29, 192–227, 238–247
　control of provinces, 192–237, 240–241
　definition, 194
　role of distance, 198–199
　strategies, 192–227
　　definition, 196–197
　　inverse, 198

pervasive, 198
emulation, provincial strategy, 202–205
encomenderos, Spanish grant-holders, 202
ethnohistory, 195
exchange, 79, 156, 158, 200, 271–276
exodus, provincial strategy, 209–214
explanation, 323

feasting, 78, 251–252, 260–261
Fermi problems, 89
figurines, 52–53, 205. *See also* ritual,
　　domestic
finance, staple and wealth, 31, 65, 240–241,
　　242–243
Flannery, Kent V., 49–50
food, 45, 250–252, 256–257
forest, clearance of, 306
fortified sites, 100

Ggantija, tower on Gozo, 148
gifts, 200
gobernador, local leader in the Spanish
　　Empire, 202
Gottman, Jean, 285
Gozo, 148. *See also* Malta
Grew, Raymond, 13
Grinin, Leonid, 32–33
groundstone. *See* lithics

Habermas, Jurgen, 176–178
Hal Saflieni Hypogeum, 149
Harappa (Pakistan), 53
Hariharalaya (Cambodia), 297
Hatunmarca (Peru), 243–245
Hirth, Kenneth G., 242, 264–265
historical data, integration with
　　archaeological data, 13
history, scholarly discipline, 7–8, 13, 23
Hohokam, 97–100. *See also* Marana Region
　　(Arizona)
holocultural analysis, 10, 169. *See also*
　　Human Relations Area Files
households, 238–247
houses, 49, 51, 174–175
Huaca de la Cruz (Peru), 243–245
Human Relations Area Files, 7, 9, 169

Ica Valley (Peru), 207
Indus Valley (Pakistan), 51–53
inequality, 31, 76–77
informaton control, provincial strategy,
　　213–216

Inka Empire, 195–227
Inkas, 238–247
integration, social, 30–34, 35
irrigation, 303–306
islands, 138–139, 154

jewelry. *See* ornaments

Kamehameha, Hawai'in king, 144
Khahajuro (India), 288
kingship, 143
Knossos (Crete), 150–153
Korea, 181–182
kurakas, Peruvian indigenous rulers, 202,
    215

labor, investment in architecture, 74–75,
    124–127, 153–155
land tenure, 143
legitimation crisis, 176–178
Levant, 47–51
Liao Valley, Western (China), 82, 104–106,
    116–133
lithics, 251–253, 266, 269–270, 272
Little Ice Age, 312

Machu Picchu (Peru), 222
Magdalena, Alto (Colombia), 81–82, 110
Mallia (Crete), 150–153
Malta, 148–150, 154–158
Mantaro region (Peru), 199–223, 243–245
Marana region (Arizona), 97–100, 116–133
Marca (Peru), 243–245
markets, 241–242
Maui (Hawai'i), 143–144, 154–158
Maya, Classic period, 32, 292–294. *See also*
    Tikal (Guatemala); Copan
    (Honduras)
Mayapan (Mexico), 311
mechanisms, 324–325. *See also* middle-range
    theory
megalopolis, 285
Mehrgarh (Pakistan), 51–53
Menorca, 146–148, 154–158
Mesolithic, 45
metal, 255–256, 273–275
Micronesia, 144–146
middle-range theory. *See* theory,
    middle-range
migration, 209–214
Mirador, El (Guatemala), 292
mobility, seasonal, 307–308

Mohenjo–daro (Pakistan), 53
Monte Albán (Mexico), 108, 206
Montelius, Gustav Oscar, 5
monuments, 74–75, 138–159. *See also* public
    works
Morelos (Mexico), 199–223, 247–248
Morgan, Lewis Henry, 5
mortuary patterns. *See* burials
Moundville (Alabama), 68–69, 116. *See also*
    Black Warrior Valley (Alabama)
My Son (Vietnam), 288

Nan Madol (Micronesia), 145–146
Natufian culture, 50
naveta (Menorcan tomb), 147
neo-evolutionary approach, 2, 26–29,
    166–167, 183
Neolithic societies, 89, 90–96
New Spain, 199–223. *See also* Spanish
    Empire
Niger Delta, Middle (Mali), 108–110,
    116–133

Oaxaca, Valley of (Mexico), 81–82,
    106–108, 116–133
objects, 45–46
obsidian. *See* lithics
Oc Eo (Vietnam), 296
ornaments, 255–256, 261, 267–268, 273
Ouagadougou (Burkina Faso), 289

palaces, 150–153
paper, bark, 270
Phaistos (Crete), 150–153
Pi`ihale (Hawai'i), 144
platform mounds, 97, 100
plazas, 100
Pohnpei, 144–146, 154–158
political economy, 124–127, 238–239,
    241–242, 276–280
political science (scholarly discipline), 23,
    321, 323
polities, size of, 300–303
Pollonaruwa (Sri Lanka), 296
Polynesia, 139–144
population, 74
    density, 74, 92
    growth, 116–121, 127–128
postmodern scholarship, 323, 326
Prambanan (Java), 288
prestige. *See* status
public works, 74–75, 122–124

Pueblo Bonito (Arizona), 69–70
Pueblo Grande region (Arizona), 97–100,
    116–133
Puuc region (Mexico), 311

Quachilco. *See* Tehuacan Valley (Mexico)

Rapa Nui (Easter Island), 139–143, 154–158
rebellions, 208–209
regional organization, 73
resistance, provincial strategy, 205–209
Rio Blanco region (Mexico), 199–223
ritual, 54–55, 77, 261
    domestic, 261

Sambor Prei Kuk (Cambodia), 296
San José Mogote (Mexico), 81, 108
San Martín Tilcajete (Mexico), 206
Santa Valley (Peru), 100, 116–133
Saudeleur dynasty, 146
scientific approach, 325–326
Scott, James, 205, 214, 326
sedentism, 49
self-similarity, 302–303
Shandong region (China), 106–108,
    116–133
shell, 274
Sitio Conde (Panama), 68–69
Skorba (Malta), 148
Smith, Adam T., 8, 327
social classes, 250–251, 262
social science history, scholarly discipline,
    322–325
social variation, 166–174
sociology, scholarly discipline, 23, 323
Soconusco (Mexico), 205
Southwestern United States, 53–56
Spanish Empire, 195–223, 227. *See also* New
    Spain
specialization. *See* craft production
Spencer, Herbert, 5
Sri Lanka, 294–296
Standard Cross–Cultural Sample, 9
standard of living, 250–251, 260–261, 262,
    278
statecraft, 196–198
states, 321. *See also* city-states, empires
status, 77–78
storage, 49, 152, 242–243, 277
Sukhothai (Thailand), 288

talayot (Menorcan tower), 146–148
Tarxien (Malta), 148
taula (Menorcan sanctuary), 147
taxation, 75–76, 122–127, 261. *See also*
    finance, staple and wealth
Tehuacan Valley (Mexico), 110–114,
    116–133
Tehuantepec (Mexico), 205
Tell Hasuna (Iraq), 49–50
Tell Mardikh (Syria), 165
Teotihuacan (Mexico), 102
Thai kingdom, 181
theory, 62, 323–325. *See also* cultural
    evolution
    middle-range, 323–325
Thomas, Cyrus, 4
Tikal (Guatemala), 292–294, 298–314
Tilly, Charles, 8
Tlahuica, 257–260
trade. *See* exchange
transport costs, 198–199
Trigger, Bruce G., 4, 6, 26, 67, 80, 327
Truwalen (Java), 288
Tunanmarca (Peru), 243–245
Tylor, Edward, 5

Umpamalca (Peru), 243–245
Upper Mantaro Archaeological Research
    Project, 243–245
Upper Paleolithic, 45, 47
urbanism, 285–315. *See also* monuments
    orthogenetic and heterarchical cities, 288
Urban Revolution, 321

Vayda, Andrew, 324
villages, 72–73

warfare, 76, 120–122, 143
wealth, 76–77
weapons, 255–256
Willey, Gordon, 285
work, 46
world systems theory, 198

Yasodharapura (Cambodia), 297
Yautepec (Mexico), 246–248
Yaxcabá (Mexico), 212
Yoffee's Rule, 165–166

Zakros (Crete), 150–153